WOMEN IN
ANCIENT GREECE

WOMEN IN ANCIENT GREECE

SUE BLUNDELL

HARVARD UNIVERSITY PRESS

Cambridge, Massachusetts

Printed in Great Britain
Second printing 1999

Library of Congress Cataloging-in-Publication Data

Blundell, Sue
    Women in ancient Greece / Sue Blundell.
    p. cm.
    Includes bibliographical references and index.
    ISBN 0–674–95473–4 (pbk.)
    1. Women—Greece—History.   I. Title.
  HQ1134.B58 1995
  305-4´0938—dc20   93–36217
                                         CIP

Designed by Behram Kapadia

Contents

ILLUSTRATIONS

Acknowledgements

I am grateful to all the students at Birkbeck and Goldsmiths' Colleges, who over the years have helped me to 'add women on' to the history of Ancient Greece. Their enthusiasm and ideas have been of immense value. Special thanks are owed to the Library staff at the Institute of Classical Studies in London, for anticipating so many of my needs; to Nina Shandloff and Carolyn Jones at the British Museum Press, for their diligence, good humour and monumental patience; to Margaret Williamson, for reading and commenting on sections of this text, and for providing sympathy and stimulation at a time when she was grappling with Sappho's Immortal Daughters; and to Caroline Heijne and Nick Bailey, for their love and moral support.

SUE BLUNDELL

Introduction

Traditionally, the study of Ancient Greece has taken as its focus the political, military and cultural activities of the male half of the Greek population. In this, of course, it differs very little from studies of other historical eras. During the last twenty years, however, this male-centred view of what constitutes a significant area in past human experience has been challenged in a number of quarters.

> It is now at least acknowledged that while men were performing the feats, building the institutions, producing the goods and cultures, ruling the peoples, and generally busying themselves with those activities we are wont to call history, women were invariably doing something – if only bearing more men to make more history and more women to permit them to do so.
>
> (Fox-Genovese, 1982, p. 6)

What women were doing – and what was being done to them – is a subject which now attracts a growing amount of attention from historians studying a wide range of historical societies, including that of Ancient Greece. Since 1975, when Sarah Pomeroy published her ground-breaking work *Goddesses, whores, wives and slaves*, there has been a plethora of books and articles which have examined diverse aspects of the lives and representation of women in the Ancient Greek world, with the focus broadening in recent years to embrace issues involving relations between the sexes. Very few overviews of the subject have been produced, however. In attempting to make good this omission, I have benefited enormously from the dedication, research and innovative thinking of numerous scholars who have preceded me.

In broad terms, this book aims to fill the gap which women, and their relationships with men, ought to have occupied in general histories of Ancient Greece. Before turning to the complex question of what the word 'women' means in this context, I must first explain the expression 'Ancient Greece'. Conventionally, the term 'ancient' is applied to a span of several thousand years in the history of Greece, extending from the emergence of a Bronze Age culture in about 3000 BC, to the Christianization of Greece in the fourth and fifth centuries AD. In this book, however, I shall be focusing on a much more limited period, beginning in 750 BC and ending in 336 BC. This comprises what are generally known as the Archaic and Classical Ages, during which a distinctive and in many ways short-lived civilisation was being shaped. The political, social, legal and cultural structures which came into being during this time were to determine the nature and quality of women's lives in a number of important respects.

The word 'Greece', in the context of the Archaic and Classical Ages, denotes a wider geographical area than the one embraced by the modern state. From about 1000 BC, Greek-speaking peoples from the mainland and the Aegean islands had been migrating to other parts of the Mediterranean basin, and to the Black Sea area, and had established flourishing Greek communities in a number of coastal regions. Potentially, then, 'Greece' refers to all the far-flung settlements inhabited by Greeks. However, the scope offered by this concept of Greece is not, unfortunately, as broad as it may seem. The majority of our sources for the history of Ancient Greece, particularly those relating to the Classical Age, derive from the city of Athens, whose literary output seems to have far exceeded that of other states. Inevitably, the 'women of Ancient Greece' will often, although by no means invariably, be represented in this book by the women of Athens.

There are many other factors which limit the identity of the 'women' who are to be the subject of this book. The study of Ancient Greece is in general hampered by a lack of detailed source material and, needless to say, those sources that do survive are concerned primarily with the activities of men. Often the women of Ancient Greece are to be encountered only in asides, inferences or vague generalisations. Very few real women are known to us as individuals, and even fewer are accorded the dignity of a name. Moreover, the class bias of the sources is such that most of the women who do put in an appearance belong to the upper echelons of the citizen body. The evidence relating to slaves, foreigners and lower-class citizen women is particularly fragmentary. If we are to avoid the danger of seeing women as an undifferentiated group, we need constantly to remind ourselves that their lives were subject to considerable social and economic variation.

The identity of the women whom we will be studying is also circumscribed in a more fundamental way. In Ancient Greece women were generally denied a public voice, and today they speak to us directly in only a very limited number of contexts. A few scraps from poems composed by a handful of women writers have survived, of which the most numerous are those representing the work of the Archaic poet Sappho – yet these amount to scarcely more than forty battered fragments. These verses tell us something about the preoccupations and attitudes of the individual woman who wrote them, but they furnish us with very little information about the experiences of the female population in general.

Almost everything that we know about Greek women is derived ultimately from a masculine source – from the things which men said about women, from the images of women which they created in literature and art, and from the informal rules and legal regulations which they constructed in order to deal with women. Both as a group and as individuals, the women of Ancient Greece are to a large extent creatures who have been invented by men. This is most obviously the case with the fictional women who feature, sometimes in an unusually prominent manner, in imaginative works such as Homer's *Odyssey* or the plays of fifth-century Athenian tragedians. But even the 'real' women who are discussed in the law-court speeches or medical treatises of the fourth century BC have to be seen in some sense as male inventions. They are presented to us only in portions – as receivers of dowries, bearers of heirs, possessors of wombs which are not behaving quite as they ought to. These portions have been selected by men, in accordance with their own personal views about what it is in a woman that makes her significant. None of these women is allowed to speak for herself. None is able to tell us what *she* thinks about her life and the place which she occupies in Greek society.

This is not to say, of course, that a Greek woman's own account of her nature, role and activities would not have been equally one-sided, equally subjective. The fact that women in Ancient Greece are a 'muted group'[1] does not mean merely that we have been deprived of a valuable source of information on what women did in the privacy of their own homes. It also means that women's subjectivity has been denied to us. The only 'truth' about Greek society which we can hope to recover is inevitably going to be a male 'truth'. The alternative female 'truth' – the way in which women viewed themselves, their menfolk, and the world in which they were living – is almost entirely inaccessible to us. Before embarking on any study of women in Ancient Greece, we have to come to terms with this tremendous drawback.

Given that we are unable to get inside the minds of Greek women, what then is to be gained from studying the texts in which they appear? I believe that the benefits are twofold. In the first place, women in the 1990s are still interested in recovering their own history; and though Greek sources have to be treated with caution, they nevertheless have something to tell us about the reality of women's lives during a significant period in Europe's past. These texts provide us with a limited amount of information about women's day-to-day experiences and, more importantly, they furnish evidence for the legal, social and economic position accorded to women. While it would obviously be a mistake to believe that these man-made regulations can tell us the whole truth about the female population of Greece, it would be equally misguided to assume that they played no part whatsoever in shaping women's reality. To one extent or another, women in Ancient Greece were obliged to live by men's rules. Secondly, the male view of women – provided that it is recognised as a partial and not a universal view – is worth studying in its own right. By examining the roles which men constructed for women, and the system of gender differences into which they were incorporated, we gain an insight into the cultural dynamics of a male-dominated society. This insight has a contribution to make to two different kinds of history. It provides a key to an understanding of one of the strands in the history of the subordination of women; and at the same time it broadens our knowledge of the history of Ancient Greece.

This book, then, has two principal objectives – the study of Greek women's social reality, and the study of their place in literary and visual representations. Inevitably, since it is only through the representations that we can attempt to reach the reality, there is going to be tension between these objectives. In Part I, on women in Greek myth, the focus will be on the second objective, since here we will be examining images of women which involve an obvious element of fantasy. Parts II, III and IV, on the Archaic and Classical Ages, pursue a chronological approach to the study of Greek women. Here, I have tried as far as possible to separate my treatment of women themselves from my treatment of representations of women. The chapters on 'Women and the poets' and 'Women in stone', in Part II, and Part IV, on 'Ideas about women in the Classical Age', are all explicitly concerned with the male view of women which is being presented in particular cultural media; while Part II's 'Women as poets: Sappho' is devoted to the one reasonably coherent expression of the woman's viewpoint to have survived from Ancient Greece. The remaining chapters in Parts II and III seek to examine various aspects of the lives of real women. But it must be borne in mind that all these women are brought to us by courtesy of male authors and artists. In these sections, the tension between representation and reality is particularly strong.

This introduction has been full of warnings, and I am going to conclude with two more. The nature of women's domestic role has altered very little in the course of history, and in Ancient Greece, where women were less involved in extra-domestic activities than they are today, their lives would have been subject to far fewer changes. The chronological treatment which they have been accorded in Parts II, III and IV may therefore seem somewhat artificial. The features which seem to us to distinguish the Archaic from the Classical Age are of a political and cultural character, and would have had a greater impact on men than they did on women. The division into Ages is probably justified, both because it is now a traditional element in the study of Ancient Greece, and because the political and ideological developments which mark the transition to a new 'Age' would have influenced male attitudes to women. But the reader should bear in mind that a Greek woman living in the Classical Age would probably have been less aware of the effect of these changes on her life than her male counterpart.

My last warning is more general. This book, like many that have been written in recent years, represents an attempt to 'add women on' to men's history. I believe that this is a necessary process if the role which women have played in historical societies is to be recognised. But it carries with it the danger that the women of the past will become ghettoised – thus reinforcing the notion that women are a special case, and do not conform to the norm of human experience. If this danger is to be avoided, then books like this one must be seen as essentially transitional. When 'general' historical studies have been broadened so as to incorporate the other half of the human race, then 'Women in . . .' books will have become redundant.

PART I

WOMEN IN MYTH

I

Myth: an introduction

WHAT, WHEN AND WHO?

The English word 'myth' is derived from the Greek *muthos*, which originally meant speech or utterance, but later came to signify a spoken or a written story. By the fifth century BC, a distinction was being made between a *logos*, a rational account, and a *muthos*, a more imaginative narrative. This is not to say that the distinction between the two was necessarily seen as one of truth versus falsehood. In Classical Greece, as today, there was a wide variety of opinion about the significance of myth. There were doubtless many Greeks who still believed that the strange events recorded in myths had actually taken place in the distant past. Some people, however, dismissed them as 'old wives' tales'; while others saw them as expressions of the relationship between gods and humans, or as allegories of scientific or moral truths.

Myths are traditional narratives in which the many-layered significance of human situations is explored through the application of fantasy. The words 'traditional' and 'fantasy' employed in this basic definition merit some further comment. In placing my chapter on myth at the beginning of this book, and separating it out as a topic from the chronological accounts, I do not want to create the impression that I see myth as a timeless entity which can be divorced from the processes of historical change. Greek myths were invented by human beings who lived in particular societies at particular points in time; and as time went on, and circumstances changed, the narratives were freely adapted and embellished to suit the particular preoccupations of their audiences. Nevertheless, myths were at the same time traditional. The same basic stories were handed down from generation to generation, and, in spite of adaptations, someone who had had a hand in shaping a tale in about 1200 BC might still have recognised it when it was being told in about 30 BC. Myths represent an element of continuity in Greek life, and cannot generally be pinned down to a particular historical period. This is the reason why I have chosen to deal with myth as a separate topic.

The notion that myths are invented, and that they involve fantasy, does not necessarily imply that there is no grain of historical truth in them. Some of the human beings named may really have lived, some of the events recounted may actually have taken place, and the background to the story – the social customs, the places and the objects mentioned – may have had some basis in reality. But all of this is overlaid with a strongly fictional element. Moreover, the versions of Greek myths which we possess were generally composed several centuries, in some cases several millennia, after the events which they purport to describe. It follows that to use myth as a source of information about historical events and societies is a rather dangerous exercise.

This brings us to the question of who made Greek myths, and when. Our main source for myth is literature, and, in particular, poetry. The earliest Greek poets to whom we can give names, and who provide us with some of our most important mythological narratives, are Homer and Hesiod, who were probably writing in about 700 BC. But although this is an early date where literature is concerned, in a mythological context it is very late. Undoubtedly, many myths would have come into being long before that time, and would have been handed down by word of mouth. In the Archaic Age, epic poems, hymns to the gods, shorter lyric songs and 'wisdom' poetry (conveying information about the gods and about important aspects of human life) were the main media through which myth was transmitted. All of them formed part of the cultural apparatus of the community, and were performed at events such as religious festivals, banquets, weddings and funerals. The invention of a system of writing in about 750 BC meant that some of these poems were also written down. In the Classical Age an important new vehicle for myth came into being, for the fifth century BC was the great age of Athenian verse drama, and epic poems in particular furnished tragedians with a rich source of material for their plots.

Mythological narratives were also constructed visually, most notably in relief sculpture and in vase paintings. Although literature remains our most important source for myth, occasionally one of the visual texts provides us with evidence for an entirely new episode in a story. More importantly, by presenting the story in a different context and a different symbolic language, these texts allow us to recover meanings of myths which may not be apparent in the literary versions.

This very concise history of Greek myth-making raises a number of points. Firstly, myths have come down to us largely in the form of the sophisticated and selfconscious versions created by educated members of the upper classes. Almost all of these people were, moreover, male. Although women may well have had a hand in early myth-making, at the stage when these narratives became embedded in the culture of the community they were being handled by and large by men (the work of the woman poet Sappho being the only notable exception). As Odysseus's son Telemachus says to his mother Penelope when she tries to cut short a recital of an epic poem, '*muthos* is the province of men' (*Odyssey* 1.356–9). We should be wary, however, of seeing women merely as the objects and passive recipients of male myths. Although Greek literature offers very little evidence for women's responses and reactions, we should not assume for this reason that these did not exist. A story which had been shaped by men could easily have been transformed in meaning when women came into contact with it. One such alternative view has, in fact, been preserved for us, in Sappho's albeit very brief treatment of the story of Helen (see p. 89–90).

The second point to bear in mind is that myths went through a constant process of adaptation. A story that began its existence in, say, 1500 BC may have come down to us in a form which was devised over a thousand years later; and such a story is probably going to tell us as much about what people were thinking in the fifth century BC as it does about the Bronze Age in which it originated. Even basic factual details could be altered. For example, according to Homer, when King Agamemnon returned to Greece from the Trojan War he was murdered by his wife's lover Aegisthus. By the fifth century BC we are being told that it was the wife herself, Clytemnestra, who did the killing (see p. 173–4). A change like this one is clearly of some significance, particularly where the attitude to women is concerned.

The third point is related to the last one. The process of adaptation means that there is no definitive version of any one Greek myth, let alone a 'bible' which serves as a hallowed source for the whole of Greek mythology. Moreover, writers often allude to only one episode in a story, assuming that their audience would be familiar with the rest of it. As a result we are frequently in the position of having to piece together a narrative from a number of different sources, and we should not get too upset if the bits do not always fit together very neatly. Often an author would try to make what he was saying harmonise with the versions of his predecessors, but this was by no means always the case, and absolute consistency cannot be expected.

This is not the place to discuss the merits of the numerous theories of myth which have been produced since the nineteenth century. However, in considering the relationship between myths' meanings and their representation of women, it is obviously of peculiar significance that the major role in shaping the narratives was played by men. These stories can help to reveal to us the response to women experienced by men living in a patriarchal society: what makes myth a very different source from, say, a philosophical treatise on the duties of a wife, is the fantasy element. Through myth we can reach the unconscious, rather than the logically-argued, notions which men entertained about women. In this way we can gain an insight into the symbolic value accorded to women – into what, in fact, the term 'Woman' meant to men. In the words of John Gould (1980, p. 55), 'myth may significantly add depth to (our) sense of the woman's role in society . . . This is because it brings into view ambiguities, tensions and fears, deep-seated fears, which the norms of law and custom are intended to control and even suppress: myth in some sense contradicts the comfortable surface normality of the social structure defined by law and custom, and points to conflict at a deeper level within the dominant structure.'

WOMEN IN MYTH: GODDESSES, ROYALS AND MONSTERS

Women are certainly not thin on the ground in Greek myth. Often they are accorded considerable prominence. In this Part, therefore, I have had to be very selective, and have chosen to concentrate on certain topics which, for one reason or another, seem to me to be fundamental. Chapter 2 deals with creation myth, which is basic both in narrative terms – it takes us back to the imagined beginnings of time – and because it includes the creation of Woman. The following chapter discusses the six Olympian goddesses, all of whom were worshipped widely throughout the Greek world by women and men. The subject of Chapter 4 is Homer, whose poems were the most authoritative source of mythological narratives for Greeks of every era. Finally in Chapter 5, on the Amazons, a myth about women will be discussed which was immensely popular in Classical Greece, and was to become a source of inspiration for twentieth-century feminists.

But before moving on to these specific topics, I offer a few general observations. The heading above refers to the three levels of being which women assume in Greek myth. The divine level is dominated by the figures of the six goddesses (Hera, Athena, Artemis, Aphrodite, Demeter, Hestia) who together with six gods (Zeus, Poseidon, Apollo, Hermes, Ares, Hephaestus) form a ruling élite known as the Olympian deities. But there are also many lesser goddesses, the relatives and associates of the Olympians; and a number of divine female collectives, such as the Fates, the Muses and the Graces. On the human level of representation, myth features women from a number of social classes. But it would be true to say that the only ones with starring roles are the queens and princesses of the ruling households, such as Helen or Electra. This is indicative of the fact that the Bronze Age, when many Greeks were still ruled by monarchs, was a crucial time for the creation of myth. Royalty was one of the bits of traditional social baggage that Greek myth carried with it into later ages, but its presence did not mean that the stories were of no relevance to women and men of other classes. When, for example, the tragedian Aeschylus was writing about the queen Clytemnestra in fifth-century Athens, where no royal women existed, his play would not have been dismissed as having no implications for the more egalitarian society of his own day.

On the third level of being there is the female monster, who is part-woman and part-animal. Examples of this type are the Gorgons, three sisters who had golden wings, boars' tusks and snaky hair, and who turned men to stone; and the Sphinx, whose form embraced that of woman, lioness and bird. These creatures speak most obviously of the fear which women inspired in men. But it is worth remembering that beings which are terrifying can also be useful, because they help to keep one's enemies at bay. So, while Freud's theory that the Gorgon's head represents the castrating female genitals should certainly not be dismissed out of hand,[1] it should also be borne in mind that antefixes in the form of these heads were commonly used to decorate Greek temples. Similarly the Sphinx, which in myth destroys those hapless passers-by who cannot answer its riddles, often served as a grave-marker in Greek cemeteries of the sixth century BC. Both these objects doubtless had the function of frightening away evil spirits. This points to the ambiguity of the male response to the female. Even the Furies, the ghastly spirits of vengeance with Gorgon-style snaky hair, who generally seem to be pretty straight-forwardly nasty, turn into kindly beings, or *Eumenides*, at the end of the play of that name by Aeschylus.

The amount of speculation prompted by the Greek goddesses in recent years makes it necessary to provide some additional comment on their history. It is a frequently-noted paradox that the societies which worshipped these prominent female deities were ones in which real women had a very low status. Many commentators have tried to account for this anomaly by resorting to a hypothetical reconstruction of the origins of Greek religion. According to this hypothesis, before the arrival of the Greeks on the Greek mainland, in about 2000 BC, the native population consisted of settled agriculturalists, who worshipped deities who were primarily female and were associated with the fertility of the earth. The Greeks then brought with them a set of strong male deities more suited to their own way of life, which hitherto had revolved around warfare, pillage and the use of horses. As the native and Greek populations combined, their religions went through a process of fusion whereby the resident females and the incoming males were brought together in a single system. The tensions generated by this development found ex-pression in mythological accounts of friction between females and males, one example being the stormy marriage of Hera and Zeus.[2]

Nowadays it is widely accepted that this reconstruction is a gross oversimplification. The culture of ancient Greece was a complex phenomenon made up of many strands, and its anomalies cannot be explained simply in terms of the racial differences which are the basis of this theory. Archaeological evidence from the Cycladic islands and from Crete, dating from the Early and Middle Bronze Age periods, would certainly seem to indicate that female deities were widely worshipped during that time,[3] and this may go some way towards explaining the prominence of goddesses in later Greek religion. There is, however, very little evidence to support the idea, still commonly encountered, that in the prehistoric era there existed a single unified Mother or Earth Goddess, who was worshipped throughout Europe and the Middle East. It seems much more likely that there were quite a few female deities, with varying functions, in early Greece. The historical process whereby these goddesses were gradually incorporated into a male-dominated pantheon cannot now be recovered, because the evidence simply does not exist. It would undoubtedly have been a complex transformation, involving social, political and cultural changes as well as external influences.

The notion of a prehistoric Mother Goddess has been linked by some people with the idea of matriarchy, or rule by women. The matriarchal era as such is outside the scope of this work, since, if it ever existed, it would have been located in the Stone and Early Bronze Ages. However, since the idea of matriarchy has influenced the interpretation of Greek myths, a brief discussion is necessary. As a theory it relies very heavily on those myths which describe the suppression of women's power. The upholders of matriarchy argue that these contain echoes of the historical transition from matriarchal to patriarchal government. But this reliance on myth makes the theory a very dubious one, since, as we have seen, the myths which we possess were the products of the adaptations worked upon them by later patriarchal societies. For example, it was probably not until the sixth century BC that the story of Agamemnon's murder was altered in order to make Clytemnestra the chief perpetrator (see p. 16). In other words, the 'matriarchal' element, the woman's attempt to rule and her violent overthrow, was added at a later stage, at a time when patriarchal domination in Greece was firmly established.

There is no clear evidence to prove that matriarchy ever existed as a historical reality. Many feminist scholars today, while accepting that some prehistoric societies were much more egalitarian than later historical ones, reject the notion of outright female dominance.[4] As a feature of myth, rule by women (which is not in fact all that common) can best be understood, not as a memory of historical events, but as a narrative 'providing justification for a present and perhaps permanent reality by giving an invented "histori-cal" explanation of how this reality was created'.[5] In other words, the myth explains why men and not women rule, and hence helps to validate and reinforce male control. It is the 'justifiable' male take-over which is the crucial factor. So, to take the example of Clytemnestra, as a ruler she is shown to be bloody and tyrannical, and the restoration of male power is seen as something to be welcomed.

A brief survey of the symbolic associations of the mythological female concludes this chapter. Prominent among these is the identification of women with the wildness of nature – that is, with whatever exists beyond the boundaries of an ordered civilisation. It is generally assumed that it is women's capacity for child-bearing, and hence their alignment with natural forces beyond male control, that prompts these commonly envisaged relationships with trees, plants, springs, birds, and so on.[6] This nature symbolism can often be found to be operating within a 'nature versus culture' model, where men are seen as the representatives of a civilised society which is somehow opposed to the forces of nature. One example occurs in Euripides' play *The Bacchae*, where the king, Pentheus, is associated with ordered life within the walls of the city, while the women worshippers of Dionysus whom he is persecuting are repeatedly linked to the savage world of the mountainside and its wild animals. That the encounter between nature and culture can be seen as leading to the destruction of men is demonstrated in this instance by the appalling fate of Pentheus, who is torn to pieces by the women when he tries to spy on them.[7]

We have already seen, in the discussion of female monsters, that women in myth can be terrifying and destructive. This is equally true of regular mortal women, among whom betrayers, avengers and murderers are legion. Not all of these women are isolated individuals: there are also whole societies of women who murder their husbands, such as the daughters of Danaus or the women of Lemnos. Men in Greek myth can, of course, do their fair share of killing, but this is usually a straightforward manly affair, in the hunt or on the battlefield. Typically, a woman employs trickery and deception in order to dispose of others; and the people disposed of are generally related to her by blood or by marriage. The ultimate negation of the woman who adheres to her proper role in life is the mother who murders her sons, and of these there are several examples. In *The Bacchae*, for instance, Agave is the leader of the band of women worshippers who tear her son Pentheus limb from limb.

Clearly these themes demonstrate a great anxiety about women – one which does not appear to be justified by any of the facts which are known to us. The question of this anxiety will be taken up again in subsequent chapters (see pp. 75, 119). For now, it should be noted that the notion of women's destructiveness can probably be linked in part to their perceived closeness to nature, and hence their perceived remoteness from civilised values. As Gould has written, 'women are not part of, do not belong easily in, the male ordered world of the "civilised" community; they have to be accounted for in other terms, and they threaten continually to overturn its stability or subvert its continuity, to break out of the place assigned to them by their partial incorporation within it. Yet they are essential to it: they are producers and bestowers of wealth and children, the guarantors of due succession ... Like the earth and once-wild animals, they must be tamed and cultivated by men, but their "wildness" will out.' (1980, p. 57).

Implicit in what Gould is saying here is a notion of women as 'liminal'. This is an anthropological term, meaning 'existing on, or crossing, boundaries'.[8] Women in Greek myth can be seen more often than not to be boundary-crossers: they are represented as anomalous creatures who, while they live in the ordered community and are vital to its continuance, do not really belong there. They are always liable to cross over its boundaries into some disorderly state of being, and for this reason they are seen as highly dangerous.

Perhaps equally as common as the destructive women of myth, though receiving far less attention, are the women who are victims. They are united with their more outgoing sisters in a basic antithesis: mortal women who are active are very often destroyers, while mortal women who are passive are very often destroyed. This is particularly true of the scores of women who are raped or seduced by gods in Greek myth: in the sexual act or in subsequently giving birth they are liable to perish, often in very nasty ways.

2

Creation myth

THE CREATION OF THE WORLD

The definitive mythological account of the world's creation is presented by Hesiod in his poem *Theogony*, written in about 700 BC. It is a strange tale, describing the origins of both the cosmos and the gods. The latter, although in some instances they correspond to parts of our world, also behave like human beings, in that they make love, give birth, and produce successive generations. According to Hesiod, Chaos was the first being to appear, but after Chaos came Gaea (Earth), Eros (Love), and Tartarus (the deepest Underworld). Gaea, without making love, then gave birth to Uranus (Sky), the Hills and the Sea. Next she lay with her son Uranus, and as a result produced a great brood of monstrous children, including the primitive gods known as the Titans. Uranus did not warm to any of the offspring he had fathered, so he hid each of them inside Gaea, and would not allow them to see the light of day. Poor Gaea groaned with the discomfort of this, and plotted Uranus' overthrow with her son Cronus, one of the Titans. She created a sickle from grey steel, and with this Cronus castrated his father when next he came to lie with Gaea. The genitals were tossed into the sea, and from them spread a foam, in which the goddess Aphrodite came into being (*Theogony* 116–210).

This story of a son's violent overthrow of his father was repeated in the next generation. Cronus made love to his sister Rhea, and she gave birth to Hestia, Demeter, Hera, Poseidon, and Zeus (that is, to the older generation of Olympian deities) and to Hades (the ruler of the Underworld). As soon as each of these children emerged from the womb, Cronus promptly seized hold of it and gulped it down, for he had been told by his parents that it was his destiny to be vanquished by one of his own offspring. Grief-stricken, Rhea managed to give birth to her youngest child, Zeus, secretly in Crete, and Cronus was then handed a stone wrapped in swaddling-clothes. Being none too bright, Cronus immediately swallowed this. Later, when Zeus was grown up, he overpowered his father, who was forced to vomit up first of all the stone, and then the rest of his children. In this way Zeus became the king of gods and men, and the Olympians were established as a powerful ruling élite (*Theogony* 453–506).

There is no reference in this narrative to the creation of the human race, which in the next episode is simply assumed to exist. Prometheus, the son of one of the Titans, organised a meeting with Zeus at a place called Mekone. Here Prometheus set before Zeus two portions of an ox, and gave him the choice between the meat of the animal wrapped up in its stomach, or its bones hidden beneath the shining fat. This was a trick, since normally the meat would have been beneath the fat. Zeus chose the less favourable of the two portions, thus ensuring that in future human beings would sacrifice only the bones of an animal to the gods and not its meat. (This was indeed the normal sacrificial practice among the Greeks.) In order to punish humans for having gained this advantage, Zeus then refused to give them fire. This would have meant (a point not made explicit by Hesiod) that they would not have been able to cook their newly-acquired meat. When Prometheus stole some fire and carried it down to mortals, Zeus retaliated by masterminding the creation of the first woman, of whom more anon (*Theogony* 535–84).

Later Zeus had to overcome challenges to his supremacy from the Titans and from a monstrous serpent, Typhoeus. This he managed to do with tremendous displays of thunder and lightning (*Theogony* 617–736, 821–86). After this he settled down to some procreation. His first wife was a goddess named Metis, but when she was pregnant with Athena Zeus swallowed her whole. He had been advised by Gaea and Uranus that in this way his royal power would be assured, otherwise Metis would eventually bear him a son who would be the king of gods and men. Later Zeus gave birth to Athena from his own head.[1] He also had liaisons with the goddesses Themis, Eurynome, Demeter and Mnemosyne, who bore him a succession of daughters. Leto presented him with twins, Artemis and Apollo. Finally he married his sister Hera, who provided him with three legitimate offspring (*Theogony* 887–926), Hebe, Ares and Ilithyia.

In this narrative, the evolution of patriarchal divine power and of an orderly cosmos are seen to be inextricably linked. Thus male domination is represented as an essential ingredient in the stability of the universe and the justice of divine rule. At the beginning of the story, Gaea emerges as a powerful goddess who can give birth to her sons alone; at the end, Zeus is the ruler, and he produces a daughter, Athena. Rule by the male has replaced rule by the female, and at the same time the gods have come progressively closer to appropriating the function of reproduction. Uranus tried to block the birth of his children, and it was from his severed genitals that the goddess Aphrodite was born. Cronus swallowed his children and then disgorged them through his mouth. These early attempts at take-over misfired because they were foiled by the feminine cunning of Gaea and Rhea. Zeus resembles both Uranus and Cronus in that he prevents the birth of a child through the act of swallowing; but he forestalls opposition by disposing of the mother as well as the infant. By this means he completely usurps the woman's reproductive role; and birth now takes place from the head, the seat of wisdom.

Zeus has managed in this way to escape from the cycle of succession, and from the hostility between father and son which was so notable a feature of the two preceding generations. By evading the future overthrow prophesied by his grandparents, he ensures that no son will ever succeed to his position. Instead of a threatening male child, he begets a loyal daughter whose perpetual virginity is a guarantee of her refusal to be the source of any further challenge to his power. This does not mean that Zeus will never father children by the normal method (far from it), or that he will never have sons.[2] It is in its tremendous potency as a symbol that the miraculous birth of Athena is significant: it sets the tone for the system of rule which it has helped to bring into being. This will be a system in which the male is utterly dominant, since even the female's role in reproduction can be dispensed with if Zeus puts his mind to it; and it will be perfectly stable, for unlike human government, it will never be disrupted by the transference of power to the next generation. At this stage the immortality of the Olympians is made manifest: if the gods are to provide us with a model of eternity, there has to be a point at which they stop behaving like human beings and therefore stop yielding power to their sons. Athena's birth and her virginity stand as signs that this point has been reached.

Moreover, the nineteen children that are born as a result of Zeus' subsequent liaisons are all daughters and all virgins. The first three, born of his second marriage to Themis, or Right, are called Order (Eunomia), Peace (Eirene), and Justice (Dike): they are indicative of the high moral tone of Zeus' government, and of the good things which can come out of the female principle once it is subject to regulation within the patriarchal system. These women are like the statues of Justice or Liberty or Industry which adorn the institutions of our own male-dominated societies.[3] In Zeus' case, they tell us in no uncertain terms that the violence which characterised the previous regimes has now been replaced by peaceful and enlightened government. The swallowing of Metis has confirmed Zeus in his power; the virgins who are then born to Zeus tell us what the nature of that power will be.

Thus the myth of creation can be seen to validate male domination on the human level by erecting a divine pattern in which the onset of patriarchy is linked to the creation of order. But among mortals the 'ideal' situation of the gods cannot be completely reproduced. In the world of humans the existence of two sexes is essential for reproduction. Men cannot survive without women, and as a result their position of dominance is never absolutely assured. It is in this context that the story of Pandora's creation is introduced.

THE CREATION OF WOMAN: PANDORA

In Hesiod's *Theogony*, the human race is punished for the acquisition of fire when the craftsman god Hephaestus, acting under instructions from Zeus, moulds from the earth the image of a virgin. Athena decks her out in some splendid clothes, and the 'lovely curse' (*Theogony* 585) is then handed over to an assembly of mortals, for whom she becomes a 'hopeless trap, deadly to men' (589). At this point, we discover that hitherto the human race has consisted entirely of males:

> From her comes all the race of womankind,
> The deadly female race and tribe of wives
> Who live with mortal men and bring them harm.

> (*Theogony* 590–92)[4]

Hesiod now lets fly with a spate of misogynistic reflection. Women do nothing to alleviate men's poverty, but they are always ready to share in their wealth. They are like the drones in a beehive, who fill their bellies up with the products of the worker-bees' labour. But,

> ... if a man avoids
> Marriage and all the trouble women bring
> And never takes a wife, at last he comes
> To miserable old age, and does not have
> Anyone who will care for the old man.
> He has enough to live on, while he lives,
> But when he dies, his distant relatives
> Divide his property ...

(Theogony 603–7)

In another of his poems, the *Works and days*, Hesiod treats us to another version of the same story. Here, a number of deities contribute to the woman's ornaments and accomplishments: Athena teaches her to weave and fits her out with a girdle and robes; Aphrodite provides charm and 'painful, strong desire' (66); Hermes gives her 'sly manners, and the morals of a bitch' (67); and the Graces adorn her with golden necklaces, while the Seasons crown her with spring flowers. The *Works and days* narrative also supplies the first woman with a name. She is called Pandora, or 'Allgifts', because she is presented as a gift by the gods. This 'deep and total trap' (83) is delivered to the human race by Prometheus' absent-minded brother, Epimetheus, who has forgotten that his more forward-looking brother warned him to accept no gift from Zeus, in case it should injure men. Up to this time, men have lived free from sorrow, disease, and the need to work. But the woman opens up her jar, and scatters all the pains and evils of the world among its inhabitants: the only thing to remain inside the jar is hope. 'Thousands of troubles, wandering the earth' (110) are released, and all of this has been willed by Zeus.

The woman created in both versions of this story is a manufactured object, moulded from clay like a piece of pottery. Men receive her as the 'free gift' that comes with their acquisition of fire; and like many a free gift, she is not all that she is made out to be. Deceptiveness is one of her outstanding characteristics: she is a mere 'image' and a 'trap', and Hermes has put into her breast 'lies and persuasive words and cunning ways' (*Works and days* 78). In the *Theogony* her appearance represents the final phase in the establishment of a separate identity for the human race. Three successive developments – the introduction of meat-eating (associated with the sacrifice trick), the use of fire and the institution of marriage (the result of Pandora's creation) – serve to bring into being a civilisation distinguished by its double-edged character. Like meat-eating and fire, women help to sustain human life, but like them[5] they are also, in Hesiod's view, potentially damaging. However, men need children to care for them in their old age, and to inherit their property when they die. So women must be endured.[6]

The female whose existence helps to characterise this human civilisation is herself only partially incorporated into the human race. In the *Works and days*, Pandora's ability to cross the boundary between the divine and the human spheres is suggested both by the fact that she is a gift to men from the gods, and by the terms in which she is described: she has a face 'like an immortal goddess' (*Works and days* 62), but a human voice and capacity for movement (61–2). She is also credited with bestial qualities – she has 'the morals of a bitch' (67) – and so can be seen to straddle another boundary, the one between humans and animals. She is in fact a thoroughly ambiguous creature, who, though an 'evil', can bring 'delight', and, though a 'ruin', will be loved by men (57–8). By incorporating within her person elements from all three levels of being, she helps to determine the intermediate status of the human race, poised between the gods and the beasts. With her coming, the distinctively human problems of sorrow, hard work and disease are unleashed.

Pandora's significance as a gift has been admirably discussed by Joseph Nagy (1981), in an article in which he draws on the work of the sociologist Marcel Mauss. In his classic study *The Gift* (1925), Mauss discusses the social function of the exchange of gifts, and points out that, because of the obligation to repay which is created, a gift can be a means by which the giver gains power over the receiver. Nagy discerns in Greek myth a common pattern whereby a theft (the negation of the gift) is paid for when the thief then accepts a gift which turns out to be other than what it appeared: it is through this 'subtle act of giving' that relations of domination and subordination are created. The ultimate example of this pattern is to be found in the story of the Trojan War, which is caused by Paris's theft of Helen, and is brought to an end when the Trojans accept from the Greeks the fatal offering of the wooden horse. In the Prometheus/Pandora myth, we are presented with a complex but logical sequence of deceptive gift, gift withheld, theft, and deceptive counter-gift. Zeus's acceptance of the ox bones hidden beneath fat means that human beings have gained one advantage over the gods: in future, in return for this paltry gift made in the course of sacrifice, the gods will have to confer favours on the human race. Zeus responds by withholding fire, and this refusal to give is countered by an act of outright theft, when Prometheus steals fire and delivers it to mortals. The final stage comes with the handing over of Pandora, who brings terrible gifts, the contents of her jar, to the human race.

According to Nagy, the female can be seen here as the ultimate gift within society: not to accept her would mean that human society would come to an end, but acceptance brings nothing but trouble. Pandora's beauty is like the fat that covers the bones, for it conceals a worthless interior. Her belly is always taking (see p. 22), but men have to put up with this if they want what her belly can also give, the children whom they need in order to survive. Through Pandora, the deceptive counter-gift, the gods finally gain the upper hand over mortals, for she ensures that human beings will for evermore be subject to the ills which mark them off from the race of the gods. Like the Biblical story of Eve, the myth of Pandora envisages the female of the species as a necessary evil whose existence helps to determine the inferior status of the human race. Although this is not the only view of Woman which is offered by Greek myth, it is one that colours many of the subsequent representations.

3

The Olympian goddesses: virgins and mothers

One of the most intriguing aspects of the Greek characterisation of their Olympian goddesses is the emphasis which is placed on virginity. All of the male Olympians are sexually active. But of the six females, three – Athena, Artemis and Hestia – are dedicated virgins, steadfast in their refusal to marry; while one – Zeus' consort Hera – is what might be called a semi-virgin, since she is able to renew her virginity annually by bathing in a sacred spring at Canathus, near Argos. Although both Hera and Aphrodite, the goddess of love, are mothers, neither of them acquits herself with any distinction in this role; and Hera in particular illustrates quite clearly the negative connotations which in Greek myths are liable to attach themselves to women who have given birth. Only one of the six Olympian goddesses, Demeter, could be said to be a true mother goddess – a being whose identity is closely bound up with her role as a parent.

Although it was of the utmost importance to most Greek men that their daughters should be virgins up to the time of their marriage, it was of equal importance that women should marry and give birth. In this respect the role model presented by the Olympian females was hardly an inspiring one. The virgin goddesses repudiate the most important function ascribed to women by Greek social values, while two of the mothers are notable for their lack of devotion to their children. Four of the goddesses, moreover – Athena, Artemis, Hera and Aphrodite – are remarkably active outside the home, contradicting the ideal of a modest and domesticated lifestyle constructed for both married and unmarried women. The mythological characterisation of the female Olympians cannot, it seems, be explained simply in terms of a reinforcement of a conventional social code. The differences between the Olympian goddesses and their female worshippers seem, if anything, to be more significant than their similarities. In what follows, I shall be discussing some of the basic characteristics of these deities, and then considering the implications of their distinctive behaviour and attributes.

ATHENA

Although Athens was by no means the only Greek state where Athena was worshipped, it is as the patron deity of that powerful city that the goddess is best known to us. The prominence of the idea of virginity in the Athenian concept of their patron is something that is highly visible even today, for Athens is still dominated by the mighty temple of the Parthenon, which housed a statue of the goddess known as the Parthenos, or Virgin.[1] Athena is generally represented as a highly androgynous figure, who involves herself in both masculine and feminine activities; and this ambiguity seems to be encapsulated in her virgin status. Although she is female, she rejects the roles of marriage and mother-hood which most Greek men saw as fundamental to a woman's existence.

Athena's feminine side is displayed most clearly in her supervision of one of the most characteristic of women's occupations. As Athena Ergane (or 'Workwoman') she was worshipped as a goddess of handicrafts, and in particular as the inventor of spinning and weaving, tasks which in ancient Greece were carried out primarily by women in the home. The goddess's association with textile production was commemorated at the Great Panathenaea, an Athenian festival celebrated every four years in her honour, where the culminating event was a procession which wound its way up to the Acropolis, displaying at its head a robe specially woven for Athena (Fig. 1).

But the dominant image of the goddess is one that links her firmly with masculine activities. Both in literature and in the visual arts, Athena is most frequently represented as an armed warrior (Fig. 34), a manifestation which is found in our earliest sources. For Hesiod, the goddess is a 'fearsome queen who brings/ the noise of war and, tireless, leads the host,/ she who loves shouts and battling and fights' (*Theogony* 925–6).[2] In Homer's *Iliad*, she is prominent among the divine partisans who constantly intervene in the warfare between Greeks and Trojans. On the battlefield she sweeps through the Greek ranks, bullying, inciting and bellowing out war-cries. She grabs the reins of chariots, guides Greek spears into enemy flesh and fends off Trojan weapons with her bare hands (see, for example, *Iliad* 5.121–32, 5.778–863, 20.41–53). Her golden helmet, massive spear and flapping aegis strike terror into the hearts of her opponents. Many Trojans bite the dust as a result of her interventions, including the noble Hector, who is enticed into making a stand against Achilles when Athena poses as his brother and offers to lend him assistance. Pausing only to hand Achilles back his spear after a mis-throw, the goddess then promptly disappears and leaves Hector to his fate (*Iliad* 22.224–305). Respect for fair play is not one of the warrior maiden's most obvious qualities.

In many of her functions, however, Athena traverses and transcends the boundary between feminine and masculine roles. Her relationship with the olive tree features in the story of her successful bid to become patron deity of the city of Athens, recounted in the sculptures of the Parthenon's west pediment. Her rival for the post was the god of the sea, Poseidon, whose offering to the city, a salt spring on the Acropolis, was countered when Athena created an olive tree in the same area. The decision went in the goddess's favour, and ever afterwards she was regarded as the guardian of olive trees (Fig. 2). This myth ascribes to Athena a traditionally feminine connection with the fertility of the earth. But it also links the goddess to masculine modes of economic production: olive oil was one of Athens' principal exports, and olive trees were cultivated by men.

Athena's role as *kourotrophos*, or nurturer of young men, similarly evokes a feminine quality; but in performing it she is brought into intimate contact with some of the most virile of Greek mythological characters. Anyone who is anyone in the roll-call of heroes seems at some stage in his career to receive assistance from the warrior maiden. Among the Greeks who fight at Troy, Achilles and Odysseus are particular favourites (see p. 53). For Jason she constructs the *Argo* in which he sails off in quest of the golden fleece. Bellerophon is presented by the goddess with a golden bridle so that he can tame the winged horse Pegasus. When Perseus cuts off the head of the Gorgon Medusa, it is Athena who guides his hand. Above all, Heracles, the archetypal hero, is able to rely on the goddess as his mentor and helpmate in many of his labours (Fig. 3).

Moreover, it is often through her adoption of aggressive masculine stances (see p. 191) that Athena's overall protective function is exercised. In this respect the snake is an appropriate symbol of the goddess's powers. There is a striking proliferation of these creatures about her person, most notably in the numerous examples which wriggle around the fringes of her magic breastplate, or aegis, and can be brandished by the goddess when she is warding off her enemies. Like the snake, Athena is an ambivalent entity whose deadliness to her enemies enables her to be kind to her friends. It was believed by some Athenians that the Acropolis was protected by a giant snake which lived in the goddess's temple and, every month, consumed the honey-cake that was left out for it. This animal can be seen to represent Athena's guardianship of the Acropolis and of the city as a whole, a role referred to in one of her most important cult titles, *Polias*, or City-goddess. Athens was not the only community which looked to the goddess for protection, and in this connection her chief temple was often located on a fortress hill, as for example in Argos, Sparta, Lindos and Gortyn, as well as in Athens.

Her defence of cities establishes Athena firmly as an urban deity, involved in many aspects of human technology and culture, in both female and male spheres of activity. Perhaps above all she should be seen as a superb manager. This side of Athena is displayed even in the midst of warfare, for she is not a goddess of uncontrolled violence but one whose contribution is strategy and discipline. When Odysseus goes on a walkabout through the Greek camp, using all his diplomatic skills to persuade the war-weary fighters not to abandon the campaign, he does so because he has been motivated by Athena (*Iliad* 2.155–82). It is Odysseus' great ability as a manipulator that especially endears him to his female champion, for, as she herself admits, this is a quality which the two of them share. In response to one of the hero's tall tales about his recent adventures, she exclaims affectionately:

> It would be a sharp one, and a stealthy one, who would ever get past you
> in any contriving . . . you and I both know
> sharp practice, since you are far the best of all mortal
> men for counsel and stories, and I among all the divinities
> am famous for wit and sharpness . . .
>
> (*Odyssey* 13.291–9)[3]

This fondness for schemes and contrivances earns Athena her reputation for wisdom. Until the fourth century BC, the word *sophia*, which we translate as 'wisdom', signified the kind of practical intelligence which skilled craftspeople and men of affairs possessed. In the fourth century, most notably in the works of the philosopher Aristotle, *sophia* began to take on the meaning of contemplative wisdom; and it was at some stage after this (perhaps not until the first century BC) that Athena came to be regarded as the personification of *sophia* in the more abstract sense.

The two factors which more than any other determine Athena's identity as a female who is different from ordinary mortal women are brought to our attention in the

Eumenides, the last tragedy in Aeschylus' *Oresteia* trilogy, produced in 457 BC. The Greek commander Agamemnon has been murdered by his wife Clytemnestra on his return from Troy, and their son Orestes has later avenged his father by killing his mother. Hounded by the Furies, the ghastly spirits of retribution, Orestes goes on trial in the city of Athens. The god Apollo defends him by maintaining that his offence was less serious than Clytemnestra's, since the mother is not the true parent of the child (see p.106), and offers as proof of this contention the example of Athena, president of the court. She is a 'Child sprung full-blown from Olympian Zeus,/ never bred in the darkness of the womb' (*Eumenides* 664–5).[4] Athena, in giving her casting vote in favour of Orestes' acquittal, endorses Apollo's argument:

> No mother gave me birth.
> I honour the male, in all things but marriage.
> Yes, with all my heart I am my Father's child.
> I cannot set more store by the woman's death ...

> (*Eumenides* 736–40)

Athena is different, then, because she had no mother and because she is a dedicated virgin who has always resisted offers of marriage. The way in which these factors are exploited in this particular context is a product of fifth-century Athenian male consciousness, and as such represents a rather late formulation so far as mythology is concerned. But both factors were long-established features of Athena's biography, and though their implications may not always have been so consciously voiced, they suggest that a denial of motherhood may always have been a part of the characterisation of the goddess. In the *Theogony* (886–900, 924–6), the poet Hesiod relates how Zeus swallowed his wife Metis whole, and later gave birth to Athena from his head (see p. 21). In other versions of the story, the part played by Metis is totally suppressed, and Zeus is represented as the sole parent.[5] From the seventh century BC onwards the birth of Athena was depicted in Athenian vase paintings (Fig. 4), and it was also chosen as the subject of the sculptural representation in the east pediment of the Parthenon (see p. 192).

Metis in Greek means 'cunning intelligence' – a suitable name for the mother of the wily Athena – and we can speculate that at one time the story was one which told of the transmission of a purely feminine wisdom. What is much clearer, however, is the significance in the surviving narratives of the downgrading or total removal of Metis' role. The myth as it now stands demonstrates that it is the father who is the predominant or sole parent, and in this way the very special relationship which exists between Zeus and his daughter is explained. Athena by her birth has secured the stability of Zeus' political regime, and has at the same time validated patriarchal control within the family.[6]

In the most extreme version of this story, Athena has had no contact at all with a woman's womb. At the same time, her own womb is denied, since she herself is a virgin who will never marry or give birth. Even a glimpse of the goddess's naked form is unforgivable: the seer Tiresias as a young man caught sight of the goddess as she was taking an alfresco bath in a spring, and was punished with blindness for this offence. The story which best illustrates Athena's antipathy to male sexual advances relates how the blacksmith god Hephaestus had once tried to rape her when she was visiting his forge to commission a new set of weapons. Athena resisted furiously, and the god ejaculated over her leg. In disgust, she wiped away the semen with a piece of wool and threw it onto the ground, causing a child, Erichthonius, to be born from the earth. Having missed by inches becoming the infant's mother, Athena consented to take charge of his upbringing (Apollodorus 3.14.6). In this way the goddess's virginity, which marks her off from ordinary mortal women, is mediated by her role as a foster mother, an aspect of her *kourotrophos* function which draws her back into the realm of human femininity. In a prayer composed by the tragedian Euripides, Athena the virgin goddess can nonetheless be addressed as 'Mother' (*Heracleidae* 771–2).

In many of her activities Athena can be seen to be like her mortal worshippers, both female and male. But she is also strikingly different – different from the females because she is a virgin, different from the males because she is female. The significance of this tension between likeness and difference will be explored in more detail below (p. 44).

ARTEMIS

The second virgin goddess is the twin sister of Apollo, and a child of Zeus by a minor deity named Leto. In some ways, Artemis can be seen as the antithesis of Athena, who is essentially an urban goddess. Artemis, by contrast, is a loner who haunts the remote reaches of the countryside. 'Let all the mountains be mine', was the request that she put to her father when she sat on his knee as a baby; and instead of girlish trinkets, she asked for a bow and a loose knee-length tunic suitable for hunting (Callimachus, *Hymn Three: to Artemis* 8–19). She is an 'arrow-pouring virgin' (*Homeric Hymn* 9.2),[7] whose most familiar image is that of the vigorous young sportswoman who strides out purposefully in pursuit of prey (Fig. 5).

In myth Artemis is also terribly destructive towards young women. In the course of a family row her stepmother Hera taunts her with the words, '"Zeus has made you a lion/ among women, and given you leave to kill any at your pleasure."' (*Iliad* 21.483–4). Along with her brother Apollo she inflicts the most horrific punishment on the mortal woman Niobe for boasting that she has had more children than the goddess Leto. Apollo and Artemis immediately spring into action with bows and arrows to rob her of this advantage, and while her twin disposes of Niobe's six sons, Artemis shoots down the six daughters.

The maiden Iphigenia is another of Artemis' victims. When the Greek fleet is about to set sail for Troy, Artemis sees to it that the winds are unfavourable and then decrees that Agamemnon, the leader of the expedition, must sacrifice his first-born child Iphigenia to her in order to make the winds blow in the right direction. Agamemnon obeys, and the capture of Troy is assured. But the deed certainly does not endear him to his wife Clytemnestra, who in many versions of the myth gives the slaughter of her daughter as the motive for murdering her husband on his return from Troy (see p. 177–8). One way or another, Artemis' treatment of Iphigenia seems to be bound up with her function as a hunting goddess: in some versions it is because Agamemnon has killed one of her sacred stags that she demands this dreadful act of expiation;[8] in others, Artemis at the last moment replaces Iphigenia with a deer and carries her off to the city of Tauris in the Crimea, where she becomes a priestess in a cult involving the sacrifice to the goddess of all the unfortunate Greeks who land on the shore.[9]

These human sacrifices are mythical, and we cannot be sure that there was ever in reality a time when men and women were offered up to Artemis. But the cult practices associated with the goddess do throw up a number of instances of ritual cruelty. At Halae in Attica, for example, a festival of Artemis was celebrated at which a few drops of blood were drawn from a man's throat with a sword. In Sparta, Artemis presided over a more gruesome and testing ordeal: at the festival of Artemis Orthia young men had to run a gauntlet of other youths wielding whips in order to grab some cheeses from an altar. It is possible, as Pausanias suggests (3.16.10), that rites such as these had at some stage been introduced as substitutes for human sacrifice. But this is a matter for speculation. Of more significance is the fact that myths and rites alike create an image of a goddess who can be deadly in her treatment of the human race.

However, these destructive tendencies are combined with a remarkable creativity. Artemis the hunter is also celebrated for her nurturing of young animals. In the *Iliad*, Homer refers to her as 'Mistress of Animals' (21.470), a long-established formula which doubtless refers to her role as a supplier of prey for human hunters; and in Aeschylus' *Agamemnon* (141–3), she is hymned as 'Artemis, lovely Artemis, so kind/ to the ravening lion's tender, helpless cubs,/ the suckling young of beasts that stalk the wilds'. Human fertility too comes within her remit. The goddess capable of destroying young women is also thought of as participating in three of the most important transitions of their lives, all of them linked to their reproductive role. She was appealed to at the onset of menstruation.[10] She was in women's thoughts just before marriage, when they dedicated to her the girdles which they had worn since puberty. Above all, 'women suffering the sharp pains of childbirth' called for her aid (Callimachus, *Hymn Three* 20–22). By the Classical period, Artemis had developed into a full-blown goddess of childbirth, and as such had merged with the more obscure birth deity Ilithyia.

Artemis' close relationship with young women was highlighted in Athens by a rite which seems to have had the function of preparing an Athenian girl for the transition into adulthood, defined as far as a female was concerned as the stage at which she became capable of bearing children and therefore marriageable. Between the ages of five and ten, girls went into service in the sanctuary of Artemis at Brauron, on the east coast of Attica. These young attendants were referred to as the 'bears' (*arktoi*), and during their time at the sanctuary – probably a year – they wore yellow dresses, and ran races and performed 'bear-dances' in honour of the goddess. According to legend, this service was an atonement for the slaughter by Attic youths of a bear which was sacred to Artemis. Its theme of propitiation points to the notion that a price had to be exacted from young women before they could be allowed to become fertile and surrender their virginity.[11] Perhaps the girls' activities at Brauron can also be seen as an acknowledgement of their natural wildness – of the part of them that wanted to 'act the bear'. Only when this had been purged could they be tamed within the institution of marriage.[12]

The creative side of Artemis is represented most graphically in the famous statue of the goddess which was the focus of her cult at Ephesus, a Greek city on the west coast of Asia Minor (Fig. 6).[13] This image, which was housed in a magnificent temple, is very different from that of the lithe young athlete honoured in the western part of the Greek world. The copies of the statue which have survived date from the Roman era, when the cult was still so popular that a mass protest meeting was organised against St. Paul's preaching by the city's replica-makers, and the theatre reverberated to chants of 'Great is Artemis of the Ephesians' (*Acts of the Apostles* 19.23–41). However, the image's iconography certainly dates back to the Greek period, if not to an earlier time. It is now generally agreed that the numerous globes attached to her chest do not represent breasts: recent suggestions identify them as either fruits or the testicles of bulls sacrificed to the goddess. It may at one time have been the practice to attach one or other of these items to a primitive wooden image of Artemis as a way of 'asking her for more' – more fruit or more bulls – while at the same time providing her with the wherewithal, seeds or semen, to produce them. After a time these temporary offerings would have been given a more permanent form in a ritual pectoral, and eventually the statue was carved with the pectoral already in position.[14] In any event, whether the objects are fruits, testicles or indeed breasts, there is little doubt that they are emblematic of the goddess's role in promoting fertility. The bulls, lions and bees which are worked into the design of her robe point in the same direction, and call to mind the Artemis who is hailed as 'Mistress of Animals'.

The juxtaposition of destructive and creative elements within the same deity may be paradoxical, but it is by no means unusual. It is a common motif in myth, and doubtless springs from a basic sensitivity to human mortality: death is the price which we have to pay to the gods for the gift of life. We are born to die, and Artemis reminds us of these two extremes of the human condition by showing us that in a very real sense our lives are sustained by death. A goddess who both nurtures and kills would certainly not seem strange to hunting or agricultural peoples, who are forever involved in the ambiguous practice of caring for young animals so that later they can be slaughtered for food. Childbirth, too, in ancient Greece at least, could very easily bring death with it; and it is not surprising that at Brauron, where young girls were set on the road to motherhood, the garments of women who had died in labour were also dedicated.[15]

Rather more difficult to come to terms with is the fact that a goddess who is so intimately associated with the fertility of animals and humans should herself be a dedicated virgin. Like Athena, Artemis defends her chastity vigorously: when the hunter Actaeon accidentally catches sight of her bathing in a woodland pool, she punishes him by turning him into a stag, so that he is torn to pieces by his own hounds. Unlike Athena, Artemis also inspires a commitment to celibacy in some of her followers. In Euripides' tragedy *Hippolytus*, the young son of King Theseus is so obsessively devoted to Artemis that he tries to suppress his own sexual identity. For this he is persecuted by the love-goddess Aphrodite, who arouses in his stepmother Phaedra an ungovernable passion for the youth: both of them come to very nasty ends. Atalanta, who as a baby was fostered by a she-bear, is another of Artemis' devotees; a formidable hunter and athlete, she expresses her antipathy to the married state by announcing that she will only become the wife of a man who can beat her in a running race, a feat which she mistakenly believes no-one can achieve. All this fervent dedication to the single life is inspired by a goddess who also presides over childbirth. Some possible explanations of this anomaly will be discussed below (p. 44–5).

HESTIA

The third Olympian virgin is the goddess of the hearth. While other deities are out and about, Hestia stays at home on Mount Olympus to keep the fires alight: as a result she has very few adventures, and generates only a minimal amount of mythology. Indeed, Hestia (whose name means simply 'hearth') seems very often to be thought of more as a set of sacred stones than as a deity with a human form, and it is not surprising that there are very few visual representations of the goddess.

Nevertheless, she was a deity of great symbolic significance, and was worshipped throughout the Greek world. The hearth was the centre of the Greek home, and as a family altar it was the site of many domestic rituals. Small offerings of food – the most basic and the most common form of sacrifice – were made there before a meal. In Athens, a rite called *amphidromia*, in which a baby was carried around the hearth a few days after its birth, probably signified the formal acceptance of the child into the family. At a wedding the bride was led from the hearth in her father's house to the new hearth which she would tend as mistress in the home of her husband. Clearly, the *hestia* was deeply rooted in family life, and not surprisingly it came to symbolise the sanctity of the Greek *oikos* or household. That the stable core of the household should be regarded as female is, of course, only to be expected.

Hestia also provided a focal point for the community as a whole. In many Greek states, the *prytaneion*, a kind of town hall, contained a public hearth which was seen as the centre of the city and as an emblem of civic unity. The one in Athens was situated midway between the agora and the Acropolis, and in it there was a statue of the goddess and a fire that was kept perpetually burning. It was here that foreign ambassadors were entertained following an invitation to dine 'at the public *hestia* of the city'. Hestia, the goddess who stays at home, represents permanence and security not only within the family, but also within the community of which the family forms the foundation.

The only significant piece of narrative attached to Hestia concerns her refusal to marry. Once when she was courted by both Poseidon and Apollo, she touched the head of her brother Zeus and swore a great oath that she would remain a virgin forever. Instead of marriage Zeus gave her high honour and a central place in the home (*Homeric Hymn* 5.21–32). Of all the virgin goddesses, she comes closest to providing a role model for young Greek women, for she is the only one of the three who exhibits anything like the required degree of passivity. Yet even here there is a paradox, for Hestia – the goddess who forswears marriage and motherhood – is also, as we have seen, a symbol of family life. This ambiguity is underlined by the writer Porphyry, when he tells us that there were two images of Hestia: one was a virginal figure, but the other was a matron with prominent breasts, representing the power of fertility (in Eusebius, *Praep.Ev.* 3.11.7).

HERA

Hera was the full sister and wife of Zeus, ruler of gods and mortals. The importance of the goddess in cult practice is indicated by the fact that two of the earliest temples in the Greek world, on the island of Samos and at Argos, were dedicated to her in the eighth century BC.[16] Primarily, she was worshipped as a goddess of weddings and marriage. She was invoked as the Uniter (*zygia*), as the Preparer-of-weddings (*gamostolos*), and as the Woman-given-in-marriage (*nympheuomene*); and in the month of Gamelion ('Wedding-month' – our January), special sacrifices were offered to her. In the *Thesmophoria-zusae*, a fifth-century comedy by Aristophanes, the female chorus addresses this prayer to the goddess:

> Be with us, sweet Hera, great Goddess and Queen,
> Take part in our dancing today!
> Defender of marriage, Protectress serene,
> Lend grace to our revels and play!

(973–6)[17]

This role as protectress of marriage is obviously linked to Hera's relationship with Zeus, and in visual representations the two deities are often shown side by side. In the Parthenon frieze, for example, Hera turns to face her husband, and raises her veil in the gesture of a bride (Fig. 7). Even in Hera's own shrines, her influential consort was liable to put in an appearance: according to Pausanias (15.17.1), a helmeted figure of Zeus stood next to the cult statue of the enthroned goddess in the temple of Hera at Olympia. Her association with marriage was perhaps responsible for Hera's strange status as a semi-virgin. Pausanias (2.38.2) tells us that near Nauplion there was a spring named Canathus where the goddess bathed annually in order to renew her virginity: for most women, virginity was an essential prerequisite of marriage, and Hera's yearly rebirth as a potential bride may well have been seen as an event which recreated and reaffirmed the marital relationship.

Hera's supervision of weddings gave her a special link with young women, and it was in this connection that she was honoured in a festival celebrated every four years at Olympia. This was the female counterpart of the famous Olympian games held in honour of Zeus, although needless to say the women's version was far less prestigious and elaborate. Very little information about the festival is recorded by ancient authors, but it is known that it began with the presentation to the goddess of a newly-woven *peplos* or robe, after which running races were held in the Olympic stadium. The competitors, who may all have been young local girls, wore short tunics which left their right shoulders and breasts exposed. The course for the races was about five-sixths of the length of the Olympic track, and the prizes were olive crowns and a share of the cow sacrificed to Hera (Pausanias 5.16).

According to one legend, this festival was instituted by the local princess Hippodamia as a thank-offering for her marriage to the hero Pelops which took place after Pelops had won a chariot race against the bride's father, an event seen by some authorities as the original contest of the men's games at Olympia. The importance of the marital relationship was in fact accorded some very visible recognition in the Olympian sanctuary: not only was the prelude to the chariot race depicted in the east pediment of Zeus's temple, but in its west pediment the story of the unsuccessful attempt by the Centaurs to disrupt a Lapith wedding ceremony was represented (see p. 189–90). The union between Pelops and Hippodamia had not been without its problems, however. The hero had managed to kill his prospective father-in-law in the course of the chariot race, and as a result had brought down a curse upon his family. This curse was to have enormous mythological repercussions, since it eventually descended to Pelops' grandsons, Agamemnon and Menelaus, both of whom experienced considerable marital difficulties: Menelaus' bride Helen absconded to Troy with Paris, while Agamemnon was murdered by his wife Clytemnestra when he returned from the Trojan War (see p. 173–4). Clearly, marriage is not being presented in these myths as a source of unalloyed delight, and much the same might be said of Hera's own relationship with the god Zeus, which is a very stormy affair.

Indeed, when we turn from Hera's role in cult practice to her representations in myth, a very different image of the goddess emerges. The revered defender of marriage features in Homer's poems as an almost comic character – an archetypal nagging wife who keeps a jealous watch over all her husband's movements, and shows considerable resentment when he fails to consult her (e.g. *Iliad* 1.536–70). Her sharp tongue and competitiveness are also displayed in the anonymous *Homeric Hymn to Apollo*, in a scene where Hera learns about her husband's do-it-yourself procreation:

> 'O stubborn and wily one! What else will you now devise?
> How dared you alone give birth to gray-eyed Athena?
> Would not I have borne her? ...

And now, I shall contrive to have born to me
a child who will excel among the immortals.'

(*Homeric Hymn to Apollo* 322-7)

In retaliation, Hera gives birth unaided to the monstrous serpent Typhoeus. But what a difference there is between the two offspring – between the clever and supportive Athena, the child of the father, and the devouring monster who is the symbol of the mother's power. There can be little doubt who is the moral victor in this particular contest.

A famous episode in the *Iliad* provides a portrait of a more subtle and manipulative Hera. In order to distract her husband from a turn of events in the Trojan War of which he may not approve, she throws herself enthusiastically into a magnificent scheme of seduction. Having bathed and adorned herself with the utmost care, she engineers a 'chance' meeting with Zeus on Mount Ida, and with the aid of a magic girdle borrowed from Aphrodite succeeds in reawakening his ardour. Their union sets in motion a series of splendid cinematic effects:

... There
underneath them the divine earth broke into young, fresh
grass, and into dewy clover, crocus and hyacinth
so thick and soft it held the hard ground deep away from them.
There they lay down together and drew about them a golden
wonderful cloud, and from it the glimmering dew descended.

(*Iliad* 14.346-51)

This description may preserve a memory of an earlier concept of Hera as an earth goddess, whose sacred marriage to the sky deity causes vegetation to spring forth. But in Homer's *Iliad* Hera is much more than a personification of the earth: she is a strong and vigorous personality, and it is to marriage on the human rather than the cosmic level that she principally relates. The model of marital relations presented in the poem could hardly be said, however, to present a positive image of women's role. When Zeus discovers that his encounter with his wife was part of an elaborate plot, he threatens her with a whipping, and reminds her of the violent punishments which he has inflicted on her in the past. For all Hera's forcefulness, the pattern of male domination is clearly reaffirmed in these glimpses into the domestic life of the Olympians.

Hera is also a member of a ruling dynasty, and within the political institutions on Mount Olympus she exercises considerable authority: her appearance in the assembly of the gods produces instant and respectful attention, and her policy decisions are readily accepted by the other deities (*Iliad* 15.84-148). But here again, the power accorded to a woman has to be viewed within a framework of overall male control. Hera's authority is shown to derive ultimately from that of her husband: in the words of Aphrodite, honour must be accorded to a goddess who lies 'in the arms of Zeus, since he is our greatest' (*Iliad* 14.213; see also 18.366).

Hera figures most prominently in myth as a wife and a queen. As a mother, she is negligible. Her marriage to Zeus produces three or four offspring – two minor goddesses, Hebe and Ilithyia, the hateful war-god Area, and, in Homer's account, the blacksmith-god Hephaestus.[18] This last child is born lame, and according to Homer his mother is so ashamed of him that she hurls him from the top of Mount Olympus (*Iliad* 18.394-405). He lands in the ocean, and in one of its underwater grottoes he receives his training in metallurgy, a skill which he later exploits in order to win revenge against his unkind parent.[19] When Hera seats herself on a beautiful golden throne which her son has sent as a gift, she is immediately clapped in invisible bonds; and frantic messages to Hephaestus that he should come and free his mother are met with the response that he has no mother. Only when he has been brought back to Olympus in a drunken stupor by the wine-god Dionysus, and has been bribed with an offer of marriage to Aphrodite, does he agree to release Hera from her shackles.

Clearly, the goddess's relationship with her son is far from ideal. Her cruelty towards the younger generation is brought out particularly strongly in the stories of her treatment of the many illegitimate offspring fathered by the persistently unfaithful Zeus. Many of these are pursued with a terrible vengeance. At Hera's command, Dionysus is torn to shreds by the Titans. The monstrous serpent Python is despatched to dispose of Apollo. Most famous of all is the punishment inflicted on the hero Heracles, who as a result of the machinations of Zeus's wife has to endure the dreadful burden of the twelve labours. Far from being a tender, caring mother, Hera is frequently in myth made to act out the role of the archetypal wicked stepmother.

The negative qualities with which Hera is invested in myth are important, for they tell us a great deal about the attitudes of Greek males to marriage and motherhood. But the mythological portrait should not be allowed to overshadow the very different picture which emerges from a study of Hera's role in cult practice. There, she was venerated as the protector of an institution which was not only central to women's experience but was recognised as a vital component of Greek social structures. To the people who took part in her rites, and more especially to her female worshippers, she must have presented a far more positive image.

APHRODITE

Aphrodite is the goddess of love and sexuality (Figs 42, 44–5). She is seen as being present in the sexual act itself: the term *aphrodisiazein* means simply 'to make love'; while *eros*, the word for physical love or desire, is also the name of a god who is Aphrodite's companion from the moment of her birth (Hesiod, *Theogony* 201). But it would be a mistake to regard the goddess as a straightforward incarnation of the erotic impulse. Though sex is her prime concern, the narratives surrounding her reveal that her powers extend well beyond the realm of physical relations.

As a divine being, Aphrodite had close links with the Semitic goddess of love, Ishtar/Astarte, who was worshipped in Mesopotamia and Phoenicia. Aphrodite often bore the title Heavenly (*Urania*), while Astarte was invoked as the Queen of Heaven; and both goddesses were honoured with incense altars and sacrifices of doves. Sacred prostitution, one of the best-publicised aspects of the cult of Ishtar/Astarte, was also to be found in some of the centres of Aphrodite's worship. The best-attested example is Corinth: in 464 BC a Corinthian athlete named Xenophon, who had won victories in two events at the Olympic Games, fulfilled a vow which he had made to Aphrodite and dedicated a number of prostitutes to the goddess's service in her temple on the hill of Acrocorinth. The offering was commemorated in an ode by the poet Pindar:

> Young women, hostesses to many, handmaidens
> Of Attraction in wealthy Corinth,
> Who burn the golden tears of fresh frankincense,
> Often you soar in your thoughts
> To Aphrodite in the sky,
> The mother of loves.

She gave to you, girls, without blame
To pick the fruit of soft youth
In beds of desire.
With compulsion all is fair...

(Pindar, fragment 122)[20]

The historian Herodotus's statement (1.105) that the oldest cults of Aphrodite in Greece had been established by Phoenician settlers may contain a broad element of truth. The goddess had very strong associations with the island of Cyprus: the city of Paphos, the site of one of her most important temples, was seen by Greek poets as the goddess's true home; and from the time of Homer onwards the epithet most commonly applied to her was Cypris, or 'the Cyprian'. It is possible that she started life as a local Cyprian love goddess who took on some of Astarte's characteristics when Cyprus was colonised by Phoenicians in the ninth century BC. From here, the cult would have spread gradually to the mainland of Greece, a process which may be partially recaptured in the story of Aphrodite's birth from the sea and her journey across the waters. This reconstruction is speculative, however, for the picture of the goddess's early development is still very unclear.

The most famous account of the mythical origins of Aphrodite is the one given by the poet Hesiod (*Theogony* 154–206). When Cronus castrates his father Uranus and throws his genitals into the sea (see p. 20), a shining white foam or *aphros* is produced. From this there arises a beautiful goddess (Fig. 40), who floats slowly to Cyprus where she steps ashore and causes grasses to spring up beneath her slender feet. Gods and mortals call her Aphrodite, because she was born from *aphros*. She is attended from the first by Eros and Himeros (Desire), and she is allotted a sphere of influence that includes 'Fond murmurings of girls, and smiles, and tricks,/ And sweet delight, and friendliness, and charm' (Hesiod, *Theogony* 205–6).

In this narrative, Aphrodite appears as a powerful and primaeval deity. She is older than any of the other Olympians, for she is present at the first stage in the formation of our world, when Earth and Sky are separated. This view of Aphrodite as a vital cosmic force emerges even more clearly from a poem entitled *On nature*, written by the fifth-century philosopher Empedocles. In this account of the physical workings of the universe, Empedocles outlines a system in which the four elements – earth, water, air and fire – are mingled together by a controlling force called Love, so as to form the visible objects of our world: 'Love is in their midst, equal in length and breadth. Gaze on her with your mind, and do not sit with dazzled eyes. For she is recognised as being inborn in mortal limbs; through her they think kind thoughts and perform the deeds of friendship, calling her Joy by name and Aphrodite.'[21]

The account of Aphrodite's birth transmitted by Hesiod may have been inspired in part by some early myth-maker's belief that her name had been derived from the Greek word *aphros*, which can mean either semen or sea-foam. Similarly, her relationship with Uranus could have been invented in an attempt to explain the goddess's title of Heavenly, or Urania. But these considerations would not in themselves have given rise to the most striking element in the story, the castration episode. The basic association implied between the act of love (symbolised by Aphrodite) and the act of castration points to a pervasive fear of female sexuality, a response which may also have helped to determine the paired but contrasting roles of Aphrodite and Athena in the narrative (see p. 21). Both goddesses are born from the male alone. But while Aphrodite emerges from

Uranus's genitals as a result of the latter's overthrow, Athena comes out of Zeus's head and helps to ensure his supremacy. Thus the birth of a goddess renowned for her sexual activity is ascribed to a period when the female principle is still strong; while the consolidation of male control is marked by the advent of a goddess who espouses virginity. The same polarisation could be said to mark the subsequent careers of the two deities: Athena is unfailingly loyal and helpful to her worshippers; Aphrodite on the other hand is often seen as the female force that lays men low.[22]

The power possessed by Aphrodite is disturbing but also essential. In the anonymous *Homeric Hymn to Aphrodite*, she is honoured as the irresistible sexual urge that operates on every level of creation. She is 'the Cyprian, who stirs sweet longing in gods/ and subdues the races of mortal men as well as/ the birds that swoop from the sky and all the beasts/ that are nurtured in their multitudes on both land and sea' (2–5). Among deities, we are told, only the virgin goddesses Athena, Artemis and Hestia are immune to her ministrations. Zeus himself cannot escape her, but on one occasion he did get his own back by inspiring her with love for a mortal man, the Trojan Anchises. Aphrodite went to visit him while he was tending his cattle, and as she strode across the wooded slopes of Mount Ida she drew with her a retinue of enchanted beasts:

> And along with her, fawning, dashed grey wolves
> and lions with gleaming eyes and bears and swift leopards,
> ever hungry for deer. And when she saw them, she was delighted
> in her heart and placed longing in their breasts,
> so that they lay together in pairs along the shady glens.

> (69–74)

In this scene, Aphrodite is pictured as a powerful nature goddess, a Mistress of Animals who, rather than tending young creatures as Artemis does, ensures that the coupling takes place which will bring them into being.

Her relationship with the world of nature may be present also in the myth of her passion for the beautiful Cyprian youth Adonis, who was born from the bark of a myrrh tree. While out hunting, Adonis is fatally gored by a boar, and from the drops of his blood which fall to the earth the goddess causes scarlet anemones to spring up. In an alternative version of the story, Adonis is still a baby when Aphrodite falls in love with him. She hides him in a chest and gives him to Persephone, queen of the Underworld, for safekeeping. But the goddess of death is so enchanted with him that she refuses to give him back, and the dispute between the two deities is eventually brought before Zeus. He decrees that the boy is to spend a third of each year by himself, a third with Persephone, and a third with Aphrodite. In this way, he becomes subject to an annual death and resurrection.

Adonis' name is clearly derived from a west Semitic word *Adon*, meaning Lord, and he may well have been in origin a god who made his way from Phoenicia to Greece in the company of Aphrodite. His myth had its counterpart in an annual festival, the Adonia, which was celebrated in various parts of the Greek world, chiefly by women. In this cult, the emphasis was on mourning the death of the god. In Athens, women planted short-lived herbs and cereals – the 'gardens of Adonis' – in pots placed on the roof-tops, and as the plants withered the women bewailed the god's passing. In Alexandria, a magnificent pageant imitating the wedding of Aphrodite and Adonis was followed on the next day by a ritual in which an image of the god was carried down to the shore, where it was cast into the sea amid loud lamentation.

The myth and cult of Adonis were seen by James Frazer (1957, pp. 426–57) as fitting neatly into his theory of the powerful nature goddess, whose annually resurrected consort symbolises the decay and revival of vegetation. But death and weeping were the central features of the cult, and it is not until the time of the Roman Empire that we hear of women rejoicing over the rebirth of the god. As a representative of vegetable life, Adonis would appear to be singularly unreliable, for the plants with which he was associated were essentially barren and ephemeral. Moreover, it is unlikely that his festivals were seen as having any link with the stages of the agricultural year, since they were not state-sponsored and were indeed looked on with suspicion by the male population.

The sexual element in the story should not be overlooked. The young lover dies prematurely as a consequence of his relationship with a powerful female. The wound inflicted by the boar can perhaps be seen, because of its location near the groin, as the equivalent of castration.[23] In the alternative version of Adonis' biography, it is Aphrodite herself who first consigns the beloved infant to the Underworld. These narratives may be thought of as expressing once again a male fear of women's sexuality. The Adonia festival, with its uninhibited exhibitions of grief and despair, clearly provided the women involved with a tremendous emotional outlet; but the association which the rite established between unrestrained sexuality and the failure of fertility perhaps spoke to them of society's need to contain women's passions within the male-dominated institution of marriage.[24]

Aphrodite is represented in Homer's poems on a much more human scale. As a personality caught up in the byzantine machinations of the Olympian deities, she cuts rather a pathetic figure. When her son Aeneas, born as a result of her affair with Anchises, is injured on the battlefield at Troy by the Greek hero Diomedes, she rushes to defend him: 'and about her beloved son came streaming her white arms,/ and with her white robe thrown in a fold in front she shielded him' (*Iliad* 5.314–15). But as a devoted mother she has very little staying power. When Diomedes wounds her in the hand she lets out a shriek and immediately drops her son. Having fled to the safety of Mount Olympus, she is taunted by the warrior Athena; and the father of the gods himself, taking her on one side, advises her to leave warfare to the others and to content herself with 'the lovely secrets of marriage' (5.429).

Aphrodite's links with marriage must surely have been seen by Greek men as somewhat disturbing, for she herself is unique among the Olympian goddesses in that she is sexually promiscuous and adulterous. Although married to the blacksmith god Hephaestus, she has well-publicised affairs with the Olympians Hermes and Ares (see p. 54), as well as with the mortals Anchises and Adonis. She also inspires adulterous desires in others. In the myth of the Judgement of Paris, Aphrodite secures for herself the award for the most beautiful of goddesses by bribing the young Trojan prince with the offer of Helen's love; but the responsibility which she thus incurs for the deadly combat of the Trojan War is referred to only obliquely in the poems of Homer. By the fifth century, however, attitudes were hardening; and in the tragic drama of this period the disruptive effects of Aphrodite's power to shatter marriages are evoked much more vividly. In Euripides' *Andromache* (289–92), Aphrodite is said, at her meeting with Paris, to have spoken 'witching words/ Most sweet to the young judge,/ But deadly too, a lewd confusion to destroy/ And throw low/ All the towers of high Troy'.[25]

It is as the source of terrible passions in married women that Aphrodite features most devastatingly in fifth-century tragedy. Most searing of all is the story of Phaedra's love for her virginal stepson Hippolytus (see p. 31). By excluding Aphrodite from his life, Hippolytus has provoked the spiteful goddess into a terrible demonstration of her power; but it is Phaedra who provides the emotional arena in which the consequences of this rejection are played out. The passion which Aphrodite inflicts on her leads eventually to the woman's suicide and to Hippolytus' brutal death at the hands of his father. As the nurse in Euripides' play comments:

> Cypris is an unbearable thing when she comes in full flood.
> She comes gently to anyone who yields, but if she finds someone out
>   of the ordinary and thinking big,
> she seizes him, and you can imagine how she humbles his pride!
> She passes through the sky; she lives in the waves
> of the sea; Cypris gives birth to all things.

> (*Hippolytus* 443–8)[26]

Underlying this narrative is the belief, present also in the story of Aphrodite's birth, that female sexuality can unhinge and destroy a man. In the work of a woman writer, a totally different view of the goddess is presented. For the poetess Sappho, Aphrodite is a gentle and accommodating deity. She descends to the earth not as a torrent of painful passion, but as one who can soothe and satisfy her worshippers. Her presence is an occasion for rejoicing:

> ... Cyprian goddess, take and pour
> gracefully like wine into golden cups,
> a nectar mingled with all the joy
> of our celebrations.[27]

The ambivalence of the male response to the goddess of love is perfectly encapsulated in an account of her given by one of the characters in Plato's dialogue *The Symposium*. According to him, there are two Aphrodites. The older one, Heavenly Aphrodite (Aphrodite Urania), is composed entirely of the male element. She inspires a love that is free from lust and is directed towards young men who are old enough to be intelligent companions. The younger goddess, Common Aphrodite (Aphrodite Pandemus), is made up equally of male and female elements. She is associated with the love experienced by the man in the street, who admires people for their bodies rather than their minds, is only interested in the sexual act, and is as likely to fall in love with a woman as a boy (*Symposium* 180d–181d). Aphrodite Pandemus was one of the goddess's cult titles, honouring her as a deity 'of the whole people', who by bringing a population together in common worship helped to strengthen the social bonds which united them. In Plato's usage, however, the ambiguity of the name has been exploited. This Aphrodite is 'common' in the derogatory sense of the word – she is a symbol of an inferior sensual love, which is distinct from the spiritual and uplifting variety which is created between males who share the same intellectual concerns.

As a sexually active goddess, Aphrodite is also inevitably a mother. Apart from the Trojan prince Aeneas, she produces a son named Hermaphroditus, the result of her love affair with the god Hermes; and according to some sources Eros is also her child. However, this aspect of her activities receives very little recognition in myth. Aphrodite is the patron of sex and sexual desire, and it seems that for the Greeks sex and motherhood do not mix. The passion which the goddess inspires is associated, in many contexts, with wildness and otherness and lack of control. To conjoin this passion with motherhood would be to accord to a female a frightening accumulation of powers which would place her beyond the orbit of male control. Hence Aphrodite is good at sex, but a failure as a mother. Our last goddess, Demeter, represents the reverse side of the process. Exemplary in her love for her child, she is negligible when it comes to sexuality.

DEMETER

Demeter's name is indicative of the most significant aspect of her identity, for *meter* is the Greek word for mother. She also has a clearly established link with the fertility of the earth. But the goddess should not be seen simply as an Earth Mother, as a straightforward personification of the powers that reside in the soil. As the patron of corn and cultivation, she is very much associated with human control of the earth: like Athena, she is a goddess of culture rather than nature.

The definitive version of the story bringing together Demeter's two roles as mother and corn goddess is presented in the anonymous *Homeric Hymn to Demeter*, which was probably written between 700 and 550 BC. One day, when Demeter's daughter Persephone was picking flowers in a meadow, she was snatched up by the god Hades, ruler of the Underworld, who carried her into the depths of the earth in his chariot. For nine days Demeter wandered through the world, with a blazing pine torch in either hand, searching for her child. Eventually the sun god Helios told her that Hades had borne her away to become his bride, and that this had happened with the consent of the girl's father, Zeus. Appalled by this treachery, Demeter deserted Mount Olympus and went to live on earth with the human race. In her journeyings she came at last to the city of Eleusis (near Athens). Here, disguised as an old woman, she found employment in the palace of the king Celeus and his wife Metaneira, who hired her as a nurse to their only son Demophoon. Under her care the baby was well on the way to becoming immortal, for Demeter secretly anointed him with ambrosia, and every night she buried him like a brand in the heart of the fire. But one night Metaneira caught her in the act, and let out a terrified scream. The angry goddess then revealed her true identity, and ordered the people of Eleusis to make amends for their lack of faith by building a magnificent temple.

Here Demeter remained, mourning for her daughter, and for a whole year she would not allow the crops to grow. The human race began to suffer from a dreadful famine, and the immortals too were becoming restless, for no sacrifices were being made to them. The various embassies despatched by Zeus left Demeter unmoved:

> She said she would never set foot again on fragrant Olympus
> and never allow the grain in the earth to sprout forth
> before seeing with her eyes her fair-faced daughter.
>
> (*Homeric Hymn* 2.331–3)

Finally the god Hermes was sent down to the Underworld to tell Hades that he must let Persephone go. Before her departure, Hades gave his bride a single honey-sweet pomegranate seed to eat, telling her that in his kingdom she would be 'mistress of everything which lives and moves' (*Homeric Hymn* 2.365). Mother and daughter were reunited at Eleusis, rushing joyfully into each other's arms. But the very first words which Demeter spoke to her offspring were these: 'Child, when you were below, did you perchance partake/ of food?' (*Homeric Hymn* 2.393–4). If she did, Demeter said, she would have to spend a third of every year in the Underworld, returning to her mother and the other immortals for the remaining two-thirds:

Whenever the earth blooms with every kind of sweet-smelling
spring flower, you shall come up again from misty darkness,
a great wonder for gods and mortal men.

(Homeric Hymn 2.401–3)

And so it turned out. Demeter made the earth teem once more with vegetation. Every year, when her daughter was restored to her in the springtime, she would do the same. Before returning to Olympus, the goddess instituted her sacred Mysteries among the people of Eleusis:

... (she) showed them the
celebration of holy rites, and explained to all
... the awful mysteries not to be transgressed, violated
or divulged, because the tongue is restrained by reverence for the gods.
Whoever on this earth has seen these is blessed,
but he who has no part in the holy rites has
another lot as he wastes away in dank darkness.

(Homeric Hymn 2.474–82)

In all subsequent versions, the essential features of this story remained unchanged. But by the fifth century BC another episode had been added. On her departure for Olympus, Demeter had taught a young man of Eleusis named Triptolemus the secrets of agriculture. He was sent off around the world with the mission of teaching the human race how to grow corn. In this way, a further dimension, an account of the origins of human civilisation, was added to the narrative. The Triptolemus incident was a very popular one in Athenian art of the Classical period (Fig. 9).

In the main narrative, Persephone's perpetual return to the Underworld is secured by the eating of a pomegranate seed. This feature of the story springs from the Greek tradition of guest-friendship: once Persephone has tasted the food that she has been offered in the Underworld, she has become subject to a sacred bond which requires that she remain loyal to the host who gave it to her. But the pomegranate was also a symbol both of fertility (presumably on account of its large number of seeds) and of death (because of the bloody colour of its juice). As a motif it stands at the heart of the Demeter and Persephone story, and encapsulates its overall theme of death and resurrection.

This myth has been subject to a large number of interpretations. Frazer's theory (see p. 38), that myths which tell of the death and resurrection of a deity were closely linked to rituals designed to promote the revival of vegetation, may appear extremely tenuous in many of its applications, but in this case it does seem peculiarly apposite. Greece was a country with very little arable land, and the threat of famine would have been a constant preoccupation in many areas, particularly in the winter months when the stock of grain harvested in the early summer was beginning to dwindle. Against this background, the reassurance offered by the myth can be easily appreciated. It provides an explanation of why the crops do not grow in winter, and at the same time holds out a promise of future regeneration. The Eleusinian Mysteries, the rites associated with the myth, were celebrated in September, just before the planting of the seed corn in October. When Persephone disappears into the Underworld, this must surely represent the burying of the seed corn in the ground; while her reunion with her mother symbolises its return to the earth in the form of crops. Thus in the period when the seed is destined to die, its resurrection is vouchsafed to the celebrants; and in this way, the renewal of human life is guaranteed.[28]

But the significance of the myth is not confined to its agricultural content. The intimate relationship between mother and daughter is an impressive feature of the story, and it is highlighted again in the fact that the Greeks often referred to them simply as 'the Two Goddesses', or even sometimes as 'the Demeters'. The psychologist Jung and his collaborator Kerenyi (1963, pp. 101–83) see the two goddesses as a dual entity, representing two distinct but complementary phases in a woman's life, maidenhood and motherhood. When Persephone and Demeter are reunited, we are reminded of the continuity which springs from the merging of these stages: the maiden becomes the mother, and the mother gives birth to the maiden. In the words of Jung, it might be said 'that every woman extends backwards into her mother and forwards into her daughter ... The conscious experience of these ties produces the feeling that (a woman's) life is spread out over generations – the first step towards the immediate experience and conviction of being outside time, which brings with it a feeling of immortality' (1963, p. 162). From the myth of Demeter and Persephone there springs an awareness of the contribution which the individual makes to the cycle of regeneration. The rebirth of the grain and the recreation of human life are to be seen as two manifestations of a divine pattern of eternal renewal which is revealed to us by the two goddesses.

However, for a woman living in ancient Greece the story may have had a more immediate and less positive significance. Marriage to a stranger, arranged by her father against her mother's wishes, and envisaged as a kind of rape, would have been a reality and not a fanciful tale for many Greek women. That the event was also seen as bringing with it a kind of death – a loss of individual identity – can be easily imagined. Indeed, the fear would always be present that marriage might be fatal in a very real sense, for many women died in childbirth. The link commonly made in myth between death and marriage can thus be seen to have its roots in a shared feminine experience. Persephone, of course, provides the ultimate example of this response, for she marries Death himself.

The more abstract implications of the theme of death have been emphasised by Burkert (1979, p. 139). He points out that the return of the maiden is very much a mixed blessing. Persephone was the queen of the Underworld, and it was in this guise that she was chiefly worshipped in ancient Greece. When she makes her annual ascent to the earth, she is bringing renewal, but she is also bringing death into our world. Looked at from this point of view, the myth becomes one of many which tell of the terms on which the gift of life is offered to the human race. Through the annual growth of crops and the ability to reproduce, Demeter and Persephone confer a kind of immortality on human beings. When the Triptolemus episode is added to the narrative, the art of agriculture becomes another factor in our survival. But the price which we have to pay for this endless regeneration is our individual mortality: 'a dimension of death is introduced into life, and a dimension of life is introduced into death' (Burkert, 1985, p. 161).

To the worshippers of Demeter and Persephone the prospect is at least held out of a better fate after death. The speech made by Demeter when she institutes the Eleusinian Mysteries hints at a distinction between the lot of the initiated and that of the uninitiated. This is elaborated on in a fragment from Sophocles' play Triptolemus: 'Thrice blessed are those mortals who have seen these rites and thus enter into Hades: for them alone there is life, for the others, all is misery' (Sophocles, fragment 837). In this respect, the symbolic value of corn appears to be very close to the one expressed in the New Testament: 'Except a corn of wheat fall into the ground and die, it abideth alone: but if it die, it bringeth forth much fruit. He that loveth his life shall lose it; and he that hateth his life in this world shall keep it unto life eternal' (St. John 12.24–25). The guarantee of some form of personal salvation is unusual as an aspect of Greek religion in the Archaic and Classical periods. But the evidence of the *Homeric Hymn to Demeter* would suggest that the Eleusinian Mysteries did encompass this belief, and there is no direct evidence to suggest that it did not go back to the origins of the cult.

Festivals of Demeter and Persephone were very common in ancient Greece. Many of them were linked to important stages in the farmer's year, and some of them, such as the festival of the Thesmophoria, had a close connection with the experience of women (see pp. 163–5). But the ritual most intimately associated with the myth of Persephone's rape and return was that of the Eleusinian Mysteries, celebrated at the town of Eleusis, fourteen miles to the west of Athens, and administered by Athenian officials. Initiation into the Mysteries was open to all Greek speakers, both male and female. Following some preliminary rituals in Athens, a procession of prospective initiates set out along the Sacred Way linking the city with the sanctuary at Eleusis. Initiation took place during the night in a huge pillared hall called the *telesterion* (the 'initiation-place'). Details of the rites were a closely guarded secret, and we have little reliable information concerning them.[29] However, it seems certain that they included the revelation of sacred objects; and some re-enactment of the myth of the goddesses was also doubtless performed. The emotional impact of Persephone's return would have been enhanced by a sudden blaze of light. Torches, carried by Demeter in her search for her daughter, were an important emblem of the cult, and there are numerous representations of them at Eleusis. The lighting of these torches to celebrate the deity's epiphany would have produced an impressive underscoring of the theme of cosmic renewal implicit in the narrative to which these rituals were linked.

CONCLUSION

There is a marked tendency in Greek mythological representations to divide powerful women up into the sexually active but hostile, and the virginal but helpful. Just one example of this antithesis can be found in Aeschylus' *Oresteia* trilogy, where Clytemnestra can be seen on one level as the wicked mother who has to be eliminated, while Athena is the friendly virgin who sets everything to rights (see pp. 27–8). Although it would be an oversimplification to analyse the Olympian goddesses purely in terms of this bad mother/good virgin polarity, it is significant that Demeter is the only one among them who presents a positive image of motherhood.

This attitude to mothers could be explained on a purely psychological basis, an interpretation which has been discussed in detail by Philip Slater (1971), who employs Freudian analysis to account for the various destructive and devouring mothers of Greek myth. According to Slater, men's natural fear of female reproductive powers beyond their control became accentuated in Classical Athens on account of the sharply dichotomised lives led by men and women. Athenian boys, who spent their formative years cooped up in the home with women who were frustrated and bitter, would have been the object of disturbingly ambivalent feelings on the part of their mothers: intense involvement springing from the need to find an outlet for repressed aspirations and sexual desires, coupled with tremendous hostility inspired by the knowledge that their sons would grow up into oppressive Athenian men. Hence the Athenian male's fear of sexually active women; and hence the violent mothers of Athenian myth and tragedy.

This reconstruction should certainly not be dismissed out of hand; but it lacks an awareness of the political dimension of the male response – of the interaction that takes place between individual psychological impulse and collective ideology. In a society in which women's reproductive powers were carefully regulated, not merely by the male-dominated institution of the family, but also by the state, there was clearly an official recognition of the crucial social role played by women as reproducers of the citizen group; and in this context a collective anxiety about women who were fertile was likely to develop (see pp. 120–1, 125–6). Thus, there would have been a political as well as an individual dimension to the invention of hostile mothers. A child-bearing woman was supposed to come under male domination, and any female who tried to evade this social truth, and to take control of events, was clearly up to no good.

Conversely, only a woman who was not fertile could be allowed, at least on the level of the imagination, to be both powerful and beneficent. Virginity in a goddess would have been seen as a mark of potency and inviolability. Since in theory wives were subordinate to their husbands both sexually and socially, it may well have been felt that the married state was incompatible with a goddess's independence, and hence with her ability to confer independence on others. The symbolic value of resistance to male domination can be appreciated in the case of all three Olympian virgins. As a goddess of war and of urban life, Athena could prevent both warriors and cities from being overpowered by their enemies. Artemis looked after hunters, and ensured that they maintained the upper hand in their struggle against the animals. Hestia, the protector of the household, guaranteed the self-sufficiency and integrity of the family units on whose survival the state depended.

This idealised construction of female virginity would have been reinforced by Greek attitudes to male sexuality. Burkert (1983, pp. 60–61) has pointed out that sexual abstinence was often a part of the preparation for war or hunting, and Athena and Artemis, the goddesses who brought success in these activities, would have served to validate this ban through their own inaccessibility. A negative version of the same message can probably be extracted from the story of Actaeon's association with Artemis (see p. 31): the hunter who breaks the taboo on sex and dares to look at a naked virgin loses the battle against the animals, and becomes the hunted instead of the hunter. Like many other people, the Greeks seem to have regarded celibacy as a precondition of physical achievement. Their view of sex as a form of bodily combat, the belief that it involved the release of vital fluids or contamination with feminine weakness, and the association with loss of self-control, may all have helped to inspire the notion that erotic activity could have a debilitating effect on a man.[30]

But what are we to make of the virgin goddesses' associations with motherhood? Part of the explanation probably lies in their fostering role: young heroes and warriors, hunters and girls approaching puberty are all cared for by these goddesses, who are allowed to display the benevolent qualities which are for the most part denied to the genuine mothers. But the idea that Athena and Artemis are boundary-crossers (see p. 19) – being capable in their case of passing over the dividing line between women and men – helps to throw a little more light on this aspect of their characterisation. As females, they would naturally be seen as sharing in the nature of women; but as females who repudiate the most characteristic of women's functions (marriage and childbirth) and engage instead in the most characteristic of masculine activities (fighting and hunting), they would also be regarded as honorary males. By combining the female and the male principles in this way, they would be able to bring women's creativity within the orbit of men's control.

This ability is best illustrated by the role of Artemis. The stages in a woman's life which she supervises – menstruation, loss of virginity on marriage, childbirth – all involve bleeding. Her task can thus be identified with that of the male, whose job it is to bring about bloodshed, whether in war, in hunting and sacrifice, or in their relationships with women. If, in the interests of reproducing society, Artemis has to make women bleed, then she must herself resemble the male: she must be active, not passive; she must shed blood but not bleed herself. As a female, Artemis can get close to women; but as a virgin she can assume a dominant position and cause the wounds through which women give birth.[31] These wounds are the price which women have to pay to a goddess whose own espousal of virginity means that it is only with reluctance that she allows women to bear children.

Comparative evidence exists which tends to bear out this interpretation. In the Bimin-Kuskusmin tribe of Papua New Guinea, fertile women are seen as possessing great power which can become dangerously polluting unless it is controlled and properly channelled by men. To assist them in this task they have a female ritual leader, the *waneng aiyem ser*, a post-menopausal woman whose gender is highly ambiguous. On assuming her position she takes on a masculine name, wears regalia that are partly female and partly male, and is allowed to share in some of the men's privileges, such as the right to speak on certain public occasions. When women are in labour, she has the role of ritual midwife; while at male initiation ceremonies she handles menstrual blood, and stands with her legs apart so that the young men can pass through them in a form of rebirth: for this reason she is sometimes called the 'male mother' (Poole, 1981, p. 117).

The anomalous virginity of the more shadowy Hestia must be explained in rather a different way. Unlike Athena and Artemis, Hestia is not androgynous and does not engage in masculine activities: she comes closer than either of her fellow-virgins to exemplifying the chaste demeanour which was expected of a young woman prior to her marriage. In Ancient Greece, life-long celibacy in real people was rarely seen as a good thing in itself. Virginity was prized rather as a form of freshness, a prelude to subsequent fruitfulness, and hence as a symbol of endless renewal. In this context Hestia can be seen to represent the powerful potential of the virgin daughter who will one day marry and produce children; and it is this which establishes her link with the regeneration of the family unit.

In Classical Athens, at least, Hestia's virginity would have carried an extra dimension, one which underpinned the patriarchal nature of the family. The virginity of a bride was one of the guarantees of the paternity of subsequent children, and this helped to establish its value in the eyes of Athenian men. It is a wise child that knows its own father: but in Classical Athens, where it was an offence to have sex with an Athenian woman before she was married, or with an Athenian woman who was married to somebody else (see p. 125), they did their very best to ensure that children knew who their fathers were, and, more importantly, that fathers knew who their children were. Virginity seen in this light can come to be associated with loyalty to the father.

J.-P. Vernant (1983) provides a further insight into the link between Hestia's virginity and patriarchal control. When a woman marries, she renounces the hearth of her own family and goes to join that of her husband. There is therefore a basic ambiguity in the symbolic association of women with the fixity and permanence of the home: it is the woman who moves from one household to another, while the man remains in the same household for the whole of his life. According to Vernant, Hestia's virginity can be interpreted as reconciling this contradiction on the level of religious representation. A real woman has this one element of mobility in her life; but through Hestia, who never marries and therefore never leaves the parental home, this element is denied. In this way, the need to import a woman from another household in order to perpetuate one's own is also denied. 'Through the goddess of the hearth, the function of fertility, dissociated from sexual relations ..., can appear as an indefinite prolongation of the paternal line through the daughter, without a "foreign" woman being necessary for procreation' (pp. 120–1).[32]

Finally, it should be said by way of an addendum that there is no close parallel, in spite of their connections with motherhood, between the virgin goddesses and the Virgin Mary. Just a glance at the lifestyles of Athena and Artemis is sufficient to tell us that they are expressing a very different ideal. While these two deities can be seen to act as mediators between female and male, the Virgin Mary serves rather to create a relationship between divine and human, by becoming the vehicle through which a mortal child with a divine father is brought into the world.[33] In this respect, the women who are much more closely comparable with the Virgin Mother are the various mortals – Alcmene, Semele, Leda, and so on – who in Greek myth give birth to the illegitimate sons of Zeus and other deities. None of these women would have been considered to be virgins in a biological sense – sexual intercourse with the god in question is generally an undisputed part of the process. But it is interesting to note that one of them, Coronis, who becomes pregnant with Apollo's son Asclepius, is referred to by the poet Pindar (*Pythian Odes* 3.34) as a *parthenos*, the word that is normally translated by us as 'virgin'.

Some scholars have argued on this basis that the significance of the term *parthenos* is social rather than biological: it denotes a woman who has reached puberty but is still unmarried, rather than one who has never been penetrated by a man. However, after a thorough examination of the evidence, Sissa (1990a, pp. 73–104) maintains that a *parthenos* is indeed a virgin, but in the case of the unmarried mothers the virginity is a sham: there is a degree of irony in the application of the term to these women, and in some instances it becomes a definite stigma – a mark of their shame. The debate is an interesting one, but it does not impinge on our interpretation of the virgin goddesses, who have all quite unequivocally foresworn sexual relations with men.

The Virgin Mary may not in her function resemble the virgin Olympians, but in one respect there is a similar pattern of thought behind her characterisation. Like Athena, Artemis and Hestia, the Virgin holds out the promise of a fertility that does not involve sexuality, and does not therefore threaten men with feminine power or feminine passion beyond their control. In this way, as Zeitlin has commented, 'Mother is denied but not denied' (1977, p. 172). Hera and Aphrodite, goddesses whose sexuality has not been suppressed, are both in their different ways seen as dangerous to men. Only in the case of Demeter did Greek mothers encounter a narrative which presented an uplifting view of the fundamental role which they played in Greek society.

4

Women in the poems of Homer

Many of the mythological images of women created by the Greeks were based on characters from the poems of Homer, which by the Classical Age had attained a hallowed place in the canon of Greek literature. Even in that period there was considerable uncertainty about when the author of the *Iliad* and *Odyssey* had actually lived. Most modern commentators assign him to the late eighth century BC, but some would put him rather later, in the seventh or even the early sixth century BC. What seems almost certain is that the poems as we know them were composed at some time in the Archaic Age, at least five hundred years after the Trojan War and its aftermath, the events which they purport to depict.[1] Few people nowadays doubt that they were the end-product of a long process of oral composition and transmission, and that for several centuries wandering bards had been taking up and embroidering the themes that eventually came down to us in the work of Homer. As a result, the poems contain descriptions of material and social items which derive from a wide range of periods, so that they cannot be assumed to represent a single well-defined historical era. This begins to cause difficulties when we try to use Homer as a source of evidence for the social history of early Greece (see p. 65). In this section, which is concerned with the cultural representation of women rather than their social reality, this lack of historical definition is not a major problem.

In what follows, I shall be examining Homer's treatment of a variety of females – mortals, monsters, and goddesses. But one group of women who play a significant part in both narratives will not be considered: Homer's characterisation of the Olympian goddesses, some of whom have a very high profile in the Trojan War, has already been discussed in the previous chapter.

WOMEN IN THE *ILIAD*

On one level, the women represented in the *Iliad* are peripheral. The *Iliad* is a poem about the Trojan War, and about the heroes who fight in it; and, in the words of the

Trojan prince Hector, 'war is men's business' (6.492). Women make very few appearances in the work, and as far as the action is concerned they are insignificant. They are, however, crucial to the poem's plot. The abduction of Helen by the Trojan prince Paris has caused the war as a whole; and the theft of another woman – the captive Briseis – forms the basis of the specific events of the *Iliad*, since the wrath of the Greek hero Achilles when Briseis is taken from him is its principal theme. When the Greek commander Agamemnon is forced to liberate his own slave-girl Chryseis, awarded to him from the booty captured in the fighting, he seizes Briseis from Achilles by way of compensation. Achilles then withdraws his services from the Greek army, and as a result disaster threatens the Greeks.

Although a woman helps in this way to determine the course of events in the poem, she features in this respect as a piece of property – as stolen goods – rather than as a human being. Briseis has been awarded to Achilles as a 'prize of honour' (9.344), and it is as a status symbol that she is valued both by him and by Agamemnon. For these two, passing Briseis backwards and forwards between them is a way of defining their relationship. 'What do you want? To keep your own prize and have me sitting here/ lacking one?' (*Iliad* 1.133–4)[2] are the words with which Agamemnon announces his intention of appropriating the slave-girl of one of his allies. When the commander later tries to come to terms with Achilles, he offers as a mark of his goodwill to return Briseis, with whom he swears he has not slept, and to send in addition 'gifts in abundance' – tripods, cauldrons, gold, horses, and seven women of Lesbos, skilled in weaving (9.119–35). This is one of a number of instances in the poem where women are ticked off as one item in a list of valuables. For example, when Achilles is organising funeral games in honour of his beloved friend Patroclus, he sets out as prizes for the wrestling match:

> . . . a great tripod, to set over fire, for the winner.
> The Achaians among themselves valued it at the worth of twelve oxen.
> But for the beaten man he set in their midst a woman
> skilled in much work of her hands, and they rated her at four oxen.
>
> (23.702–5)

Like Briseis, the woman who is being offered here as a prize would have been a slave, and as such might be expected to be the object of proprietorial attitudes. But women given in marriage are also seen as gifts (see pp. 23–4, 67–8), and like slaves they can serve as the instruments of men's political relationships. This practice tends to invest women with a symbolic worth, over and above the value which they possess as workers, as sexual partners and as bearers of children. For this reason, the women who feature in poetry can easily become the vehicles of meaning: the symbolism ascribed to them in real life converts them into figures that are well suited to the literary function of commenting on the activities of men. In the *Iliad*, this is particularly apparent in the case of Briseis, whose transfers stand in the narrative as a token for the initial disaffection and subsequent reassimilation of Achilles into the Greek army.

Throughout these transactions Briseis remains by and large a shadowy figure, whose own responses to her treatment at the hands of her male masters are not recorded by the poet. But it would be unfair to Homer not to mention that there is one occasion when he allows us to see her, not as a commodity, but as a human being with a personal history and powerful feelings. When Briseis is eventually returned to Achilles, she immediately catches sight of the mangled corpse of the hero's beloved friend Patroclus, slain in the fighting. She takes him up in her arms, and in the impromptu lament that follows she exclaims on the misery of her life. When her husband and three brothers had all been killed in battle (the former by Achilles himself), Patroclus comforted her and promised to persuade Achilles to marry her. 'Therefore I weep your death without ceasing. You were kind always' (19.300).

Helen, like Briseis, seems to bear only a token relationship to the masculine encounters related in the *Iliad*. She makes only three appearances in the work, a fact which seems in itself to be indicative of her true status in the general hostilities. But Helen is a princess and not a slave, and as such is represented in the poem as a more interesting and complex personality than Briseis. When she does appear, the question of her responsibility for the war is inevitably raised, although in this respect the role attributed to her is notable for its ambiguity. Her arrival on the high tower in Troy is greeted by the old men gathered there with whispered comments on her beauty: 'still, though she be such, let her go away in the ships, lest/ she be left behind, a grief to us and our children' (3.159–60). Helen herself, when speaking to Priam (Book 3) and to Hector (Book 6), refers to herself as a 'slut' (3.180) and a 'nasty bitch' (6.344), and wishes that she had died (3.173) or been swept away by a storm (6.345–48), before becoming the cause of so much unhappiness.

But Helen is seen as a victim as well as a cause. Priam, when he meets her on the tower, speaks gently to her and assures her that he does not blame her: 'to me the gods are blameworthy/ who drove upon me this sorrowful war against the Achaians' (3.164–5). Later, when Aphrodite has rescued Paris from the battlefield and is bullying Helen into paying him a visit, it is Helen herself who bitterly expresses her sense of victimisation. Go to Paris yourself, she says; comfort him; stay with him forever: 'I am not going to him. It would be too shameful' (3.410). But in the end the goddess prevails, and Helen departs, subdued and frightened by Aphrodite's threats. This is Helen at her most sympathetic, viewed as a mere plaything of powerful deities. But at the same time her intimacy with the goddess of love makes her appear a somewhat mysterious and dangerous character.

Helen, then, is both blameless and blameworthy. Her treatment in the *Iliad* provides us with an example of what some modern critics refer to as 'double motivation', a device whereby two contradictory explanations of the course of events – divine control *and* human agency – are juxtaposed. In this case, the double motivation is made all the more conspicuous by the fact that at one point it is expressed by a single character: Helen refers to herself as 'a nasty bitch evil-intriguing' (6.344), and then five lines later asserts that 'the gods had brought it about that these vile things must be' (6.349). As readers, we are left to decide between these two different interpretations of causality. We are not, however, invited to see the war as something that the fighting parties have brought upon themselves. The responsibility lies either with the gods, or with a woman.

Apart from the women who are seen as both the causes and the rewards of strife among men, mortal females feature in the *Iliad* largely as wives and mothers. Again, their appearances are few and far between. The outstanding wife – the only wife apart from the dubious Helen to receive any significant individual treatment – is Andromache, who is married to the Trojan prince Hector. When her husband returns from the battlefield and she runs to meet him at the city gates, she begs him not to go back to the fighting. Her parents and her seven brothers are dead, Andromache says. 'Hector thus you are father to me, and my honoured mother,/ you are my brother, and you it is who are my young husband./ Please take pity on me then, stay here on the rampart,/ that you may not leave your child an orphan, your wife a widow . . .' (6.429–32). Here is a woman whose place in the world is defined by her relationship with men, and who will be helpless once those men are no longer there to protect her.

Hector's reply to his wife shows genuine concern about the treatment she will receive once Troy falls and she is enslaved. But in spite of this he is not prepared to stay out of the battle, although he knows that one day he is bound to be killed. Andromache, demonstrating a rather surprising insight into military matters, has advised him to remain in the city and look to the defence of a vulnerable section of walling; but Hector rejects the suggestion with a pronouncement which reaffirms the fundamental division between masculine and feminine spheres of activity:

> Go therefore back to our house, and take up your own work,
> the loom and the distaff, and see to it that your handmaidens
> ply their work also; but the men must see to the fighting,
> all men who are the people of Ilion, but I beyond others.

(6.490–3)

The scene between Andromache and Hector is nevertheless an intimate and moving one. By allowing the reader this brief glimpse of their affectionate marriage, the poet skilfully introduces into the narrative a contrasting perspective, one which temporarily locates the hero in the normal society which exists beyond the exceptional events of the battlefield. At the same time, the death of the hero, the end of the marriage and the collapse of the society are foreshadowed with the utmost pathos. Later, when Hector is slain by Achilles and Priam finally brings his body back to Troy, the laments of the women serve to remind us once more of the personal relationships binding the warrior to the city whose continued existence is now under threat. The words of Andromache in particular also recreate the personal pain of a woman bereaved by warfare:

> ... but for me passing all others is left the bitterness
> and the pain, for you did not die in bed, and stretch your arms to me,
> nor tell me some last intimate word that I could remember
> always, all the nights and days of my weeping for you.

(24.742–5)

The earlier interview between Andromache and Hector at the gates has suggested to some critics that one of the important functions assigned to female characters in the *Iliad* is the exertion, or attempted exertion, of a restraining influence over the men: the heroes' refusal to be restrained then underlines their courage and nobility.[3] This could be called the 'man's gotta do what a man's gotta do' syndrome. It comes to the fore on a number of other occasions, most notably when Hector's mother Hecabe, just before her son's final, fatal encounter with Achilles, stands on the walls above the battlefield and, holding out one of her breasts to Hector, pleads with him not to accept the challenge to single combat (22.79–92).

But there are also a few instances where women take on the opposite role, of inciting men to fight. When Helen joins Paris in his bedchamber, she taunts him with cowardice and tells him to go back to the battlefield, then immediately adds, 'No, better not, you will probably get killed' (3.432–6). Helen's contradictory character is certainly on display here; but she is also fulfilling the 'white feather' function of attempting to shame men into action. A story told to Achilles by his old tutor Phoenix describes how, when the hero Meleager had withdrawn from a war, he eventually gave in to his wife's tearful entreaties not to allow his city to be captured (9.529–99). Achilles himself has a mother, the sea-goddess Thetis, who may not exactly urge her son on to fight, but who accepts that it is his glorious destiny to beat back disaster from the Greek forces. When Achilles determines to return to the fighting, Thetis volunteers to fly off to Mount Olympus to commission a new set of armour for him, even though she knows that his death will soon follow the slaying of Hector (18.65–137).

In all their roles the female characters of the *Iliad* are being used by the poet to comment on the world of war and the values of the fighting men. The function assigned to them in both the narrative and the society which it represents is not necessarily downgraded, but they are nevertheless seen as peripheral to the real business of life. Women provide causes and rewards, encouragement or restraint; they reflect the sufferings of warfare and represent the social ties which form the background to the battle scenes. Always, they exist only in relation to their menfolk. Although they are implicated in life's most serious transactions, they do not take an active part in them.

WOMEN IN THE ODYSSEY

In passing from the *Iliad* to the *Odyssey*, we encounter women who, instead of standing in the wings, occupy very often the centre of the stage. Far from being passive, most of them are represented as powerful and vigorous personalities. This indeed is one of the most striking and refreshing aspects of the *Odyssey*. The power of these women is often seen in a negative light, however. On his return voyage from Troy the hero Odysseus, who has incurred the enmity of the marine god Poseidon, is forced to spend nine years roaming the seas in his attempt to reach his native island of Ithaca. Many obstacles are placed in the way of his homecoming, and it is significant that the great majority of these are female (the most notable exception being the one-eyed giant Polyphemus). On the more positive side, marriage gradually emerges as one of the central themes of the poem, and its importance for both women and men is often brought home to us. As Odysseus says to the princess Nausicaa, 'for nothing is better than this, more steadfast/ than when two people, a man and his wife, keep a harmonious household' (6.182–4).[4]

Of the female obstructions encountered by Odysseus on his epic journey, some of them present obvious physical dangers. The hero and his men have to negotiate their way between the whirlpool Charybdis, who sucks down water and then vomits it up again, and the dreadful Scylla, who reaches down from her cavern high above the straits, and with her six heads and eighteen rows of teeth snatches up and devours six of Odysseus's companions (12.73–126, 222–59, 426–46). These monsters are unmistakably female, and their significance probably extends beyond that of the natural hazards faced by sailors on the high seas. The imagery associated with them suggests that women are to be seen as having the power to engulf and obliterate men if they become too closely involved with them: that this engulfment is of a sexual nature is an impression evoked by the symbols of the yawning chasm and the man-eating monster. The Sirens, whose seductive songs lure sailors to a lingering death on their beach (12.39–54), are associated not just with physical obliteration, but with the temptations of a godlike but debilitating omniscience. 'Over all the generous earth we know everything that happens' (12.191) are the words with which they advertise their attractions. Odysseus, who has plugged his sailors' ears with wax, is himself, with unblocked ears, lashed to the mast of his ship so that he can hear but not follow their magical music.

The nymph Calypso poses a similar threat, in that she too can offer Odysseus a superhuman but ultimately paralysing existence. The first time that we meet the hero he is sitting on the beach of Calypso's island, 'breaking his heart in tears, lamentation, and sorrow' (5.83). Calypso has been detaining him for the last seven years, hoping to make him her husband; and now the restless sailor is longing to return home. Modern readers may feel little sympathy for a man who protests continually that he is desperate to see his family once more, but who for seven years has apparently made little attempt to tear himself away from the arms of his lover. To many women, this will seem like a piece of very familiar male hypocrisy. But there is no doubt that Homer wants us to see Odysseus's residence with the nymph as an enforced one and his grief as perfectly genuine. Calypso has not, however, been a cruel mistress. She rescued Odysseus from the sea after all his companions had been killed, and since then has cherished him fondly, in a golden-age environment of trees, flowers and fountains. As she confesses to the god Hermes who instructs her to release the hero, 'I had hopes also/ that I could make him immortal and all his days to be endless' (5.135–6). But Odysseus prefers the norm of a painful but vigorous humanity to the blissful transcendence represented by the female figure.

At an earlier stage in his journey the hero enters another female-dominated environment while visiting the island of the immortal enchantress Circe.[5] Here too Odysseus finds himself in a kind of paradise, where the meat and fine wine are unlimited and there is incessant feasting at silver tables. Like Calypso, Circe when first encountered in the poem is seated at a magnificent loom, singing in a sweet voice. The fantastic islands ruled over by both of these goddesses are wild and uncultivated: agriculture, the quintessential economic activity of the male, is nowhere to be seen. But women's work, in the form of spinning and weaving, is ever-present, a fact which helps to underline the upside-down nature of these magical countries. Wool-working and music establish the predominance on the islands of female domestic values, and speak of women's ability to entice and entrap men with their beautiful designs.

Initially, Circe appears to be far more sinister than Calypso. Conversely, once she is disarmed she becomes much more positively helpful. When a detachment of Odysseus' men first approaches her dwelling, they come across a group of lions and wolves who mysteriously haunt the glade. The audience soon learns why there are so many animals about the place, for Circe puts a drug into the men's drink to make them 'forgetful of their own country' (10.236), then touches them with her wand and turns them all into pigs. Odysseus, setting out to investigate his men's disappearance, is supplied by the god Hermes with an antidote to the drug. Once inside the house, having failed in spite of his hostess's ministrations to turn into a pig, he rushes at the mystified Circe with his drawn sword. She at once invites him to join her 'in the bed of love' (10.335), but Odysseus refuses to oblige until she has sworn a solemn oath that she will not devise any evil against him: without this, 'when I am naked you can make me a weakling, unmanned' (10.341). After the oath and the love-making, Circe turns the 'nine-year-old porkers' in her pen back into men (10.390), and for a whole year entertains Odysseus and his restored companions lavishly in her home. When Odysseus finally asks her to help him on his way home, she immediately agrees, and provides him with a detailed itinerary and much useful advice.

In this episode, the sexual imagery seems fairly explicit. The reduction of men to animals – animals who are disturbingly submissive and fawning – suggests the mindless bestiality which is seen as the consequence of sexual domination by a woman. This notion is amplified in the 'Delilah-type' characterisation of Circe, who is a woman capable of reducing men to impotence once they are naked. The answer to this, in Odysseus's case, is a forcible assertion of masculinity – and here we can surely be confident that the drawn sword has the phallic connotations which Freudianism would attribute to it. As soon as he has demonstrated by word and deed that he is the one who is in control, then sex can be safely enjoyed by the hero; and in these circumstances the woman's love, which is otherwise so damaging, becomes positively beneficent.

Like Circe, though in a far more subtle fashion, the princess Nausicaa fulfils the dual role of female helper and hindrance. When Odysseus is shipwrecked on the coast of Scheria, the land ruled by Nausicaa's father, he is apparently charmed by the plucky young woman whom he encounters on the beach and who directs him towards the assistance which he so badly needs. Nausicaa herself, as she admits to her maids, is smitten by the stranger's handsome appearance: 'if only the man to be called my husband could be like this one . . .' (6.244). Later on in the palace, the idea of a marriage with Nausicaa is tentatively put to Odysseus by her father: 'how I wish that . . . / you could have my daughter and be called my son-in-law, staying/ here with me. I would dower you with a house and properties,/ if you stayed by your own good will' (7.311–15). Odysseus does not pursue this offer, and one does not feel that in this instance he is seriously tempted to abandon his homecoming. Nevertheless, the temptation is there, and once again it is a woman who provides it. When Nausicaa bids goodbye to the handsome wayfarer, she is still full of admiration; and Odysseus' reply to her suggests, perhaps, a little regret: '. . . I will pray to you, as to a goddess,/ all the days of my life. For maiden, my life was your gift' (8.467–8).

Unequivocal female aid is provided by the goddess Athena, who works continuously behind the scenes to bring her favourite hero back to his native land, and time and again pops up in one disguise or another in order to supply assistance or encouragement. Athena on one level can be understood as the benign counterpart of the goddess Calypso, whose succour is stifling and ultimately destructive; and here one remembers that the lure presented by Calypso is a sexual one, while Athena is a virgin goddess. The contrast helps to reinforce the notion that it is a woman's sexuality which is potentially so threatening to a man's independence. The asexual Athena is the only female in the poem whose commitment to Odysseus' return is totally unambiguous.

The poem also includes representations of women who, though not directly involved in Odysseus' journey, serve to illustrate the varieties of homecoming experienced by the heroes who fought at Troy. Notable among these is the beautiful Helen, whom Odysseus' son Telemachus encounters when he goes off in quest of news of his father. His visit to the palace at Lacedaemon provides an intriguing glimpse of the domestic life enjoyed by Menelaus and his celebrated wife, reunited after so many years of bitter warfare. Not surprisingly, their relationship, though smooth on the surface, seems to bristle with an undercurrent of tension. Helen treats Telemachus to a story about one of his father's exploits, when he went on a spying mission to Troy, and on receiving some aid from Helen revealed to her all the secrets of the Greek war strategy: '. . . my heart/ was happy, my heart had changed by now and was for going back/ home again . . .' (4.259–61). But this tale of remorse is immediately capped by one from Menelaus, who describes how Odysseus restrained the Greeks crouching inside the wooden horse when Helen walked three times around the animal impersonating the voices of the concealed men's wives. Menelaus courteously prefaces this account with the placatory comment, 'you will have been moved by/ some divine spirit who wished to grant glory to the Trojans', but he immediately adds, 'and Deiphobos, a godlike man, was with you when you came' (4.274–6), mentioning the name of the Trojan whom the supposedly repentant Helen had married after the death of Paris. This needling exchange instils in the reader even more forcibly than the scenes in the *Iliad* a notion of Helen's highly ambivalent allegiance in the war fought to regain her.

One of the functions which the representation of Helen fulfils in the poem is to throw into relief the remarkable fidelity of Odysseus's long-suffering wife Penelope. There are two other portraits of adulterous wives in the poem – both created in stories-within-the-story – which produce the same effect. One of them involves the goddess Aphrodite, whose affair with the god Ares is unmasked by her husband Hephaestus, the blacksmith god, when he rigs up an invisible steel net above the marital bed and during a pretended absence succeeds in entangling the lovers in its meshes. This cautionary tale, the subject of a song sung by a bard at the court of Scheria, is recounted in a singularly light-hearted fashion. The gods who in the story gather round to witness the discomfiture of the unhappy couple are doubled up with laughter; and when Apollo, in a nudge-nudge aside to Hermes, asks whether he would mind being trapped in bed with Aphrodite, Hermes replies that he would not object if there were 'thrice this number of endless fastenings' (8.340).

No such levity accompanies the story of the adulterous Clytemnestra, whose exploits exemplify the bad homecoming. When Odysseus visits the Underworld, one of the departed heroes whom he interviews is Agamemnon, who gives a bitter account of his murder at the hands of his wife's lover Aegisthus. At the thought of the 'sluttish woman' (11.424) who was Aegisthus's accomplice in this act of butchery, Agamemnon exclaims:

> So there is nothing more deadly or more vile than a woman
> who stores her mind with acts that are of such sort...
> ... she with thoughts surpassingly grisly
> splashed the shame on herself and the rest of her sex, on women
> still to come, even on the one whose acts are virtuous.
>
> (11.427–34).

Although Odysseus will never suffer such a fate at the hands of the 'circumspect Penelope' (11.445), he must nevertheless be careful on his return not to tell her everything, for 'there is no trusting in women' (11.456). Odysseus certainly seems to take this warning from Agamemnon to heart, for when he eventually arrives in Ithaca the secret of his identity is kept from his wife for many a long day.[6] In the end, of course, her loyalty to her husband is affirmed and celebrated. But Penelope is perhaps to be seen as an exception: in the last book of the poem, when Agamemnon down in the Underworld hears the news of Odysseus' successful homecoming, he enlarges on the comparison between Penelope and his own wicked wife (daughter of Tyndareos):

> '... Thereby the fame of her virtue shall never
> die away, but the immortals will make for the people
> of earth a thing of grace in the song for prudent Penelope.
> Not so did the daughter of Tyndareos fashion her evil
> deeds, when she killed her wedded lord, and a song of loathing
> will be hers among men, to make evil the reputation
> of womankind, even for one whose acts are virtuous.'
>
> (24.196–202)

There are two notable instances in the *Odyssey* of women whose political impact is viewed in a far more positive fashion. Queen Arete, wife of the king of Scheria, is said to be a woman of great intelligence, who is regarded as a god by all her people, and who 'dissolves quarrels, even among men' (7.74). Both the princess Nausicaa and the goddess

Athena advise Odysseus that if he wants to make a good impression at the palace he must bypass the king in his chair of state and make straight for the queen as she sits spinning by the hearth: 'for if she has thoughts in her mind that are friendly to you,/ then there is hope that you can see your own people, and come back ... to the land of your fathers' (6.313–15; 7.75–7). Arete is not a woman who rules in her own right, but she does seem to be credited with a degree of recognised political authority. In this, however, she is seen to be an exceptional case: in the words of Athena, her husband has given her 'such pride of place as no other woman on earth is given' (7.67). It is worth bearing in mind here that the land of Scheria possesses some of the features of a Utopia. Its climate is always mild, the fruit never fails on the trees (7.117–21), the ships understand men's minds, and the sailors never come to grief (8.557–63). In the utterly magical countries inhabited by Calypso and Circe, it is possible for women to be in complete control; while in a place like Scheria, midway between the everyday and the fantastic, a female can be accorded a measure of power.

Odysseus' wife Penelope, who belongs more obviously to the real world, seems in her husband's absence to come close to wielding power in the palace at Ithaca. It was through the cunning device of unravelling her weaving at night that Penelope succeeded in stringing her suitors along for over three years (2.94–110, 19.138–56). Since the exposure of this fraud, she has played for time by more subtle methods, holding out hope to each man, but offering definite acceptance to none of them (2.91–2). In the light of this information, Penelope certainly emerges as a clever and determined woman, who is quite capable of evading the pressures placed on her both by the suitors and by her own family (19.158–61). But in order to achieve this she employs the weapons traditionally associated with females; the deceptive use of weaving and of words is typical of the behaviour ascribed to women in the *Odyssey*, and it lends Penelope a shady and ambiguous character not unlike the one accorded to Helen.

In some respects, however, Penelope exerts authority in a more direct fashion. She roundly rebukes the suitors for their violent behaviour and their schemes against the life of Telemachus (16.409–47); she reproves her son for allowing a guest in the palace to be insulted (18.215–25); and she receives and cross-examines this same guest, the disguised Odysseus (19.96–599). In this interview she reveals her sense of personal responsibility for the maintenance of order in the household – 'my property, my serving-maids, and my great high-roofed house' (19.526) – and her painful awareness of the damage which her failure to remarry is causing. It is to make good some of the depredations brought about by the prolonged stay of the suitors that she has skilfully extracted courtship presents from them (18.274–303), a move which meets with considerable secret approval from her husband.

That a woman whose lord was absent at the wars might have exercised the kind of power attributed to Penelope is easily imaginable: Penelope herself confirms that Odysseus before departing for Troy had placed everything in her charge (18.266). However, this period of dominance seems to have been drawing to a close even before the return of Penelope's husband. Her son is now grown up and is beginning to assert himself. When his mother attempts to cut short the performance of a song about the return of the Greeks from Troy, Telemachus immediately countermands her instructions: she must go back into the house and resume her spinning, 'but the men must see to discussion,/ all men, but I most of all. For mine is the power in this household' (1.358–9). Penelope is amazed by her young son's assertiveness, but she does not hesitate to obey him.

The issue of Penelope's powerfulness is open therefore to diverse interpretations. Her own awareness of the limits of her authority is revealed in her conversation with the disguised Odysseus. Without a husband to take care of her, she tells him, she cannot resist the injuries inflicted on her home by her powerful suitors (19.127–61). As for assistance to strangers, this is impossible, since 'there are none to give orders left in the household/ such as Odysseus was among men' (19.314–15). Penelope's inability to deal satisfactorily with guests, one of the main social obligations in the Homeric world, is later confirmed by her son Telemachus, who attributes this failing to his mother's shortcomings as a judge of character. She is all too ready, he says, to honour bad men, and to send the good ones packing (20.131–3).

Penelope's power, then, can be seen to be restricted. It is also peculiar, in that it has arisen out of the unusual circumstances of Odysseus' extraordinarily long absence. The topsy-turvy nature of the situation which has developed on Ithaca is underlined in the poem by the use of what one critic has referred to as 'reverse similes', an image involving a comparison with someone of the opposite sex.[7] When, for example, Odysseus first greets Penelope, he tells her that her fame is like that of 'some king who . . . / . . . ruling as lord over many powerful people,/ upholds the way of good government . . .' (19.109–11). Her relief when she is eventually reunited with her husband is compared with that felt by a shipwrecked sailor who has finally made it to dry land (23.233–40). Such similes suggest both the authority of Penelope and her close identification with her husband, a genuine king and a man who has been shipwrecked on numerous occasions. But they also serve to make the point that what has occurred on Ithaca during Odysseus' absence is an inversion of the normal order of things. A woman has been playing a man's role, and though she has shown great bravery, resolution and cunning – great heroism, in fact – she has not been able to prevent the disruption of the established social and economic structures.

With the slaying of the suitors and Odysseus' revelation of his true identity, normality can at last be restored. But both the hero's and the audience's uncertainty about Penelope's intentions is maintained even now.[8] The need for some renegotiation of the respective roles of Odysseus and Penelope is indicated by the latter's remarkable reluctance to recognise her husband, in spite of his decisive action and his acceptance by the rest of the household. After a splendid scene in which the reader encounters the two of them sitting in silence on either side of the fire, eyeing each other warily, Penelope finally responds to her husband's accusation of stubbornness by giving orders that a particular bed, one which Odysseus himself had constructed, should be made up for him in the hall. Odysseus reminds her that this bed cannot be moved, since one of its posts was carved out of a live olive tree; and it is through this ultimate token of his identity that Penelope's recognition is finally secured. The bed which the couple shared long ago stands as a symbol of their marriage, and it is only when its permanence and stability have been acknowledged by Odysseus that Penelope is willing to renew their relationship.

In this way, the conclusion of the *Odyssey* demonstrates the centrality of marriage in the lives of both women and men. It is through this institution that their separate but complementary roles are defined and regulated. Penelope and Odysseus may operate in different spheres, but their close affinity is brought home to the reader time and time again, not least by the similarity of their characters, for both are remarkable for their cunning and perseverance. This model of gender relations is in some ways quite different from anything which can be derived from the later literature of the Classical Age, in which the spheres of activity of male and female are seen as fundamentally distinct. In the

Homeric world, where political power is rooted in the royal household, the boundary between the domestic and the political, between the private and the public, is not nearly so rigid. The roles of men and women overlap, and it is for this reason that a woman can come close – in the absence of her husband – to the exercise of political power.

That said, the story of Penelope and Odysseus nevertheless makes it clear to us that their relationship, though complementary, is also asymmetrical in terms of power and status. A woman is ultimately dependent on her husband for the maintenance of orderly relations within society at large, and when he is present her position can never be anything other than subordinate. In Homeric as in later Classical society, a woman's duties are anchored firmly in the household. It is her job to protect what is permanent and unchanging, while the male, through his involvement in the wider concerns of the world, has a part to play in the movements of history and time. These two characters – Odysseus the wanderer and Penelope the guardian of the home – were to survive as potent symbols of gender difference, not just for later generations of Greeks but for peoples of many subsequent ages.

5

Amazons

A large number of ancient writers tell us about a race of warrior women called Amazons, who lived without men, wore masculine clothing and took part in activities – hunting, farming and, above all, fighting – which among Greeks were normally exclusive to males. The Amazons are placed in a variety of geographical locations, but the one mentioned most frequently is the area bordering on the south-eastern shore of the Black Sea (in present-day northern Turkey), around the city of Themiscyra and the river Thermodon. According to one ancient historian, Diodorus Siculus (3.52–5), there was also an earlier race of Amazons who were natives of Libya in North Africa.

The era when the Amazons are supposed to have lived also varies a great deal, but most commonly they are assigned to the period before and during the Trojan War, that is, to a time at least five hundred years before the earliest reference to them, which is in Homer's *Iliad*. For most writers, then, the Amazons are a phenomenon of the distant past, and no author claims ever to have seen them, or even to have met anyone who has seen them. In *Airs, waters, places*, a treatise ascribed to the fifth-century physician Hippocrates, some Amazon-type characteristics are attributed to the warrior women of the Sauromatians, a nomadic tribe who in the Classical Age inhabited territory in southern Russia to the east of the River Don. But the author is not describing a race of women living apart from men, and he himself does not refer to them as Amazons. The geographer Strabo in the first century BC mentions stories about Amazons which were current in his own time, but is clearly not inclined to believe them himself.

Only one set of narratives places the Amazon story in a specific historical context, that of the late fourth century BC. Several writers refer to a tale about a meeting between Alexander the Great and a troop of Amazons, under their queen Thalestris, in the far north of the Persian Empire.[1] The historian Arrian gives a slightly different version, referring to a story that Alexander received from the governor of Media a gift of a hundred armed and mounted women, whom the governor called Amazons; the circumspect conqueror at once dismissed them, fearing that his troops would not treat them with much respect, but promised that one day he would visit their queen and make her pregnant (Arrian, 7.13). The episode is not given much credence by the majority of the authors mentioning it: Arrian says that it is not included in the most reliable sources for Alexander's life, and that he himself doubts whether Amazons still existed at that time.

Amazonian customs receive a great deal of attention from ancient authors, as well they might. Strabo says that in order to reproduce themselves, the Amazons set aside two months every year for visits to the mountainous area on the border between their own country and that of the Gargarians. The men from the other side of the border made their way to the same region, and sexual intercourse took place in the dark, and at random. At certain fixed times, then, the Amazons' total rejection of men gave way to participation in promiscuous sexual relationships. If the babies which were born as a result were female, they were kept by the Amazons; if they were male, they were handed over to the Gargarians (Strabo, 11.5.1). A number of writers tell us that the right breasts of the girls were either cut off or seared with red-hot bronze instruments when they were infants: this was done to prevent them getting in the way during their later careers as fighters.[2] According to the author of *Airs, waters, places*,[3] this was also the custom among Sauromatian women, and had the effect of diverting all the strength and bulk to the right shoulder and arm, which wielded weapons. But the idea that the Amazons lacked one breast must have become popular at quite a late date, since in the numerous visual representations of them produced in the fifth century BC they are always shown with the normal two. Clearly one reason why the story caught on was that it offered an explanation (almost certainly a fanciful one) of their name: the Greek word *a-mazon* could be translated as 'without a breast'.

Needless to say, the absence of men in the Amazon community excites a great deal of comment. The fifth-century tragedian Aeschylus calls them 'man-hating' (*Prometheus Bound* 723–8) and 'manless' (*The Suppliants* 287–9). As far as Strabo is concerned, it is this feature of their way of life which makes their existence hard to credit, for 'who could believe that an army of women, or a city, or a tribe, could ever be organised without men ...?' (11.5.3). Not only did they manage to survive without men, but they also of course fought against them. They are 'a match for men', says Homer, who locates the Amazons in southern Asia Minor and says that the hero Bellerophon (*Iliad* 6.186) and Priam the king of Troy (*Iliad* 3.189) had both encountered them in battle. For Lysias, an Athenian orator of the Classical period, the Amazons 'seemed to surpass men in their spirit'; they also pioneered the use of iron and horses in battle, and with these assets they succeeded in enslaving their neighbours and ruling over many lands (2.4–6). The Amazons, then, reject what for a Greek was the ultimate female experience, marriage, and instead engage in the most characteristic of male activities, fighting. The reversal is emphasised by the nature of their religious practices: their favourite deities are said to have been Artemis, the virgin goddess, and the war god Ares.

According to Diodorus (2.45–6, 3.53–5), the lifestyle of both the Libyan and the Black Sea Amazons involved an inversion of normal sex-roles rather than complete separatism. In Amazon communities the women were the fighters, rulers and administrators, while the men, 'like married women in our own society' (3.53.2), looked after the home, reared the children and carried out the orders given to them by their wives. While female infants had their right breasts seared to improve their prowess as fighters, the boys were mutilated in their legs and arms so as to make them unfit for war (2.45.3). Both races of

Amazons were renowned for their military accomplishments, and succeeded in conquering large parts of Syria and Asia Minor; but eventually both were overwhelmed in battle by the Greek hero Heracles, who 'thought that it would ill accord with his resolve to be the benefactor of the whole of mankind if he should allow any race to be under the rule of women' (3.55.3).

For other ancient authors the Amazons, in spite of their separatist habits, were not immune to the lure of sexual desire. The fifth-century historian Herodotus recounts how some Amazons from Themiscyra who had been taken prisoner by a Greek force succeeded in murdering their captors while they were on board ship (4.110–18). They eventually landed on the northern shores of the Black Sea, in the territory of the people known as the Scythians, where they at once stole some horses and took up the profitable pursuit of marauding. When the Scythians at last discovered the sex of these mysterious raiders, they embarked on a deliberate campaign of seduction. A stray Amazon was waylaid by a Scythian, and readily agreed to have sex with him. On the next day they each brought along one of their friends, and before long the entire population of both camps had been brought together by this blind date process. The Amazons were nevertheless reluctant to be drawn into conventional Scythian society, since their customs were incompatible with those of the local women, and it was agreed that the couples should establish a new community to the north-east. This, according to Herodotus, was the origin of the Sauromatian race, whose women in his own day still engaged in hunting and warfare, and wore the same clothes as the men; they also had a law which forbade a woman to marry until she had killed an enemy in battle.

For Herodotus, then, the Amazons' opposition to men could be overcome by the power of sexual attraction. For others it was the force of arms which finally put paid to their unique way of life. The latter was in fact by far the more common explanation of how the Amazons eventually came to grief, and it features in some of the most prominent of their myths. At least as old as the fifth century BC[4] is the story that Heracles, for his ninth labour, was given the job of bringing back to Greece the girdle of the Amazon queen Hippolyta. To achieve this, he and his followers fought a battle against the women warriors, in the course of which – according to some accounts – Heracles killed Hippolyta and took the girdle from her dead body.

Some of the versions of the Heracles episode relate how the hero was accompanied on this adventure by his Athenian comrade, Theseus. The latter either captured in battle, or received as a prize, or was amorously pursued by, Hippolyta's sister Antiope – the details vary from story to story, and indeed according to some narratives it was Hippolyta herself rather than Antiope who became the consort of the legendary Athenian king.[5] But one way or another, Theseus came home with an Amazon, thereby precipitating one of the major events in Athens' mythical past. In order to free their queen (or simply, in some versions, in pursuit of their lust for conquest), the Amazons invaded Greece from the north and marched on Athens. From their base on the Areopagus hill they launched a siege of the Acropolis, which was only lifted three months later when the women's army was finally defeated by Theseus' forces.[6]

One final Amazonian exploit features the later queen Penthesilea, who after the death of Hector brought her army to Troy to help defend the city against the Greeks. The hero Achilles faced her on the battlefield, and it was only after his spear had pierced her breast that he came to realise her beauty and to fall in love with her – too late, of course (Fig. 8).[7] Here, the two most common causes of the defeat of Amazonian resistance – physical force and love – are combined, and we encounter an analogy frequently made in Greek myth between violent domination and the sexual act. These erotic connotations can be discerned in some of the other Amazonian episodes – Heracles captures the queen's girdle, Theseus carries off an Amazon bride – and were certainly not lost on the sculptors of the Classical Age (Fig. 10).

It is impossible to ascertain whether or not the Amazon myth had any substantial basis in reality. No archaeological evidence has been uncovered which would remotely suggest the existence, in the Bronze Age or at any later time, of a community consisting entirely of female warriors; nor are there any material remains or contemporary written records which can confirm the notion that the myth preserves a memory of a time when a matriarchal society in Asia Minor was struggling for survival in the face of the growing patriarchal dominance of the incoming Hittite peoples.[8] At present, the most likely candidates for the role of Amazonian prototype seem to be the women of the Sauromatian race, who according to Herodotus and the author of *Airs, waters, places* (17) used before their marriages to engage in riding, hunting and fighting. Archaeological evidence provides some confirmation of these activities: a few Sauromatian female burials of the sixth to fourth centuries BC contain weapons and armour.[9] Travellers' tales about these strange female practices may in themselves have been sufficient to give rise to Amazon myths, especially if the hearer began to speculate, as Herodotus evidently did, about the women's distant ancestors. Genuine warrior women seem often to have excited the male imagination, and it would not be surprising if some such group in the course of time had been mentally transformed into an entire race of female fighters.[10]

Although the origins of the Amazon myth are obscure, there is no doubting its popularity, particularly in Classical Athens: confrontations with Amazons were mentioned frequently by poets, orators and historians, and were a common theme in sculpture, frescoes and vase paintings. Presumably, then, it was a myth that meant something to the population at large; undoubtedly, it had gained a place in the official iconography of Athens, since it was chosen for depiction on some very prominent public buildings, including the Parthenon (see pp. 191, 193). When we come to consider why this high profile was accorded to the women warriors, the question of whether or not they ever existed becomes irrelevant. No-one in fifth-century Athens would have expected ever to encounter an Amazon, or would have believed that this race posed any threat to their city in real life. Nevertheless, the Amazon story seems to have been important to the Athenians.

Whatever the reason for this, we can be sure that it had nothing to do with heartwarming messages about the empowerment of women. The Amazons were outstanding fighters, and they conquered many nations, but in the end they were always beaten by Greeks – by Heracles, by Achilles or, most significantly for the Athenians, by Theseus. According to Lysias (2.4–6), their encounter with the courageous defenders of Athens brought out the Amazons' basic feminine weakness: 'they died here and paid the penalty for their folly. They made the memory of our city imperishable because of its bravery, and rendered their own country nameless because of their disaster here.' Clearly on one level the Amazon theme in Athenian art can be interpreted as a form of patriotic display. The self-glorification inspired by the myth became very pronounced after the Persian invasions of Greece in 490 and 480 BC (see p. 95). Like those other legendary foes the Trojans, the Amazons lived in an area which in the early fifth century was part of the Persian Empire, and their incursion into Greece was seen as foreshadowing the recent Persian onslaughts, which had been directed in particular at the city of Athens.[11]

The identification between Amazons and Persians is confirmed by numerous fifth-century Athenian vase paintings in which the women warriors are provided with Persian dress and weapons – leggings, leather caps, curved bows, axes and hide-covered shields (Fig. 11). There can be little doubt that the Amazons were favoured by Greek artists partly as an example of the 'defeated barbarian' type. In the sculpture which decorated Greek temples, it was customary to refrain from depicting recent historical events, for fear that the gods might be offended by human boastfulness. But myths which provided parallels to those events were quite acceptable; and this would have been one reason why the female invaders were chosen to adorn the Parthenon, the temple which was constructed to replace the one destroyed by the Persians when they sacked Athens in 480 BC. In these scenes from Athens' heroic past there were intimations of more recent achievements.

However, it is difficult to avoid the conclusion that the Amazons were important to the Greeks, not simply as barbarians, but also as women. Certainly in sculpture their female characteristics are frequently on show, with one breast left exposed, and the buttocks emphasised. These creatures who were so feminine in their physique were nevertheless masculine in their behaviour, and this would have presented a paradox which Greek men would have found stimulating but also instructive. In the literary accounts the Amazons can be seen to represent an inversion of everything which a Greek male (in particular, an Athenian male) would have expected of a woman. They were active in the public arena; they were experts in warfare; they were in political control of the state in which they lived; they refused to marry; they were either asexual or sexually promiscuous; and they valued girl babies more highly than males. In later versions of the story, they also, in cutting off a breast, performed a symbolic denial of the characteristic role of women, motherhood. Athenian men may well have found all this female assertiveness very sexy, but they certainly would not have wanted to recommend it to their own womenfolk.

But recommendation was not, of course, what the Amazon myth was offering. This fantasy of a horde of rampant women could be safely enjoyed because of the cautionary nature of its ending: the Amazons were everything that an Athenian woman ought not to be, and ultimately they failed. There can be little doubt that, in a society like that of Classical Athens, one of the myth's functions was the provision of a negative role model. When the men in Aristophanes' comedy *Lysistrata* want to egg each other on to oppose the rebellious women of Athens, they remind each other of a famous painting which shows 'the Amazons on horseback fighting against men' (678–9). The message of the myth for both males and females alike was that in a civilised society women are passive, chaste and married. The alternative – behaving like an Amazon – was a mark of barbarism, and its consequences were disastrous both for the women themselves and for the state over which they ruled. In this way the personal and political dominance of men was justified and reinforced.[12]

It would be interesting to know whether the Amazon myth was always 'correctly' decoded by the Athenian women who encountered it. It is possible that some of them would have found these assertive females inspiring, in spite of their failure. But of course we have no inkling of women's reactions. Presumably the role invented for the Amazons – that of vanquished barbarian invader – would have ensured that the majority of women subscribed to the prevailing view and rejected the warrior women's example.

PART II

THE ARCHAIC
AGE: 750–500 BC

The period in Greek history referred to as the Archaic Age involved political and social changes of enormous consequence. In central and southern Greece, on the Aegean islands, and on the west coast of Asia Minor (to which Greeks had been migrating from about 1000 BC) there were already a number of well-established independent communities which came to be known as *poleis* (singular, *polis*). In physical terms, a *polis* was an area of agricultural land with an urban centre, where many of the inhabitants lived and where they also traded their goods, assembled in public meetings and collectively worshipped their deities. Most of the *poleis* were relatively small, with populations in the low thousands, but in political terms they were self-governing states. In the course of the Archaic Age this type of structure was to develop into the basic framework for political organisation in Greece, so that by the end of the period the Greek world was divided into literally hundreds, if not thousands, of *poleis*. They were a fundamental aspect of the Greek way of life, and many of the notions about freedom and collectivity that were subsequently framed can be linked to their existence.

The economy of any *polis* was always basically agrarian – the great majority of the inhabitants earned their living one way or another from farming. But there were regional variations to this pattern. *Poleis* like Corinth, Miletus and Athens soon began to include a minority of residents whose livelihood was derived entirely from trade or manufacture. In the early Archaic Age political power in most *poleis* resided with small groups of aristocratic families who also owned most of the land. They ruled through institutions like Councils and magistracies, and their authority was based on their economic power, on their ancestry, and on marital and kinship connections with other aristocratic clans both within and outside their own states. It is clear that there was growing conflict between these aristocrats and the rest of the population, exacerbated by rapid population growth in the eighth century, and by a widespread problem of debt. One of the consequences of these economic difficulties was a wave of emigration, which from about 750 BC onwards carried the Greeks to southern Italy, Sicily, the shores of the Black

Sea, and, to a lesser degree, to North Africa, southern France and north-east Spain. From the start the 'colonies' which they founded were politically and economically independent – they were *poleis* in their own right.

In some of the older Greek communities, increasing civil disorder led to the seizure of power by non-constitutional rulers, who were known as tyrants. In other states, growing protest against the aristocrats' monopoly of judicial sanctions led to codification and in some instances revision of the laws. In Athens, for example, the early sixth-century lawgiver Solon introduced economic and constitutional reforms which were to lay the foundations for the later development of Athenian democracy. Both tyranny and the codification of the laws were important stages in the transition from aristocratic rule to more widely-based forms of government. By the end of the sixth century the aristocratic monopoly of political office was a thing of the past, and the majority of states had either oligarchic or democratic constitutions. In the former, wealth rather than birth became the qualification for office, and real power rested with small groups of prosperous landowners. In the latter, all adult male citizens were able to participate in government. In democratic states in particular, citizenship had become a valued and jealously-guarded privilege. At the same time, the development of chattel slavery on a substantial scale had created in oligarchic and democratic states alike a class of persons who, in theory at least, had no rights at all.

Many of the cultural innovations of the Archaic Age were linked to the institution of the *polis* as a framework for artistic production. Homer's massive epic poems the *Iliad* and *Odyssey*, which probably assumed their present form shortly before 700 BC, harked back to a bygone era of heroic achievement. Epic poems continued to be written, but the creative emphasis had shifted to the composition of lyrics, short songs which were performed to a musical accompaniment at religious festivals, men's drinking parties or family celebrations. Monumental architecture began to appear in the form of temples, which were the visible expression of a state's veneration of the gods. In sculpture, the life-size, free-standing statue arrived on the scene, and became a vital element in the public display of art. Another important development at this time was the emergence of prose composition, and its use in the writing of philosophical and historical treatises. But perhaps the most significant overall characteristic of culture in the Archaic Age was a growing sense of Greekness, which ran counter to the entrenchment of the *polis* system and the particularism which this engendered. Although it could never overcome the intense competitiveness and aggressive political stances which the division into a multitude of small states produced, the construction of a specific Greek identity, fostered by alliances, trade, literature and common religious festivals, was to be a crucial determining factor in the shaping of a distinctive civilisation.

1 Eastern section of the Parthenon frieze: slab V, *c.*440 BC. Left to right: female attendant; priestess of Athena; the basileus and child, with the robe; Athena; Hephaestus.

2 View of the west end of the Erechtheum, on the Athenian Acropolis, with the olive tree. The caryatid porch is on the right.

3 Heracles cleans the Augeian stables, under the direction of Athena. Metope from the temple of Zeus at Olympia, *c*.460 BC.

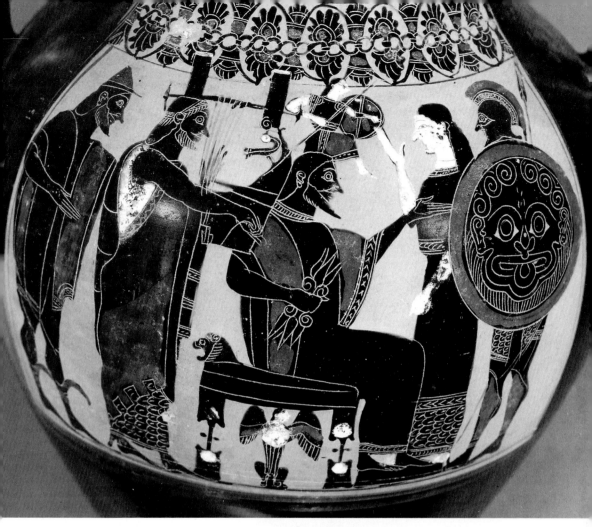

4 The birth of Athena from the head of
Zeus. Black-figure Athenian amphora
attributed to Group E, *c.*540 BC.

5 Artemis and Actaeon. Athenian red-
figure krater by the Pan Painter, *c.*470 BC.

6 Artemis Ephesia, a Roman copy.

7 Eastern section of the Parthenon frieze: slab V, *c*.440 BC. Nike, Hera, Zeus.

8 Achilles and Penthesileia.
Athenian black-figure
amphora by Exekias,
*c.*540 BC.

9 Demeter and Persephone
with Triptolemus, who is
about to take corn to the
human race. Athenian red-
figure skyphos attributed to
Makron, *c.*480 BC.

10 Greeks versus Amazons: frieze from the temple of Apollo at Bassae, c.425 BC.

11 Amazon in Oriental dress on horseback. Athenian red-figure amphora, c.420 BC.

12 OPPOSITE Mourning women at a bier. Black-figure loutrophoros, c.500 BC.

13 'The Berlin goddess'. *Kore* statue from Attica, early sixth century BC.

14 OPPOSITE 'Croesus'. *Kouros* from Anavyssos, *c.*520 BC.

15 OPPOSITE RIGHT *Kore* number 670 from the Acropolis, Athens, *c.*520 BC.

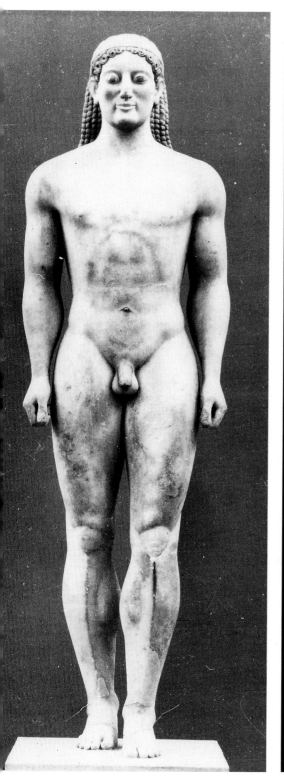

16a *Kore* number 680 from the Acropolis, Athens, *c.*520 BC.

b *Kore* number 672 from the Acropolis, Athens, *c.*520 BC.

17 Anal intercourse, shown on the inside of an Athenian red-figure wine cup, *c.*470 BC.

18 A nude woman using two dildoes, on the inside of an Athenian red-figure wine cup by the Nikosthenes painter, *c.*520 BC.

19 'Lesbian' scene: a naked woman holding a perfume jar is touched by another, squatting, woman. Inside of an Athenian red-figure wine cup by Apollodorus, *c.*510 BC.

20 A wedding procession. From an Athenian red-figure pyxis attributed to the Marlay painter, *c.*440 BC.

22 OPPOSITE Women at the fountain. Athenian black-figure hydria, *c.*520 BC.

23 OPPOSITE RIGHT Women spinning and weaving. Athenian black-figure lekythos by the Amasis painter, *c.*540 BC.

21 Three women washing at a basin. Athenian red-figure krater, *c.*500 BC.

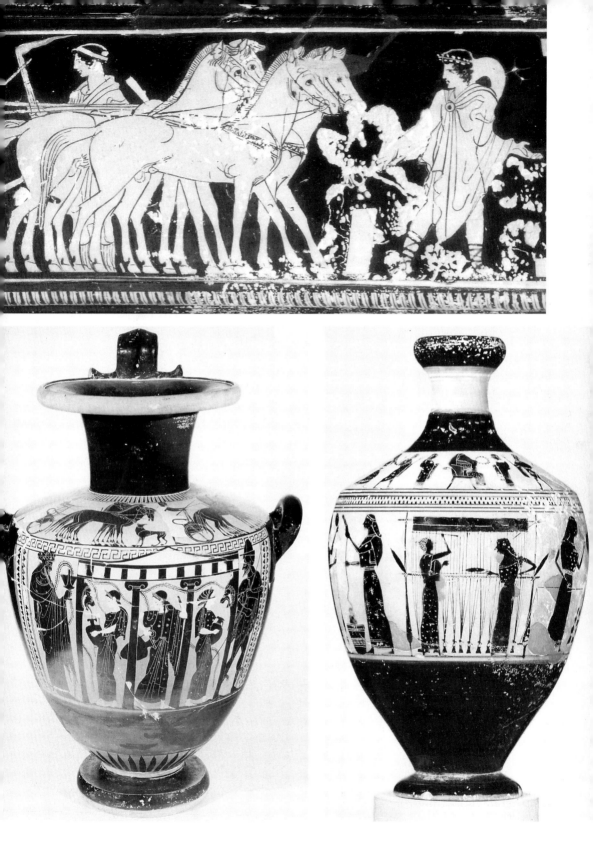

25 RIGHT Grave stele of Hegeso. From Athens, c.400 BC.

24 Grave stele of Ktesileos and Theano. From Athens, c.410 BC.

26 RIGHT Grave stele of Ampharete and her grandson. From Athens, c.420 BC.

6

Women in an age of transition

The Archaic Age was a critical period for women. The transformations which took place in society at large naturally affected its female members, and it was within the developing framework of the *polis* that the laws and customs were established which were to determine the position of women for several centuries to come. This being the case, it is unfortunate that the evidence for the role and lives of women during this period is extremely limited.

Much of the evidence for the early part of the age is drawn from the poems of Homer and Hesiod (see above, pp. 20–24, 47–57), whose use as sources for social history raises a number of difficulties. Both works present us with a male view of women's status and activities, and both involve a strong element of fantasy. In addition, there is the problem of deciding to what extent the attitudes to women voiced by these poets can be seen as typical of male responses in general. As Culham (1987, p. 16) has remarked, when we are using a dateable work of literature as a historical source, all that we can be absolutely sure about is that at that point in time a particular thought became thinkable. We can never be certain that a lot of people were thinking the same thoughts as Homer and Hesiod. However, the oral character of Greek poetry during this period – the fact that poets had to produce work that was meaningful for fairly large audiences – does at least mean that their views are likely to have been less individualised than is the case with today's poets.

With Homer, there is the additional problem of deciding which historical period he is representing (see above, p. 47). It is generally agreed that the physical objects which Homer mentions belong to a variety of periods, and that some of them, such as bronze swords, are correct for the time of the Trojan War. But many scholars believe that the social structures outlined are for the most part the ones that were in existence at the end of the Dark Ages and the beginning of the Archaic Age.[1] This is an argument which I myself have accepted. However, it must be borne in mind that there is an inevitable uncertainty attached to the 'dating' of Homeric society.

For the later part of the age, we are reliant on literary sources which are for the most

part late (Classical and post-Classical) and therefore unreliable. Moreover, the information which they yield is generally very scrappy, so that it is difficult to build up a
picture of the overall social context. Archaeological evidence ought, on the face of it, to
provide a better picture of the reality of women's lives, but it tends to be very random,
and consists largely of tomb excavations. While these tell us something about women's
material possessions, they are hardly eloquent when it comes to the behaviour,
thoughts and feelings of the people who used them. Happily, one authentic female voice
– that of the poet Sappho – has survived from the late Archaic period. But on the whole
the women of this time remain shadowy figures; and the nature of the social transformations which shaped their lives is the subject of considerable speculation.

How many women?

Did men outnumber women in the population of early Archaic Greece? There is some
evidence, cited by Pomeroy (1975, p. 46), to suggest that they did, although it is far from
conclusive. It is possible that the exposure of new-born girl babies (leaving them out to
die) was being employed by the Greeks at this time as a way of controlling population
growth, and that this produced a sexual imbalance in the adult population. Female
infanticide could probably never have been practised on a regular and generalised basis,
as this would have had a catastrophic effect in terms of population decline.[2] But it may
have been used, as Harris (1982) has argued, as a temporary expedient at times of high
natural increase in the population, or at times when more girls than boys were being
born. In the absence of firm data, however, the point can certainly not be proved.

Kinship and marriage

It is clear from the work of both Homer and Hesiod that the typical family of the early
Archaic Age was not a particularly extended one. It consisted of husband, wife,
unmarried children and (where these existed) married sons and their wives and children.
In the course of the age, this family group, or *oikos*, was established as the basic unit in the
social fabric of the *polis*. As the focus for political organisation the *polis* took on the role of
providing the family with protection from its enemies, and in return the family owed it a
variety of obligations, including military service. For this reason it was in the interests of
the *polis* that a sufficient number of families should be maintained to keep the state
supplied with soldiers. This meant that families had to be guaranteed a livelihood, and
hence new systems of inheritance came into existence which underpinned the social
dominance of the family unit.

In Archaic Greece, inheritance was patrilineal: when a man died his land was divided
equally between any sons who survived him. But whereas in the early part of the period
it seems that in the absence of sons property automatically passed to more distant
relatives, most *poleis* by the end of the age had developed systems which allowed some
power of disposal to a head of household who had no sons. A daughter did not inherit,
even when she had no brothers. But again by the end of the age, provision seems to have
been made in many *poleis* for property to be transmitted via a daughter to her own sons.[3]
In this way the survival of the *oikos* was ensured.

The Archaic Greek *oikos* was a patriarchal institution. The head of a household – its
kyrios – was always a man, and his wife and children came under his guardianship. When
a son came of age, this guardianship lapsed; but a daughter spent the whole of her life

under the legal control of a male guardian – her father, husband, son, or next-of-kin. Marriages were arranged by the prospective groom and the prospective bride's guardian, and the wife usually (although not always) went to live with her husband's family. In the early Archaic Age, to judge from the evidence of Homer's poems (e.g. *Odyssey* 4.5), male members of the upper classes generally married women who were not related to them, and who came from different areas. This upper-class habit of exogamy – marrying outside the community – was related to the political importance which marriage possessed in these circles. Marriage exchanges were one of the means by which noble families created political alliances with groups living in other areas, and in this way they made a considerable contribution to the aristocracy's stranglehold on power. This practice survived to the end of the Archaic Age. However, with the emergence of the *polis*, exogamy began to give way in some places to endogamy – to marriage within the community. For the upper classes, this meant marriage within a tight circle of aristocratic families living in the same *polis*.[4]

Marriage arrangements always involved a transfer of property, and it seems clear that in the Homeric period the most significant element in these transactions was the bridewealth, or *hedna* – the gifts which were given by the groom to the bride's father when a marriage was agreed. Hector, for example, had paid 'countless gifts' for Andromache when he took her from the house of her father Eetion (*Iliad* 22.472). The details of the system are not easy to recover, but the various pieces of information derived from Homer's poems suggest the following scenario for the arrangement of an upper-class marriage in the early Archaic Age. The process of competing for the hand of a powerful man's daughter began with an exchange of courtship gifts (or *dora*) between the suitors and the prospective father-in-law, a ritual which served to establish friendly relations between the two parties. The suitors then put in their 'bids' for the young woman by making promises of bridewealth (*hedna*) which would only be accepted once the marriage had been definitely agreed. It was on this basis that the father made his decision. Sometimes, if the groom was going to be particularly useful to his future father-in-law, he might win his bride without presenting any gifts. When Agamemnon, for example, is trying to persuade Achilles to rejoin the Greek forces, he offers to let him have one of his daughters, plus many gifts, 'without bridewealth' (*anaednon*, *Iliad* 9.146).[5]

Occasionally – it is hard to know in what circumstances – promises of *hedna* were replaced by a competition as a method of determining which of the suitors should win the girl's hand. These marriage contests had probably been quite common in Bronze Age Greece (they crop up frequently in myth); but in the Archaic Age they were clearly not employed very often. The most graphic instance involves Cleisthenes, tyrant of Sicyon in the early sixth century BC, who spent a whole year entertaining the thirteen suitors for the hand of his daughter Agariste. During this time, they were subjected to a wide range of tests, including chariot races, wrestling matches, personal interviews and group discussions. One of the favourites, Hippocleides, was pipped at the post by his fellow Athenian Megacles when, on the day Cleisthenes was due to make his decision, he got drunk at a banquet and insisted on demonstrating his dancing skills. He had reached the point of performing handstands on the table when Cleisthenes cried out to him, 'You have danced away your wife,' (Herodotus 6.127–31).

The women involved in all of these marriage arrangements seem, unsurprisingly, to have had little or no say in their own futures. Clearly, among the upper classes of Archaic Greece marriage was seen as an institution that established a relationship, not so much between a woman and a man as between a father-in-law and a son-in-law. The wealth of the two parties, as well as their political power, might be a factor that was taken into account. It seems likely that this consideration was becoming more meaningful in the latter part of the Archaic Age, when money was beginning to replace birth as a source of political influence. The sixth-century lyric poet Theognis apparently sees this tendency as typical of the degeneration of his own age, when he writes that '... a good man does not hesitate to marry a base woman from a base father, provided he gives much money; nor is a woman ashamed to be the wife of a base man if he is rich, preferring wealth to birth' (Theognis 183–90).

Occasionally, sexual attraction seems to have been a motive for marriage. Periander, who became tyrant of Corinth in the late seventh century, is said to have fallen for his future wife Melissa when he caught sight of her in a field, wearing a simple tunic and pouring wine for some workmen (Athenaeus 13, 589F). However, Melissa's own feelings do not appear to have been taken into account; and in her case physical attraction would seem to have been a particularly unreliable basis for marriage, since her husband later murdered her in a fit of jealousy, and then had sexual intercourse with her dead body (Herodotus 3.50 and 5.92).

By the end of the Archaic Age an important change had taken place in the nature of the property transfer which occurred when a marriage was arranged. Bridewealth – gifts from the groom to the bride's father – had faded into insignificance, while dowry – property allocated by a father to his daughter when she married – had emerged as a substantial element. Dotal marriage – marriage with a dowry – was to remain standard practice throughout the Classical period, and it distinguished the Greeks from other contemporary European peoples, such as the Celts and the Germans, who paid bridewealth for their wives. Clearly, the development was a significant one. It took place at a time when the *polis*, by establishing various legal requirements for the conclusion of a marriage, was beginning to provide a framework for the organisation of relationships between men and women. Unfortunately, however, it is not easy to see why this transformation should have entailed the predominance of the dowry, but a number of factors can be suggested.

It is likely that the change was linked in some way to inheritance patterns. A dowry was an allocation of property to a woman (although it was managed by her husband). Since by the end of the Archaic Age the dowry generally took the form of money or valuables, it allowed a father to provide for his daughter while ensuring that the most significant element of his property, the land, remained intact and could be handed on to his sons. One effect of the dowry system was that it gave a bride's father a greater stake in her marriage. If a divorce took place, a man was obliged to return the dowry to his ex-wife's father or guardian. Thus the dowry might function as a guarantee of reasonable behaviour on the part of the husband: he himself would be deterred from pursuing a divorce for frivolous reasons, while the threat of a divorce instituted by his father-in-law, and the consequent loss of dowry, might prevent him for maltreating his wife. At the same time, the dowry would ensure a decent standard of living for a married woman. The system can therefore be linked to the increasing stress being placed by the end of the period on the greater protection of women within marriage.

A perceived need for protection implies a lowering of the status of women, and this may have resulted from the gradual takeover of the handling of political relationships by the constitutional machinery of the *polis*. In a situation in which the power of the aristocracy was being ceded to state institutions, the alliances created by marriage exchanges would have lost a great deal of their significance. This would have meant that women were losing much of their value as commodities, and in these circumstances it may no longer have been thought necessary to make substantial contributions to their fathers' property – the bridewealth – in order to secure them as wives. Consequently, there would have been a greater obligation on fathers to contribute a dowry both as a means of attracting a wealthy husband, and as a fund for the maintenance and protection of their daughters.

In some respects, this system operated in the interests of the woman's natal family. The right to end the marriage and reclaim the dowry could be exploited in order to transfer a woman to another marriage, one which might furnish an heir for her father's *oikos* if it had failed to produce one of its own.[6] The growing emphasis on the preservation of the individual *oikos*, recognised as an important element in the stability of the *polis*, may therefore have been another element in the development of dotal marriage.

All the data discussed so far relates to upper-class marriages. About marriages among the lower classes we have much less information, but it is safe to assume that they were far less complex affairs. According to Hesiod (who probably represents the preoccupations of the peasant class) men marry in order to produce sons who will look after them in their old age and inherit their property when they die. In this way, they ensure that their land will not pass to distant relatives (*Theogony* 602–7). Here too, then, it can be seen that the survival of the individual family is seen as a matter of great concern. Hesiod advises a man to marry when he is thirty, and to choose a virgin who is in the fifth year following puberty, and lives nearby (*Works and days* 695–700). Changes in marriage customs associated with the emergence of the *polis* presumably affected the lower classes much less than the aristocracy, since the former were already in the habit of marrying women from their own communities. Hesiod also recommends having only one son, because of the expense of rearing more, although he recognises that in the long run a larger family might mean bigger profits (*Works and days* 376–80). Daughters are not mentioned by the poet.

MARRIAGE AND SEXUAL MORALITY

It was obviously important in the Archaic Age that a woman should be a virgin at the time of her marriage. To ensure this, the princess Nausicaa went to bed at night with two handmaidens guarding her on either side (*Odyssey* 6.18–19). However, young women were apparently not kept in physical seclusion, and had a reasonable degree of freedom of movement. Nausicaa was able to go down to the river to do the family washing, and though she was accompanied by slave-girls and all of them were veiled, there was no man present in the party, and the veils were later removed when they were playing a ball game (*Odyssey* 6.99–101). When she apologises to Odysseus for not accompanying him into the city, Nausicaa herself implies that some young women were in the habit of making friends with men before they were married, although she herself deplores such behaviour (*Odyssey* 6.251–315). Unmarried women of the lower classes would presumably have had even greater freedom, since the practicalities of life would have meant that they could not be confined to the home, and they had no slaves to look after them. Many of them would no doubt have carried out the same task as the wives and daughters of the Trojans, who before the war used to do their washing in springs and stone troughs outside the city walls (*Iliad* 22.153–6).

Upper-class Greek men in Homeric society seem to have had only one wife at a time, and there is no indication that any of them practised the polygamy ascribed to King

Priam of Troy, who is credited with 'many wives' and sixty-two children (*Iliad* 21.88, 6.244–8). On the other hand, the wife of a member of the Greek ruling classes may sometimes have been expected to share her home with a concubine. Agamemnon (*Iliad* 1.111–15) declares his intention of taking the Trojan captive Chryseis back home with him, because he likes her better than his wife Clytemnestra; while his brother Menelaus has a son, Megapenthes, who was born to him of a slave-woman, although only after it had become clear that his wife Helen was not going to have any more children (*Odyssey* 4.11–14). However, there are signs in the poems of Homer of the shaping of a new morality, which placed a higher value on loyalty to the family. Achilles' tutor Phoenix (*Iliad* 9.450) declares that his father 'dishonoured' his mother by keeping a mistress, while Odysseus' father Laertes is said to have refrained from sleeping with the slave-woman Eurycleia, although he had purchased her for that specific purpose, 'for fear of his wife's anger' (*Odyssey* 1.433). Casual adultery on a man's part was another matter, and none of Homer's heroes is ever criticised for the liaisons which he forms while away from home.

There are double standards here, of course. Wives were expected to be faithful to their husbands. In order to ensure this, King Agamemnon on his departure for Troy gave instructions to the resident bard to keep a close watch over his consort (*Odyssey* 3.267–9). However, it is possible that a wife's adultery was not seen as the horrendously serious business that it was to become in the late Archaic and Classical Ages. Helen's sexual past does not seem to have involved her in any kind of social disgrace: she takes her place by Menelaus' side when guests are present, and makes a lively contribution to the conversation. It would be dangerous, however, to draw too many conclusions from the example of Helen, since she is a very unusual woman with more than a passing connection with the Olympian deities. This is true to an even greater extent, of course, of the adulterous goddess Aphrodite, who is also treated with considerable leniency (see above, p. 54). Helen's sister Clytemnestra is much more roundly condemned, although even she is not seen as the prime mover in the affair which she conducts with Aegisthus (*Odyssey* 3.265–75).

The somewhat ambivalent attitude towards women's adultery displayed in the poems of Homer can perhaps be seen as a survival from a time when there was less anxiety about the paternity of a child within an individual family unit. However, in the course of the Archaic Age the growing stress placed on the preservation of the *oikos* would have meant that a new concern about the integrity of the family was developing. By the end of the period, adultery involving a wife had come to be regarded in some *poleis* as an issue of vital importance. In Athens in the early sixth century BC the lawgiver Solon introduced legislation which prescribed death for a wife's seducer if caught in the act, while the woman herself was subjected to a form of excommunication (see below, p. 125). With two exceptions, [7] all the early law codes which we know about made similar provision for the social ostracism of an adulterous wife.

The chastity of unmarried women also seems to have been a cause for concern at this time. In Athens, a law introduced by Solon prohibiting the enslavement of Athenian citizens contained one exemption: the head of a household retained the right to sell into slavery an unmarried daughter who had lost her virginity. From now on a preoccupation with the purity of their womenfolk began to figure quite highly in the masculine code of honour. It would be wrong, however, to interpret this as a straightforward case of moral hypocrisy. The fact that the man responsible for a wife's adultery was punished even more severely than the wife suggests that the object was not so much to enforce an ideal of female chastity, as to prevent a child who was not entitled to be a family member from being foisted on to the *oikos*. This relationship between social structures and attitudes to women will be discussed at greater length below (pp. 74–7).

MALE ATTITUDES TO MARRIAGE

As Finley (1978, pp. 128–9) has commented, there is no relationship between male and female described in the poems of Homer which can match in its depth and intensity the one between the warriors Achilles and Patroclus portrayed in the *Iliad*. Although marriage is important to the hero Hector, and even more so to Odysseus, it could not be said to be central to the existence of either of them. During his epic voyaging Odysseus often expresses a sorrowful yearning to return to his homeland; but it is to Ithaca itself that his thoughts chiefly turn, and very often his wife is not even mentioned. Clearly, the hero's long absence from home has been a source of much greater psychological pain to Penelope than it has to her husband.

Nevertheless, Homer's account of the Hector/Andromache and Odysseus/Penelope relationships indicates that there could be genuine affection between husbands and wives (see above, pp. 49–50, 56). It seems that during the early Archaic Age a value system was developing which allowed a poet like Homer to acknowledge that a man's feelings for his wife might form a significant part of his motivation. Hence, Hector is able to tell Andromache that, when he contemplates the capture of Troy, he is distressed not so much by the pain which will come to the Trojans, or by the suffering of his parents and gallant brothers, but by the thought of his poor wife being dragged off into captivity (*Iliad* 6.450–65). Hector is here describing an ascending scale of loyalties – city, kin and wife – in which his wife stands at the pinnacle.

Certainly, Homer's view of marriage seems very positive when it is compared to that of the poet Hesiod. In the Pandora narrative in the *Theogony* (see above, pp. 22–3), a wife is seen as a financial burden whose only function is to produce an heir. Elsewhere the poet admits that 'no prize is better than a worthy wife'; but 'a bad one makes you shiver with the cold;/ the greedy wife will roast her man alive/ without the aid of fire' (*Works and days* 702–5). Avarice and duplicity seem to be the feminine failings which Hesiod finds most alarming: 'Don't let a woman, wiggling her behind,/ and flattering and coaxing, take you in;/ she wants your barn: woman is just a cheat' (*Works and days* 373–5). There is no hint here of the mutual affection which is described by Homer. The possible reasons for this anomaly will be discussed below (pp. 74–7).

WOMEN'S ACTIVITIES

The evidence for women's day-to-day lives in the Archaic Age is severely limited. Much of it is derived from Homer's *Odyssey*, which means that it relates to the early part of the period, and that it comes to us via a male writer. However, it seems likely that the picture is a broadly accurate one, and that it would in many respects have remained true for the whole of the Archaic Age. Social change during this time may have produced entirely new perceptions of the female role, but the tasks women performed as nurturers and carers would probably have altered very little.

Women of all social classes were responsible for the smooth running of the household. Supervision of the storechamber and, in the case of an upper-class woman, of the domestic slaves was an important part of their duties; and even where the family's food was cooked by slaves, the wife might have the job of serving it if no guests were present.

That women's lives were seen as being characterised by domestic activities in Archaic Athens is indicated by the contents of graves, which contained not only jewellery but also items like spindle whorls and cooking pots (see Pomeroy, 1975, p. 43). Woman also looked after the physical comfort of men by bathing and anointing them, a job which was apparently not reserved for slaves or sexual partners: even Polycaste, Nestor's virgin daughter, performed this task for Telemachus when he visited her father's palace (*Odyssey* 3.464–6).

In addition, women made a vital contribution to the household's economic activities, in that they were entirely responsible for the production of the textiles used by its members. Even goddesses and queens are to be found spinning and weaving in Homer's poems, and their close involvement in the work is strikingly suggested by the fact that two of the royal women, Arete and Penelope, are perfectly capable of recognising cloth that had been woven some time before on their own looms (*Odyssey* 7.238 and 19.215–57).

Women's concern for their male offspring is demonstrated on a number of occasions in Homer's poems. Andromache when she hears about her husband's death immediately thinks of the hardship which her young son will endure without a father to protect him (*Iliad* 24.726–38); and Penelope, anxious for the safety of her son Telemachus, says that she grieves more for him than she does for her husband (*Odyssey* 4.810–23). One hears little in the poems about relationships between mothers and daughters, but this does not mean that these were not affectionate, only that the poet was not particularly interested in them. The reader is offered one rare glimpse of a mother and daughter scene, when the weeping Patroclus is compared to a little girl with streaming eyes who plucks at her mother's skirt and begs to be carried (*Iliad* 16.7–10).

Women of all classes were dependent on their fathers, husbands or adult sons for their livelihood. A woman from the lower classes whose husband had died might face severe financial hardship, and would have had to find some kind of work for herself. In the *Iliad* (12.433–5) Homer mentions a careful widow weighing out wool in scales in order to earn a meagre pittance for her children; while Hesiod (*Works and days* 602–3) advises the farmer to hire a female labourer during the summer months, but to avoid one who is nursing a child. Women such as these may have had to travel about looking for work: at Eleusis the goddess Demeter, disguised as an impoverished elderly woman, sits down by a well in order to ask the girls who come there whether they know of a household that will employ her as a nurse or housekeeper (*Homeric Hymns* 2.98–144). Even a woman with a husband might be poor, of course: Hesiod advises the farmer not to allow himself to sink to the condition of a man who has to beg for food with his wife and children (*Works and days* 399–400).

Participation in religious ritual was always a vital part of women's activities outside the home (for a fuller discussion of this subject, see below, pp. 160–9), and in this area the services which women performed for the dead were of particular importance. On one level, this can be seen as an extension of their domestic role, since they were responsible for washing, anointing and dressing corpses, and for keeping graves tidy and supplied with offerings of food and drink. But the main burden of mourning also seems to have fallen on females, whose grief was expressed both in ritual gestures and in the performance of funerary laments, a type of song associated particularly with women. This close relationship with the dead can be explained in a number of ways. Women were free to indulge their emotions in public in a way in which men were not. They were also regarded as the chief sustainers of the bonds which united family members, even after death. Finally, the perceived marginality of women may have been a factor: they were seen as intimately associated with the end as well as with the beginning of life.

In the Archaic period, many female mourners would have had no blood relationship with the dead person. The Greek hero Patroclus is to be mourned by captive Trojan women (*Iliad* 18.339), and when Hector's body is laid out, women who seem to be professionals are brought in to sing mournful dirges. But the latter are also joined by Andromache, Hecabe and Helen, each of whom sings an individual lament over the corpse (*Iliad* 24.717–75). The prominence of women on these occasions is confirmed by vase paintings of the Archaic Age showing funeral scenes (see Fig. 12). Among the figures around the bier whose sex can be distinguished, women predominate: they are shown with their arms raised to their heads, or performing ritual dances, or tearing their hair and lacerating their foreheads and cheeks. The excavation of Athenian tombs reveals that women themselves might be given rich burials in the Archaic Age. The fact that more male than female funerals are depicted in vase paintings indicates that the former were thought to be more worthy of representation, but not necessarily that men were given a more elaborate send-off than women.[8]

Although upper-class women in the Archaic Age could not mix freely with men, they were clearly not kept in anything approaching physical seclusion. Penelope has her own quarters in the upper part of the palace at Ithaca, where she spins and weaves with her slaves, sleeps, and also presumably dines. But when the men have finished eating in the great hall, she is quite likely to put in an appearance. The same is true in other palaces: after a meal Helen brings her spinning into the hall; and Arete is also to be found there seated at her loom next to the hearth. All three women play a lively part in cross-questioning travellers. They all, however, have their handmaidens present with them, and Penelope at least is veiled. Women also have some freedom to move about outside the home, though they are always accompanied by slaves. Andromache, for example, goes up to the great tower in Troy to watch the progress of the fighting, and might also go out to visit relatives (*Iliad* 6.378–84). Women of the lower classes would have had fewer restrictions on their movements: the cityscape depicted on the shield of Achilles shows housewives standing at their doors watching a wedding, and city walls defended by wives (*Iliad* 18.495–6 and 514–15).

The role played by royal women in the political structures of Homeric society has already been discussed (see above, pp. 54–7): it can be summarised here as one which carried a limited amount of authority, deriving from the woman's relationship with a member of the male ruling class. Later on in the Archaic Age, women in the ruling aristocratic families might occasionally become involved in male political intrigues, as when the womenfolk of the Alcmaeonids in Athens gave protection to some of the supporters of the would-be tyrant Cylon.[9] However, there is no doubt that men were socially and politically dominant even in the early part of the period. In the course of the age, as power passed from royal or aristocratic households to the political institutions of the *polis*, the recognised role of women in government was reduced from limited to non-existent. At the same time, there would undoubtedly have been a considerable erosion of the potential for informal influence.

FEMALE SLAVES

In the Homeric Age it seems to have been the Greek custom to kill or ransom male prisoners-of-war, and to enslave only women and children. So, for example, when the city where Briseis lived was sacked by the Greeks, her husband and her three brothers were slaughtered, but she herself was taken into captivity by Achilles (*Iliad* 19.291–5). This probably explains why the majority of slaves referred to in Homer's poems are female. Kidnapping, a secondary source of supply, was probably also directed chiefly at women, although it could produce a few male slaves. Odysseus' swineherd Eumaeus had himself been kidnapped as a boy, and in his father's house he had been looked after by a Phoenician nurse, whose slavery had begun when she had been snatched by raiders as she came home from the fields one evening (*Odyssey* 15.425–9).

These forms of enslavement can be seen as typical of a society where political alliances were established through guest-friendship and marriage exchanges. Anyone who was outside this network might be treated as an enemy, and his territory became a legitimate target for pillage, warfare and rape. Within the system a woman served as a commodity through which friendly relations with other communities were cemented; outside it, she could easily become a valuable form of booty. The precariousness of life was such that few women could be sure that at some stage in their lives they were not going to have to cross this dividing-line. Hector knows that, if Troy is ever captured by the Greeks, his honoured wife Andromache will become just another slave toiling away at the loom or the well (*Iliad* 6.450–65).

Female slaves were assigned a variety of domestic duties. In Odysseus' palace at Ithaca there are fifty female slaves (*Odyssey* 22.421), who perform tasks like wool-working, serving at table, washing and cleaning, grinding corn, making bread, carrying lamps, preparing beds for guests, fetching water and making up fires. A specially-prized slave might also have the job of sleeping with the head of the household. Male slaves are far fewer in number, and they are mainly responsible for farmwork. In a poorer household a female slave might have to work both inside and outside the home. Hesiod's advice to the farmer is: 'First, get a house, a woman, and an ox/ for ploughing – let the woman be a slave,/ unmarried, who can help you in the fields' (*Works and days* 405–6). How well a slave was treated would depend on her status and the temperament of her owners; but brutality could never be ruled out. After the slaughter of the suitors in Odysseus' palace, the twelve handmaidens who had been their sexual partners are first of all ordered to clean up the mess, and are then collectively hanged (*Odyssey* 22.465–72).

Most aristocratic households would almost certainly not have contained as many slaves as Odysseus' palace. But it is likely that the preponderance of female servants was something that was maintained up until the sixth century, when the growing use of slaves for agricultural and industrial purposes began to produce a much greater demand for males.

THE STATUS OF WOMEN

In the poems of Homer, there are few traces of outright misogyny, and women are sometimes represented as being worthy of great respect. In the poems of Hesiod, misogyny is rampant. It is possible, as Arthur (1973) has argued, that this discrepancy in the treatment of women was the product of class difference. Homer was writing from the perspective of the aristocracy, and in this sector of society the growing social significance of the nuclear family may have fostered an ideal of mutual co-operation between husband and wife. In the poems of Hesiod, on the other hand, we are in the world of the peasant farmer, and here the limited availability of land would have meant that the maintenance of the family unit was far more problematical. In this class a woman's most important contribution was considered to be the provision of an heir, whose existence helped to ensure that the farm did not pass to more distant relatives. Hence a woman's biological function would have been seen as a potential asset but also as a threat: if she were infertile, or unfaithful, or produced too many children, then she failed to compensate for the economic burden of supporting her. This explanation of the diverging attitudes of Homer and Hesiod seems plausible, but it is largely speculative. In the absence of corroborating sources, one cannot be sure that the discrepancy was determined by social factors and not by the differing temperaments of the two poets.

What can be said with more certainty is that Hesiod's poems reflect an anxiety about women which towards the end of the Archaic Age manifested itself in the legal structures of a number of Greek states, including Athens. In the early sixth century BC, the Athenian lawgiver Solon introduced legislation which was to have repressive effects on women. Laws whose overt objective was the control of excess and extravagance seem to have been directed chiefly at women: limits were placed on the size of their trousseux, and restrictions were introduced on their public appearances at funerals. As we have seen, measures controlling their sexual behaviour were also introduced. Much of Solon's social legislation seems to have had the aim of ensuring the survival of the property-owning family or *oikos*; of particular importance here was a law which allowed a man without sons to make a will disposing of his property to an adopted heir, thus ensuring that his land did not, as before, pass to the wider network of relatives. Many of the laws regulating the role of women can be interpreted in the same light, the clearest example being offered by the provisions relating to the *epikleros*, or woman without brothers. When her father died she was obliged by law to marry his male next-of-kin, and the property eventually passed to the sons that were born of the marriage. In this way, she became the vehicle through which the property was kept within the family.[10]

Much of this legislation points to the development of a legal structure which prescribed the subservience of women in the interests of the transmission of property. The principal aim was to maintain the existing number of families and hence to ensure the stability of the *polis*. Women were thus involved in a twofold subordination, within the family and within the state. This interest in women on the part of the state suggests that their role in reproducing the existing social order was now recognised as a crucial one. At the same time, women's rights were minimal. The awareness of this anomaly might well have produced ambivalent feelings about the female members of society, feelings which were to become more apparent in the succeeding Classical Age.

In other *poleis* apart from Athens, legislation regulating the behaviour of women had been introduced by the end of the Archaic Age. Not all states were as repressive as Athens. In Sparta and Gortyn things were certainly different, but neither of these was a typical Greek *polis*; and since much of the information about them relates to the fifth century, they will be discussed in the following Part (see pp. 150–9). Other states probably came closer to Athens in their treatment of women, although detailed information about them is unfortunately lacking. Certainly where Athens is concerned, the Archaic Age can be considered a crucial period in the history of the subordination of women.

If, as Godelier has written (1981, p. 11), 'several causes hierarchically combine to produce both the general effect of male domination and the variation in its form', what are the factors which came together to produce the intensification of the patriarchal system experienced in the course of the Archaic Age? In the rest of this chapter I shall be outlining some of the developments which may have contributed towards this end.

Doubtless the most important overall factor was the emergence of the *polis*, and the opposition to aristocratic domination which arose within it. The power of the aristocratic clans was underpinned by relationships with ruling groups in other areas, created in part by marriage exchanges. In the *polis*, the role of handling relations between communities was increasingly taken over by political institutions, and women's significance as a means of communication between men was diminished. One by-product of this change may have been the gradual development of the dowry system. The new system for creating political relationships was associated with a change in marriage practices, and women to a growing extent married within their own communities. This enabled heads of households to maintain a degree of control over their daughters even after they married, and if the need arose they might now be used as alternative suppliers of male heirs. Again, the dowry system may have contributed to this control.

Within the *polis*, women's social role was increasingly limited to that of reproducing the *oikos*, whose economic independence was considered crucial to the stability of the state. In order to guarantee that its members possessed adequate property, complex laws of inheritance were introduced. At the same time, the integrity of the *oikos* was protected by state legislation regulating the sexual behaviour of women.

A switch in the early Archaic Age from pastoral to agrarian farming may have contributed to a new ideological view of the female. Pastoralism was a more leisurely and less labour-intensive means of production. With the switch to labour-intensive agrarian farming, the division of labour between husband and wife in the peasant class would have become more obvious. To a writer like Hesiod, it may have appeared that women were not doing their share. Women were seen as being economically unproductive, and therefore as having no significant role to play in the functioning of society. At the same time, rapid growth in population would have produced a diminution in women's biological status. Too many children were a burden, and the role of reproducing society which was increasingly being accorded to women was at the same time being downgraded. A wife who was seen as having no contribution to make as an economic producer was also not valued as a reproducer. Once she had given birth to the requisite male child, her usefulness was over, and she was regarded as a parasite.[11]

The emergence of the *polis* was associated with a movement away from an estate-centred way of life to one based on an urban centre. The city rather than the home became the focus for the conduct of social life. This, coupled with the restraints on the behaviour of women, would have produced a sharper division between private and public spheres. The institutions which grew up in the city were male-dominated and revolved around characteristically male activities – politics, warfare, athletics and drinking parties. These activities, embedded within the formal apparatus of the state, operated as elaborate and prestigious arenas for male competition. The home was increasingly seen as the woman's domain, while at the same time male domination of the *oikos* was regarded as a key element in the maintenance of social and political stability. This urbanisation of culture was associated with the emergence of a new element in the masculine code of honour. Within the competitive arena of the *polis*, the protection of the chastity of women, which guaranteed the integrity of the *oikos*, would have become an important aspect of masculine behaviour, and would have come to be regarded as a worthwhile end in itself.

From this brief summary there emerges a picture of an exceptionally complex network of factors, linked to fundamental changes in the social, political, economic and cultural structures of ancient Greece. Much of what I have written is speculative, and while it seems likely that all of these factors had a role to play in transforming gender relations, their precise relationship is barely understood. Much more research is needed before we can comprehend the significance of this important phase in the history of women's oppression. Moreover, the inadequacy of the sources will probably mean that our knowledge will always be severely limited. Sadly, one aspect of the subject – the way in which these crucial changes were experienced by women – will never be illuminated.

7

Women and the poets

The performance of songs by solo artists or choirs formed an important element in the culture of Archaic Greece. These poems, sometimes referred to as lyrics, often contained expressions of personal feeling, but it would be going too far to say that they were purely individual in their significance.[1] Many of them were sung at events such as drinking parties, weddings or religious festivals, where the poet would have hoped to create an atmosphere of harmony and cohesion; and even if the sentiments voiced were genuinely those of the author – which is by no means certain – they would presumably have been ones with which many of the listeners were able to identify. When images of women occur in these poems, it is probably safe to assume that they had a degree of general acceptability. However, we must bear in mind that most of the poets were men, and they may have been addressing primarily the male members of their audience.

The abuse of women may have been a regular poetic theme at this time.[2] Rampant misogyny has already been encountered in the work of Hesiod (see pp. 22–3), and it crops up again in a long fragment from a poem written in the seventh century by Semonides, in which he sets out his theory of the origins of womankind. Different types of women, he explains, were fashioned out of different animals – the sow, the vixen, the bitch, the donkey, the weasel, the mare, the monkey and the bee; in addition there are a couple that were made out of elements, the earth and the sea. Between them, these females display a whole host of failings – dirtiness, nosiness, inconstancy, thievishness, vanity, extravagance, and, most prominent of all, greed, laziness and sexual insatiability. The only worthwhile character is the woman made from the bee, who is beautiful, affectionate and hard-working, and never sits around with the other wives gossiping about sex. Most men marry one of the other types, and have to endure poverty, backbiting and humiliation. 'Yes, this is the greatest plague that Zeus has made, and he has bound us to them with a fetter that cannot be broken' (7.115–16).[3] Like Hesiod, Semonides sees a wife as a disastrous economic burden who is nonetheless essential to a man's existence.

Most lyric poets, however, did not hate women. Quite a number of them professed to love them. But the awareness of the interdependence of male and female which can sometimes be perceived in the work of Homer is absent from the lyric poetry of the age. The women who are mentioned in the surviving poems are not wives, or potential wives. They are the objects of physical desire; and often it is the desire itself, rather than the woman who has inspired it, which is the main focus of the poet's interest. Personalities rarely emerge; and when they do, it is generally in the context of a sexual encounter. Eroticism, a striking feature of some of the exuberant vase paintings produced towards the end of the Archaic period, is also a dominant strain in Archaic lyric.

Now for the first time Eros the god of love appears in verse as an irrepressible games-player who creates havoc in human lives. For Alcman in the seventh century he is 'wild Eros, who plays like a child' (58).[4] For the sixth-century poet Anacreon he is a boy tossing a purple ball (358), a boxer (396), or a dice-player (398).[5] Sometimes love is viewed as a serious enemy rather than a sporting opponent, as when the seventh-century poet Archilochus likens the stricken lover to a warrior overpowered on the battlefield:

> Wretched and full of desire, I lie
> lifeless, pierced to the bone
> by this divine and dreadful pain.

(193)[6]

But still the experience of love is depersonalised; or rather, the other human being involved is dissociated from the emotion to such an extent that the emotion itself is accorded the status of a person, and is transformed into a wanton boy or a mortal foe.

When a woman does put in an appearance in one of these love poems, she is more often than not anonymous. Animal imagery is also quite common. For Archilochus, a prostitute is a working ox (35), while in another of his poems the girl whom the speaker is seducing is likened to a timid fawn (196A; see below, p. 80). When Alcman compares a beautiful woman to a horse, 'a sturdy, thunderous-hoofed prize-winner' (1.48),[7] the device is intended to express admiration and awe. But it also conveys a sense of the wildness and 'otherness' of the female, an idea which comes over even more strongly in a poem by Anacreon where the horse-riding metaphor is used to suggest sexual taming and domination:

> 'Thracian filly, why do you look at me from the corner of your eye and flee
> stubbornly from me, supposing that I have no skills? Let me tell you, I could
> neatly put the bridle on you and with the reins in my hand wheel you round
> the turnpost of the racecourse; instead, you graze in the meadows and frisk and
> frolic lightly, since you have no skilled horseman to ride you.'

(417)[8]

This theme of erotic pursuit and capture is frequently used by Archaic lyricists to represent men's relations with women. The most elaborate example occurs in a poem by Archilochus, in which the poet creates a tense mini-saga out of the successful seduction of an innocent young girl. At first the speaker in the poem employs gentle coaxing, and when the girl demurs he promises to take special precautions: 'for I will stop/ within your grassy garden plot' (196A.23/4). At this point, the would-be lover lets fly with a piece of nasty invective against a woman called Neobule, an ex-mistress, or perhaps just someone he once fancied:

> Neobule another man may take!
> She's [doubly] ripe . . .

the bloom is off her maidenhood,
the charms she had are gone, for she
can never get her fill . . .

but, frenzied, shows the measure of her shame.
Crows take her! . . .

It's you I want

for you don't deal in lies or treachery,
where she is sharp and takes
a hundred [friends] –

indeed I fear she'll bear litters premature
and blind, for she's as eager as
the fabled Bitch.

(196A.24–41)

Finally, the outcome of the exchange between the speaker and the girl is reported:

So much I said. I took the girl and couched her
where the blossoms opened full,
wrapped her soft

inside my cloak and put my arms about her.
[She trembled] like a fawn in fear
[but then grew still]

beneath the soothing hands that claimed her breasts
where Hebe's touch was openly displayed
upon her new-made flesh,

and then my fingers learnt her lovely body well
before I let the white sperm go,
touching her golden hair.

(196A.42–53)[9]

The juxtaposition of crude abuse and tender eroticism in this poem is very striking, and is by no means incidental. As Burnett (1983, p. 89) has written, this is no 'tale of a lover and his lass, invaded by invective, any more than it is a simple poem of abuse incomprehensibly decked out as a valentine'. The 'virgin and the whore' approach to women stands at the crux of the piece. The two female characters inhabit the opposite poles of womanhood. One is lascivious, promiscuous, active, past her best; the other is sweet, innocent, passive and fresh. One is a bitch, the other a trembling fawn; and naturally it is the latter who inspires in the speaker the lust for the chase.

The drama's ending is ambiguous. Did he take the girl's virginity after all? or did he fulfil his promise not to go all the way? Burnett (1983, p. 95) sees in the dénouement an attempt on the poet's part to overcome the masculine sense of disgust engendered by sexual conquest: through 'a form of sexual activity that will allow chastity to survive though its owner is possessed', the speaker succeeds in attaining the object of his desire without destroying it. An alternative interpretation is possible, however. It is by no means clear that the girl's chastity is preserved at the end, and one might say with equal justification that the swift climax, the sudden spurt, and the abrupt conclusion constitute a final twist which instantly demolishes the contrast between the two women so carefully built up in the preceding lines. What this elaborate performance produces in the end is simply a bit of 'white sperm', while the girl is nothing but a 'lovely body' and some 'golden hair'. Though the ultimate ambiguity leaves a question mark over the status of the girl, there is no uncertainty about the role which she plays in this fleeting love affair. By the close of the poem her passivity is complete, and she has been reduced to a much-handled physical object.

There is one set of male lyrics whose images of women stand out from the rest. Songs performed by choirs to the accompaniment of a lyre or a flute were an important feature of religious festivals and family celebrations, and in Sparta the poet Alcman became famous for his *Partheneia*, or Maiden-songs, written for choirs of young women. These poems, which were evidently sung in honour of a deity, are remarkable for their uninhibited displays of emotion and physical appreciation. In one of them, the girls sing of the 'limb-loosening desire' which is apparently inspired by a woman described in these terms: 'and she looks (at me?) more meltingly than sleep or death, and not in vain is she sweet. But Astymeloisa makes no answer to me; no, holding the garland, like a bright star of the shining heavens or a golden branch or soft down ... she passed through with her long feet' (3.61–70). In the longest fragment, the chorus-leader Hagesichora is praised for her hair, which 'has the bloom of undefiled gold' (1.53–4), for her silver face (1.55), and for her beautiful ankles (1.78). But fairer still is Agido: 'And so I sing of the brightness of Agido; I see her like the sun' (1.40–1). This woman, we are told, is like a Venetic racehorse, while Hagesichora, the second in beauty, resembles a Colaxaean steed which runs as pacemaker to a swifter horse (1.50–9). Later in the same poem a girl's words of yearning are imagined: 'If only Astaphis were mine, if only Philylla were to look my way and Damareta and lovely Ianthemis'; no, Hagesichora guards me' (1.74–7).

It must be remembered, of course, that these sentiments are being put into the girls' mouths by a male poet. Moreover, it is not always certain that they are meant to represent the girls' own feelings and not somebody else's. We must be cautious, therefore, in our interpretation. Calame (1977, vol. 2) believes that the Spartan girls' choir may have been an element in a formal religious structure which initiated young women into their civic and sexual duties, and that homosexual relations between senior and junior members of the choir may have been actively encouraged. This theory is based to a large extent on the poems themselves,[10] and though they certainly contain powerful erotic overtones, this does not necessarily indicate that the singers had sexual relations with each other. However, if the feelings being described are to be understood as those of the girls themselves, it does seem likely that strong emotional ties, at the very least, were expected to exist among them, and that the public voicing of these emotions was seen as perfectly acceptable.

Whatever the nature of girls' relationships may have been, it is worth bearing in mind that the language of the poems is often masculine in tone. The similes comparing women with thoroughbreds spring from a male interest in horse-racing and breeding; and in Greek the gender of the horses is masculine and not feminine – these girls are not fillies but stallions. The word *helios*, or sun, used to describe Agido, is also masculine, and as a deity Helios was always perceived by the Greeks as being male. In Alcman's Maiden-songs, women are endowed with a much more positive and vibrant presence than in most of the other lyrics, but they are still represented in terms of male perceptions. When we turn to the poetry of Sappho, the picture changes completely.

8

Women as poets: Sappho

THE PERSON

There is an anonymous Greek epigram, probably written in the second century BC, which lists eight great lyric poets of Greece, all of them male. It then adds 'Sappho is not the ninth of men, but is inscribed among the lovely Muses as the tenth Muse'.[1] This is a compliment, certainly, but it does suggest that the most famous female poet of the ancient world was consciously placed in a different category from the male writers. A woman who wrote poetry was obviously a kind of goddess.

We possess only one complete poem by Sappho, plus a number of fragments which are either very short or have major gaps in them. Of these, only about forty consist of more than a couple of words. Clearly, when considering Sappho as a poet, we do not have a lot to go on. This has not prevented people from writing a great deal about her, a practice that can be traced right back to the Classical Age, when her personal history seems to have aroused as much interest as her poetry. Nowadays, the sensational aspects of these ancient treatments are viewed with scepticism, and attention has switched to the role which Sappho played in contemporary society, a topic which is obviously of some relevance where the experience of women in the Archaic Age is concerned. Though Sappho's biography is certainly of less significance than her poems, it is impossible to ignore it completely.

Sappho was born in about 612 BC, and lived on the island of Lesbos, which was also the home of the male lyric poet Alcaeus. An important trading centre which had close contacts with the kingdom of Lydia in western Asia Minor, Lesbos seems to have had a long tradition of cultural refinement. From the more or less reliable data which we have on Sappho herself, we can deduce that she probably came from an aristocratic family, that she was probably married to a man named Cercylas, and that she probably had a daughter called Cleis. One of the less credible features of her biography is a famous story relating how she leapt to her death from the White Rock of Leucas while in pursuit of a handsome ferryman named Phaon with whom she was passionately in love. This tale has mythological associations – Aphrodite, for example, is supposed to have made the same leap in the same place on account of her love for Adonis – and it may have originated in a comic play written about two hundred years after Sappho's death.

Unquestionably, Sappho's poetry was much admired in the ancient world. In addition to the large number of written allusions to her and her work, there are also imaginary portraits of her on pots and coins dating from the late sixth century BC to the third century AD. The great reverence which her poems inspired is well illustrated by a story told of the sixth-century Athenian poet and legislator, Solon. In his old age he heard his nephew performing one of Sappho's songs at a drinking party, and asked the young man to teach it to him, 'So that having learned it, I may die'.[2]

Jokes were also made at Sappho's expense. From the fourth century BC onwards she appeared as a character in a number of comic plays but, as none of these has survived, we have little notion of why she was considered to be funny. Her amorous activities are quite likely to have featured in some way, but these were not necessarily represented as homosexual: we know that in two comedies she was credited with two male poets as lovers, and that in another, by Menander, the notorious affair with the ferryman Phaon was mentioned.

Elsewhere, her sexual proclivities were certainly brought under scrutiny. In the third or second century BC, commentators were beginning to mention the fact that she had been criticised for her physical involvement with women, an allegation which some authors were at pains to refute. This suggests that the poems which were still in existence then were no more explicit about her sexual behaviour than the ones which we possess today. It would also seem to indicate that female homosexuality had by this time come to be regarded as not very nice.[3] By the second century AD, it was seen as far worse than that, at least by the early Christian fathers. For example, Tatian (*Ad Graecos* 53 A) castigates Sappho as a 'nymphomaniac fornicator who even writes poems about her own debauchery'.

Whether or not the growth of Sappho's reputation as a homosexual was linked to the spread of a similar idea about the women of Lesbos in general is a debatable point. The word 'lesbian' is a modern invention: it only began to be used to denote a female homosexual in the late nineteenth century, as the result of the publicity created by a scholarly controversy over Sappho's own sexuality. In Classical Greece, women from Lesbos were apparently noted for their uninhibited and imaginative approach to heterosexual couplings. Hence the verb *lesbiazein* ('to lesbianise') can mean to practise fellatio on a man. The one clear allusion to homosexual behaviour on the part of Lesbian women occurs in a dialogue between two prostitutes written by the satirist Lucian in the second century AD. One of the characters reveals that she is having an affair with a rich woman from Lesbos, who loves her 'just like a man', and her friend goes on to comment, 'They do say that there are women like that in Lesbos, of a masculine appearance, who refuse to have sex with men but want to be with women as if they themselves were men' (*Dialogues of prostitutes* 5). But in the same conversation we hear about another butch woman from Corinth, a city renowned in the ancient world for its prostitutes and diverse sexual delights. Lesbos may well have enjoyed a similar, non-specialised, reputation. The ancient Greeks did not make a rigid distinction between homosexual and heterosexual activity, and if Lesbian women were famous for sex they are likely, as Dover has pointed out (1978, p. 183), to have practised a number of different varieties.

The evidence for Sappho's own homosexuality lies in the poems themselves; and, as always, we have to be wary about treating these as straightforwardly autobiographical. This said, there can be no doubt that on occasions she expresses feelings of considerable tenderness for young women. But there is only one reference to physical love, in a poem of farewell in which Sappho reminds a departing friend of the pleasures they shared in the past:

> for many wreaths of violets,
> of roses and of crocuses
> ... you wove around yourself by my side ...
>
> and on a bed, soft and tender
> ... you satisfied your desire ...

(94; Balmer 32) [4]

We cannot be sure, of course, that Sappho herself was involved in this moment of gratification, or indeed that it ever took place at all. The precise degree of physical contact which she enjoyed with young women is not a subject which the poems can ever make clear to us, and it is in any case of no great significance. What the poems do reveal is that on the level of the imagination Sappho was a lover of women.

The question of Sappho's sexuality is inextricably linked with the much wider issue of the role which she played in Lesbian society. The internal evidence of the poems suggests that Sappho belonged to a group of women who were united by bonds of affection and by a love of music and poetry. Education may well have been one of the functions of this group: one later commentator on Sappho's work speaks of her as 'educating the best not only of her compatriots but also of those from Ionia'.[5] Some modern critics see the circle as an unofficial gathering of friends, and suggest that it may have been traditional in aristocratic Lesbian society for young women to meet together to receive instruction in music and poetry from an older woman. Others regard the group as a more institutionalised body, formally organised for the worship of Aphrodite, the Graces and the Muses. According to this interpretation, Sappho's poetry would have been intended for public performance and would have had a ritual significance.

These two roles were not necessarily incompatible, but the distinction does raise questions about Sappho's audience, and the general level of acceptance of the values which she was expressing. If her poems were sung before private, women-only groups, then her representation of love between women might be seen as an aspect of a female counter-culture which had grown up in reaction to a set of male-dominated social institutions. If, on the other hand, performances were public and were a recognised element in the civic and religious life of the community, then it would have to be admitted that mutual female passion was accorded what would appear to us to be a surprising degree of official encouragement. It is virtually impossible for us to know which kind of audience Sappho was addressing, though we should bear in mind that it need not have been the same on every occasion. Some of her poems (the wedding songs and hymns to deities) are in a form which suggests that they were intended for presentation at social or communal events, though even here we cannot be sure that the poet has not applied a traditional form to a piece written for private hearers. The majority of the fragments, however, offer no clue as to the nature of the occasion at which they were performed.

Public performance is not necessarily ruled out by the nature of the sentiments which the poet is voicing. The Greeks did not regard homosexual love between men as abnormal or as fundamentally opposed to heterosexual activity (see pp. 102–5), and it is possible that their ideology also encompassed the fostering of relations between women.

Hallett (1979) has argued that, since women's social value in the Archaic Age was defined mainly in physical and sexual terms, it is quite likely that Greek society would have institutionalised the sensual education of upper-class women. She believes that Sappho's poems represent 'a social vehicle for imparting sensual awareness, and sexual self-esteem, to women on the threshold of marriage and maturity' (pp. 456–7). It is certainly not out of the question that Sappho's songs, and the real-life activities of the group to which she belonged, fulfilled a function of sexual initiation. But this theory too must remain on the level of speculation.

What, finally, can Sappho tell us about the creativity of Greek women in general? Some modern commentators have suggested that in aristocratic society during the Archaic period women had greater freedom than in some later communities to engage in literary activities and gain public esteem for their work. But this claim is based to a large extent on the existence of Sappho herself, so that the argument becomes a circular one. We do not know the names of any other women poets living on Lesbos in the Archaic Age, although this is not to say that they did not exist. Some of Sappho's friends, if her poems are to be believed, were also singers, and music and poetry may have been the regular mode of expression within their group.[6] Outside Lesbos, there is only one other woman poet who can be assigned with any certainty to the Archaic period. This is Megalostrata of Sparta, who was praised by the poet Alcman in these lines: 'This gift of the sweet Muses was displayed by one blessed among girls, the yellow-haired Megalostrata' (Alcman 59B).[7]

It is impossible to build any substantial theories about Archaic women's cultural involvement on foundations as shaky as these. Indeed, we have more information about women poets living in the Classical Age than we do about Archaic ones. Four of these – Myrtis, Corinna, Praxilla and Telesilla – are known to us by name. From the work of one of them, Corinna, we possess three fragments of a reasonable length; Myrtis is mentioned as the teacher of Corinna; and the other two survive in a few scattered lines. All of them, however, seem to have earned for themselves considerable reputations, both during their lifetimes and in later antiquity. Corinna is even said to have defeated the renowned Pindar in poetry competitions. But even they cannot be said to represent a trend, being so few in number.

However, one must be cautious about dismissing the idea of a female literary movement altogether. Modern researches have shown very clearly that women's achievements in the arts are all too easily neglected by a male cultural establishment. There is one area of activity at least that points to the traditional involvement of women in the composition of songs: in both the Archaic and Classical ages, funeral laments were generally performed by females, and some of these were probably adapted by the women themselves to suit the particular circumstances of the deceased. At Hector's funeral, for example (see p. 50), there were professional mourners who would have performed set dirges; but the laments uttered by his closest female relatives were more personal, and may have been seen as pieces improvised on the spot, using traditional motifs.[8] This practice suggests the existence of a long tradition of specialised oral composition on the part of women. But there are also indications that this practice was sometimes frowned upon by men,[9] and it must remain uncertain whether females were in the habit of performing their songs at other semi-public events.

THE POEMS

Sappho herself was writing within a tradition of lyric poetry created and dominated by men. But in her choice of subject-matter, in her poetic language and in the structure of her thought, she demonstrates the way in which a medium shaped by masculine values can be appropriated and transformed by a woman writer. Much of her surviving work can be characterised as love poetry. But even in the poems that do not belong to this genre, she shows herself to be almost exclusively concerned with the world of women – with their everyday lives, their dress, their occupations, their rituals, and their feelings. In one of the fragments she writes:

> I have a beautiful daughter, golden
> like a flower, my beloved Cleis,
> for her, in her place, I would not accept
> the whole of Lydia, nor lovely...

> (132; Balmer 75)

This incomplete snatch of verse contains one of the few expressions of the value of the mother-daughter relationship to be found in the whole of Greek literature. In stating her love, Sappho touches, albeit very briefly, on a wider theme which is explored more fully in one of the longer fragments (see pp. 89–90). In the last line she introduces the question of evaluation, and for a moment she transforms her child into a commodity in order to assess her worth. Cleis, she declares, exceeds in value all the wealth and power symbolised by the prosperous kingdom of Lydia. The poet refuses to enter into exchange, and in doing so asserts her overriding preference for the emotional experience of women.

The few fragments which have survived from Sappho's epithalamia, or wedding-songs (frags. 30, 108–15), testify to her recognition of marriage as a crucial element in women's experience. But marriage also brought the pain of parting from family and friends, since it involved the transference of a woman to another household, and often to another community. This may well have been the cause of the separations which form the background to a number of Sappho's poems. In one, she speaks to a woman named Atthis about her friend, who is now far away in Sardis:

> [Atthis,]
> although she is in Sardis,
> her thoughts often stray here, to us...

> [... for you know that she honoured] you
> as if you were a goddess
> and, most of all, delighted in your song.

> But now she surpasses all the women
> of Lydia, like the moon,
> rose-fingered, after the sun has set,

> shining brighter than all the stars; its light
> stretches out over the salt-
> filled sea and the fields brimming with flowers:

the beautiful dew falls and the roses
and the delicate chervil
and many-flowered honey-clover bloom.

But wandering here and there, she recalls
gentle Atthis with desire
and her tender heart is heavy with grief...

(96; Balmer 33)

None of the lyrics written by male poets has brought us as close to women's feeling as this poem does. It takes us inside its characters' minds, and recreates the pain of absence which is a vital part of women's experience of love. But at the same time it cancels distance by representing the two-way flow of thought through which absence is contradicted. Atthis is invited to imagine the woman in Sardis imagining her, a process which is underlined by the imagery of the moon, whose rays, as they stretch out over the water, form a visible link between the two friends. Here, there is no division into active and passive partners: each woman is both the subject and the object of thought. The pattern of conquest and domination which characterises the male lyricists' idea of love is replaced in Sappho's verse by a model founded upon reciprocity; and the tension which underlies the poem is created, not by a 'will the lover get the girl?' scenario, but by the context of the enforced parting.

Sappho's distinctiveness can also be discerned in the metaphors which she applies to women. Unlike the male lyricists, she never compares women with animals: for her, horses are associated, not with a wild feminine beauty, but with masculine desire (see pp. 89–90). Similarly, we can contrast Alcman's simile of the sun (p. 81) with the moon imagery which in fragment 96 conjures up the brilliance of the woman in Sardis. Fruit and flowers are the items most frequently brought into service when Sappho wishes to create a visual image: for example, a woman may be like a 'sweet-apple/ turning red at the top of the highest branch' (105a; Balmer 68). But the use of imagery to suggest a woman's appearance is not, in fact, particularly common in Sappho's poems, which tend to focus on the emotional effect created by a woman, an effect reinforced by the physical objects around her. In the flowers, the perfumes and the soft linens with which women surround themselves we experience the sensuousness which radiates from their presence. Explicit references to their personal beauty are often not felt to be necessary.

The creation of a sense of private space is a significant feature of Sappho's poetry. Women, excluded from the public arenas devoted to masculine achievement, are provided in her verse with an enclosed and woman-centred environment, secure from external pressures. In a prayer to Aphrodite, the goddess is invited to visit her sanctuary, where 'far away beyond the apple branches, cold streams/ murmur, roses shade every corner/ and, when the leaves rustle, you are seized/ by a strange drowsiness' (2; Balmer 79). In fragment 96, the space which unites the women is one created by light and by mutual thought. Elsewhere, it is a shared memory which brings them together and cancels the distance between them:

... frankly I wish that I were dead:
she was weeping as she took her leave from me

and many times she told me this:
'Oh what sadness we have suffered,
Sappho, for I'm leaving you against my will.'

So I gave this answer to her:
'Go, be happy but remember
me there, for you know how we have cherished you,

if not, then I would remind you
[of the joy we have known,] of all
the loveliness that we have shared together;

for many wreaths of violets,
of roses and of crocuses
... you wove around yourself by my side

... and many twisted garlands
which you had woven from the blooms
of flowers, you placed around your slender neck

... and you were anointed with
a perfume, scented with blossom,
... although it was fit for a queen

and on a bed, soft and tender
... you satisfied your desire ...'

(94; Balmer 32)

It is in this fragment that the self-effacing nature of women's love is most clearly expressed. The reminiscence begins with an evocation of the loveliness which the speaker and her partner have shared. But after this, there is an ever-increasing concentration on the body of the other woman – on the wreaths which she weaves around herself, the garlands placed around her neck, the anointing of her body, the satisfaction of her desire. The speaker is still there for a moment beside her as she weaves, but then she disappears from view altogether. This total absorption in the activity and fulfilment of the other partner suggests a lack of self-consciousness which is absent from the 'male as desiring subject/female as desired object' relationships so often constructed by other lyric poets.

In one of Sappho's poems the idea of pursuit and capture is taken up by the poet, but only in order that it may be turned upside down. Fragment 1, the only complete poem by Sappho which has survived, takes the form of a prayer addressed to Aphrodite:

Immortal, Aphrodite, on your patterned throne,
daughter of Zeus, guile-weaver,
I beg you, goddess, don't subjugate my heart
with anguish, with grief

but come here to me now, if ever in the past
you have heard my distant pleas
and listened; leaving your father's golden house
you came to me then

with your chariot yoked; beautiful swift sparrows
brought you around the dark earth
with a whirl of wings, beating fast, from heaven
down through the mid-air

to reach me quickly; then you, my sacred goddess,
your immortal face smiling,
asked me what had gone wrong this time and this time
why was I begging

and what in my demented heart, I wanted most:
'Who shall I persuade this time
to take you back, yet once again, to her love;
who wrongs you, Sappho?

For if she runs away, soon she shall run after,
if she shuns gifts, she shall give,
if she does not love you, soon she shall even
against her own will.'

So come to me now, free me from this aching pain,
fulfil everything that
my heart desires to be fulfilled: you, yes you,
will be my ally.

(1; Balmer 78)

Here, a famous image of Aphrodite created by Homer is reversed. In the *Iliad*, the wounded goddess escapes from the dangers of the battlefield and goes racing up to Olympus in Ares' chariot, to be comforted by her mother. In this poem, by contrast, she whirls down to earth in a flurry of amused concern to bring relief to a suffering worshipper.[10] This turning inside-out of a familiar scene prepares the reader for the reversal which is to come. The poet employs one of the traditional elements of male courtship when she evokes a sense of opposition between lover and loved through her use of the language of conflict ('subjugate', 'wrongs', 'runs away', 'run after', 'ally'). But in this case, there is a subtle shift which subverts the usual pattern of domination and submission. The speaker in this piece is no combatant confident of her own powers of seduction. She needs Aphrodite's help, and what the goddess vouchsafed her in the past was not conquest, but an equilibrium achieved through the passage of time. A woman who fled would in the future pursue; one who did not love would later experience love against her will. In the world of women, love may not always be mutual, but at least the roles which they play are interchangeable, and someone who is now an object of pursuit may one day become a pursuer.

In fragment 16 we encounter another familiar Homeric character.

Some an army of horsemen, some an army on foot
and some say a fleet of ships is the loveliest sight
on this dark earth; but I say it is whatever you desire:

and it is perfectly possible to make this clear
to all; for Helen, the woman who by far surpassed
all others in her beauty, left her husband –
the best of all men –

behind and sailed far away to Troy; she did not spare
a single thought for her child nor for her dear parents
but [the goddess of love] led her astray
[to desire ...]

        [... which]
reminds me now of Anactoria
although far away,

whose long-desired footstep, whose radiant, sparkling face
I would rather see before me than the chariots
of Lydia or the armour of men
who fight wars on foot...

(16; Balmer 21)

At first glance, Sappho seems in the first verse to be drawing a contrast between male and female systems of value.[11] Male notions of beauty all focus on impersonal military formations, while that of the woman speaker revolves around a loved individual. But on closer examination it can be seen that what the speaker is proposing is a more general definition of beauty, one that embraces the opinions expressed in the first two lines: the loveliest sight on earth is not 'this, that, or the other', it is whatever a person desires. In this way, the common male assumption that war is a more serious business than love is exposed: for them, war *is* an object of love.

The reference to Helen is notable for two reasons. In the second verse, we hear of her beauty, and expect her to be presented as an example of the loveliest sight on earth, pursued by the men who value armies and fleets of ships. But then we learn that she is not the object but the subject of desire – the active partner who is prepared to abandon her husband, child and parents in order to follow the person she loves. The second point to note is that she is not condemned for her action. Nor is she being blamed for the butchery of the Trojan War. By placing her in the same position as the desiring males at the beginning of the poem, the speaker may even be implying that responsibility for the outbreak of the War is to be shared between the two parties. Helen's choice in favour of love was no more a cause of the fighting than was the male delight in battle. This account of Helen's actions is very different from the one provided by Sappho's fellow-countryman Alcaeus, who in one of his poems describes how Helen was driven crazy by love, and how for her sake many warriors were laid low on the Trojan plain (fragment 283).

These reflections remind the speaker of the object of her own love, the absent Anactoria. She now reveals that she sets a much higher value on what she desires than on what men desire: Anactoria's radiant face is for her far superior to Lydian chariots and armies of infantry. At the end of the poem, the all-embracing definition proposed in the first stanza breaks down, and the speaker registers her particular opposition to the dominant masculine values of the day.[12]

One of the best-known of Sappho's poems focuses on the feelings which a woman's voice and laughter arouse in the speaker:

It seems to me that man is equal to the gods,
that is, whoever sits opposite you
and, drawing nearer, savours, as you speak,
the sweetness of your voice

and the thrill of your laugh, which have so stirred the heart
in my own breast, that whenever I catch
sight of you, even if for a moment,
then my voice deserts me

and my tongue is struck silent, a delicate fire
suddenly races underneath my skin,
my eyes see nothing, my ears whistle like
the whirling of a top

and sweat pours down me and a trembling creeps over
my whole body, I am greener than grass;
at such times, I seem to be no more than
a step away from death;

but all can be endured since even a pauper...

(31; Balmer 20)

As Winkler has pointed out (1990, pp. 178–9), in many discussions of this piece 'androcentric habits of thought' have allowed the anonymous male of the first line to assume 'a grotesque prominence'.[13] Winkler himself argues very plausibly that the man should not be seen as an actor in the imagined scene – as a husband or lover who has inspired the speaker's jealousy – but rather as an element in a traditional formula of praise. A similar rhetorical cliché is employed, for example, by Homer in the scene where Odysseus tells Nausicaa (see p. 53) that the man who can win her as his bride is blessed beyond all others (*Odyssey* 6.158–61).

Two people dominate the scene: the speaker and the other woman. Here, the speaker does not fade quickly from view, as she does in fragment 94. On the contrary, as the physical effects of her overwhelming passion are described, we are brought into intimate contact with the various parts of her body – her heart, her breast, her tongue, her skin, her eyes, her ears. But at the same time the force of her presence is denied, for she gradually loses her various senses, until she approaches death itself. The mutuality of women's love evoked in other pieces is not present in this fragment – at least not as far as we can tell, in the absence of the poem's ending. But it does describe a subtle shift in the power relations of love, one that allows a loved object to deprive a subject of sensation, and sweet speaking to rob a speaker of speech. Like so much of Sappho's work, this narrative offers an insight into women's consciousness and women's values. Happily, Sappho's voice was not in reality stifled, and through it an alternative perspective on the cultural and emotional preoccupations of Greek people in the Archaic Age is presented. For once, we can see things as a woman saw them. We can only regret that Sappho's voice is so isolated, and is sometimes so difficult to hear.

9

Women in stone

Prominent among the visual representations of women in the Archaic Age were the large-scale, free-standing stone figures of *korai* (young women or maidens) which, along with their male equivalents the *kouroi* (young men), made their first appearance in Greek art soon after 650 BC (Figs 13–16b). These statues seem always to have been exhibited publicly. In cemeteries, they served as grave-markers, and depicted the dead persons. In religious sanctuaries, they were dedicated to the presiding god or goddess, and here the subject of the representation may have been either the worshipper making the offering, a deity, or possibly a young person in the deity's service; the precise significance is often difficult to determine.[1] Generally the images are life-size or a little larger; a few of them are colossal. For over a century, they comprised one of the most notable branches of sculptural production in the Greek world.

The fact that females were frequently represented is interesting in itself, for it suggests a public acknowledgement of women which one might not otherwise appreciate. It appears, for instance, that in the last thirty years of the sixth century BC a large number of *korai* figures were erected in the sanctuary of Athena on the Acropolis at Athens (Figs 15–16b). These images must surely have served to create a very feminine atmosphere, which nowadays is absent from the site, and which indeed seems largely to have disappeared in the course of the fifth century. The statues were damaged when the Persians sacked Athens in 480 and 479 BC, and were replaced in the main with figures of male athletes and heroes.

A study of sixth-century sculpture reveals that Greek artists were making great strides in terms of the naturalistic representation of the human body. But certain conventions were maintained throughout the period. One is so pervasive that we tend to take it for granted: all the young women are clothed, while virtually all the young men are naked. This gender-specific treatment of nudity, the reverse of the one generally encountered in modern western society, was to remain a feature of Greek art for over two hundred years. While the absence of female nudes may seem remarkable to a twentieth-century observer, in the context of Archaic Greece it is hardly surprising, since the importance attached to the chastity of women would have inhibited public displays of female nudity.[2]

Rather, it is the convention of the male nude which requires explanation. It is true that to a certain extent male nudity was a fact of public life, in that men performed athletics naked. They did not, however, appear in the nude in most of the situations in which they are represented as such by Greek artists (fighting battles, taking part in religious processions, and so on). The social acceptance of homosexual activity among Greek men makes it likely that erotic appreciation of the male form was one of the factors determining these representations; but this is probably only part of the answer. A number of art historians have suggested that archaic images are to be understood as examples of conceptual art [3] – they represent the general concept or idea of a man rather than particular individuals – and the nudity of the *kouros* can probably be seen as reinforcing this understanding. It serves to underline the essential nature of the figure: here is man as he exists throughout eternity, divorced from the movements of history and time. As Kenneth Clark has written in his study of the nude, the confidence displayed by the Greeks in their depictions of nudity 'expresses above all their sense of human wholeness' (1956, p. 21).

The female, who is never represented nude, must therefore be seen as somehow less whole, less essential, less eternal than the male. It is the male figure which provides the model for the human anatomy, and for the human condition; the female figure retains its drapery, and in this way is proclaimed as a special case, a departure from the universal norm. According to the Athenian historian Thucydides (1.6.5), the nudity of male athletes was a feature that distinguished Greeks from barbarians, and nudity in general might also have been seen as affirming the superiority of men over women.

Another gender distinction can be discerned in the statues' poses: all the *kouroi* stand with their legs apart and their arms held stiffly down by their sides, while the majority of the *korai* are shown with their legs together or only slightly apart, and their arms extended upwards. Males, it seems, have the potential for movement, and can operate in the outside word; females are fixed and static. This, of course, is a reflection of the polarised roles played by men and women in real life. The immobility of the female figure becomes particularly striking when the *kore* is employed in the place of a column, in order to support a roof. Female statues of this kind were called caryatids, and are most famously represented in the Classical versions from the Erechtheum at Athens (Fig. 2); but examples had already appeared in the Archaic Age in the treasuries of the Siphnians and of the Cnidians at Delphi. The motif may well have originated in women's habit of carrying burdens on their heads; but when the burden is a roof, then the notion is forcibly expressed that women, by remaining rooted within the home, provide its main element of support. The female's role as guardian of the household's wealth is suggested by the use of the caryatids in treasuries.

The difference in the positioning of the statues' arms can perhaps be seen as simply underlining the difference in the legs: males adopt the 'walking' stance, while females are doing things with their arms which require them to stand still. However, it is worth noting that the location of the arms sometimes draws attention to the two areas most associated with a woman's reproductive function, the breasts and the genitals, and that many of them are holding pomegranates (Figs 13, 16a), a symbol of fertility. Contemporary morality may have dictated that women in stone had to be clothed, but it would be wrong to see these images as entirely asexual. Often the material of the dresses is stretched tightly across emphatically rounded buttocks (Fig. 16b), and it is known from elsewhere that female bottoms were an important erotic feature (see below, pp. 101; 107–8). When we bear in mind that the women represented in these statues were unmarried virgins, these sexual references may seem somewhat surprising. They tend to confirm the notion (see above, p. 45) that virginity was not revered as a good thing in itself, but rather on account of its potential for fruitfulness.

The ideological significance of the *korai* figures can perhaps be summed up very simply. Women should be nubile but modestly draped, they should stay in one place, and they should be fertile. Their calm beauty, it is true, is suggestive of a publicly-acknowledged appreciation of the female principle which stands in refreshing contrast to the spirit of the age which followed. But at the same time the emergence in the course of the Archaic Age of the male nude as the leading art form is symptomatic of the male–centred character which the culture and institutions of the *polis* were gradually assuming.

PART III

THE CLASSICAL
AGE: 500–336 BC

T he beginning of the Classical Age is marked by political events of far-reaching
significance. In the course of the sixth century, the Greek settlements on the
western coast of Asia Minor had been overrun by the Persians, who soon came
to control a vast empire extending from Egypt in the west to the Punjab in the east. A
revolt on the part of some of these Greek states, assisted to a very modest degree by
Athens, provoked the Persians into two invasions of mainland Greece early in the fifth
century. The first invasion, launched by king Darius in 490 BC, was halted by the victory
of the Athenian forces at the battle of Marathon. The second, led by king Xerxes, was a
more massive operation. It was only after the Persian army had occupied over half the
country that they were finally defeated by a coalition of thirty-one Greek states.
Prominent among these were Athens and Sparta, whose forces played a vital part in two
decisive victories, at the battle of Salamis in 480 and at Plataea in 479 BC. The successful
defence of their territory against the onslaught of the mighty Persian Empire helped to
produce in the Greeks a strong sense of their own identity and values, which they began
to see as fundamentally opposed to those of the Persians. This perceived antithesis
between 'Greek' and 'barbarian', which was paralleled in some contexts by the
male/female antithesis, coloured much of Greek thought in the Classical Age.

From 479 BC onwards, the Athenians took advantage of the collapse of Persian power
in the Aegean area in order to create a naval league whose objective was the defence of
Greek cities against further Persian aggression. Its members included a majority of the
Greek states on the Aegean islands and along the west coast of Asia Minor. From the
start, the alliance was dominated by Athens, and it soon began to be referred to as the
Athenian Empire. As the Persian threat began to recede, the league's navy was used more
and more to further Athens' own interests. In this way she managed to acquire what was
virtually a monopoly of trade in the Aegean area, and she became by Greek standards
very prosperous.

Athens' wealth – the wealth both of the state and of the several hundred men who were its richest inhabitants – was to make a considerable contribution to the Athenian cultural achievement in the Classical Age. Magnificent temples and sculpture, productions of drama, the pursuit of philosophical enquiries – none of these would have been possible without financial resources. Wealth was also important in the development of the Athenian slave economy. It is estimated that there may have been as many as 100,000 slaves in Athens by 431 BC, while the adult male citizen population at the same time may have been about 40,000. This proportion of slaves would probably have been far higher than that possessed by any other Greek state. Slaves were used as domestic, agricultural and industrial labour; and while it is debatable how far down the social scale slave ownership went, there can be no doubt that it liberated some men from involvement in economic activity, and enabled them to devote their time to political and cultural concerns. At the same time the institution of slavery helped to foster an awareness of the value of freedom. The majority of Athenians would always have had to work for a living – most of them were peasant farmers – but all of them could appreciate that as free citizens they enjoyed a status which was distinct in every way from that of the slave.

Athens' democratic system attained its most radical form around the middle of the fifth century. It was characterised by its participative – as opposed to representational – quality. All important decisions were made on the basis of a majority vote in an Assembly which all adult male citizens were entitled to attend. Executive and administrative functions were carried out by men who were chosen annually by lot from the whole citizen body. Boards of judges were also chosen by lot, and ten generals were elected annually. It was a remarkable system, in which equality of opportunity was underpinned by payment for public office, thus ensuring that poor men were not prevented from participating. But it has to be admitted that private wealth and aristocratic birth were still instrumental in acquiring for certain individuals an influence in the Assembly which made them into unofficial popular leaders. This is most obviously the case with Pericles who, between 442 and his death in 429 BC, was elected as a general every year and played a major part in shaping Athenian policy during this time. It must also be remembered that Athenian democracy only ever involved a minority of the adult population. Slaves, resident non-Athenians and women were all excluded.

During the fifth century Athens' dominant position in the Aegean area was matched by the hegemony exercised on the mainland by the state of Sparta. By 600 BC, Sparta had occupied the regions of Laconia and Messenia in the southern half of the Peloponnese, making her by far the largest of the Greek *poleis*. As a result, Sparta was in the unusual position for a Greek state of being self-sufficient in food. For this reason she never developed significant trading relations with other communities, which in part accounts for the cultural backwardness for which she was notorious in the Classical period.

Of even more relevance is the fact that Sparta, when incorporating conquered territory during the Archaic Age, had converted the native populations of those areas into a kind of serf class. These people, who were known as the Helots, greatly outnumbered Spartan citizens, perhaps by more than seven to one. They formed a compulsory labour force which carried out all the agricultural work for their Spartan masters. So, while other states imported slaves from outside their own territory, and thus acquired a workforce consisting of people from many different regions, Sparta adopted the dangerous alternative of keeping a whole population, with a sense of common identity, in subjection at home. As a result, there was an ever-present danger of Helot uprisings, which did in fact break out on a number of occasions.

It is believed that the constant need to be on their guard against the Helots was the main factor in the emergence of the intensely militaristic way of life led by the Spartans. Their highly unusual social system, which took shape in the late seventh and early sixth centuries BC, dictated that all Spartan citizens were full-time professional soldiers. They were trained for this role from boyhood, and up to the age of thirty they lived continuously in barracks. After that, they could set up their own domestic establishments, but for the rest of their lives they ate every night in a common mess. Military prowess and a capacity for absolute obedience were two of the qualities for which they were famed.

The Peloponnesian League, which Sparta created towards the end of the sixth century, included nearly all the states in the southern region of Greece, and was the basis of Sparta's dominance of the Greek mainland. By the middle of the fifth century, two power blocs had emerged, one headed by Athens and her navy, and the other by Sparta and her army. They were soon in open conflict, and in 431 BC a major war broke out. After many reversals of fortune, great loss of life and considerable expenditure of resources, the Peloponnesian War ended in total defeat for Athens. In 404 her entire navy was captured and her empire was brought to an end.

The war had destroyed the balance of power between Athens and Sparta, and in the fourth century a wide-ranging series of conflicts was unleashed as a number of states vied for leadership. By the middle of the century a power vacuum had developed. This was soon to be filled in a way which few Greeks would have anticipated. Philip II, the ruler of Macedonia in the far north of Greece, had by 350 BC converted his once obscure state into a considerable military force. Gradually and with the utmost skill he insinuated himself and his army into mainland Greece. In 338, after he had defeated Athens and Thebes at the battle of Chaeronea, he assumed control of the whole country. Greek autonomy was now at an end; and when Philip was assassinated two years later, the Classical Age too, according to most of the modern time-charts, came to a close.

Athens in particular is noted for the remarkable creativity which she generated during the Classical period. In the course of about 150 years, the city produced an amazing succession of writers, artists and thinkers. The dramatists Aeschylus, Sophocles, Euripides and Aristophanes, the historians Herodotus and Thucydides, the sculptors Phidias and Praxiteles, the philosophers Socrates, Plato and Aristotle – these are just some of the men who lived and worked there during this time. In addition, there were many painters, sculptors and architects employed in the city whose names are frequently unknown to us. In particular, the building programme on the Athenian Acropolis, carried out in the second half of the fifth century, brought together numerous artists of outstanding calibre.

It is difficult for us fully to understand today the reasons why these creative energies were released in Athens during this period. No overall explanation can ever be considered adequate. But among the factors which may be thought to have made a contribution, one can mention Athens' wealth, the role which she had played in defeating the Persian invaders, her trading contacts with other cultures, her slave economy and her democratic constitution. Women, of course, were excluded from the operations of democracy, and were not involved in any of the acknowledged fields of cultural production. Their way of life ensured that they were even barred in many respects from an appreciation of culture. When considering the nature of the Classical achievement, it is important to remember that women's experience of this phenomenon may well have been very different from that of their male compatriots.

10

Women's bodies

The Hippocratic writings

A large part of our information about the physical side of women's lives in the Classical Age is derived from a collection of writings known as the Hippocratic corpus. These are medical treatises by a variety of anonymous authors, most of whom were probably writing in the late fifth and fourth centuries BC. In antiquity, some of these works were attributed to the great fifth-century doctor Hippocrates, but nowadays it is doubted whether any of them was by Hippocrates himself.

Since eight of the works in the corpus are devoted to the subject of women, it seems clear that females formed a significant part of the clientele of Hippocratic doctors. As one might expect, the professional treatment of women's illnesses in the Classical Age was handled very largely by men. Although there is some evidence to show that there were at least a few women doctors in fourth-century Athens (see below, p. 145), these were doubtless very much the exception. Childbirth, which in normal circumstances was dealt with by midwives, would appear to be the one medical situation in which a woman might expect to be attended solely by other women (see below, p. 110). When treating a woman patient a doctor sometimes relied on a female assistant, or on the patient herself, to carry out an internal examination and report the results back to him; but in many instances it is clear that the examination was performed by the doctor.[1] Female assistants might also be used for manual tasks: in an operation to remove a dead foetus, four females hold a woman by the arms and legs and give her a series of violent shakes (*On the excision of the foetus* 4).

Among the Hippocratic works there is no treatise on the diseases of men to match those assigned to women. Although Hippocratic doctors seem to have treated their female patients no less scrupulously than the males, their writings do indicate that they viewed women as a special case, a deviation from the masculine norm. This should serve to forewarn us that there is an element in the medical treatises which runs counter to the writers' emphasis on empirically-acquired knowledge, and which derives from an ideological view of the physical nature of women. In the discussions of women's reproductive systems in particular, ideas about women's physiology can be seen to reflect and reinforce ideas about their social and moral identity.

PUBERTY AND MENSTRUATION

According to the philosopher and natural scientist Aristotle, girls' breasts start to swell and they begin to menstruate after they have reached the age of thirteen (*History of animals* 581 a–b). Some of the Hippocratic writers see the onset of puberty as a time when young women are particularly vulnerable. The author of the treatise *On virgins* advises his readers that girls at the menarche are liable to suffer from hallucinations, because the mouth of the womb is not yet opened up through sexual intercourse, and therefore all the blood cannot flow out. Instead, it rushes up to the heart and lungs, and they become feverish and sometimes suicidally insane. Some of them have visions which encourage them to throw themselves down wells and drown themselves. 'My prescription', the author continues, 'is that when virgins have this trouble, they should marry as soon as possible. If they become pregnant, they will be cured ... Among married women, the sterile ones are more likely to suffer from this condition.' Hippocratic theory maintains that intercourse and pregnancies have the effect of opening up a woman's body and creating within it the unobstructed space that is the mark of a fully-operational female. The advice is totally in accord with the common Greek practice of marrying girls off very soon after they reached puberty.

In Aristotle's view (*History of animals* 581b), masturbation is another of the perils threatening pubescent females: 'Girls who experience sexual gratification become even more licentious, as do boys, if they do not guard against one temptation or another.' In general, it seems that for various reasons girls who had reached puberty were thought to be difficult to control. This helps to account for the association, often expressed metaphorically, between young women and wildness: the term 'filly', for example, is used to denote a woman of marriageable age; and by the same token a girl's marriage can be said to involve her 'taming' or 'yoking'.[2]

Little is written about menstruation itself outside the medical texts. During their periods women apparently wore woollen rags, perhaps the remnants of wool which had been made up into garments. The Hippocratic writers' chief concern is the way in which menstruation affects reproduction. In one treatise, we are told that if a woman is healthy her blood will flow (significantly enough) like that from a sacrificial animal. Women whose periods are abundant and last for more than four days are generally sickly, and find it difficult to carry children. When periods last for less than three days and are meagre, the women are healthy and stolid, with a masculine appearance; but they are not interested in bearing children and do not become pregnant (*On the diseases of women* 1.6). Failure of menstruation is most likely to occur in celibate women, and can prove fatal if it lasts for more than two months (*On the diseases of women* 1.2).

The same treatise gives an explanation of menstruation which is based on the idea of a distinctive female physiology. A woman's flesh, the author says, is softer and more sponge-like than a man's. Consequently, she absorbs more moisture and becomes overfilled with blood, which needs to find an exit; the fact that a man works harder than a woman is also relevant, because physical labour draws off excessive fluid (*On the diseases of women* 1.1). In this analysis, the female constitution is seen as inferior to that of the male: menstruation is believed to supply a necessary corrective to its inherent defects.

In many societies, menstrual blood is regarded as a source of pollution, but this was apparently not the case with the Greeks. There is no evidence to indicate that menstruating women were prohibited from entering religious sanctuaries in the Classical Age.[3] The only example of a belief in the magical properties of menstrual blood is furnished by Aristotle (*On dreams* 459b–460a), who reports that if a woman who is menstruating looks into a very clean mirror, its surface will become tarnished because the surrounding air is disturbed in some way by her eyes. However, there is no suggestion that a woman in this powerful condition poses any kind of threat to the men whom she encounters. Similarly, there appears to have been no taboo on sexual intercourse during menstruation. Aristotle (*Generation of animals* 727 b12–23) informs his readers that a woman will not conceive if she has sex while she is menstruating, and elsewhere says (rather less helpfully) that the best time for conception is immediately after the period has finished (*History of animals* 582b). The Hippocratic author of *On the nature of woman* (8) positively recommends sexual relations during menstruation in the case of women who are being treated for erratic periods.

SEX AND REPRODUCTION

In the Classical Age, a woman's chief value was seen as her ability to bear children. This ideological view of women inevitably permeated the works of the Hippocratic writers, a number of whom express the opinion that not having sex can seriously damage a woman's health. One example of this kind of thinking has already been encountered (see p. 99). The author of the treatise *On the seed* (4) provides a physiological explanation of the damaging effects of female celibacy: 'if (women) have intercourse with men their health is better than if they do not. For in the first place the womb is moistened by intercourse, whereas when the womb is drier than it should be it becomes extremely contracted, and this extreme contraction causes pain to the body. In the second place intercourse by heating the blood and rendering it more fluid gives an easier passage to the menses.'[4] Men, according to this view, can have a therapeutic effect on women. Another medical writer records a case of a woman who suffered from bad headaches, which disappeared completely as soon as she became pregnant (*Epidemics* 5.12).

The most bizarre phenomenon associated with celibacy in a woman is the one which a modern critic has termed 'the wandering womb'.[5] A graphic account of its cause is supplied by one of the characters in a dialogue by Plato, who tells us that the womb is an animal within a woman which is desirous of bearing children (*Timaeus* 91). If this desire remains unsatisfied for a long time, the womb becomes restless and starts to wander about the body; as a consequence, the passages for breath become blocked, and this causes distress and 'disorders of all kinds'. The problem will continue until the woman has sex with a man and becomes pregnant.

Medical writers provide a more mechanical explanation of the same phenomenon. When a woman does not have intercourse, her womb becomes dry, and is liable to be displaced (*On the diseases of women* 1.7). The various itineraries embarked upon by the errant womb are described. It may move towards the bladder, causing strangury (*On the diseases of women* 1.7), towards the head, causing suffocation, sleepiness, and foaming at the mouth (*On the diseases of women* 2.123), or towards the upper abdomen, which brings on drowsiness and loss of voice (*On the diseases of women* 2.126). Sex and pregnancy are the ultimate cures (*On the nature of woman* 8); but the Hippocratic authors do recommend a variety of interim treatments, involving fumigations, pessaries, potions, and hot and cold baths. For example, a womb that is lodged in the abdomen should be treated with a pessary dipped in Egyptian perfume, myrtle, or marjoram; the insertion of a feather into the nostrils to induce sneezing and inhalations of vapour are also suggested (*On the diseases of women* 2.126). In a case where the womb has moved towards the liver, a doctor is advised to push the womb down with his hands, and then to tie a bandage below the ribs to stop it from rising up again (*On the nature of women* 3).

This curious notion may have been inspired by knowledge of uterine prolapse; but no reliable evidence can have existed for the other routes which wombs were thought to follow. The idea is not confined to the medical treatises, and it may well have had a long history in Greek thought.[6] It provides us with the most obvious example of an ideological interpretation of women's illnesses in ancient Greece: the restlessness of the womb is suggestive of a basic physiological instability to which a woman inevitably falls victim unless a man intervenes in her life. But even here it cannot be assumed that the diagnosis was always totally misguided. The social pressure to marry and produce children was such that some women may well have suffered from stress and its associated physical problems if for any reason they failed to acquire husbands at the appropriate time. It must also be admitted that the Hippocratic doctors do not always insist on the beneficial effects of sexual intercourse for women: as Lloyd (1983, pp. 84–5) points out, they recognise that in some illnesses it is dangerous for women to become pregnant.

Hippocratic writers could be woefully ignorant about the nature of a woman's orgasm: one pronouncement informs the reader that 'once intercourse has begun, she experiences pleasure throughout the whole time, until the man ejaculates' (*On the seed* 4).[7] This, the writer explains, is because the sperm, when it arrives in the womb, extinguishes its heat, and hence it is at this point that the woman's pleasure reaches its climax. The interest in women's sexual gratification is determined by its supposed link with reproduction; the same treatise refers to a woman's emission of seed at the moment of orgasm, while another writer offers the information that conception is particularly likely to occur if the woman experiences desire (*On the diseases of women* 1.24). Aristotle, on the other hand, says that women can conceive without feeling pleasure, and feel pleasure without conceiving (*Generation of animals* 727b).

Greek men did at least recognise that sex might be a source of mutual enjoyment to male and female. Xenophon, in discussing male homosexual activity, tells us that 'a boy does not share in a man's pleasure in intercourse, as a woman does' (*Symposium* 8.21). When heterosexual sex is represented by male vase-painters, the women are sometimes shown, by their smiling faces, to be enjoying themselves.[8] However, although their participation may be enthusiastic, the postures which these women adopt are nearly always indicative of their subordinate role. As Dover (1978, pp. 100–102) has pointed out, generally the women are either in a supine position, or they are bent over and are being penetrated from behind. Sometimes it is clear that the penetration is anal and not vaginal (Fig. 17). We have no way of knowing how often in real life anal intercourse was practised, but it did have the advantage of being the most reliable contraceptive technique available to the Greeks, and may also have been preferred by men on its own account (see pp. 107–8).

Sometimes, masculine awareness of the pleasure which women derive from sex can be construed as a comment on feminine lust and lack of self-control. This is the case with a number of the female characters created by the comic playwright Aristophanes. When, for example, Lysistrata reveals that her grand design to bring war to an end will involve a sex strike on the part of the women, she is at first greeted with a horrified refusal.

'Anything, anything you want. If I had to, I'd walk through fire. Anything rather than give up penises. Lysistrata, dear, there's nothing like them!' (*Lysistrata* 133–5). This notion of women's capacity for sexual gratification was also enshrined in myth. When Zeus and Hera were having an argument about whether men or women derived the greater pleasure from sex, they referred the matter to the prophet Tiresias, who had spent seven years of his life as a woman and was therefore in a good position to know. He informed them that if sexual pleasure were divided into ten parts, only one part would go to the man, and nine parts to the woman.[9] This rather extreme assessment is, however, contradicted by the Hippocratic writer who tells us that a man's orgasm is briefer than a woman's, but is more intense (*On the seed* 4).

It is clear that some Greek men did not approve of female sexual desire, at least as far as wives were concerned. Married women were thus subjected to the double bind of being limited to a biological role, and being criticised if they showed too much appreciation of the sexual act. In Euripides' play *Medea* (569–73), Jason taunts his deserted wife with these words: 'But you women have reached a point where, if all goes well in the marriage-bed, you are perfectly happy, but if there's a problem in bed then all that is fairest and best is bitter to you.' According to Xenophon (*Mem.* 2.2.4), sexual enjoyment was not the object of marriage: men acquired wives in order to raise a family, not to satisfy their lusts, which were amply catered for in the streets and the brothels.

A rather more inspiring view of marital relations is provided by a scene in the *Lysistrata* (845–958) in which a husband desperately tries to persuade his wife to come to bed with him. Her eventual refusal is not motivated by any lack of desire on her part, but by her loyalty to the strategy of the sex-strike. This particular insight into married life might be dismissed on the grounds of comic exaggeration or the very unusual circumstances, but it is hard to believe that married couples did not sometimes enjoy the sexual side of their relationship. However, it may well have been the case that many men neglected their wives, at least when they could afford the alternative of a slave or a prostitute. In a scene in the *Lysistrata* (108–10) in which the heroine is lamenting the deplorable effect of the war on women's sex lives, she complains: 'Since the Milesians deserted us, I've not even seen a six-inch dildo that might have brought us some relief in a leather form' (dildoes were apparently a Milesian export). There are a number of Athenian vase paintings where naked women are shown brandishing these objects (see Fig. 18). It would not be at all surprising if many Greek women found a sexual outlet in masturbation.

No discussion of the sexual status of women in ancient Greece would be complete without a consideration of the role which homosexual relations played in Greek society. However, it would probably be a mistake to believe that the existence of erotic attachments between men seriously affected the amount of sexual attention which women received from their husbands. Homosexual activity was regarded as perfectly acceptable, but it generally took a very particular form, and should more properly be referred to as pederastic activity. Dover (1978, p. 84) has written that 'homosexual relationships in Greek society are regarded as the product not of the reciprocated sentiment of equals but of the pursuit of those of lower status by those of higher status'. This difference in status seems generally to have been created by a difference in the ages of the homosexual partners. In Classical Athens (to which the bulk of our evidence relates), it appears that the older partner was most commonly a young man in his twenties, while the junior partner was a youth whose beard had not yet begun to grow. The word *erastes* (or lover) is sometimes applied to the older partner, while the junior partner is often referred to as a *pais* (or boy).

Since the majority of men in Athens probably married at about the age of thirty, homosexual activity may therefore have been confined by and large to unmarried men, although we do hear about a few homosexual relationships which were maintained after marriage.[10] According to Plato (*Symposium* 192b), some male lovers were extremely reluctant to marry and produce children, and only did so as a result of severe social pressure. However, even where an extramarital homosexual attachment did exist, the wife may not have made any distinction between this and an affair with another woman. Recent discussions have demonstrated quite clearly that most Greeks were unaware of any fundamental barrier separating homosexual from heterosexual behaviour: indeed, they possessed no words equivalent to our 'homosexual' and 'heterosexual'. Sexuality itself – the notion of sexual taste as a basic and formative element in one's personality – was an alien concept to them.[11] Consequently, a man who was an *erastes*, or even in some cases a *pais*, might at the same time be having a love affair with a woman. Hence male and female are sometimes seen as interchangeable where sexual activity is concerned: Plato, in referring to a successful athlete who was engaged in a rigorous training programme, tells us that 'he never touched a woman, nor a boy either' (*Laws* 840a). In Ancient Greece, the most significant distinction was not between homosexual and heterosexual activity, but between active and passive roles. The age difference between *erastes* and *pais* signified a difference in status which determined how each would act within the relationship. The older man was the dominant partner, the one whose role was to make love (*aphrodisazein*); the younger man was subordinate, and his role was to be made love to (*aphrodisiazesthai*). Greek sexual behaviour can thus be seen as hierarchical: erotic relations between active and passive participants reflected the wider social relations that existed between adult male citizens and young men who had not yet acquired political rights.

Seen in this light, the absence of any distinction between male and female sexual partners can be viewed as a facet of the social system. Women too lacked political rights, and women too played a passive role in sexual relationships. They could be identified with boys because their place in the system was very similar. Greek – and in particular Athenian – sexual behaviour was the product of a situation in which a relatively small élite was invested with a considerable political competence which sharply differentiated it from the subordinate groups that made up the bulk of the population. These groups comprised not only boys and women, but also resident aliens and slaves.[12] The active stance of the dominant members of society permeated all their dealings with these subordinates, including their sexual dealings.

So far, in speaking of the absence of a male/female distinction, I have been referring to the absence of any necessity, on the part of a young *erastes*, to make an overall choice about which sex would be the object of his erotic attentions. But it would be a mistake to believe that boys and women were seen as playing an absolutely identical role in sexual relations, either in physical or in social terms. One difference manifested itself in the positions adopted in intercourse, as revealed in pornographic vase paintings. Scenes of anal intercourse between men are rare. Male partners generally face each other, with the junior partner standing upright, and the senior partner, who is taller, bending his knees and his head. Intercourse is intercrural – the *erastes* inserts his penis between the thighs of the *pais*. In heterosexual intercourse, on the contrary, the positions of the men reflect their dominant status and, as we have seen, the women are generally either prone or are being penetrated from behind.

There was also a difference between boys and women in terms of the sexual responses that were expected of them. Junior partners were not supposed to derive any pleasure from intercourse, and in vase paintings they are usually depicted without erections and with entirely expressionless faces. Women, on the other hand, were often thought of as enjoying sex all too much. Unlike men, they were considered to be incapable of controlling their sexual desires. In Euripides' play *Hippolytus* (966–7), Theseus is anticipating a recourse to a familiar argument when he says: 'Perhaps you'll tell me that lasciviousness is not to be found in men, but is innate in women?' In a junior homosexual partner, this masculine self-control was carried to extremes, and was maintained even in the throes of the sexual act. It was in the nature of women to be overpowered by pleasure, but a *pais* could always contain himself.

These behavioural distinctions were symptomatic of a broader social antithesis. The role of *pais* was a transitional phase. The junior partner would one day acquire the rights of a citizen, and at about this time he could also graduate to the position of an *erastes*. The loved one could become a lover, the pursued could turn and become a pursuer. Indeed, there is reason to believe that male homosexuality was viewed by Athenians in the Classical Age as an institution which aided the passage from boyhood to citizen status.[13] But a woman would always be a woman. Unlike the *pais*, she would remain subordinate for the whole of her life.

The stance and behaviour expected of a *pais* in sexual encounters may have served as indicators of the crucial distinction between a future citizen and a woman. Subjection to anal intercourse was perhaps the greatest mark of a woman's inferior status, since there is evidence to show that this act was symbolic of humiliation. In an Athenian vase painting of the fifth century, a man in Persian costume (the defeated enemy) is being approached by a Greek who is holding his half-erect penis in his hand: the caption reads 'I am Eurymedon. I stand bent over', and the Persian is shown in the appropriate position. An Athenian male caught in adultery could be punished by having a large radish pushed up his anus (see below, p. 125). Such treatment, it would appear, was deemed suitable for barbarians, for disgraced Athenians, and for females.

The existence of sexual relations between males in Classical Athens is well documented. Female homosexuality, on the other hand, receives very little publicity. Some of the literature of the Archaic Age points fairly clearly, as we have seen, to the recognition of erotic attachments between women in Lesbos and Sparta (see pp. 81, 84–5). Athenian sources, however, yield only two pieces of possible evidence. One is an Athenian pot of the late sixth century BC on which a woman is shown kneeling before another woman and touching her genitals (Fig. 19); this, however, could be interpreted as a scene in which one prostitute is anointing another in preparation for the work ahead of her. The sole literary reference is to be found in Plato's dialogue the *Symposium* (189c–193d), in which one of the participants, Aristophanes, gives an imaginative account of the origins of human love. The first human beings, he explains, were circular in shape, and had two sets of genitals. Since being sliced in two on the orders of the god Zeus, each of them has longed to be reunited with her or his other half. Those who were hermaphrodites in their circular existence, with one set of female and one set of male genitals, have become lovers of the opposite sex. Women who are halves of a female whole, with two identical sets of genitals, direct their affections towards other women and pay no attention to men; and males who are halves of a male whole pursue other men.

This story provides a model of different types of human love, and should not perhaps be seen as referring to real-life situations. The male who makes love to both men and women is not, after all, taken account of in Aristophanes' scheme, and yet we know that this was a relatively common mode of behaviour.[14] But the narrative does at least demonstrate an awareness of the possibility that sexual relations could exist between women. Dover (1978, pp. 172–3) has suggested that, in Classical Athens, male anxiety about female homosexuality may have rendered it a taboo subject, and in support of this draws our attention to the fact that the comic plays of the period, not generally noted for their reticence where sexual matters are concerned, make no reference at all to the practice. If such a taboo did exist, it would seem unlikely that anything resembling an overt female homosexual subculture was to be found in Classical Athens. In Archaic Lesbos and Sparta, the situation may well have been different; and in Sparta at least the acceptance of erotic attachments between women may still have been maintained in the Classical Age. Plutarch (*Life of Lycurgus* 18), without being specific as to the period, tells us that in Sparta official approval of homosexual love as an educative factor was such that it even existed among females, and that noble and respectable women were in love with unmarried girls (see below, pp. 152–3).

CONCEPTION

A woman's ability to conceive is naturally an important topic for the Hippocratic writers. They record a number of tests which can be carried out in order to ascertain whether or not a woman is fertile. For example, in *Aphorisms* 5.59, the recommended method is to wrap the woman up in a cloak and to burn incense beneath her. If the smell of the incense seems to pass right through her body and can be detected in her mouth and nose, then she is capable of conceiving; otherwise, she is not. Like the belief in the therapeutic effects of intercourse (see p. 99), this test relies on the notion that the ideal woman is an empty vessel, whose internal space is unobstructed and available for occupation by men and babies. In another treatise (*On the diseases of women* 3.213), a dozen different causes of sterility in women are discussed. These all involve some form of internal impediment: for example, the mouth of the womb may be at too oblique an angle to the vagina, or it may be partially or totally closed. There is little recognition on the part of the medical writers that failure to conceive may be caused by infertility in the male partner, although advice offered to would-be fathers on diet and general health (*On superfetation* 30) suggests that their physical condition was not a factor which was totally ignored.

Treatments for female infertility usually had the aim of softening and opening up the mouth of the womb. Fumigations of crushed laurel leaves, myrrh, wormwood, bees-wax, sulphur, garlic and a number of other substances are recommended. Another method is to apply ointments of (among other things) goat fat, cyclamen juice, fig tree juice or cardamom seed. The third option is the insertion of pessaries into the neck of the womb: one prescription involves a woollen pessary which has been dipped into a mixture of marrow of ox, goose fat, rose oil, and thapsia root; this is to be left in for four days, and the woman meanwhile should drink a potion made of leek juice and white wine (*On superfetation* 32–3). Using remedies such as these, Classical Greek doctors can have made little progress in their treatment of infertility: they were greatly handicapped by their ignorance of the existence of the ovaries, which were not discovered until the third century BC.[15]

Not surprisingly, some women resorted to more mystical methods in their efforts to conceive. Various deities might be applied to, including Asclepius, the god of medicine. His sanctuary at Epidaurus specialised in 'dream cures', whereby supplicants slept in a dormitory on the site and had dreams which restored them to health. Sterility occurs quite frequently among the ailments mentioned in inscriptions commemorating the cures. One such memorial records the experience of Andromache from Epirus, who dreamt that a beautiful young boy undressed her, and that the god Asclepius then touched her with his hand; after that she gave birth to a son. Other dreams featured the sacred snakes that were kept in the sanctuary, emphasising their phallic significance: Agameda of Ccus, for example, dreamed that a snake lay on her belly, and afterwards she produced five children.

If all else failed, then a desperate woman might have recourse to the black market in babies, at least if the comic playwright Aristophanes is to be believed. In a catalogue of crafty dodges perpetrated by women, one example cited is that of a woman who had to keep up a sham labour for ten days while the midwife was looking for a suitable child. Eventually a baby was brought home concealed in a jar: the husband was hurried out of the room, the beeswax which had been used to stop the baby's mouth was removed, the baby cried, and everyone was delighted (*Thesmophoriazusae* 502–18). A male writer who specialises in comic fantasy is not, of course, the most reliable of sources on the activities of women. But in Classical Athens the pressure to produce children was such that it seems more than likely that deals such as this one did occur.

One cannot discuss the question of conception without considering the notorious problem of Greek belief concerning the respective contributions of male and female. One extreme view of the matter is put forward in Aeschylus' *Eumenides*, in the speech which Apollo makes in defence of Orestes (see p. 28):

> The woman you call the mother of the child
> is not the parent, just a nurse to the seed,
> the new-sown seed that grows and swells inside her.
> The man is the source of life – the one who mounts.
> She, like a stranger for a stranger, keeps
> the shoot alive unless god hurts the roots.
>
> (*Eumenides* 658–61)[16]

This notion of the mother as a mere vessel for carrying the embryo may have occurred in the main on the level of popular belief. Its principal authoritative support is to be found in the work of Aristotle, but there is an important difference between the philosopher's theory and the one expounded by Apollo. According to Aristotle (*Generation of animals* 716a, 727a–729b, 765b), the female contributes not only space but also matter to the developing embryo. This matter, however, is seen as entirely passive; it is the male who supplies the principle of movement and life. Generation occurs when the active ingredient, the semen, comes into contact with menstrual blood and gives form to this inert raw material. A child, the philosopher maintains, can be said to come from both mother and father only in the sense that a bed can be said to come into being from both the wood and the carpenter.

This analysis of the reproductive process is based on Aristotle's belief in the essential inferiority of the female: 'a woman is, as it were, an infertile male. She is female in fact on account of a kind of inadequacy' (*Generation of animals* 728a). Both semen and menses, he asserts, are secretions of the blood, but the latter is less thoroughly 'concocted' on account of the coldness of the female constitution. Hence menstrual blood is more plentiful than semen, but it is also less pure and concentrated, and is incapable in itself of activating generation. Elsewhere (*Generation of animals* 783b–784a), Aristotle informs us that women have the nature of children; they are, as it were, constitutionally retarded, and for this reason they cannot produce semen.

Mythological precedents for the belief in the dominant reproductive function of the male are provided by stories of deities, such as Aphrodite and Athena, who are born from the male parent alone. But even in myth the notion of the self-reproducing male does not go unchallenged: the goddess Hera is also seen to be capable of single-handed generation (see p. 34). Among scientific philosophers, it would seem that the weight of opinion ran counter to what was being propounded by Aeschylus and Aristotle: Alcmaeon, Parmenides, Empedocles, Anaxagoras and Epicurus all taught that the mother as well as the father contributed seed to the embryo.[17] The same theory is outlined by a number of Hippocratic writers. One author tells us that the seed produced by both partners 'mixes together' in the womb and then condenses because of the heat (*On the nature of the child* 12). Another writes that the child will bear a closer resemblance to the parent, either mother or father, from which it draws more seed, stating that it will never resemble one parent in all respects and the other in none (*On the seed* 8). On the basis of the available evidence, the theorists who discounted women's role in reproduction do not appear to have been in the majority.

CONTRACEPTION

In Classical Greece, large families were probably exceptional. It was the practice throughout the Greek world for a man's property to be divided among his sons when he died, so there was a considerable incentive to produce only a single male heir and thus avoid the splitting up of the estate. The cost of providing dowries would have similarly inhibited the desire for daughters.[18] A number of factors may have contributed towards the limitation of family size. The practice of abortion, the exposure of new-born babies, the sexual neglect of wives, and infant and child mortality probably all played a part. Homosexual activities may also have had some effect; according to Aristotle (*Politics* 1272a), relations between males had been deliberately introduced into Crete as a way of keeping down the birth-rate. The extent to which contraception was responsible for the small size of Greek families is very debatable. There is little direct evidence for its use in the Classical period. This, however, need not indicate that it was not employed, only that male writers were not particularly interested in it. It seems likely that the main responsibility for contraceptive techniques rested with women.

Moral or religious objections to contraception seem to have been rare in the ancient world. Where they did exist, they were associated with minority groups such as the Pythagoreans, who believed 'that one should eliminate any coupling which is unnatural and violent, and leave only ... those which take place for the restrained and lawful procreation of children' (Iamblichus, *On the Pythagorean life* 210).

Where heterosexual intercourse is depicted in fifth-century vase paintings, it is quite often of the anal variety (see p. 101). Oral sex (fellatio rather than cunnilingus) is also represented on occasions. These, of course, would have been very effective methods of contraception, and as such they would have been favoured in particular by prostitutes, whose activities the vase-painters may well have had in mind. In Aristophanes' comedy *Wealth* (149–52), prostitutes in Corinth are said to present their anuses to rich customers as soon as they arrive. We have no way of knowing to what extent these practices featured in marital relationships, but in Aristophanes' *Peace* (869) a slave reporting on the progress of wedding preparations announces, 'The bride's had her bath, and her bum's looking lovely!'. This form of penetration may have been a male preference, irrespective of any contraceptive advantages which it offered.

Aside from anal intercourse, there seem to have been few if any contraceptive techniques where the initiative rested with the male. There is no evidence for the use of anything resembling a condom in ancient Greece, and there is only one, very dubious, reference to *coitus interruptus*, in Archilochus' seduction poem (see p. 80). The ancient world's most detailed account of female contraceptive measures is provided by Soranus, a Greek medical writer of the early second century AD. It cannot be assumed that the methods which he discusses were already in use in the Classical Age, but most of them are homely and straightforward, and it is hard to believe that they were not the product of a long tradition of women's wisdom. The objective in most of them is either to block the mouth of the womb or to cause it to contract. One recommended procedure is to smear the mouth with various substances, including old olive oil, honey, cedar resin, juice of balsam, and a paste made from myrtle oil and white lead. Another is to stuff it with a tuft of fine wool. Suppositories of various kinds are also suggested: one involves a plant known as tanning sumach, which is to be rubbed with wine and wrapped in wool. The suppository, if left in for two to three hours, will make the mouth of the womb contract, and is to be removed just before intercourse.

None of these methods can have been very effective, and it is impossible to know to what extent they were used. It is interesting that the Hippocratic writers, who have so much to say on the subject of remedies for sterility, were virtually silent when it came to contraception. The ideological view of the female as a child-bearing vessel may have been effective in suppressing the notion that motherhood was something that women might sometimes want to avoid, and it is possible that contraception was often practised without men's knowledge. This is not to say that Greek men were in favour of large families: but for them the freedom to expose unwanted babies may have provided an adequate fallback solution.

PREGNANCY

Pregnancy is seen by ancient writers as a delicate and difficult condition. According to Aristotle (*History of animals* 584a), pregnant women begin to suffer from sickness and headaches soon after conception; they are also subject to rapid changes of mood, and to cravings which are referred to by some as 'ivy-sickness', and which are particularly acute if the child that is being carried is a girl. The Hippocratic author of *On superfetation* (18) reports cases of pregnant women who eat earth and coal, and adds the vague warning that if this happens the child when it is born will bear the mark of these activities on its head.

Another Hippocratic treatise offers the information that women are most likely to miscarry during the first three or four months of pregnancy (*On the diseases of women* 1.21, 25). Miscarriages can occur because the womb is too large or too small or has too wide an opening; they can also be brought on if the woman picks up a heavy weight, is beaten, takes violent exercise, eats too much or too little, drinks an excessive amount, or suffers from a fright. In order to enhance the health of the unborn child, Plato recommends that women should take part in prenatal gymnastics (*Laws* 789a–d), while Aristotle (*Politics* 1335b) advises them to eat well and take plenty of exercise. But mental exertion, he adds, is better avoided. Aristotle approves of sexual intercourse during pregnancy, however, noting that women who have sex shortly before giving birth are delivered more quickly (*History of animals* 584a).

Pregnant women were also thought to be vulnerable to the dangers of pollution. When in Euripides' play *Iphigenia in Tauris* (1226–9) the priestess Iphigenia is about to lead the matricide Orestes through the streets of the city, she warns pregnant women to keep away. They do not, however, seem to have been regarded as a source of pollution themselves, and were not prohibited from visiting religious sanctuaries.

Perhaps the greatest threat to the health of pregnant women arose from the practice of marrying girls off soon after the onset of puberty. A large proportion of them may have become pregnant for the first time in their mid-teens. Aristotle certainly recognised the dangers of this, stating that intercourse at too young an age was liable to produce defective children, and that very young women had more difficult labours and were more likely to die in childbirth (*Politics* 1335a). If this awareness was shared by others, it did not, in Athens at least, give rise to any change in social practice.

ABORTION

There is no evidence to suggest that any Greek law code contained a blanket prohibition on abortion. In Athens, however, there do appear to have been some legal restrictions, although it is unclear whether these involved some form of time limit, or a stipulation that a married woman must first obtain the consent of her husband.[19] The existence of religious sanctions is suggested by Aristotle's statement (*Politics* 1335b) that, in accordance with 'divine law', an abortion ought to be procured before the embryo has acquired life and sensation. But here too the position is uncertain. In a fourth-century cathartic law (a sacred law relating to purification) in operation at the sanctuary of Artemis in Cyrene, no distinction is made between voluntary and involuntary abortions when these are listed as a source of pollution; this may indicate that the pollution was of a purely ritual character, and did not imply any guilt on the part of those involved.

Generally speaking, abortion was not condemned by philosophers. In Plato's ideal state, it and exposure are the two methods prescribed by law for the disposal of the products of sexual relationships between people beyond the legal age of child-bearing (*Republic* 461b–c; see p. 183). Aristotle recommends it as a way of restricting population growth (*Politics* 1335b). The only philosophical school which was opposed to it seems to have been that of the Pythagoreans, who believed that an embryo was imbued with life from the moment of conception (Ps.-Galen, *Against Gaurus: on the question of whether embryos are ensouled*, p. 34, 20).

One of the most unequivocal pronouncements on abortion – 'I will not give a pessary to cause abortion' – occurs in the Hippocratic Oath, which probably dates to the fourth century BC. The force of this declaration is somewhat negated, however, by the inclusion in some Hippocratic treatises of prescriptions for abortive drugs (e.g. *On the nature of woman* 32). In addition, one author describes quite openly the treatment which he once administered to a prostitute owned by one of his relatives (*On the nature of the child* 13). The girl was worried that she was pregnant, because she had heard from her friends that when a woman is going to conceive, the 'seed' remains inside her and does not flow out after intercourse. The doctor told her to jump up and down, touching her bottom with her heels at every leap. She followed his instructions, and at the seventh leap the 'seed' fell out onto the ground. Soranus in the second century AD mentions this episode in referring to a distinction made by some people between abortions procured by drugs, and those brought on by shaking and leaping (*Gyn.* 1.60). Some doctors, it seems, believed that the second method did not come under the Hippocratic prohibition, which specifies the use of pessaries.

Oath or no oath, some doctors were no doubt prepared to assist women with abortions; but it is possible that the majority were induced by the mothers themselves. One Hippocratic writer reports that when a woman has damaged herself through an abortion, 'as many women are doing all the time', she will recover if treated promptly, but will remain sterile (*On the diseases of women* 1.67). The same author states that women who have abortions undergo great risks, 'because it is impossible to abort the embryo without violence, whether by drugs, potions, food, pessaries or something else' (*On the diseases of women* 1.72). Surgical abortion, the most dangerous method, is not mentioned, and would appear to have been rare.

CHILDBIRTH

'I would rather stand three times in the line of battle than give birth to a single child' (Euripides, *Medea* 250–1). These words, spoken by Medea in her long recital of women's woes, remind us of the dangers confronting the majority of Greek women in the course of their lives. The incidence of death in childbirth is unknown, but estimates for prehistoric societies in general are in the range of ten to twenty per cent.[20] In ancient Greece, poor standards of hygiene and the young age at which many women would have borne their first child would have contributed considerably to mortality. But the fact that it was a relatively common occurrence did not mean that it was seen as an unremarkable event. Although manner of death was rarely alluded to on Classical Athenian tombstones, an exception was occasionally made in the case of women who had died in childbirth, who were commemorated with appropriate reliefs.[21] Sometimes, the pathos of such a scene was reinforced by an epitaph:

> Mnasylla, the daughter you lament,
> Neotima, dead in childbirth
> In your arms, lies still in your arms
> On your tomb's pediment, the carved
> Eyelids misty. Aristotle,
> Her father, rests nearby his head
> On his right hand. A stricken group:
> Whose grief, even in the relief
> Of death, in stone goes unrelieved.[22]

How many times in her life would a woman have had to face the ordeal of a confinement? The fact that most Greek families seem to have been small is not necessarily of any relevance, since exposure and infant mortality may to a large degree have been responsible for this. Clearly, numbers would have varied in accordance with both individual and political circumstances. At the time of the Peloponnesian War, for example, there may have been a decline in the birthrate. But the rough average was perhaps five or six confinements per woman.[23]

In normal circumstances childbirth appears to have been handled exclusively by women. For all their interest in gynaecological matters, the Hippocratic writers produced no treatise on obstetrics, which probably indicates that doctors were only called in if special difficulties were being experienced. Generally, a woman would have relied on a midwife (*maia*), and a network of female friends and neighbours; in Aristophanes'

Women in the Assembly (526–34), the heroine explains her early-morning absence to her husband by telling him that she had to rush out in the middle of the night to assist a friend who had gone into labour. Deliveries normally took place in the home, probably in the women's quarters.

Female wisdom concerning childbirth was doubtless handed down by word of mouth. Consequently, we possess very little information about normal deliveries. It seems that women usually gave birth in a seated position, either on a birthing stool,[24] or, in an emergency, on the lap of one of the helpers. It was probably unusual for a woman to be delivered lying down, but it was certainly not unknown. A number of Hippocratic sources refer to the use of drugs to speed up delivery (e.g. *On the diseases of women* 1.77), and sometimes labour would have to be induced; one Hippocratic author describes a rather violent method whereby four female assistants seize the woman by the legs and arms and give her at least ten firm shakes, then place her on a bed with her legs in the air and subject her to more shaking by the shoulders (*On cutting up the embryo* 4). Extracting the afterbirth might also prove difficult. A number of pessaries and potions are recommended by the Hippocratic writers, and in addition there is a description of an ingenious procedure which involves placing the baby on two water-filled goatskins before the cord is cut: the goatskins are pierced, and as the child sinks slowly towards the ground the afterbirth is gently pulled out by the cord (*On the nature of woman* 32; *On superfetation* 8).

At the moment of birth the mother's helpers uttered a ritual cry of joy – an exultant *ololuge*. Once the afterbirth had been expelled, mother and child were given a ritual bath to cleanse them of the defilement of the birth process. In many places it was customary for a newborn baby to be wrapped in swaddling-bands, apparently in the belief that its limbs would become misshapen unless they were moulded into their natural form while still soft. The birth was announced to the community at large by pinning appropriate symbols on to the door of the house – an olive crown if the baby was a boy, and a tuft of wool, indicative of her future dedication to textile production, if it was a girl.[25] The midwife's duties doubtless involved the care of mother and child for several days following the birth. One unpleasant task that seems to have fallen to her was the organisation of the exposure of the baby, if for any reason it was decided that it should not be reared (Plato, *Theaetetus* 151c). Although childbirth was considered a source of ritual pollution, it does not appear to have been a very serious one. Cyrene's cathartic law of the fourth century BC[26] states that anyone who has been inside a house where a woman has been in childbirth will be polluted for three days. The mother's own pollution may have lasted up until the child's name-giving ceremony on the tenth day after its birth (Euripides' *Electra* 654, 1124–33).

At some stage after giving birth, a woman visited a shrine of one of the birth-goddesses in order to give thanks for her delivery. Artemis and Ilithyia were the goddesses most frequently honoured, and it was common for them to receive an offering of clothing. In the inventories of the treasurers of Artemis, dating to the fourth century BC, the list of dedications made to the goddess at her shrine at Brauron includes such splendid items as 'a spotted, sleeved tunic in a box', 'a short tunic, scalloped and embroidered, with letters woven into it', 'an embroidered purple tunic' and 'a woman's cloak with a deep wavy border in purple'. According to Euripides (*Iphigenia in Tauris* 1464–7), the garments of women who had died in childbirth were also dedicated at this sanctuary. The goddess was evidently remembered even when her visit to a woman in labour had been a harsh one.

THE MENOPAUSE

According to Aristotle (*History of animals* 585b) most women ceased to menstruate in about their fortieth year, but some continued to be fertile up to their fiftieth birthdays, and pregnancies at this age were not unknown. There is very little discussion of the menopause in Greek literature. Perhaps, as Pomeroy (1975, p. 85) has suggested, it generated much less interest than the menarche because far fewer women lived long enough to experience it. But the low valuation placed upon non-fertile females could also have contributed to the neglect of this stage in a woman's life.

DEATH

The average life expectancy of Greek women is impossible to estimate. The age at which people died is rarely recorded on Greek tombstones, and the evidence of literature is hopelessly selective. On the basis of his study of skeletons from Classical Athens, Angel (1972, p. 94, table 28) has calculated that the median age at death (that is, the age by which fifty per cent of the population had died) was 34.6 for women and 44.5 for men. As Garland (1990, p. 245) has pointed out, the information derived from analyses of this type is far from reliable, and there may be a considerable underestimation of ages. But it does seem likely that the life expectancy of women was lower than that of men, a conclusion which is confirmed by Aristotle's statement that men naturally live longer than women because they have more heat in their bodies (*On the length and shortness of life* 466b).

II

Women in Athenian law and society

Most of our knowledge about women in Classical Greece relates to Athens, the city which has provided us with the bulk of our source material for this period. Inevitably, Athenian women occupy a large proportion of this chapter on the Classical Age. But one must be cautious about allowing the female residents of Athens to represent Greek women in general. Athens was in many ways an unusual city. It was bigger and richer and more powerful than most. It included in its population far more slaves and resident aliens than the average Greek state, and its democratic constitution, while not unique, was probably more radical and innovative than those established elsewhere. All of these factors would have affected the lives, status and images of women. It is difficult for us to know to what extent the experience of other Greek females diverged from that of their Athenian sisters, but evidence relating to Sparta and Gortyn (discussed in a later chapter) indicates that in some states at least the legal and social role accorded to women might be very different.

In this chapter, I shall be examining the position of women within Athenian society, as defined both by law and custom; while in the one that follows, I shall be attempting to look beyond this legal and normative framework and to consider the reality of Athenian women's lives. Both chapters will draw on a wide variety of source material – law-court speeches, historical writings, comic and tragic drama, philosophy, instructive treatises, inscriptions, archaeological sites and vase paintings. All of these sources present us to some extent with ideas as well as with 'facts' about women; but in two of them – drama and philosophy – the ideas are more consciously formulated and more extensively expressed than elsewhere, and therefore these literary genres will also be studied as distinct discourses in Part IV.

In separating out drama and philosophy in this way, I am not suggesting that the other sources which are being used are necessarily more objective and value-free. For example, law-court speeches, most of them composed in the fourth century BC, will provide much of the information discussed in this and the following chapter. The data which they furnish about the content of Athenian law may be thought to be reasonably factual, but even here it must be borne in mind that the speaker's interpretation of the law will have been influenced by the need to argue his case. Even more caution must be exercised when it comes to evaluating the glimpses into women's lives which the speeches offer, for these were public utterances whose object was to convince the jurors of the respectability of the speaker and his family. They were spoken by men and addressed to male audiences; and neither party would have been free from preconceptions about women and their activities.

LEGAL STATUS

In law an Athenian woman had no independent existence. She was always assumed to be incorporated into the *oikos* which was headed by her *kyrios*, or male guardian. Until she was married, a woman came under the guardianship of her father, or male next-of-kin. On her marriage, her husband took over the role of *kyrios*: if she was subsequently divorced or widowed, and she had no sons, she returned to her original guardian. But if she was widowed and had sons who were still minors, she could choose to stay in her late husband's *oikos* under the guardianship of her sons' *kyrios*, while if her sons were already of age she could pass if she wished into their guardianship.

The function of a woman's *kyrios* was, in general, that of protection. As well as being responsible for her economic maintenance and her overall welfare, he acted as an intermediary between the private domain occupied by the woman and the public sphere from which she was excluded. This mediation would have been most frequently undertaken in dealings which had a legal significance, such as the making of contracts or the arrangement of a marriage. If any of these dealings ever necessitated a court appearance, this too would have been handled by the *kyrios*. An Athenian woman was barred from conducting legal proceedings on her own behalf, and there is reason to believe that normally she could not even give evidence in court. It seems instead to have been presented by her *kyrios*.[1]

PROPERTY: DOWRY AND INHERITANCE

Athenian women could not by law enter into any contract 'beyond the value of one *medimnos* of barley' (Isaeus 10.10): a *medimnos* was a measure of grain, and its value in relation to barley was perhaps sufficient to keep a family fed for five or six days.[2] This amount would therefore have been large enough to account for the petty trading activities, such as selling vegetables, which we know some Athenian women engaged in; but it would certainly have ruled out any major transactions.[3] Although this prohibition may not always have been observed, people were sufficiently aware of it to see it as a mark of male dominance: in Aristophanes' comic fantasy *Women in the Assembly* (1024–5), women who have just taken over the government of Athens introduce a law which reverses this situation by imposing the restriction on men instead of women.

It would be wrong, however, to assume on this basis that Athenian women were legally barred from owning property. Ownership is a complex concept; and as Foxhall (1989, p. 28) has argued, the existence of a regulation under which women were not able to dispose of property proves only that one of the several relationships which people might have with property was not available to them. Another relationship was free usage, and Athenian women do seem to have enjoyed this right within the household, particularly in relation to slaves and moveable goods such as furniture, clothing and jewellery. In one sense, then, Athenian women can be regarded as property-owners; but they were always much more limited in the amount of control which they had over their possessions than men were. Moreover, unlike the woman herself, a women's *kyrios* did have the right to dispose of her property, and it is doubtful whether he even needed to obtain her consent before doing so.[4]

The three principal means by which a woman might acquire rights over property were gifts, dowry and inheritance. The most significant gifts which she would have received would generally have been the *anakalupteria*, gifts to new brides from their husbands or relatives. Dowries, inheritance and the *epiklerate* (a specialised form of inheritance through the female line) will be discussed in some detail in the rest of this section.

Dowry

The most significant form of property acquired by a woman would have been her dowry, or *proix*, which her *kyrios* provided when she was married. He was probably not under any legal obligation to do so, but by the fifth century dowries were a well-established convention, and the moral pressure to produce one was undoubtedly very strong. Finding a husband for a woman without a dowry was, if some of the men pleading their cases in the law-courts are to be believed, a thankless business, 'for who would ever have taken a dowerless wife from a man who was penniless and in debt to the treasury?' (Demosthenes 59.8).

The dowry was usually handed over at the *engue*, or betrothal, but a later date, such as the marriage itself, could be agreed upon by the parties. Its principal component was generally a sum of money, but furniture and other moveable goods might also be included. Land might also be an element, but this would not have been common, since most men would want to keep their estates intact for their sons. Property other than money was assigned a monetary value at the time of its transfer. A large dowry, as well as being an eloquent expression of a man's wealth and social status, was undoubtedly useful in attracting eligible suitors, as had been the case with the wife of the statesman Alcibiades (Isocrates 16.31).

The proportion of the value of a man's estate represented by the dowry seems to have ranged from over 20 per cent to well under 10 per cent.[5] In many cases it is unlikely that the income created by investing the dowry would have been enough to cover a woman's maintenance, though doubtless there were some instances where a tight-fisted man refused to spend the whole of the income from a generous dowry on his wife. Theophrastus (*Characters* 28.4) says of one such skinflint: 'His wife brought him a talent in dowry, and has borne him a son, but he only gives her a couple of coppers for treats, and makes her wash in cold water on festival days.' The dowries of poor men's daughters were sometimes supplemented by contributions from more affluent relatives, where these existed.[6]

A dowry was a woman's share of the patrimonial inheritance, received on marriage rather than on the death of her father. However, the woman herself would not have been legally capable of disposing of it, and her husband would have made all the arrangements for investing the money and for spending the major part of the income which it produced. But most husbands would have been very cautious about touching the capital sum. On divorce, a man was obliged to return the dowry to his wife's original *kyrios*: if he failed to do so he had to pay interest on its value at the high rate of 18 per cent per annum, and he could be sued if he did not keep up with these payments. These regulations applied, it would appear, irrespective of which partner had initiated the divorce, and also irrespective of its grounds; it seems probable that the dowry had to be returned even if the divorce had been brought about by the wife's adultery.[7] The dowry was also returned if the marriage was terminated by death and the couple had no children, or if a widow was left with daughters.[8] But if there were sons, and the wife died, the husband retained control of the dowry until the sons were old enough to inherit it. If the husband died, and the wife chose to return to her natal *oikos*, she took her dowry with her; if she chose to remain in her dead husband's *oikos*, then the dowry was managed by her sons' *kyrios* until they came of age. Daughters did not, apparently, inherit their mothers' dowries.

These regulations throw an interesting light on the Athenian concept of marriage. The dowry has been described as 'a fund or an estate created by the bride's relatives to give her as it were a stake in the *oikos* to which she is by marriage transferred' (Harrison, 1968, p. 45). It constituted an element of protection for the wife, since the obligation to return the dowry would have been to some extent a safeguard against a frivolous divorce initiated by the husband, while her family's right to terminate the marriage and reclaim the dowry would have acted as a deterrent against ill-treatment. The power which a well-dowered woman might possess within the marriage is suggested by Plato's comment that, as a result of his proposed abolition of dowries, 'there would be less arrogance among women, and less servility and abasement and lack of freedom among men on account of money' (*Laws* 774c).

The dowry might with equal validity be said to provide the woman's family, rather than the woman herself, with a stake in her marriage. The father's ability to initiate a divorce and get back a dowry which could then be used as the basis for a further marriage gave him a continuing control over the woman's person. Sometimes, another marriage would seem desirable, either because it was more advantageous than the first one in terms of wealth or political connections, or because the first union had not produced any children and the woman's family needed to import a male heir. This facility will be discussed in more detail in the conclusion to this section.

Inheritance

In a society which was predominantly agricultural, inheritance was a vital issue, and would have affected members of the lower classes as well as the wealthy. A large proportion of Athenians would have owned land which had to be passed on when they died, and the stability of the state as a whole was very much bound up with the transmission of this crucial economic resource. Direct inheritance by a woman, while it was certainly possible, would have been comparatively rare. If a man had a son or sons, either natural or adopted, then they inherited his property, sharing it equally between them, and perpetuated his *oikos*. Daughters and their descendants were excluded. If a man had no sons but did have a daughter, then the property and the *oikos* were transmitted via the daughter to his grandsons: this system, known as the *epiklerate*, will be discussed below. However, in the absence of both sons and daughters, a man's property passed to a group of close relatives called the *anchisteia*, and women did feature in this, although males took precedence over them at every level.

The most probable order of succession within the *anchisteia* is as follows: brothers of the deceased and their direct descendants, without limit; sisters and their direct descendants; paternal uncles and their children and grandchildren; paternal aunts and their children and grandchildren; brothers by the same mother but a different father, and their direct descendants; sisters by the same mother and their direct descendants; maternal uncles and their children and grandchildren; maternal aunts and their children and grandchildren.[9] Thus, relatives on the mother's side were included as well as those on the father's; and among relatives on both sides women's rights to the property were among the first to be exercised: sisters, for example, got precedence over paternal uncles.

However, the transmission of property through this system would have been an eventuality which most Athenian men would have wished to avoid. If a man had no children and his estate passed to the *anchisteia*, then his *oikos* died out. This was an outcome which was socially unacceptable, since it was in the interests of the Athenian state to see that the number of *oikoi* was maintained and that wealth did not become concentrated in too few hands. It would also have been unacceptable to the individual concerned: quite apart from considerations of family pride, there would also have been a strong desire to leave behind someone who would perpetuate the ancestral cult of the *oikos*, and would tend the family graves and make sacrifices on behalf of the deceased and his forebears. Wherever possible, then, a man tried to have sons; if nature failed him in this respect, then in accordance with a law introduced by Solon (see p. 75) he could make a will in which he adopted a son and heir. Through the latter, the *oikos* would be perpetuated as a distinct entity, for the adopted son was required to renounce all rights of succession within his own natal *oikos*.[10]

The epiklerate

If a man had no natural sons, his *oikos* could be perpetuated through a daughter. The term *epikleros* which is applied to such a woman is often translated, misleadingly, as 'heiress'. The word means literally 'with the property', and it encapsulates her status very neatly. The *epikleros* did not herself inherit the property, but at the same time she could not be separated from it: no man could take it over without first of all marrying her. There was nothing to prevent a man who had only a daughter from adopting a son, as a childless man could, but in this case the adoptee was obliged to marry the daughter. He would then become the direct heir. If there had been no adoption, then the order of succession to the daughter's hand was the one that existed among male candidates in the *anchisteia*. The property of a man with a daughter would thus follow a similar route to the property of a childless man, but in the former case the *oikos* of the deceased man was perpetuated.

If a candidate was unwilling to marry the *epikleros*, then she passed, along with the property, to the next in order of succession. Her paternal uncle would be the first who had a right to marry her: this relationship was not considered incestuous by the Athenians, and the situation would sometimes have arisen where a young girl just past puberty found herself obliged to marry a man who was more than thirty years her senior. The next in line was her paternal uncle's eldest son, and so on.[12] If the *epikleros* was already married to somebody else, and her father had not taken the precaution of adopting her husband as his heir, then a claimant could force her to divorce her existing husband, although it is possible that this only applied if she had not already produced a son.[13] If the claimant was himself already married, then he had to divorce his existing wife or give up his claim. One such situation is described in a speech attributed to Demosthenes (57.41), where a poor man called Protomachus is said to have arranged for his wife to marry an acquaintance of his so that he himself was free to take on an *epikleros* and the large estate that went with her.

The next-of-kin who married an *epikleros* did not, however, have unconditional control over the property to which she was attached. He held it in trust until the son or sons that were born of the marriage came of age, at which point they became its owners.[14] But up to this time he enjoyed the income which the estate produced, which in some cases might be considerable. The *epikleros*, then, could be a great asset to her husband. But it is clear that her true function was to supply her deceased father's *oikos* with an heir, and thus ensure its continued existence. This illuminates the rationale behind two laws introduced, according to Plutarch (*Life of Solon* 20.2–3), by Solon. These stipulated that an *epikleros*'s husband was to have sex with her at least three times a month; and that the *epikleros*, if her husband was incapable of intercourse, had the right to marry his next-of-kin. In view of the fact that the husband might be an elderly man, it was evidently thought to be necessary to safeguard against a situation where he might take the money and then fail to fulfil his marital duties.

Not surprisingly, relatives sometimes quarrelled about who was entitled to the hand of an *epikleros*. These disputed claims were referred to the courts, where, if Aristophanes is to be believed, juries might sometimes settle the woman's future in a very cavalier fashion: 'If a father dies and leaves his daughter to someone as an *epikleros*, we tell the will to get stuffed even though it's so solemnly covered in seals. We give her to whoever wins us over by his entreaties', says a juryman in *The Wasps* (583–6). At best, an *epikleros*, in terms of the control which she had over her own life, would have been in no worse a situation than any other Athenian girl whose marriage was arranged by her father, for it would often have been the case that her husband was chosen by adoption. At its worst, she was at the mercy either of the inheritance system or of the law courts. The men who so earnestly pursue these tangled inheritance cases in the courts generally show no recognition at all of the fact that they are deciding with whom a young woman will spend the rest of her life.

Conclusions

While she herself in normal circumstances was excluded from direct inheritance, an Athenian woman could potentially play a crucial role in reinforcing patrilineal succession. Firstly, as an *epikleros* she could produce the son which her father had lacked. Secondly, even when she did not possess the status of an *epikleros*, she could supply other members of her family with adoptive sons. When a childless man adopted an heir in order to avoid the extinction of his *oikos*, he was in theory free to choose anyone he liked; but in practice he generally adopted a close relative, such as his sister's son. 'Thus the legitimate children which a woman bore even within another *oikos* created, as it were, an alternative supply of heirs for her natal *oikos* should the need arise' (Just, 1989, p. 94).

These factors help us to understand why it was in the interests of a family to retain residual rights over a woman after she was married – the right to reclaim both the woman and her dowry and to transfer them elsewhere should she become an *epikleros*, or should her existing marriage prove childless. Ideally, the line of descent was maintained through the male, but if necessary this could also be achieved through the female. Since any woman could potentially be called upon to play this role, it was important that her links with her natal *oikos* should never be completely severed. In her social function a woman can therefore be seen to be liminal, in that she straddles the social boundary which separates the *oikos* of her father from the *oikos* of her husband. The awareness of this ambiguity in status could well have reinforced the mythological concept of a woman as a boundary-crosser (see p. 19).

The important part played by Athenian wives in the transference of property can now be appreciated. Firstly, they could be employed to bridge a gap in the male line of descent. Secondly, whether supplying heirs for their father's or for their husband's *oikos*, they were responsible for conferring legitimacy, which was an essential qualification for inheritance. Finally, after 451/0, when a law was introduced which made Athenian parentage on both sides the qualification for citizenship (see pp. 120–1), they became instruments in the transmission of citizen rights; and in Athens only citizens were allowed to own land. The unease aroused by the uncertainty as to which *oikos*, father's or husband's, was the object of a woman's loyalty would have been augmented by the anxiety generated by the utter liminality of her role in the inheritance system. Though she stood at the core of the system, in terms of economic power she was marginal. As Just (1989, p.102) has pointed out, if women had played no role at all in the transmission of property, they might have been more free from the constraints and designs of men. As it was, the essential nature of their contribution produced the need to control them.

It was in the interests of the Athenian state that the individual *oikos* should be maintained as a viable economic unit, both because this ensured a continuing supply of soldiers and sailors, and because the economic self-sufficiency of the *oikos* was an important factor in keeping at bay the civil strife which increasingly racked so many other Greek states in the Classical period. It was against the background of this overall political stability that Athenian democracy was maintained and strengthened in the fifth century. Thus there was a merging of women's private and public roles: as contributors to the survival of the individual *oikos* they were central not just to the well-being of their families but also to the vitality of the democratic state. This idea is expressed quite simply by the female chorus in Aristophanes' *Lysistrata* when it states, 'I have a share in public service. For I contribute men' (651). Women's liminality can therefore be seen to encompass a political dimension. Though democracy needed them, they were excluded from its institutions; and though, after 451/0, they were given a role in the transmission of citizens' rights, they themselves did not enjoy full citizenship.

MARRIAGE

It is difficult to know whether many women remained unmarried in Classical Athens. There are very few references in literature to individual spinsters, but this could be explained by the Athenian male's lack of interest in non-reproducing females. Spinster-hood was viewed by men as a disastrous fate. According to the orator Lysias, for example, one of the evil consequences of the reign of terror instituted by the Thirty Tyrants at the end of the Peloponnesian War was that women had been robbed of potential husbands (12.21). In Aristophanes' *Lysistrata* (493), the heroine who is trying to put a stop to war expresses the sorrow she feels for 'maidens growing old in the bridal chambers'.[15] An unmarried woman would have been financially dependent on her male next-of-kin, and one whose relatives were poor might have faced destitution or have been driven into prostitution (Demosthenes 59.113). Although there was some work available to women in Athens, it was probably scarce and certainly unremunerative (see p. 145).

Most Athenian girls were probably married for the first time between the ages of fourteen and eighteen. Evidence is limited, but where it exists it indicates that the younger end of the age range may have been favoured: for example, the new bride in a treatise by Xenophon is aged fourteen (*Oeconomicus* 7.5); and the sister of the orator Demosthenes was to be married at fifteen (Demosthenes 27.4 and 29.43). Most men on the other hand probably married at about the age of thirty. The reasons for early female marriage are not at all clear. Since in normal circumstances most Greeks were probably keen to limit the size of their families (see p. 107), it seems unlikely that the motive was the maximising of breeding potential. Perhaps in general it was the perceived need to control women that was responsible for the practice. The belief that women became wild and ungovernable at puberty, the stress on premarital virginity and the fact that the girl's father (who would have been over thirty when she was born) might die in the near future, may all have made early marriage appear desirable. A husband might also prefer a young wife whom he could educate to run the household in the way that he wished (see Xenophon, *Oeconomicus* 7.4–5). The disparity in the ages of husband and wife would have helped to foster the notion of the intellectual inferiority of the female, and would have reinforced patriarchal attitudes towards women.

A woman was legally incapable of arranging her own marriage, and this responsibility normally fell to her guardian. There is scarcely any evidence to show that the woman was allowed any say in the matter.[16] When, for example, a speaker in a lawsuit (Isaeus 2.3–9) is describing how Menecles, a close friend of his deceased father, asked him and his brother for the hand of their sister, he remarks: 'Knowing that our father would have given her to no-one with greater pleasure, we gave her to him in marriage.' Later on, when Menecles decided that in view of their childlessness his wife ought to be given the chance to remarry, her brothers did at least insist that she herself would have to agree to the divorce; but again there is no suggestion that she played any part in choosing her new husband.

There was, however, a good chance that the bride would at least have had some social contact with her new husband. In Classical Athens, close-kin marriages were relatively common, even when not dictated by the *epikleros* system. Marriages between first cousins appear to have been particularly favoured;[17] but marriages between uncles and nieces, second cousins, cousins once removed and siblings with the same father but a different mother are also known. This tendency to look for partners within the extended family probably sprang from a traditional loyalty towards one's kinsfolk. If a man had a favour to confer in the form of a daughter and her dowry, he would prefer that it went to someone to whom he was closely related, and whose character and material resources would be well known to him.

If the extended family did not yield a suitable candidate, then a woman might be offered to a close friend of her father, as in the case of Menecles' wife. But marriages to men who were unconnected with the family also occurred, and sometimes a bride may not even have set eyes on her husband-to-be prior to their betrothal. The amount of wealth available on both sides would certainly have been an important consideration when these unions were arranged, at least among the upper classes. Whether the creation of political alliances was also a factor is open to doubt: as Humphreys (1983, pp. 25–6) has suggested, the masculine network of friendships forged at drinking parties and in the gymnasium was probably more significant in this respect, and marriage ties may have functioned as declarations of political allegiance rather than as a means of establishing it.

In 451/0 Pericles introduced a law which stipulated that in order to qualify as an Athenian citizen a man had to be of Athenian parentage on both sides, and not just, as previously, on that of his father. This would have deterred the great majority of Athenians from seeking brides both in other parts of Greece and among the non-Athenian population of Athens. The citizenship law was reinstated in 403/2, having apparently fallen into disuse, and at some point in the following century it became positively illegal for an Athenian citizen to marry a non-Athenian. From the middle of the fifth century onwards, then, Athenian society became officially endogamic, in that it was from marriages within the community that the citizen body was created. There has been much speculation about the purpose of this law. The two most favoured suggestions are that it was introduced in order to limit the influence of aristocratic families over foreign policy, by effectively preventing them from arranging dynastic marriages with powerful families in other states; or that its chief objective was the creation of an exclusive and limited citizen body at a time when citizenship carried considerable privileges within the democratic state.[18] In general, the system of endogamy can be seen as contributing towards the cohesion of the Athenian state, since the exchange of women between citizens would have created a network of kinship relations binding together different *oikoi*.

The seriousness with which men viewed the rights and responsibilities exercised by women as conferrers of citizenship is illustrated by the famous case against Neaera, which was heard in the Athenian courts in about 340 BC. In a speech attributed to Demosthenes, two men are prosecuting Neaera, a Corinthian courtesan, for living with an Athenian citizen Stephanus as his wife, contrary to the laws of Athens. One of the chief accusations which is made in the course of this case is that Stephanus had passed off Neaera's alien children as his own by a former marriage, and had twice given her daughter in marriage to Athenian citizens: any children born as a result would have fraudulently exercised the rights of citizenship.

In this passionate oration, citizenship is viewed as a precious gift which has been cheapened by men like Stephanus, who has subverted the laws which are the basis of the state's integrity. Interestingly, women are singled out as the members of society most threatened by his actions: the sacred duties of citizen women are debased when an alien and a prostitute is allowed to share in them, and if men believe that they can live with women like Neaera with impunity, then poor Athenian women will be unable to find husbands. 'I want each one of you to bear in mind that you are casting your vote, partly in the interests of your wife, partly in the interests of your daughter, partly in the interests of your mother, and partly in the interests of the state and of the laws and of religion, so that women such as these should not appear to be held in the same esteem as a prostitute, and that those who have been brought up by their relatives with great care and in the utmost modesty, and have been given in marriage in accordance with the laws, should not appear to be sharing their privileges with someone who in so many obscene ways has consorted so many times a day with so many men . . .' (Demosthenes 59.114). Clearly, an appeal to the popular view that women were in need of the state's protection was likely to prove effective in the Athenian courts.

Was love never a motive for marriage in Classical Athens? Dover (1973, p. 69) has suggested that, while love-matches may not have existed among the upper classes, lower down the social scale segregation of the sexes would not have been feasible, and young people must sometimes have met and had love affairs. However, there is only one reference to such an affair in Classical literature, in a comedy of Aristophanes in which a young woman waits to welcome her lover while her mother is out (*Women in the Assembly* 920). There is no suggestion at all that this is expected to lead to marriage.

Certainly, there seems to have been little room for the concept of love in the official ideology surrounding marital relations in Athens. When the speaker in the case against Neaera tells his listeners 'We have courtesans (*hetaerae*) for pleasure, concubines to take care of our day-to-day bodily needs, and wives to bear us legitimate children and to be the loyal guardians of our households' (Demosthenes 59.122), his object is to distinguish between the various types of sexual relationship which an Athenian male might enter into; but at the same time he gives voice to a strictly utilitarian view of the purpose of marriage, one with which he would presumably have expected his audience to sympathise. 'Love and marriage' is a scenario which is largely absent from the imaginative literature of the Classical period. Yet, in the early Hellenistic Age, the comic playwright Menander wrote plays in which young men fell in love and were anxious to marry the objects of their affection. This was undoubtedly new as a theme, and its appearance in the theatre is indicative of the growing acceptability of privatised aspirations. It is, on the other hand, hard to believe that the experience itself was an entirely novel one. However, the fact that Menander's plots focus on the removal of the seemingly insuperable social obstacles standing in the way of wedded bliss suggests that love and marriage may not have been viewed as natural partners. Whether in the Classical Age this had led to a great deal of frustration it is impossible to say: there is certainly no indication of this in the sources for the period.

The legal definition of marriage in Athens is unclear, but it seems likely, as Patterson (1991, p. 60) has argued, that it should 'be understood not as a simple legal event but as a composite process', involving a number of actions or events. One of these was certainly the procedure known as *engue*, which is often translated as betrothal. It consisted of a private verbal contract made between the bride's *kyrios* and the groom (or the groom's *kyrios*, if the groom himself was not yet of age). Proof of *engue* was vital if the legitimacy of one's children was ever called into question, so that it was advisable to perform it in front of witnesses. The agreement was probably sealed by the traditional formula, 'I hand over this woman to you for the ploughing of legitimate children' (Menander, frag. 720, Kock), a phrase which seems to echo one used when agricultural land was leased, but which also makes use of a common metaphorical association between women and the earth.[19] Normally the dowry would have been transferred at the *engue*, and its monetary value agreed upon. In most cases the cohabitation of the couple probably commenced shortly afterwards, but in some situations there might be a considerable interval: Demosthenes' sister, for example, was betrothed at the age of five when her father was on his deathbed (Demosthenes 28.15). *Engue* was not apparently a legally binding contract, since the groom could withdraw at any point prior to cohabitation, on condition that the dowry was repaid.

Apart from *engue*, the wedding celebration (*gamos*), cohabitation (*sunoikein*), and the production of children may all have been regarded as indicators of the existence of a marriage. None of the sources provides us with a complete description of the *gamos*, the set of rituals which accompanied the handing over (*ekdosis*, literally, 'giving out') of the bride to the groom: the account which follows has been pieced together from various visual and literary texts.

At some point prior to the ceremony, a sacrifice was performed by the bride's father, and it may have been at this stage in the proceedings that the bride cut off her hair, and removed and consecrated to a goddess such as Artemis or Athena the girdle which she had worn since puberty. Both these actions were symbolic of her imminent transfer to a new status. She was then given a ritual bath in water that had been drawn from a sacred spring and carried in a special vessel known as a *loutrophoros*: if a girl died unmarried, one of these pots was often buried with her, and was sometimes represented on her tombstone. The public part of the ceremony began with a wedding feast in the house of the bride's father. At nightfall, the partially veiled bride, the groom and the groom's best friend were carried to the couple's future home in a nuptial chariot drawn by mules, accompanied by a torchlit procession of friends and relatives singing nuptial hymns (Fig. 20).

At their destination the bride was greeted by her mother-in-law, who was carrying torches, and was formally conducted to the hearth, the focal point of her new home. Meanwhile, bride and groom were showered with nuts and dried fruits, emblems of fertility and prosperity, and a boy crowned with a wreath of thorns and acorns circulated among the guests distributing bread from a basket shaped like a winnowing fan. The presence of this child, who had to have both parents still living, signified that the proper end of the couple's union was the birth of children; but at the same time the acorns, the bread and the words that he spoke – 'I escaped the bad, I found the better' – were symbolic of a prehistoric transition from a raw to a domesticated diet, and were suggestive of the dual role played by agriculture and marriage in the progress from savagery to civilisation (see p. 42). The climax of the proceedings came when the bride was led by the groom towards the bridal chamber, while a wedding hymn was sung by the guests. It may have been at this point that she removed her veil with a ritual gesture. On the following day, which was called the *epaulia*, gifts were presented to the couple by the bride's father and other relatives; they were carried in procession to the house, and included many items – a wool-basket, pots, furniture, jewellery, fine garments, combs, perfume – which alluded either to the domestic role or to the sexual identity of the new wife.

These ceremonies emphasised the fundamental nature of the transition in which the bride was involved. One obvious motif was that of alienation: by being veiled, the bride was converted into a non-person in her old home so that she could be reborn as a married woman in the new one. There were also suggestions of a theme of abduction: at the start of the wedding procession the bride was lifted on to the chariot by the groom; and as she was led towards her new home, and again when she was conducted around the hearth, the groom held her by the wrist, a gesture indicating control and possession. Jenkins (1983, pp. 139–40), citing the work of several anthropologists, argues that the mock abduction represented a ritualisation of the family's resistance to the idea of giving up the bride, and of the bride's own feelings of grief caused by the separation and her imminent loss of virginity. It also expressed the passive status of the bride, who in this transfer was powerless to decide her own destiny.[20]

Several writers have noted that many of the rituals performed at weddings – such as the purification and adornment of the bride, the cutting of the hair, and the procession accompanied by song – were paralleled by ones that took place both at funerals and at sacrifices.[21] The equation between marriage and death is also to be found in literature. It stands at the core of the story of the rape of Persephone, and is frequently encountered in tragedy: when, for example, Antigone goes to her grave, her lament includes the exclamation 'I shall be married to the lord of Acheron (river of the Underworld)', and 'Oh tomb, oh bridal-chamber' (Sophocles *Antigone* 816, 891). The identification of the bride as victim, or corpse, underlined not just the critical nature of the transformation, but also the themes of loss, sorrow and helplessness. Although in the course of the ceremony the bride was pronounced 'blessed' by the assembled company, the occasion was hardly viewed, in ritual terms, as 'the happiest day of her life'. Nor, in all likelihood, would she have experienced it as such. The idea of rebirth and renewal, which was a vital element in sacrifice, was present also in a marriage, but the bride herself may not have been particularly conscious of it.

A marriage did not bring about any change in the legal or political status of the bride: she merely passed from the control of one male to that of another. Nonetheless, symbolically, socially and emotionally, this was the most important transition which she would ever undergo. She was passing from childhood into adulthood, from virginity into wifehood, and from the *oikos* in which she had grown up to the one in which she was to spend the rest of her life. The occasion may also have involved her transference from one community to another, if, as Osborne (1985) has suggested, there were as many marriages between couples from different *demes* (local communities) as there were between those belonging to the same *deme*. It would not be surprising if the experience were a traumatic one, especially since it preceded the loss of her virginity to an older man who may have been almost a complete stranger to her. Sophocles, in a fragment from one of his plays, has probably captured her feelings very well:

> It is my belief that young women in their fathers' homes lead the sweetest lives of all. For ignorance always keeps children secure and happy. But when we reach womanhood and gain some understanding, we are thrust out and sold away from our ancestral gods and our parents. Some go to live with strangers, some with foreigners, some go to joyless homes, some to unfriendly ones. And all these things, once a single night has yoked us to our husbands, we are obliged to praise, and consider a happy outcome.
>
> (frag. 524, Nauck)

CONCUBINES

The variety and hierarchical nature of the sexual relationships available to an Athenian man are revealed by the maxim about courtesans, concubines and wives already quoted (pp. 121–2). In Classical Athens, the term concubine (or *pallake*) was applied to any woman living with a man on a more or less permanent basis who had not been given to him by the process of *engue*. Among the upper classes, the practice of keeping a concubine appears to have been relatively common. Normally these women would have been slaves or foreigners, but it seems that some of them were free-born Athenians, who had been handed over to their partners in a semi-formal manner: 'even those men who give their women as concubines first come to some agreement about what benefits the concubines are to enjoy' (Isaeus 3.39). Most probably, the women who ended up in this position were ones whose families were poor and could not afford a dowry. There was some recognition of their status in law, since they came under their partners' guardianship, and were included in the list of women with whom it was illegal for another man to have sex (see p. 125).

Generally concubines were set up in separate establishments, but in some cases they may have lived alongside a man's legitimate wife as part of a *menage à trois*. As Humphreys has pointed out (1983, p. 63), there are a number of fifth-century tragedies in which this situation occurs, and these may well have had a contemporary relevance. It can be easily imagined that the antagonism attributed to the female characters involved in these arrangements would also have arisen in real life. Deianeira, the wife in Sophocles' *Women of Trachis*, expresses her feelings in this way: 'But share the house with her, and share the husband – / It's more than any woman can do . . . I know,/ I see how it is: the one with youthful beauty/ Ripening to its prime, the other falling away' (545–8).[22]

The status of the children who were born as a result of these relationships has been much discussed. It seems likely that in the Classical period they were barred from inheriting their father's estate, and could only receive what was referred to as an 'illegitimate portion'. In normal circumstances they may also, as illegitimates, have been excluded from citizenship. There is some evidence to suggest that during the temporary emergency of the Peloponnesian War a law was passed which gave citizen rights to the children of concubines. But this does not prove, as some have maintained, that during this time bigamy was legalised in Athens. Unions with concubines could have acquired a more formal status without being recognised as marriages.[23]

ADULTERY

The Greek word which is normally translated as adultery is *moicheia*, a term which in fact had a much wider meaning. It signified unauthorised sex with any Athenian woman who came under the guardianship of another Athenian citizen, and who was not working as a prostitute. *Moicheia* was a punishable offence, and this meant that it was illegal for a man to have sex with another Athenian's wife, widowed mother, unmarried daughter or sister or with his concubine. Where relations with Athenian women were concerned, he was therefore limited to his own wife or concubine, or to prostitutes.

Any citizen who caught a man in the act of having sex with a woman under his guardianship had the right to kill him on the spot. Alternatively, he could accept financial compensation from him, holding him prisoner until he could provide sureties for the sum agreed upon; or he could subject him to various bodily humiliations, including, it seems, what Aristophanes refers to as 'radishment' – that is, having a large radish stuffed up his anus.[24] If the guardian had not succeeded in catching the couple *in flagrante*, or if he had decided not to take matters into his own hands, he could prosecute the man either for seduction or for rape. The maximum penalty for both offences was probably death, but a fine might be imposed as an alternative.

A man who killed a seducer on the spot ran a great risk, since he might subsequently be prosecuted for homicide by the man's family. This is the background to a speech by Lysias (1: *On the murder of Eratosthenes*) written for an Athenian named Euphiletus who, having killed a young man whom he had allegedly caught in his wife's bed, was later prosecuted by the man's relatives. It seems likely that by the Classical period very few men were willing to take the chance that Euphiletus did, and that instead they had recourse to compensation or the courts.

The penalties inflicted on the woman involved in a love affair were less severe than those which the man suffered, but they might nonetheless have a devastating effect on her life. A law which allowed a man who caught his daughter or sister *in flagrante* to sell her into slavery (see p. 70) had probably by now fallen into disuse. But the husband of an adulterous wife was legally bound to divorce her, on pain of the suspension of his citizen rights, and she was henceforth barred from participation in all the religious activities of the state, which meant that she was cut off from the one form of public involvement available to women in Athens. Any man who met her at a public religious rite could tear off her clothes and beat her, although he must stop short of killing her: 'the lawgiver seeks to disgrace such a woman and make her life intolerable' (Aeschines 1.183).

One revealing aspect of these regulations lies in the fact that any Athenian citizen, and not just the woman's guardian, could prosecute a seducer or a rapist. The offences, in other words, were treated as public ones, a good indication that the protection of the integrity of the *oikos* was considered to be in the interests of the community as a whole. Any male child which a married Athenian woman gave birth to would eventually receive the benefits not just of inheritance, but also of Athenian citizenship. A woman's chastity was therefore the concern not just of herself and her family, but also of the state.

It is in this context that the moral outrage aroused in particular by the crime of seduction has to be viewed. Lysias (1.33) tells us that 'the lawgiver prescribes death for adultery ... because the man who gains his end by persuasion in this way corrupts the mind as well as the body of the woman ... and gains access to all a man's possessions and casts doubts on his children's parentage'. The activities of the seducer were seen to be more dangerous than those of the rapist, firstly because he won the wife's confidence and could steal the household goods which she protected; and secondly because a seduced woman was more likely than a raped one to pass off the adulterer's child as her husband's. If she was detected, the parentage of all her children would be in doubt, and claims both to inheritance and to citizenship would be thrown into confusion. Euphiletus, it is worth noting, is careful to make the point that his wife's alleged affair with Eratosthenes had only begun after the birth of their son (Lysias 1.6–8). It goes without saying that the sufferings of a raped woman were legally of no concern. But on the level of personal morality a rape may have been viewed with more disgust, and a playwright like Euripides could be sensitive to the wrongs which the woman had suffered even when her attacker was the god Apollo (*Ion* 941–4).

Whatever the rationale behind them, the effect of the Athenian regulations on adultery was to give official sanction to double standards of sexual morality. An Athenian man was certainly not free to make love wherever he might, but there was no legal or apparently moral bar on sexual relations with concubines, prostitutes, slaves or resident aliens. An Athenian woman, on the other hand, was in theory confined for the whole of her life to relations with a husband. It is impossible to know how often women were involved in illicit love affairs, but it seems unlikely that they were very common, if only because women had so few opportunities for meeting men outside the family circle. In the only detailed account which we have of an (alleged) adulterous relationship, the wife of Euphiletus is said to have been seen for the first time by her future lover Eratosthenes at the funeral of Euphiletus's mother, which suggests that a religious ritual was one of the rare occasions when a woman might encounter other men. The circumstances, as we can readily imagine, were not particularly conducive to seduction. Eratosthenes is said to have approached the wife indirectly, using as a go-between the household's slave girl, whom he met on her way to market. Eventually he began coming to the house when the husband was away at his country estate (Lysias 1.8–20).

Some of Aristophanes' female characters, however, refer to women's extramarital affairs as though they were a regular occurrence. In *Women in the Assembly*, for example, Praxinoa when extolling the traditional values of women says: 'They bake cakes, as they've always done. They annoy their husbands, as they've always done. They hide lovers in the house, as they've always done' (223–5). These allusions seem to stem from a male fantasy about the female sexual appetite, and can be located within an ideology which pictured women as wild, instinctive and in need of male control. But they inevitably create a doubt as to whether Athenian women in reality always maintained the rigid chastity which Athenian sexual mores sought to impose. Speakers in the law courts who refer to the modesty and dignity of Athenian women (see, for example, p. 135) are not necessarily any more reliable than a comic fantasist as witnesses for real-life behaviour of citizen wives. At the end of the day, only Athenian women knew which of these two discourses was closer to the truth; and not only do they not speak to modern readers, but they were of course unlikely to speak to their husbands about such matters.[25]

DIVORCE

Divorce was a relatively easy matter in ancient Athens. It could be achieved by mutual agreement, or it could be initiated either by the husband, or by the wife or her family. When the husband was the instigator, it seems that he was required to do nothing other than dismiss his wife from the house: divorce was established by the fact of separation rather than by any legal process. He was, however, obliged to repay the dowry (see p. 115–6). The regulations concerning divorces initiated by the wife or her family are not very clear. It seems almost certain that a father had the right to terminate his daughter's marriage against her wishes;[26] but even where the woman herself wanted a divorce she may always have had to rely on members of her family to act on her behalf. Again, it was the woman's removal from the home of her husband that was the decisive element; but it seems that divorces initiated on the wife's side also had to be registered with the Archon, the chief magistrate. He does not appear, however, to have had any power of decision in the matter.

There were three situations in which a husband was obliged by statute to divorce his wife: if she had committed adultery; if she had become an *epikleros* and had to be married to the next-of-kin; and (from the fourth century BC onwards) if he had discovered subsequent to the marriage that she was an alien. Otherwise, the most common motive for divorce was probably childlessness: according to Aristotle, 'Children ... are a bond between parents, which is why childless marriages break up more quickly' (*Nicomachaean Ethics* 1162a). The desire for children would undoubtedly for many men have been linked to considerations of inheritance.

In one very unusual situation, the reason for an attempted divorce was the husband's behaviour. Hipparete, the wife of the general Alcibiades, grew tired of her husband's habit of bringing courtesans home with him, and took herself off to the house of her brother Callias. Later she tried to register the divorce with the Archon, but for some reason her brother was not present. Alcibiades appeared, picked her up, and carried her off through the agora to his house. The unfortunate Hipparete continued as Alcibiades' wife, but died not very long afterwards (Plutarch *Life of Alcibiades* 8, and Andocides 4).

A woman's family may sometimes have been motivated by the prospect of a more profitable match. In a fourth- or third-century comedy by an unknown author, one woman begs her father not to see this as a reason for ending her marriage:

> If (my husband) has offended against me, I should take note of it. But I know nothing of it; perhaps I am stupid, I couldn't deny that. Yet, father, even if a woman is a silly creature when it comes to judging other matters, about her own affairs perhaps she has some sense. Explain to me how by whatever he has done he has done me wrong. There is a covenant between man and wife; he must love her, always, until the end, and she must never cease to do what gives her husband pleasure. He was all that I wished with regard to me, and my pleasure is his pleasure, father. But suppose he is satisfactory as far as I am concerned but is bankrupt, and you, as you say, now want to give me to a rich man to save me from living out my life in distress. Where does so much money exist, father, that having it can give me more pleasure than my husband can? How can it be just or honourable that I should take a share in any good things he has, but takes no share in his poverty? Tell me, if the man you now want me to marry ... in turn loses his property, will you give me to another husband? How long will you go on tempting fortune in the matter of my life, father? ... So in the name of

Hestia don't rob me of the husband to whom you have married me; the favour that I ask of you is just and humane. If you refuse it, you will be enforcing your will and I shall try to bear my fate properly and avoid disgrace.

$$(GLP\ 185-7)^{27}$$

The provisions of the law relating to the children of divorced parents are obscure, but in most circumstances they probably remained with the father. Remarriage for a divorced wife (or a widow) who was not past child-bearing age appears to have been quite normal, for divorce did not apparently carry any stigma.

POLITICAL STATUS

Athenian women were not considered to be *politai* – a word which is normally translated as 'citizens', but which more specifically signifies citizens with full political rights, who were always male. Instead, the word *astai* was applied to women, and this can be taken as referring to their possession of civil rights. We are often forced, for lack of a corresponding term in our own language, to translate *astai* as 'citizens'; but it must be borne in mind that for Athenian women 'citizenship' meant only that they had a share in the religious, legal and economic order of the Athenian community.

No Greek state ever enfranchised women. In Athens, they could not attend or vote at meetings of the Assembly, sit on juries, or serve as Council members, magistrates or generals. Their exclusion from the political arena extended even to public speech: although collectively women were often made the basis of emotional appeals in law-court orations, there was a great reluctance to mention respectable upper-class females by name, even in speeches where their activities were of considerable relevance. Instead, they were specified in terms of their relationship with a male – they were generally someone's wife, daughter, sister or mother.[28] A similar taboo is reflected in the famous pronouncement with which Thucydides (2.46) rounds off the funeral speech attributed to Pericles: 'the greatest glory of a woman is to be least talked about among men, whether in praise or blame'.

There are some indications in law-court orations that women might exercise an influence over the public decision-making of their menfolk. For example, at the end of the speech against Neaera, the speaker imagines what will happen if the jurymen acquit her and are later questioned about the case by their female relatives: 'And the women, when they have heard your account, will say, "Well, what did you do?" And you will say, "We acquitted her". At this point the most virtuous of women will be angry at you ...' (Demosthenes 59.111). But references such as this amount to little more than emotional reminders of men's duties as protectors of women. In Aristophanes' *Lysistrata* (518–20), the heroine comments forcefully on her total lack of influence over her husband in political matters: 'And if I so much as said, "Darling, why are you carrying on with this silly policy?" he would glare at me and say, "Back to your weaving, woman, or you'll have a headache for a month."'[29] A husband named Critobulus tells Socrates that there are few people to whom he talks less than he does to his wife (Xenophon, *Oeconomicus* 3.11).

But if some women did manage to exert pressure on their husbands, this should probably not be interpreted as 'power behind the throne', because, as Just has said (1989, p. 22), in a democracy 'there were no thrones from behind which women could rule ...'. In Classical Athens, power had been officially transferred from the individual to the collective. It has already been suggested that the development of democracy in Athens may have been a parallel phenomenon to the subordination of women, in that both were linked in some degree to the emphasis placed on the economic independence of the *oikoi* (see p. 119). Democracy might also be said in a very real sense to have robbed some women – those belonging to aristocratic families – of the influence which they had exercised in former times. More pervasively, since democracy created a growing dichotomy between activities which were public and collective, and those which were private and individual, it accentuated the disparity between males and females. Increasingly, men in the democratic state were defined by their active involvement in political life, and women were defined by their exclusion from that sphere.

This is not to say that there were no distinctions between Athenian women and the other excluded groups – slaves and resident aliens. Socially, the difference would in many cases have been very great. After the introduction of Pericles' citizenship law, there would also have been a considerable difference in the way in which Athenian women, as distinct from alien women, were viewed by men. Athenian women became important as channels through which political as well as economic rights were transmitted to the next generation of citizens.

12

The lives of women in Classical Athens

The legal definitions of the role of women which were examined in the previous chapter provide important evidence for the way in which women in Athens were expected to behave. Clearly, women's lives would have been influenced to one degree or another by these regulations. However, not all areas of behaviour are taken account of by the law, and even legally enshrined roles can be negotiated and manipulated. In this chapter I shall be attempting to bypass the legal statements and explore the reality of women's day-to-day experience, but not without supplying the usual reminder about the masculine and upper-class bias of our sources.

EXPOSURE

Although there seems to have been no legal or moral bar on the exposure of infants of either sex, the sources record no single real-life instance. The references to it are all either general, metaphorical or fictional, and although it seems likely that exposure did sometimes take place, it has to be admitted that we are basically ignorant about the extent to which it was practised.

The babies who were most at risk, regardless of their sex, were probably those who were illegitimate, sickly or handicapped. Socrates, in Plato's dialogue *Theaetetus* (161a), prior to investigating an argument to see whether it is ill-formed, asks the man who has produced it, 'Will you be able to bear seeing (your child) examined, and not get angry if someone takes it away from you, even though it is your first delivery?'; while Aristotle recommends that there should be a law forbidding the rearing of disabled children (*Politics* 1335b). Whether the Athenians were in the habit of exposing healthy legitimate children is unclear. Modern scholars who believe that they did have generally maintained that more girls than boys would have been disposed of in this way. Their arguments have rested in the main on the low valuation of daughters (see pp. 131–2), which is hardly conclusive, and on demographic speculation, which is more persuasive.

Golden (1981), for example, has suggested that an oversupply of marriageable females, brought about by a combination of the practices of early marriage and frequent remarriage for women, could only have been avoided if the Athenians had exposed as many as 10 per cent of all females born. There is some literary support for this view, although it comes from the Hellenistic period: a third-century comic poet Posidippus writes, 'Everybody raises a son even if he is poor, but exposes a daughter even if he is rich' (fragment 11, Kock).

But, as Golden recognises, the suggestion is open to objections. The non-infanticidal death rates of males and females are unknown, so that we cannot be sure that the surplus was not wiped out in other ways (for example, infant mortality could have affected more girls than boys because of inferior care). Moreover, the practice of keeping concubines and worries about young women who will not be able to find husbands (see pp. 115, 119) could be seen as indicating that some surplus of marriageable women did in fact exist. There would certainly have been periods, most notably at the time of high casualty rates during the Peloponnesian War, when the state would have wanted to maintain this surplus, in order to increase the citizen birth-rate: one measure which helped to achieve the latter was, as we have seen (pp. 124–5), the granting of citizenship to the children of concubines. Where individual motives for infanticide are concerned, the cost of providing dowries would very likely have deterred men from rearing daughters; but having too many sons would have been equally undesirable, since the estate would have to be divided among them.[1] The subject, in short, is fraught with difficulties. Probably the most that can be said is that there may have been times in the Classical Age when the Athenians were exposing more girls than boys, but it is unlikely that the practice was generalised.

The passage from Plato's *Theaetetus* quoted above indicates that the wishes of a mother may not have been taken into account when the decision was made to expose a child. The responsibility, in the case of legitimate children, would have rested with the father, the child's *kyrios*. But the deed itself would often have been performed by the midwife or a household slave, who would have placed the baby in a deserted spot, or possibly near a rubbish-heap, shrine or crossroads where there would have been a chance that someone wanting a child would have picked it up. Mothers who decided to expose illegitimate children would naturally have found the process an agonising one, as Euripides recognises when he creates the character of Creusa, who has been haunted all her life by the memory of her baby, the product of a rape, stretching out his arms to her as she wrapped him in a shawl and tearfully laid him on the ground (*Ion* 954–63).

Girlhood

Children of both sexes received just one personal name. Most girls' names were feminine forms of those given to boys, and often seem to us to be singularly inappropriate – 'Hegesistrata', for example, means 'army-leader'. Sometimes, however, they were more obviously feminine: they might denote abstract entities, such as Euphrosyne (Happiness) or Eirene (Peace), or the qualities which women were expected to display, as in Malthake (Soft), or Eukoline (Contented). The latter, however, were rare among citizen women in Classical Athens.[2]

There is evidence to suggest that daughters were less highly valued than sons. One of the 'crafty dodges' attributed to females in Aristophanes' *Thesmophoriazusae* (564–5) involves a woman who exchanged her girl baby for a slave's boy and passed the latter off as her own; and in *Women in the Assembly* (549), a man who is complaining bitterly about his wife's absence at a friend's confinement is told, 'Never mind, it was a boy'. The desire for an heir to perpetuate the family would have been partly responsible for these reactions, though the rapture that greeted the birth of a boy would doubtless have become an embedded cultural response. Girls may also have been less well fed than boys. Xenophon reports that in Greek states other than Sparta girls lived on the plainest fare and were often allowed no wine; he points out in addition that their sedentary lives were hardly conducive to health (*Constitution of the Spartans* 1.3).

Nevertheless, some men may have been quite happy to be presented with a daughter once the obligatory son had appeared on the scene. Athenian plays are not short of references to elderly men's affection for their female offspring: for example, in Euripides' *Suppliant Women*, Iphis, remembering how his daughter used to cradle his head in her arms and kiss his face, says, 'To an aged father there is nothing more sweet than a daughter. Boys have greater courage, but they are less given to tender endearments' (1101–3).

When they were small, girls probably mixed quite freely with boys. But at about the age of six, when boys began to go to school (see below), the dichotomy between the public male sphere and the domestic female sphere would have started to enter the lives of children. Girls who stayed at home with their mothers learning how to perform household tasks would have had far fewer opportunities for socialising with members of their own sex than did boys, who in addition to school also went to the gymnasium and to athletics festivals. As girls neared puberty, the segregation from males would have become more of an object of conscious concern. A young unmarried woman might not be sent on an errand, because 'it is not nice for girls to creep through the crowd' (Euripides, *Orestes* 108), and she ought not to be seen even standing on the roof of her house (Euripides, *Phoenician Women* 93–4). Athenian feelings on this matter seem to have been shaped as much by a concern for maintaining appearances as by a desire to keep young women away from the danger of male contact. Whether young women had many opportunities for evading segregation is difficult to ascertain, but among girls of the lower classes surveillance may have been much less strict.

EDUCATION

When Xenophon (*Memorabilia* 1.5.2) refers to a dying man's desire to find a trustworthy person to look after his son's education and protect his daughter's virginity, he is probably highlighting a common dichotomy in the upbringing of males and females. Whereas many boys between the ages of about six and fourteen attended small private schools, there is very little indication that girls received any education outside the home.[3] Some women, nevertheless, seem to have been literate. In a law-court speech, for example, a guardian accused of having defrauded his nephews of their inheritance is said to have been challenged on his administration of the estate by the boys' mother, who appears to have been perfectly familiar with the contents of an account book found by her sons (Lysias 32.14–15). Vase paintings in which women are shown in a domestic environment holding book-rolls may represent the activities of real-life females from the privileged upper classes.[4]

But the evidence for literacy among women is scanty, and it would almost certainly have been the exception rather than the rule. Only one of the women in Athenian tragedy – Euripides' Phaedra (*Hippolytus* 856–81) – is represented as knowing how to write, and in another of Euripides' plays (*Iphigenia in Tauris* 582–7), Iphigenia has had to ask a Greek prisoner to write a letter for her. In a society which relied heavily on the spoken word, illiteracy would certainly not have been as great a handicap as it is perceived to be today, and the level of literacy even among males may not have been very high. But there can be no doubt that more males than females would have been able to read and write, and this discrepancy would have reinforced the notion of the intellectual inferiority of women. Most Athenian girls, it must be remembered, would have been married off at an age when boys were still living at home with their parents and still in some cases receiving formal education. As Sourvinou-Inwood has pointed out (1988, p. 78, n. 84), a girl's maturation was considered to be complete when she became capable of bearing children; that of a boy was a much more protracted affair, and involved initiation into the civic and military duties and rights of a future citizen.

Literacy may even have been regarded as a dangerous accomplishment in a woman: a later writer of comedy warns that a man who teaches his wife to read is giving additional poison to a horrible snake ([Menander] frag. 702, Kock). In general, female ignorance would have been viewed by some people as an important part of the barrier erected between women and the outside world: in Xenophon's treatise on household management, a husband Ischomachus reports that before their marriage his wife had been carefully supervised, 'in order that she might see and hear as little as possible, and ask the fewest possible questions' (Oeconomicus 7.5). The only woman in Classical Athens known to have displayed intellectual accomplishments of any note is Pericles' mistress Aspasia, who was a foreigner (see p. 148); and none of the female poets whose names have been preserved (see p. 85) was Athenian.

Those women who did learn to read and write were probably taught at home by their mothers. Some scenes on vases suggest that privileged Athenian girls may also have had lessons in music and dancing from outside tutors; and lyre-playing may have been one of the skills acquired by some upper-class women.[5] But undoubtedly the most common form of instruction received by girls in the home would have related to their domestic role. This would often have taken the form of helping out with tasks such as cooking, cleaning, caring for younger children, and handicrafts. Even Ischomachus's sheltered young bride had learned how to make a cloak out of wool and hand out spinning to the slave-girls (Xenophon, Oeconomicus 7.6).

There is no evidence to suggest that Athenian girls were given any kind of systematic athletics training in the gymnasium, as boys were; but some interesting vase paintings of the sixth and fifth centuries indicate that they may not have been so rigorously confined to the home as might be otherwise imagined. One pot of the late sixth century represents a scene in which young women are bathing naked in the open air, apparently in a creek. Some are swimming, some diving, some anointing themselves with oil, some combing their hair, and two stand under makeshift showers. We cannot be sure that the viewer was intended to see these as citizen girls; but there is nothing in the representation to indicate that they are either Amazons, nymphs or prostitutes, as some have suggested.

Fragments of pottery from the sanctuary of Artemis at Brauron (see p. 30) show girls who are taking part in running races. This activity would certainly have had a ritual significance, and the nudity of some of the older running girls perhaps points to a rite performed prior to the completion of the period of service, in which the shedding of the bears' yellow gowns symbolised the approaching bridal night and the imminent transition to womanhood. There are no other depictions of real-life female athletes on surviving Athenian pots, but there are a number of representations of the mythical sportswoman Atalanta, who is sometimes shown engaged in a wrestling match with the hero Peleus, and in one example is seen leaning on a pick-axe, the tool used by wrestlers to break up the earth in the competition area. It is difficult to believe that Atalanta's habitual costume in these paintings – skull-cap, bra and shorts – was not based on something worn in real life. Finally, scenes in which fully-grown girls are shown washing at a basin and using a strigil (an athlete's scraping implement, Fig. 21) can perhaps be interpreted as depictions of post-athletic ablutions. The presence of an element of fantasy in these representations should not be overlooked, and none of the material indicates with any certainty that it was considered acceptable for Athenian girls to engage in sporting activity outside a restricted ritual context. However, the idea should not be dismissed out of hand.[6]

THE RELIGIOUS ROLE OF ATHENIAN GIRLS

In Aristophanes' comedy *Lysistrata*, a chorus of Athenian women gives a recital of the honours conferred on them by their city when they were girls. These take the form of a progression of religious offices: 'As soon as I was in my seventh year I became an *arrhephoros*. Then I was an *aletris*. At the age of ten in honour of the *Archegetis* I was an *arktos* shedding the yellow gown at the festival at Brauron. Then as a beautiful girl I acted as a *kanephoros*, wearing a string of figs' (*Lysistrata* 641–7).[7]

An *arrhephoros* ('bearer of secret things') was one of two or possibly four girls, chosen by the magistrate in charge of religious affairs, who resided 'for a certain time' (Pausanias 1.27.3) on the Acropolis in Athens (Fig. 37a), and who made a mysterious nocturnal visit to an underground shrine of Aphrodite in the gardens on the north slope of the hill, carrying unnamed sacred objects on their heads.[8] They were also entrusted with a less arcane task, helping the priestesses to set up the loom for the weaving of the sacred robe presented to Athena at the Panathenaea (see p. 26). The *arktos*, or bear, was the girl who served Artemis, possibly for as long as a year, at her sanctuary at Brauron in eastern Attica (see p. 30): the title *Archegetis*, or first leader, is probably being applied here to Artemis, the leader of the band of girls, and 'shedding the yellow gown' may refer to the races which the girls ran in the nude (see p. 133). Very little is known about the other two roles mentioned by the chorus. An *aletris* ('grinder') may have ground meal for a special cake offered to a goddess, possibly Eleusinian Demeter. The cults of a number of divinities had *kanephoroi* ('basket-bearers') attached to them; these were young women, probably chosen among other things for their good looks, who in religious processions carried baskets containing sacred objects. The nature of the particular ritual mentioned in the *Lysistrata* is unknown.

There is little evidence to support Brelich's theory (1969, pp. 229–311) that the chorus's recital alludes to what at one time had been a system of universal female initiation based on four successive grades. The number of girls engaged in all these roles was very small, and with the possible exception of service at Brauron, there is no reason to believe that it had ever been any larger.[9] Their initiatory quality is also debatable. The only one which seems to have involved a ritual of segregation prior to entry into a new life is service at Brauron, where girls in the pre-menstrual phase who dressed up as bears may have been acting out a period of non-human existence preceding their socialisation as fully adult wives and mothers. The other roles do not appear to have included any initiatory element, other than that of temporary separation from their families. This in itself, however, while certainly not amounting to a full-scale rite of passage, would at least have helped to prepare a girl for the trauma of her marriage and her permanent removal from her home. At the same time she would have been introduced to the role which she was to play as an adult in the religious life of the community.

Young women in Athens were accorded a number of other ritual duties. The weaving of Athena's sacred robe was carried out by a team of girls, the *ergastinae* (or workers), who were chosen from the aristocratic families of Athens. In the spring month of Munychion, girls carrying boughs of sacred olive wrapped in wool walked in procession to the temple of the Delphinium, where they made supplication to the presiding deities Apollo and Artemis (Plutarch, *Life of Theseus* 18.2). A little later in the year, the temple of Athena Polias on the Acropolis was given its annual spring-clean: girls who were called 'Washers' and 'Bathers' removed the ornaments from the ancient statue of the goddess, and in the procession that followed Athena's robes were probably carried away to be washed (Plutarch, *Life of Alcibiades* 34.1). Musical performances were also a part of the religious life of girls: during the festival of the Panathenaea a chorus of young women kept up an all-night vigil on the Acropolis, and danced and sang in honour of the goddess.[10]

SEXUAL SEGREGATION

In the first half of this century much of the scholarly discussion about the position of women in Classical Athens centred on the issue of their seclusion.[11] Nowadays, there seems little doubt that sexual segregation did at least exist as an upper-class ideal. Xenophon (*Oeconomicus* 7.30) produces a classic statement of it when he puts into the mouth of Ischomachus the words, 'So it is seemly for a woman to remain at home and not be out of doors; but for a man to stay inside, instead of devoting himself to outdoor pursuits, is disgraceful'. According to Plato (*Laws* 781c), women are a race 'accustomed to an underground and shadowy existence'; while the spectacle of Athenian women crouched in doorways, asking passers-by for news of their husbands, fathers or brothers after a disastrous defeat in battle, is described in one speech as 'degrading both to them and to the city' (Lycurgus, *Against Leocrates* 40). The market-place was apparently included in the public locations deemed unsuitable for respectable females, for it seems to have been common for husbands or slave-girls to do the shopping.[12]

The segregation of male and female citizens was also applied to those occasions when the social life of the *polis* penetrated the private house. The *symposium*, the party where men drank and talked with their friends, was not an event for citizen women, although mistresses and female entertainers might attend. If a woman went out to parties with a man, this was regarded as proof that she was a courtesan and not his lawful wife (Isaeus 3.13–14). In her own home a wife would not be expected to have any contact with male visitors. She was not present when guests were entertained, even if the invitation had been an impromptu one (Lysias 1.23). To say that a woman talked to men, or even that she opened the front door herself, was tantamount to calling her a trollop (Theophrastus, *Characters* 28).

The home was the arena devoted to the private life shared by males and females, and any violation of the home might be interpreted as an affront to the modesty of its womenfolk, even if the incursion had manifestly been made for other purposes. This aspect of the code of honour is highlighted in a number of law-court speeches. In one, the speaker relates how his opponent Simon, in the course of a drunken raid on his house, had entered the women's rooms and encountered the speaker's sister and niece, 'who had lived so modestly that they were ashamed to be seen even by relatives'. Even

Simon's companions felt that this was a monstrous act (Lysias 3.6–7). In another oration, the speaker is careful to contrast his own behaviour with that of his opponent's associates. Before entering the house of his opponent Theophemus in order to seize some surety for equipment which should have been handed over to him, he had first ascertained that Theophemus was unmarried (Demosthenes 47.35–38). He was not, in other words, likely to run across any women. But later, when Theophemus's brother and brother-in-law broke into the speaker's house, they confronted his wife and children in the courtyard. The resulting commotion brought one of the neighbours running up, but even in these circumstances he did not like to enter the house in the absence of its master (Demosthenes 47.52–61).[13]

The issue of sexual segregation is a complex one, however. Those scholars who in the past were anxious to defend Athenian men against accusations of locking up their womenfolk often made much of the fact that in tragedy and comedy females seem to have little difficulty in leaving the house.[14] This, one might argue, is a necessity arising from one of the conventions of Athenian drama, which often deals with relations between family members but is almost always set outside the home. It is also thematically significant, since the interaction between private (feminine) concerns and public (masculine) ones is something which interests many Athenian dramatists, and symbolically the threshold of the house is the location where this occurs (see p. 179). Moreover, male characters in drama sometimes express their discomfort at seeing women engaged in exchanges in a public place. Euripides' Achilles is desperately embarrassed when he is forced into conversation with a free-born woman, Clytemnestra, in the Greek camp (*Iphigenia in Aulis* 821–34); and Electra is warned by her husband that 'It is shameful for a woman to be standing with young men' (Euripides, *Electra* 343–4). In comedy, too, a woman who leaves the house may be suspected of having an assignation with a lover (Aristophanes, *Women in the Assembly* 520).

Nevertheless, it is important to note that in many references it is the fact that women are seen conversing with unrelated males, rather than their appearance out of doors, which is found to be offensive. Segregation is not the same thing as seclusion, and some people may have thought it acceptable for women to emerge from the house occasionally provided that they kept apart from male company. The belief that 'a woman's place is in the home' is not linked solely to the aim of protecting her chastity. Many women would have had plenty of work to keep them there as well. When a character in the *Lysistrata* says 'It's difficult for a woman to get out of the house', she adds 'What with dancing attendance on her husband, keeping the servant-girl on her toes, putting the baby to bed, bathing it, feeding it . . . ' (Aristophanes, *Lysistrata* 16–19). The domestic and time-consuming nature of women's work must have contributed greatly to the notion that a woman who was seen too much out of doors must be up to no good, so that neglect of one's housewifely duties would have become synonymous with a lack of modesty.[15]

For many women of the lower classes, complete confinement to the home would not have been feasible. In a democratic society, Aristotle asks, 'who could prevent the wives of the poor from going out when they want to?' (*Politics* 1300a). In those homes where there was no well in the courtyard, and no slave to fetch water, women would have to go to the public fountain. The female chorus in Aristophanes' *Lysistrata* (327–31) speaks of the crowd that gathers round the fountain in the morning, and scenes like this are also depicted in vase paintings (Fig. 22); there is no reason to assume that all the women represented in these are to be seen as slaves, aliens or courtesans. Lower-class women also went out to work, and even where they were employed indoors (for example, as midwives), they would of course have had to leave the house in order to get to their jobs. Although many of the working women in Athens were probably the wives of resident aliens, there is evidence that citizen women worked as grape-pickers (Demosthenes, 57.45), and that some of them sold goods – such as ribbons, garlands, vegetables and bread – in the market.[16] When Lysistrata summons the 'seed-and-pancake-and-green-grocery-market-saleswomen' and the 'garlic-selling-barmaid-breadwomen' among her female followers, she is probably referring to Athenian rather than to alien women (Aristophanes, *Lysistrata* 457–8).

Clearly, lower-class women – the majority of the female citizen population – had a number of legitimate reasons for appearing out of doors. Segregation does not necess-arily break down in these circumstances. Most of the activities which took women out of the home would not have necessitated a great deal of converse with men, and as Gould (1980, p. 48) has suggested, citing comparisons with modern rural Greece, there may still have been a 'residual sense of boundary . . . marking them off from the strange males with whom they must have come face to face'. Women who lived in the country, who may have been responsible for tasks such as tending gardens and feeding chickens, probably had more cause to leave their houses than town-dwellers.[17] The strictest segregation was likely to have occurred in the city, where there were far more unknown men on the streets, and where public space may always have been regarded primarily as male space, occasionally penetrated by females. Until 431 BC, the majority of the Athenian popu-lation lived outside the urban centre, but this picture changed when the outbreak of the Peloponnesian War necessitated the evacuation of the Athenian countryside. The women who at that stage came to live in the overcrowded city may have experienced an intensification of the constraints upon them. It is interesting to speculate that the frustration of these countrywomen, coupled with a growing need for women to go out to work (see pp. 138, 145), may have produced an increasing disjuncture between male expectations and female behaviour.

Sexual segregation was often a feature of social gatherings in Athens, but there were some events – such as funerals or weddings – where women would have been in mixed company. These would have been mainly family affairs, but women did attend the large state funeral which was conducted for men who had died in the Peloponnesian War (see pp. 128, 198), and they were also present at state festivals (see pp. 160–3). However, occasions such as these probably provided little or no opportunity for converse with unrelated males (see p. 126).

There is no reason to believe that women were isolated from companions of their own sex. Many women, particularly in the lower classes, would have had their own circle of friends and neighbours, part of an autonomous sphere of female relationships which existed in parallel with the masculine social network. Women went to help each other when they were in labour (see pp. 131–2), and might pop into a neighbour's house to borrow some salt, a handful of barley, or a bunch of herbs (Theophrastus, *Characters* 10). When Euphiletus's wife (see p. 126) slipped out one night, she told her husband that she had gone next door to relight a lamp (Lysias 1.14). One speaker in a lawsuit informs his hearers that his own and his opponents' mothers had been close friends, 'and used to visit each other, as was natural when both lived in the country and were neighbours, and when, moreover, their husbands had been friends when they were alive' (Demosthenes 55.23–4). Female friendships, unlike their male equivalents, were formed and conducted within the home, and some men may well have been suspicious of these 'hidden' relationships. It is, after all, a male playwright who puts these words into the mouth of a female character, Hermione: 'our homes are a sink of evil. Against this/ double-lock your doors and bolt them too./ For not one wholesome thing has ever come/ from gadabout female callers – only grief' (Euripides, *Andromache* 949–53).[18]

The seclusion of women, while it may have existed as a masculine ideal, could probably only have been put into practice by the affluent classes. As an effective demonstration of a man's ability to protect the purity of his womenfolk, it would have been a mark of masculinity, of status and of wealth, and it is little wonder that it was mentioned by speakers in the law-courts who were anxious to stress their respectability. But by the end of the fifth century a tension may have been developing between ideal and reality. Euripides' Andromache reveals a contradiction between expectations about women and their actual behaviour when she delivers this personal apologia:

> First, since a woman, however high her reputation,
> Draws slander on herself by being seen abroad,
> I renounced restlessness and stayed in my own house;
> Refused to open my door to the fashionable chat
> Of other wives.

(*Women of Troy* 648–52)[19]

In comedy, a woman might well be one of the 'other wives' who ignored her husband's wishes: 'If we visit a friend for a celebration, wear ourselves out and fall asleep, you men turn up and search the place from top to bottom, looking for "the bane of your life"' (Aristophanes, *Thesmophoriazusae* 795–6).

The same tension can be perceived in attitudes to women of the poorer classes. In the fourth century, a man named Euxitheus could be deprived of his citizen rights because his mother, having worked as a nurse and a ribbon-seller, was suspected of not being Athenian; and yet, he argues (Demosthenes 57.45), many Athenian women have become nurses, wool-workers, and grape-pickers, on account of our city's misfortunes (probably the aftermath of the Peloponnesian War). 'We do not live', he points out, 'in the way we would like' (57.31). The theory that it was the mark of an Athenian woman to stay quietly at home had certainly not been demolished, but it was obviously being put under great pressure at a time of considerable economic hardship.

Scholars who earlier this century argued against the Athenian practice of seclusion were troubled by the notion of contempt for women which they believed it implied. In this, they were imposing their own standards of judgement on the men of ancient Athens. It is perfectly possible for women to be 'valued' but also to be denied the same rights as men, and the ideal of seclusion would undoubtedly have been viewed by Athenian males as indicative of their great regard for women and of their own diligence in protecting them. It is perhaps only by women today that it is construed as a mark of a lack of freedom and equality for women which has nothing to do with either contempt or its opposite. Of the extent to which Athenian women themselves felt compelled to challenge the ideal we know very little; but there are at least some clear signs that they were on occasions able to evade male vigilance, and to build up an alternative system of female friendships which ran counter to prevailing notions of feminine decorum.

HOUSES

Our knowledge of Athenian houses is limited, since very few have been excavated, and the literary sources contain no detailed descriptions of them. The evidence that exists suggests that in the city they were situated on narrow winding streets, and that even those belonging to upper-class families were very simple in design and construction. The walls were of mud-brick on stone bases, and the rooms were grouped on two or more sides of a small courtyard, which sometimes had a well. In some cases there were upper storeys. There seems to have been very little in the way of elaborate decoration, and furniture and ornaments were sparse. The port of Piraeus, which attracted a growing population in the fifth century, had similar houses, but they were arranged in regular blocks. Country dwellings also had much the same plan, but some of them had larger courtyards, with porticoes along one side.

The boundary between the public world of males and the private world of females was encountered even within the home, at least among the upper classes. Male guests were entertained in the *andron*, the men's dining room, which was a place for talk and also for flirtations with female entertainers and handsome youths; while women spent much of their time in the *gynaikeion*, the women's quarters. The latter consisted of either a single room or a suite of rooms, and might be located on either the ground floor or, where one existed, on the upper storey. It was here that women did wool-working, looked after their children and entertained themselves. The unmarried women of the household and the female slaves would also have slept there, as might the wife on those occasions when she did not join her husband. Even a humble home which had no slaves may have had a room restricted to the women's use, although there is no direct evidence for this.

The most detailed literary account of household space is to be found in the speech in which Euphiletus defends himself against a charge of murdering his wife's alleged lover (see p. 130). Euphiletus explains that his small dwelling had two storeys, and that at first the women's quarters were upstairs, and were equal in extent to the men's quarters below. However, when their child was born, this arrangement was reversed, and the women's quarters were moved to the ground floor so that his wife would not have to keep going downstairs to wash the baby. This presumably means that there was a well in the courtyard. His wife often slept downstairs so that she could feed the infant in the night. On one occasion when Euphiletus came back unexpectedly from the country, the baby began crying, and he insisted that she go down to feed it. She taunted him with wanting to get his hands on the young slave-girl in her absence, and playfully turned the key in the lock when she left, only returning at dawn. Later, he says, he realised that the lover had been in the house, and that the slave had been making the baby cry on purpose (Lysias, 1.9–14).

Excavated Athenian houses tend to support this picture of partial segregation within the home. Where men's and women's quarters can be identified, they are often, when both are on the ground floor, on different sides of the courtyard, and the men's rooms are generally near the street door or opposite to it. Sometimes, rooms in which loom-weights have been found have the remains of staircases in them, which suggests that women might have been able to move from their workroom on the ground floor to the sleeping area above without having to emerge from the women's quarters. The houses generally had only one entrance, so that there was no back door where women might have a casual chat with neighbours.[20] A husband who was suspicious of female friend-ships would therefore have found it relatively easy, when at home, to police his wife's activities.

WOMEN IN THE HOME

Although rigorous seclusion may seldom have been put into practice, it is clear that on the level both of ideology and of real life the home was a woman's predominant sphere of activity. The most comprehensive account of the ideal is given by Xenophon in the treatise *Oeconomicus* (7–10), where the 'model' husband Ischomachus describes in detail the education which he gave his young wife when they were first married. To modern readers Ischomachus may well come over as an insufferably pompous and patronising character, but credit must be given to the respect which he shows for his wife's managerial role within the home. It must be borne in mind, however, that his attitude probably does not represent the norm among Athenian males, who were more likely to have placed a low value on women's domestic work.

In instructing his young bride, Ischomachus warmly recommends a sexual division of labour which determines that husband and wife will play complementary parts in establishing and maintaining an orderly household. Human beings, he says, need shelter for the storage of goods, for the rearing of children and for the production of food and clothing. While men are constitutionally suited to productive labour in the open air, women are by their natures – being more soft, tender and anxious than men – suited to indoor tasks. According to Ischomachus, a woman is like a queen bee: she despatches others to their jobs outside the home, supervises those who work inside and stores, administers and distributes the goods that are brought into the house. In addition to these duties, Ischomachus' wife will be responsible for training and managing their slaves, and for looking after anyone in the household who falls sick. She has to organise the household equipment and personal belongings according to a rational scheme. When this tractable wife asks for her husband's advice on how she can best maintain her looks, Ischomachus' prescription is to avoid too much sitting about: she should stand over and supervise her slaves when they are weaving, baking or handing out stores, and should go on tours of inspection of the house; when in need of a more vigorous work-out she can knead and roll out dough, shake coverlets and make the beds.

Ischomachus' bride, we are led to believe, welcomes her new duties with enthusiasm, and demonstrates her considerable intelligence by her dutiful response to her husband's training. When she modestly points out that none of her work would be of any use if Ischomachus were not such a diligent provider, he replies that his labours too would be to no avail if he had no-one to guard what he had produced: 'Do you not see what a pitiful situation those unfortunate people are in who are forced to pour water into sieves for ever ...?' Theirs is a partnership in which their separate natures and roles perfectly complement each other.

A similar if rather less fulsome testimony to the importance of the woman's role is contained in a fragment from the play *Melanippe*, by Euripides: 'Women manage homes and preserve the goods which are brought from abroad. Houses where there is no wife are neither orderly nor prosperous. And in religion – I take this to be important – we women play a large part ... How then can it be just that the female sex should be so abused? ...' (*Select papyri* 13, Page). Euphiletus (see p. 126) shows little respect for the value of his wife's work, which is hardly surprising in the circumstances; but he does make it clear that although he had watched her carefully when they were first married, he had begun to trust her with the control of his possessions once their son had been born (Lysias 1.6). Although women were not allowed to engage in monetary transactions of any significance (see p. 114), it would seem that they were often responsible for managing the domestic finances. Lysistrata supports her contention that women are quite capable of controlling the treasury of Athens by pointing out that they have been in charge of the housekeeping for years (Aristophanes, *Lysistrata* 492–7); and Plato claims (*Laws* 805e) that men in Greece hand over control of the money to their wives.

In addition to the duties already outlined, women in poorer families with no domestic slaves would of course have been responsible for all the cooking, baking, cleaning and washing. They and their more affluent sisters would also have been involved in caring for and educating their children, in the case of the girls probably up until the time they left home (see pp. 132–3). Some reasonably well-to-do women, such as Euphiletus's wife (see p. 139), breastfed their own children, but it seems to have been a fairly common practice to engage a wet-nurse: free-born Athenian women were preferred, but slaves and resident aliens were also employed, especially by the poor.

Women of all social classes would have engaged in the important task of wool-working. Although better-off women had slaves who did the bulk of the work, literature and vase paintings indicate that their mistresses assisted and guided them in their labours (Fig. 23). Textile production was a vital part of the domestic economy, and some households would have been completely self-sufficient in this respect, even producing their own wool, although raw wool could also be bought on the market. Women in the home were responsible for preparing fleeces, for spinning thread and for weaving lengths of cloth on the loom. Wool was by far the most common fibre, but flax was also used by the better-off, since linen was prized as a material from which finer garments could be made.

Weaving in particular was viewed as the quintessential female accomplishment, and it was common for women to honour a deity with a gift of a fine piece of work. As well as producing the material, they were also responsible for making it up into finished articles. However, most of the clothes worn by the Greeks required a minimum of sewing, since they consisted in the main of simple rectangles of cloth which were belted or pinned into place. Much of the interior decoration of a home was also supplied by its womenfolk, in the form of wall-hangings, bedcovers and cushions. The best items would probably have been displayed in the men's dining room, the most public part of the house, where they would have served to demonstrate the skill and devotion to duty of the female members of the family. Weaving must have been back-breaking and laborious work, but there can be no doubt that for Athenian women their handicrafts would have been a source of pride.

According to Ischomachus, women naturally have more affection for newborn children than men (Xenophon, *Oeconomicus* 7.24). This affection must often have been a source of grief to Athenian women. Golden (1990, p. 83) estimates that the infant mortality rate may have been as high as 30–40 per cent in the first year of life, and that the majority of Greek mothers could have expected to bury at least one child in their lifetime. In addition, some of them would have had to cope with the exposure of an infant (see pp. 130–1). Some modern scholars have suggested that, in circumstances such as these, mothers become conditioned not to feel too great a sense of loss at the death of a child, and that the experience of maternal love is consequently not such a potent element in women's lives as it is at other times or in other places.[21] Golden (1990, pp. 82–9), however, believes that children in ancient Greece received loving attention from their mothers, but that their grief at a child's loss was diffused through ritual mourning practices and through sharing their sorrow with other adults involved in their care. The existence of the practice of exposure, he suggests, tells us nothing about the response of parents to the death of any child whom they had decided to raise: it is even possible that children are less likely to be neglected in societies where infanticide is permitted, since the children that are reared are positively wanted.[22]

There is certainly no shortage of references in Classical Greek literature to the agony experienced by mothers at the loss of a child. Aeschylus (*Agamemnon* 1417–18), Sophocles (*Electra* 530–81) and Euripides (*Electra* 1020–29 and *Iphigenia in Aulis* 880–end) all allow Clytemnestra to speak of the grief which she feels at the sacrifice of her daughter Iphigenia. Hector's widow Andromache, in Euripides' *Women of Troy* (757–62), utters a heart-rending speech of farewell to her young son when he is taken away to be executed:

> ... Dear child, so young in my arms,
> So precious! O the sweet smell of your skin! When you
> Were newly born I wrapped you up, gave you my breast,
> Tended you day and night, worn out by weariness –
> For nothing, all for nothing! Say goodbye to me
> Once more, for the last time of all...[23]

The concern of real-life mothers for their children is revealed by Aristotle when he describes how some women (presumably those who are poor or unmarried) give their children up to others to rear, and are content to see them getting on well, and to go on loving them, even though the children are ignorant of their true parentage and cannot love them in return (*Nicomachaean Ethics* 1159a). Numerous dedications were made to healing deities such as Asclepius by mothers on behalf of their sick children; and in one Athenian epitaph of the fourth century a woman named Xenocleia is said to have died of grief for her young son (*IG* 2.2, no.12335).

Greek tragedy, and Greek myth in general, are nevertheless remarkable for the amount of violence that takes place between parents and children.[24] The tendency to focus attention on murderous mothers can perhaps be attributed to an underlying anxiety about sexually active females which found its most forthright expression in imaginative literature (see pp. 173–80). Although such acts of violence were doubtless not unknown, there is no evidence to suggest that in real life they were any more common than they are in our own society.

A more realistic picture of relations between women and their adolescent sons is probably to be found in a section of Xenophon's *Memorabilia* (2.2) in which Socrates chastises his sons Lamprocles for being bad-tempered with his mother, and treats him to a long recital of the selfless toil undertaken by mothers. Even so, Lamprocles replies, no-one could possibly put up with my mother's vile temper. Admittedly, she hasn't done me any physical injury, but she says things which one wouldn't want to listen to for anything in the world. In Aristophanes' *Clouds* (42–74) there is a portrait of a more indulgent parent. Young Pheidippides, according to his father, has been hopelessly spoiled by a mother who resented her marriage to a social inferior and helped to foster her son's expensive passion for chariot-racing. These sketches, which hardly present a positive view of mothers, probably reflect more accurately than tragedy the conscious responses of the average Athenian male to the institution of motherhood. A pervasive downgrading of the mother's role was perhaps responsible for the relative dearth of images of mothers and children in Greek art.

These rather bleak representations of motherly love must be considered alongside the adverse publicity which wives often receive in Athenian literature. In tragedy, wives may be murderous, like Clytemnestra, bitterly jealous, like Hermione and Deianeira (see above, p. 124 and p. 206, Ch. 11, n. 22), lustful, like Phaedra (see p. 31), or horrifically vindictive, like Medea, who murders her own children in order to rob her faithless husband Jason of his triumph over her. Tragedy's only significant depiction of a loving relationship between husband and wife is to be found in Euripides' *Alcestis*, in which the heroine agrees to die in place of her husband Admetus. In Aristophanes' comedies, wives are less violent, but are often seen as wily, devious, prone to adultery and overfond of alcohol. In the fourth century the comic playwright Eubulus provided this ironic comment on wifely virtue: 'Oh honoured Zeus, am I the man ever to speak ill of wives? Zeus, may I perish if I do, for they are the best of all possessions. If Medea was an evil woman, Penelope was a good thing. Some will say that Clytemnestra was wicked. But Alcestis can be set against her as good. Perhaps someone will speak badly of Phaedra. But ... by God, there must be another good wife. Who? Alas, poor me, I've already got through all the good wives, and I've still got so many of the terrible ones to talk about' (frag. 116, 117, lines 6–15, Kock).

However, although most Athenian men probably had a utilitarian attitude to matrimony, this would not necessarily have prevented a loving relationship from developing in the course of a marriage. Ischomachus is anxious to point out to his new wife that he has not married her for reasons of passion, but because he believes that she will make a suitable partner in the home and in the rearing of children (Xenophon, *Oeconomicus* 7.10–11); but, by his own account at least, a bond of mutual affection does appear to develop between the couple. To the somewhat unreliable testimony of male writers on the subject of marital relations there can be added the fact that from about 420 BC onwards there was a considerable increase in the popularity of family burial plots, and that in grave-reliefs of this period joint commemoration of a husband and wife was relatively common (Fig. 24). These changes can perhaps be attributed to a gradual privatisation of male concerns, allowing a growing acknowledgement of the part played by one's domestic life in the securing of personal fulfilment.[25] Nevertheless, the expression of love for a wife remains a comparatively rare feature of Classical Greek literature. Aristotle may express the most common male view of relations between husband and wife when he says that their affection for each other is 'in accordance with merit: the husband, as the superior, receives the greater share' (*Nicomachaean Ethics* 1161a).

Few Athenian authors are prepared to acknowledge that the position of Athenian women in the home may have amounted to one of power. Yet references to female control of a household's possessions (see pp. 140–1) invite speculation on the possibility of a domestic inversion of public authority patterns, bolstered by the institution of the dowry (see p. 116). More circumstantial evidence is provided by some law-court speeches. In one, we hear about a family meeting where a mother, in a very competent and forceful manner, tackles her sons' guardian (her own father) about his mismanagement of their estate, at the same time demonstrating her sound knowledge of the family finances (Lysias 32.10, 12–18). Women might also be present at discussions about the terms of a family member's will, and might even represent their husbands on these occasions (Demosthenes 41.17–19). Aeschines in one of his speeches (1.170) refers to rich young men whose fathers were dead and whose mothers were administering their property.

In many instances women would have wielded power through the more indirect methods of nagging or doing things behind their husbands' backs. Euphiletus (see p. 139) bears unwitting testimony to the operation of this power: he clearly sees himself as master in his own home, yet his account reveals that his wife was able to speak to him very freely, that her 'joke' of locking him in the bedroom came off, and that she was moreover able for some time to get away with conducting a love affair under his nose. Aristophanes' comedies are a rich source of information on similar female strategies. In *Thesmophoriazusae* we hear about infertile women who sneak babies into the house (407–9), and wives who have duplicate keys made so that they can smuggle extra provisions out of the larder (418–28). Praxagora in *Women in the Assembly* (520–727) is always ready with a smart and often abusive retort in her verbal exchanges with her husband. On the basis of the *Lysistrata* we can surmise that withholding sex may have been another female ploy for gaining control over a spouse. Methods such as these were viewed with disfavour by men, but Aristophanes is quite prepared to acknowledge that they could prove very effective. The contrast between the vigorous and outspoken women characters of comedy and the silent and submissive female of the Athenian ideal can probably be explained in part by the fact that inside some homes at least the public face of family life disappeared, and the obedient wife of male discourse was transformed into a genuinely powerful one.

Comedies and law-court speeches offer in this way a valuable insight into a side of Athenian life rarely referred to in the bulk of Athenian literature, which generally focuses attention on public power structures and views the home, if it is mentioned at all, as an extension of the masculine sphere of authority. In legal terms this authority certainly existed, as we have seen; and the ideal of masculine government of the household is forcibly expressed in works such as Xenophon's *Oeconomicus* (see p. 140). Yet between the cracks of the legal and normative framework there appear these glimpses of an alternative and informal pattern of female power. This may to a small extent have filtered out into the public arena as a result of wifely influence over husbands on political and legal questions (see p. 128). The close relationship established between *oikos* and *polis* in Athenian ideology meant that the importance of male domination of the home was recognised; but it also permitted at least a hypothetical reversal of the flow of power. If women and not men were dominant in the private sphere, were the effects of this not bound to be felt in the public domain?

Few Athenian men would have been willing to voice this question openly. But Athenian awareness of the possibility is demonstrated by the frequency with which tragic and comic playwrights envisage a situation in which women intrude into the world of public affairs. This topic will be discussed in detail in a later section (see pp. 172–80), but one particular instance can be noted now. In the *Lysistrata* (567–86) the heroine produces a brilliant analogy between the processes involved in the preparation of raw wool for weaving and the tactics required to create political cohesion in the city. Aristophanes, for one, seems to have been conscious of the fact that the overlap between private and public concerns meant that women, by drawing on their domestic skills, might be capable of making an intellectual as well as a physical contribution to the well-being of the state. Too much should not be made of the issue of female power, for the allusions to it are rare and, in the case of comedy, may be highly imaginative. But it is by no means impossible that a whole area of alternative power structures has been ignored or suppressed by the patriarchal literature of Classical Athens. Once again one must regret the absence of an authentic female voice from the sources for this period.

Athenian Women Workers

In addition to the jobs already mentioned (pp. 136–7), Athenian women of the lower classes took employment as washerwomen (Lefkowitz and Fant, 1982, nos. 50 and 51), wet-nurses (Demosthenes 57.35), and midwives (see p. 110). The majority of these activities involved a marketing of the skills which women had acquired as providers of food or childcare. A fifth-century vase painting records one type of female employment not related to the domestic sphere: in a scene representing a potter's workshop, a woman sits to one side of a group of men applying paint to a large pot (see Bérard, 1989, p. 10, fig. 1). Such a woman may well have been an alien or slave rather than Athenian; and the occupation was doubtless an unusual one among members of her sex. The most elevated female profession recorded belongs to a woman of the mid-fourth century named Phanostrate, whose tombstone states that she was both a midwife and a doctor: 'she caused pain to none, and all lamented her death' (Lefkowitz and Fant, 1982, no. 52). There is no evidence to suggest that women doctors were at all common in Athens, but there is perhaps a grain of truth in a story told by a later Latin writer about an Athenian woman named Hagnodice who was forced to disguise herself as a man in order to practise obstetrics, and later demonstrated her true sex by raising her tunic in court when accused of seducing her patients (Hyginus, *Fabulae* 274).

Opportunities for paid work within one's own home must have been severely limited, but one example is recorded by Xenophon (*Memorabilia* 2.7.1–12). In a conversation with the philosopher Socrates, a man named Aristarchus once complained that as a result of the political turmoil produced by an oligarchic coup in Athens an assortment of homeless female relatives had moved into his house, and as a result he had to support no less than fourteen people. Socrates suggested that these relatives be put to work making clothes. Though Aristarchus was at first reluctant, he finally set his womenfolk up in a wool-working business, and as a result they not only succeeded in providing for their own maintenance but also achieved great job satisfaction.

It is impossible to assess what proportion of Athenian women took on paid work, or how easy it was for them to find it. It is clear that in the fourth century there was still a stigma attached to the working woman (see p. 138); but the economic troubles which Athens experienced as a consequence of the Peloponnesian War and her subsequent loss of empire would have undoubtedly produced an increase in the number of women seeking employment, and some of them may, like Aristarchus's relatives, have been relatively well-born.

Resident Aliens

As a busy trading centre, Athens in the Classical period attracted a large number of immigrants, mostly from other parts of Greece but also from the Near and Middle East. Non-Athenians who were given permission to live in Athens were known as metics, and by the start of the Peloponnesian War they and their families may have comprised as much as one-sixth of the total population. Their status was always an inferior one, since they were excluded from citizenship and were not allowed to own land. Most of them probably had humble occupations such as metalworking, building, carpentry, retailing and farming rented land. But a notable few made large fortunes in industry or banking, and would have mixed on equal terms with members of the Athenian upper classes. Slaves who were given their freedom by their owners were also accorded metic status.

The majority of women in the metic class would have been the wives and daughters of male immigrants or their descendants. A significant disability was imposed on the daughters of metics in 451/0 BC, when Pericles' citizenship law (see pp. 120–1) removed from those of them who were married to Athenian men their right to give birth to Athenian citizens. A metic woman's chance of marrying an Athenian husband would have been vastly reduced at this point; but some of them would have lived with Athenian citizens as their concubines (see p. 124). A small minority of metic women would have come to Athens independently and registered in their own right as resident aliens; most of them were probably prostitutes.

We know very little about the lives of metic women, but as they were not in most cases (in all cases, after 451/0) vehicles in the transmission of citizenship, it is possible that masculine control over their behaviour was less rigorous than in the case of Athenian women. A larger percentage of them would have had jobs outside the home, and the range of occupations which they undertook may have been wider. The majority of metics appear to have lived in the city rather than the countryside, and it is possible that as neighbours they mingled quite freely with Athenian women of the lower classes, whose lives would have resembled theirs in most respects. However, a difference in status marked by their exclusion from the religious role of Athenian women may have produced a social barrier.

SLAVES

Most members of Athens' sizeable slave class (see p. 96) were males, who worked in mining, agriculture or manufacturing industry. It is difficult to know how far down the social scale ownership of slaves went, but it may have been the case that most peasant farmers would have tried to keep at least one slave to help with work on the farm. 'Middle income' citizens would in addition have been able to afford at least one domestic servant: Euphiletus (see p. 126), who tells us that his house was a small one, employed a single slave-girl in his home. But no Athenian household appears to have contained enormous squads of slaves; even among the wealthiest citizens it seems to have been rare for the number to have exceeded ten. Most of the slaves employed in houses appear to have been female, and their jobs included shopping, cooking, cleaning, childcare and wool-working. In an affluent household some of the female servants had specialised roles, such as housekeeper, cook or nurse. Only specially-favoured slaves were allowed to marry and rear children, and casual sexual relations with fellow-slaves may also have been prohibited in most cases: Ischomachus puts a stop to nocturnal assignations by fixing a bolt on the door of the women's quarters (Xenophon, *Oeconomicus* 9.5). Sexual relations with the master of the house were probably another matter, but the fact that the wife of Euphiletus taunts her husband with wanting to get his hands on their slave-girl (see p. 139) suggests that these affairs were not accepted as a matter of course. The children born as a result of such associations would almost certainly have been disposed of by exposure.

Euphiletus's slave-girl performed an additional, unofficial, duty when she was employed as a go-between by his wife's lover, a desperate and dangerous measure, for the girl later informed on the couple when Euphiletus threatened her with a whipping and being thrown into a mill (Lysias 1.18, 23). Female slaves must often have been their mistresses' confidantes in matters where their complicity was less problematical, for the relative seclusion of upper-class women would have meant that many of them developed close relationships with their slaves. In tragedy, Medea and Phaedra discuss their deepest feelings with their old nurses; and Athenian tombstones often depict intimate scenes involving the deceased woman and her slave-girl (Fig. 25). It is possible that a sense of their common exclusion from the masculine world of public affairs would have produced a degree of identification between Athenian women and their slaves.

PROSTITUTES

Women's work was not generally valued by Athenian males, and as a consequence the only form of female employment about which we have any detailed information is prostitution. The majority of prostitutes were probably women, although establish-ments where one could hire young men were apparently quite common. Both male and female prostitution seems to have been legal, since the people employed in both categories paid a special tax. The port of Piraeus and the Ceramicus or Potter's quarter were two of the better known 'red-light' districts of Athens.[26]

Making love to a respectable Athenian woman who was not one's wife or concubine was an enterprise fraught with difficulty, not to say danger (see p. 125), and brothels provided men with a readily available and cheap alternative. The range of what was on offer is described by Xenarchus in this fragment from his comic play *The Pentathlete*, written in the fourth century:

> ... in our city ... there are, after all, very good-looking young things in the whore-houses, whom one can readily see basking in the sun, their breasts uncovered, stripped for action and drawn up in battle formation by columns, from among whom one can select whatever sort one likes – thin, fat, squat, tall, shrivelled, young, old, middle-aged, full-ripened – without setting up a ladder and stealthily entering [another man's house] ... For the girls themselves grab people and drag them in, naming those who are old men 'little father', those who are younger 'little bro.'. And each of them can be had without fear, affordable, by day, towards evening, in every way you like.
>
> (frag. 4).[27]

Squandering one's money in brothels was certainly not regarded as a respectable way of passing one's time, but it was not considered to be anything out of the ordinary if a young man paid an occasional visit to a prostitute, and the activity would have been within most men's means. In the Classical period the sixth-century lawgiver Solon was credited with having purchased slave women and put them to work in brothels at prices which everyone could afford. This measure was seen, at least by a character in a comedy written by Philemon in the late fourth or early third century, as one which was in accordance with the democratic tendencies of Solon's other reforms: 'But you found a law for the use of everyone; for you were the first, Solon, they say, to discover this practice – a democratic one, by Zeus, and a saving one (I should know, Solon!): ... you bought and stationed women in various public locations, equipped and fitted out as common possessions for all. They stand there naked, so you won't be fooled: what you see is what you get ...' (fragment 4).[28]

There were in fact a wide variety of sexual partners available for hire in Classical Athens.[29] The most affordable were the *pornai*, the common prostitutes who staffed the brothels, the great majority of whom were probably slaves owned by the brothel-keeper. Of a slightly higher class were the prostitutes who walked the streets, most of whom were either freed slaves or free women, either metics or Athenians, who had been forced into the trade by poverty. The female dancers, flute-players and acrobats who were hired to perform at upper-class male drinking parties provided sexual services as well as entertainment.[30] They were probably mostly slaves, but as skilled artists they would have been more expensive than the average prostitute.

Sometimes a favourite prostitute might, if she were a slave, be purchased by a wealthy client and set up as his concubine. This had been the fate of the hapless Neaera (see p. 121), who as a prostitute in Corinth had been bought by two young men for the large sum of thirty minae. When they were about to be married and had no more use for her, they offered to let her buy her freedom (generously granting her a discount on her original purchase price) on condition that she did not ply her trade in Corinth. Neaera raised the required twenty minae by organising a whip-round among her old clients, and came to Athens with the one who had contributed the most, a man named Phrynion. He introduced her to fashionable society by taking her out to upper-class drinking parties; women who appeared at these gatherings were not considered respectable, and Neaera's activities on these occasions were apparently more scandalous than most. According to her accusers, Phrynion used to have sex with her in front of the other guests, and at one particularly wild party she bestowed her favours on a large number of the men present, including some of the slaves (Demosthenes 59.29–33). Not surprisingly, Neaera eventually left Phrynion.

At the top end of the sexual market were the women known as *hetaerae*, or 'female companions', often referred to nowadays as courtesans. These were sophisticated beauties, occasionally Athenians but more often metics, who charged very high prices for a single night in their company, and who sometimes reserved themselves for a few chosen lovers. They represented the only significant group of economically independent women in Classical Athens. The most famous *hetaera*, and indeed the most famous woman of fifth-century Athens, was Aspasia, who had been born in Miletus, graduated to being a controller of other *hetaerae* and finally became the mistress of the statesman Pericles. She was renowned for her intelligence and political astuteness. According to Plutarch (*Life of Pericles* 24.3), she used to receive visits from Socrates, accompanied by some of his pupils, and other men used to take their wives along to listen to her. In Plato's *Menexenus* (235e–236b), Socrates in what is admittedly a jesting frame of mind claims that Aspasia taught him and other men, including Pericles, the art of rhetoric, and credits her with having been the true author of Pericles' famous funeral oration.

After divorcing his wife, Pericles lived with Aspasia until his death. The degree of influence which she exercised over him is impossible to assess, but a number of Athenians seem to have regarded her role as an illegitimate intrusion into the male-dominated political system. She was the object of some vicious caricatures in comic plays, and her name has been found inscribed on a lead curse tablet. According to Plutarch, Pericles was induced by Aspasia to declare war on the Samians, because this would benefit the people of Miletus (*Pericles* 25.1); and Aristophanes (*The Acharnians* 515–39) concocts a fantastic story, featuring the abduction by some men from Megara of two of Aspasia's prostitutes, in order to explain Pericles' motive in introducing a notorious ban on Megarian trade which precipitated the outbreak of the Peloponnesian War. At one stage Aspasia was prosecuted for impiety and for procuring, but was passionately and successfully defended by Pericles at her trial. Undoubtedly Pericles' mistress was serving in all of this as a vehicle for indirect attacks on Pericles himself; but one can easily imagine that in the exclusive and patriarchal ranks of Athenian citizens there would have been a hostile reaction to the possession by an individual foreign woman of a power which may well have been quite considerable.

OLDER WOMEN

The age difference between males and females at marriage would have meant that quite a large number of Athenian women were in their late twenties or early thirties when they were widowed. Some of them, as Garland (1990, p. 212) has pointed out, would also have become grandmothers at about the same age. The youthful appearance of a woman named Ampharete who is seen on an Athenian tombstone of the late fifth century cradling her grandson in her lap is therefore not at all surprising (Fig. 26). The epitaph which relays her words to the passer-by is indicative of the close relationship which might exist between a woman and her grandchildren:

> I hold the dear child of my daughter, whom I held in my lap when we were alive looking on the light of the sun, and hold now when he is dead as I am dead.

A widow was still of child-bearing age would have had a good chance of remarrying, especially if her dowry was a substantial one. If she remained single and had a son or sons, she would generally have remained in her late husband's *oikos*; if there were no sons she could either return to the *oikos* into which she had been born or stay on in her old home with her husband's heir. The person on whom the guardianship of her dowry had fallen – her son, her nearest male relative or her husband's heir – was obliged by law to support her. Speakers in the law-courts often use their widowed mothers' dependency as a way of arousing the sympathy of the jurors.[31] Bonds of affection may often have united these sons and their mothers: one tombstone of the fourth century BC announces that Telemachus is buried at the right-hand side of his mother, and is not deprived of her love (*IG* 2.2 7711). But non-relatives might be far less respectful in their attitudes towards elderly women, and might, like Aristophanes (e.g. *Women in the Assembly* 938–1111), picture them as sex-starved 'old bags'.

One compensation for ageing enjoyed by women who had passed the menopause was the greater freedom of movement allowed to them by male notions of propriety. A significant number of the women workers already discussed (p. 145) were probably post-menopausal; nurses seem often to have been elderly women, and according to Socrates (see p. 130), midwives had to be beyond child-bearing age. The attitude behind this relaxation of restraint is probably summed up by the fourth-century orator Hyperides when he states that 'a woman who leaves the house ought to be at the stage in life where people who meet her ask, not whose wife she is, but whose mother' (frag. 205, Jensen). If this relative lack of concern about the comings and goings of older women was indicative of their diminished value in men's eyes, this would not necessarily have troubled the women concerned.

13

Sparta and Gortyn

Sparta and Gortyn are the only Greek states apart from Athens for which we possess detailed information on the role of women. Most of the evidence comes from Classical and post-Classical sources, but many of the legal provisions and customs referred to probably date back to the Archaic era. Where Gortyn is concerned our knowledge is confined to the legal framework; but in the case of Sparta some assessment of the reality of women's lives can be attempted. In both states the legal and social position of women appears in some respects to have been very different from what it was in Athens. Both, however, possessed unusual social institutions, and it cannot be assumed that the rights which they extended to women were matched in other parts of Greece. While Classical Athens may have been unusually repressive in its treatment of women, Sparta and Gortyn may have been unusually liberal.

WOMEN IN SPARTA

Throughout history, Sparta's unique social system (see pp. 96–7) has been capable of arousing strong feelings, either of admiration or of antipathy. Much the same might be said of Spartan women, at least as far as the responses of ancient writers are concerned. Some respected them for their vigour and outspokenness, others were horrified by their independent ways. None of these writers was Spartan, and all, of course, were male, so that our source material is doubly distanced from its subject matter. The tendency to use the behaviour of women as a benchmark for an alien society's entire character doubtless helps to explain why writers living elsewhere were prone either to idealise or to condemn the women of Sparta.

The ideology of the Spartan state was such that the family was, in Finley's words (1975, p. 166), 'minimized as a unit of either affection or authority, and replaced by overlapping male groupings'. In this way, the state sought to ensure that a man's interests were channelled into public life, which in Spartan terms meant military life. At the age of seven a Spartan boy was taken away from his home, and up to the age of thirty he lived in barracks with other males, although he generally married when he was in his twenties. When he was thirty he was allowed to reside with his wife and children, but even then he would have spent most of his time away from the domestic environment, engaged in military training and campaigns, hunting, political decision-making and eating meals every evening in a common mess-hall. One result of this system was that the authority of the individual father was downgraded, a tendency which was positively encouraged by Spartan custom; all older men were addressed as 'father' by Spartan boys, and had the right to discipline and punish them (Xenophon, *Constitution of the Spartans* 2.2, 2.10–1; Plutarch, *Life of Lycurgus* 15.8, 17.1).

There can be little doubt that one effect of the undermining of the father's role would have been to enhance that of the mother, who by the time her husband moved into the family home would have established her pre-eminence there, and would subsequently have had little difficulty in maintaining her position in view of her partner's frequent and sometimes prolonged absence. In Classical Athenian society, the degree of largely unacknowledged power which women exercised within the home is a matter for speculation (see pp.143–4); but the recognition of the interconnection of public and private interests did at the very least foster an ideal of male dominance in the household. In Sparta, no such ideal appears to have existed. There, the more radical separation of the public and private spheres,[1] on both an ideological and on a material level, would have ensured that female domestic power was accepted and possibly even officially encouraged.

Until his departure for the barracks at the age of seven, a boy would probably have spent most of his time at home with his mother. He would have had little or no contact with his father: as Kunstler (1987, p. 33) has pointed out, by the time a man moved in with his family his son or sons might have already left home. If a boy's emotional ties with his parents were not completely obliterated by the state education system, then it is likely that the strongest of these would have been with the mother. As we shall see (p. 157), there is evidence to suggest that this was indeed the case.

For a Spartan girl the father would also have been a remote figure, and she would have seen very little of her brothers once the barracks had claimed them. Up to the time of her marriage, at about the age of eighteen, she would have lived in a household which was controlled by her mother, and would have developed an intimate relationship with her. This experience of a virtually all-female environment would doubtless have helped to foster the independent outlook for which Spartan women were renowned. Nor would the model presented by her mother have been an entirely domestic one, since servants relieved Spartan women of many onerous household duties, and sedentary pursuits such as weaving were not considered a fit occupation for a free woman (Xenophon, *Constitution of the Spartans* 1.3–4).

The home was not the only context for the creation of same-sex relationships among women. In Sparta, by contrast with Athens, the upbringing of girls to a certain extent paralleled that of boys. Physical fitness was considered to be as important for females as it was for males, and girls took part in races and trials of strength (Xenophon, *Constitution* 1.4). Plutarch (*Lycurgus* 14.2) includes running, wrestling, and throwing the discus and javelin in the list of their activities. They also learnt how to manage horses; they drove carriages in processions (Plutarch, *Life of Agesilaus* 19.5), and at the Hyacinthia, a festival of Apollo and Hyacinthus, they raced in two-horse chariots (Athenaeus 4.4, 139c–f). It is very likely that girls' athletic events were often a part of cult practice, and that some of them took place during all-female ritual occasions.[2] Their training would probably have been in the control of older women: women, at any rate, are referred to in an inscription as the 'officers and overseers for life of the most sacred games of the Hyacinthia'.[3]

It is possible that girls and boys sometimes performed athletics side by side in the same stadium. Certainly, Spartan girls do not appear to have been at all times segregated from males, for they were in the habit of mocking young men who had misbehaved themselves, and of singing the praises of those who had acted bravely (Plutarch, *Lycurgus* 14.3). Like males, girls may have taken part in athletic events in the nude, even in front of mixed audiences. This is certainly the implication of the account given by Plutarch, who denies that there was anything indecent in this, 'for modesty attended them, and there was no wantonness in their behaviour' (*Lycurgus* 14.4). Sixth-century bronze figurines, which are thought to have been manufactured in Sparta, depict girl runners who are wearing tunics, although one of them has one of her breasts bared (Fig. 27), recalling the description given by Pausanias of the girls' athletics at Olympia.[4] On the other hand, Sparta was unusual among Greek states in that in the late Archaic Age it produced statuettes of female nudes, which suggests that Spartans may have been more accustomed than other Greeks to witnessing displays of female nudity. According to Plutarch, Spartan girls also appeared naked in ritual processions and dances which were watched by young men (*Lycurgus* 14.2).

The stress on physical fitness is in line with Xenophon's statement (see p. 132) that girls in Sparta were better nourished than those elsewhere. It was largely responsible for the great reputation which Spartan women earned among other Greeks for a muscular style of beauty, referred to in an exchange which takes place in Aristophanes' *Lysistrata* (78–82), when the Spartan woman Lampito comes to join the Athenian women in their sex strike:

> *Lysistrata* Welcome, Lampito, my dear Spartan friend. Darling, you look simply beautiful. Such a healthy complexion, such vigour. You look as though you could throttle a bull.
> *Lampito* I should think so too, by the two goddesses. I do gymnastics, and high-jumps – kicking my heels right up to my bum.
> *Lysistrata* And what marvellous breasts . . .

According to Plato, the Spartan system of education for girls included compulsory instruction in the arts as well as athletics (*Laws* 806a), and in Sparta 'there are not only men but also women who pride themselves on their intellectual culture' (*Protagoras* 342d). Certainly, silence does not appear to have been one of the virtues cultivated in Spartan women (see p. 157).

Young women were also brought together in choirs which performed lyrics such as the Maiden-songs written by the poet Alcman (see p. 81). Here too, the context for participation was almost certainly one of cult practice. Calame has suggested that by educating girls in the areas of sexuality, marriage and maternity, these rites may have prepared them for their incorporation as adults into the civic community. For these purposes they may have been divided into age classes similar to the ones into which boys were placed for their military training. The details of this reconstruction are largely hypothetical; but the homosexual character of the bonds uniting the girls with each other and with their instructors is suggested both by Alcman's poems, and by Plutarch's statement (*Lycurgus* 18.4) that in Sparta the degree of approval for homosexual love was so great that even maidens found lovers among good and noble women. Although the reputation which Spartan men gained elsewhere in Greece for their homoerotic preferences may have been engendered in the main by prejudice,[5] there is evidence to show that relationships between youths and men were officially encouraged; and it is possible that a parallel system of female liaisons was openly acknowledged.

By Greek standards, Spartan women married relatively late, 'not when they were small and unsuited to intercourse, but when they were in their prime and fully matured' (Plutarch, *Lycurgus* 15.3). Women may have been about eighteen and men about twenty-five when they entered into matrimony.[6] There is no evidence to show that Spartan women had any more say than their Athenian sisters in the choice of their husbands. References to marriage arranged by a woman's father (Herodotus 6.57.4, 6.71.2) probably reflect the general practice. Although Spartan marriage is said to have taken place 'by capture', this phrase seems to have alluded to the unusual set of rituals which accompanied it, and there is no reason to believe that in the great majority of cases the consent of the bride's father had not first been obtained.[7]

On the eve of a marriage a bridal attendant cut the bride's hair close to her head, dressed her in a man's cloak and sandals and laid her on a mattress alone in the dark. The bridegroom ate as usual at the common mess hall, and then slipped secretly into the room where the bride lay, loosened her girdle and carried her to the marriage bed. Having spent a short time with her, he returned composedly to the barracks and slept with the other young men. These furtive visits continued for some time (presumably until the groom reached the age of thirty and left the barracks). The young husband was ashamed and fearful of detection when he visited his wife, who collaborated with him in arranging stolen interviews. In this way men might become fathers before they had ever seen their wives by daylight (Plutarch, *Lycurgus* 15.3–5).

As in the Athenian marriage ceremony (see p. 123), the motif of abduction may have had a purely symbolic significance, suggesting the violence of the transition which the bride was undergoing. The cutting of the bride's hair would similarly have denoted the new status which she was about to acquire. However, her masculinisation is more difficult to explain. It was not entirely unique,[8] and can perhaps best be seen as a remnant of a full cross-dressing ritual in which the donning by each partner of the clothing of the opposite sex was intended either to confuse evil spirits, or to underline sexual complementarity by introducing a temporary reversal of the roles which each would play in their subsequent relationship.[9] In the surviving form of the rite, however, the sexual ambiguity was all on the female side, and as Kunstler has suggested (1987, p. 40), this may have had the effect of easing the emotional threat which marriage represented to a man whose loyalty had hitherto belonged solely to all-male groups.

According to Plutarch (*Lycurgus* 15.5), the secrecy of the couple's subsequent meetings ensured that their relationship was not staled by easy access, but always retained a spark of mutual longing. Xenophon believes that the heightening of the couple's desire produced healthier babies (*Constitution* 1.5). Alternative explanations suggested by modern scholars are that the practice was a survival from a time when Spartan men were not permitted to marry until the age of thirty; or that it may indicate a kind of trial marriage, only made official when the woman had conceived or given birth.[10] The latter theory is not contradicted by the story that the Spartan king Anaxandridas II was so devoted to his wife that he refused to divorce her even though she was childless (Herodotus 5.39–40), for this indifference to childbearing capacity was clearly seen as exceptional. If trial marriages were a reality, then Spartan men may not have been particularly concerned about the virginity of their new brides. They certainly differed from other Greek men in their attitude to a wife's sexual behaviour after marriage.

The aspect of Spartan life which non-Spartans must have found most horrifying was the practice of wife-sharing. This seems to have involved two different but parallel arrangements. Polybius (12.6b.8) reports that it was an ancestral custom and a current practice for three or four men, or more if they were brothers, to share one wife, and for the children to be regarded as belonging equally to all. In addition, when a man had produced enough children, it was both honourable and customary for him to pass his wife on to a friend. Both Xenophon (*Constitution* 1.7–9) and Plutarch (*Lycurgus* 15.6–9) elaborate on the circumstances in which the loan of a wife might occur. If an elderly Spartan had a young wife, he might introduce her to a younger man of good character and physique; alternatively a man who did not wish to live with a wife but who wanted children might choose a distinguished woman who had produced fine offspring, and endeavour to obtain her husband's consent to a sexual relationship. The object in either case was the begetting of children. According to Plutarch, these customs promoted the cause of eugenics, for it was recognised that it was illogical to select the best parents when breeding dogs and horses but not to do so when rearing humans.

From these accounts it appears that men in Sparta were monogamous, while women might on occasions be polygamous, or polyandrous – they might, as in the first situation described by Polybius, have more than one husband. In addition, wife-borrowing was practised, apparently by men who were not already married themselves, or at any rate had not produced children. Selective breeding may have been the official Spartan explanation for customs such as these; but, as Hodkinson (1989, p. 90) has suggested, arrangements which had the effect of dividing one woman's fertility between two or more men may in reality have been designed to limit the number of legitimate children fathered by individuals, and hence prevent the splitting up of estates (see below, p. 156).

The implication of the ancient descriptions of wife-sharing is that men had absolute control over the process, and that the women were passed around from male to male without being consulted. However, it is possible that male authors have glossed over some of the realities of the system. Assertive Spartan women were perhaps unlikely to have allowed themselves to be used in quite so cursory a fashion, and we can speculate that some of the men who asked a husband's permission to go to bed with his wife had first of all made contact with the woman concerned. It seems probable, at any rate, that there was no strict supervision of women's sexual activities, and that they themselves may have initiated some extramarital liaisons. The frequent absences of their husbands would have made this perfectly feasible; and there is some literary evidence to support the idea. When the ex-king Demaratus cross-questioned his mother about his paternity, he assured her that she would not be the first Spartan wife to have taken a lover – 'many women have done the same' (Herodotus 6.69); and the Athenian general Alcibiades during his sojourn in Sparta is said to have had an affair with the wife of king Agis, Timaea, who was not ashamed to admit to friends and servants the true identity of the father of a child she bore (Plutarch, *Life of Alcibiades* 23.7–9).

Whatever their precise implications for sexual morality, Spartan marriage practices would almost certainly have contributed towards the diminution of the power of the father. When Cartledge (1981, p. 103) states that they formed an element in the effort to devalue family life, he does not go on to point out that this would have applied only to the male role within it and not to that of the female. The mother who had children begotten by more than one father would have been the dominant stable figure in the family, an outcome hinted at by Xenophon when he gives as one motive for the marriage system the fact that some women wished to run two households (*Constitution*

1.9). Even if they were passive pawns in the sexual side of the arrangements, as mothers these women would have been far more prominent. In Hodkinson's words (1989, p. 111), 'the status of the woman was *underlined*, not undermined'.

Ample grounds have already been uncovered for the reputation which Spartan women earned among other Greeks for licentiousness. To these there can be added the fact that Helen, the most famous 'loose' woman of myth, was a Spartan; in Euripides' *Andromache* (595–6) a disapproving elderly man calls her a vile creature, but adds that no Spartan woman could ever be respectable. Female dress was also a contributory factor. Women in Sparta wore the Doric peplos, whose split side allowed freedom of movement, earning for its wearers the epithet 'thigh-showers' (e.g. Ibycus, frag. 58, Page). Myths about the sexual proclivities of foreign females have often been concocted from ingredients less substantial than these.

The dominance of Spartan women over their menfolk is attested by a number of sources. When Agis IV, a reforming Spartan king of the third century BC, was attempting to institute a redistribution of wealth, his mother helped to popularise his ideas by organising a women's conference, for 'the men of Sparta always obeyed their wives, and allowed them to intervene in public affairs more than they themselves were allowed to intervene in private ones' (Plutarch, *Life of Agis* 7.3). In the fourth century BC Aristotle, one of their severest critics, believed that Spartan women were allowed a degree of licence and luxury which was damaging to the aims of the constitution and to the well-being of the state. He clearly attributes the political decline which Sparta experienced in his own lifetime to the influence of females, whose management of affairs could be traced back to the time of the wars fought in the Archaic Age, when the men were away from their homeland for long periods (*Politics* 1269b–1270a). Plutarch informs us that during military campaigns women were given more regard than they should have been and were accorded the title of mistress (*Lycurgus* 14.1). They became too bold, behaving in a masculine fashion even in front of their husbands: not only did they have absolute control over their households, but also in public affairs they expressed their opinions very freely on the most weighty of subjects (*Comparison of Lycurgus and Numa* 3.5).

Whatever the origin of their power, it seems likely that Spartan women's dominant position in domestic matters was fully institutionalised, and that even their 'behind the throne' role in public affairs may have been openly acknowledged. This unusual situation can be attributed to a number of interconnected factors, prominent among which are the female education system, the military way of life imposed on the males, the relatively small age-gap between husbands and wives, and the fact that the family was downgraded as an object of loyalty for men while at the same time being promoted as the locus for the reproduction of the citizen class. To this list there can be added the fact that women in Sparta were owners of landed property.

The Spartan system of land tenure is a subject which has provoked a great deal of debate,[11] but it seems probable that by the fifth century BC most land was in private ownership. Aristotle (*Politics* 1270a) identifies the unevenness of the distribution of private property as one of the basic weaknesses of Spartan society, and singles out for particular criticism the fact that by his time almost two-fifths of the land was owned by women. He gives two causes for this: there were many heiresses (*epiklēroi*), and no restrictions about who might receive them in marriage; and dowries were very large. Although the rules of inheritance are far from clear, it seems likely that a Spartan woman was capable even if she had brothers, of inheriting a share of the family estate – perhaps half of the portion which was due to a son, as in Gortyn (see below, p. 159). If she had no natural or adopted brother, then she probably inherited the whole estate, and was not, if betrothed by her father prior to his death, obliged to marry the next-of-kin.[12] Spartan heiresses seem to have had the right to dispose of their own property: Plutarch reports that in the third century BC king Agis IV as part of his reform programme asked rich women, including his own mother and grandmother, to give up their wealth (*Agis* 4.1, 7.1–7); his mother, we are told, was rich enough to lend money to many people (*Agis* 6.7).

There is some uncertainty about the dowries mentioned by Aristotle. According to Plutarch (*Moralia* 227f), the Spartan lawgiver had legislated against dowries, believing that character rather than wealth should determine the choice of a bride. It is possible, as MacDowell suggests (1986, p.82), that a law forbidding the payment of dowries by contractual agreement was circumvented by wealthy men who gave large informal gifts of landed property and moveables to their daughters on marriage. Alternatively, it may have been the practice in Sparta, as in Gortyn, to give a daughter her share of the family estate on marriage, as a 'pre-death inheritance' (Hodkinson, 1989, p. 82). If this were the case, then Aristotle, in his statement about 'heiresses' and 'dowries', could have been referring, somewhat inaccurately, to two different types of female inheritance, one where the daughter inherited the entire estate, and one where she received a share of it on marriage.

Whatever the precise workings of the system, there can be no doubt that by Aristotle's time Spartan women were substantial owners of property, and that this was linked in some way with the drastic decline in the number of male citizens which occurred in the late fifth and early fourth centuries BC. By the third century, according to Plutarch (*Agis* 7.4–5), the greatest part of the land was in the ownership of women, and some of these intrigued against king Agis because his proposed redistribution of property would have deprived them of the wealth on which their power was based.

Hodkinson (1989) has argued that women's property rights may have been associated with short-term instability, in that land was constantly being reallocated from one lineage to another (since daughters were inheriting from both their fathers and their mothers, and were passing property on to children whose fathers may have been from another lineage), and estates were subject to greater division on death (since daughters as well as sons were inheriting). He believes that marriage arrangements such as polyandry would have helped, from the standpoint of individual families, to reduce these difficulties by limiting the number of heirs, and that practices such as close-kin marriages and the relatively age of marriage for women would have contributed to the same end. If enough households were engaging in these practices, they would have led to concentrations of property, and to a reduction in the number of citizens. The threat of declining citizen numbers would have become apparent by the late fifth century; but prominent wealthy Spartans would have had a vested interest in maintaining the status quo. One additional reason, Hodkinson suggests, why no radical measures were introduced to solve the problem may have been the influence of wealthy married women, who were concerned to promote the economic interests of their own children. By the third century the situation had reached crisis proportions; but although some notable royal women are said to have helped to promote reforms (see Plutarch, *Agis*, 6.7, and *Cleomenes* 1.3, 6.2), others, according to Plutarch, were reluctant to surrender the influence which their wealth had brought them (*Agis* 7.5–7).

One fundamental issue relating to the role of Spartan women centres on the question of whether they had been liberated from personal dominance by their husbands only in order to be subordinated to the all-embracing interests of the state. There can be little doubt that, in Sparta's state ideology, considerable stress was placed on the child-bearing function of women. According to Xenophon, the Spartan lawgiver believed that 'child-bearing was the most important activity of freeborn women' (*Constitution* 1.4); and the attention paid to the physical fitness of females was said to have been motivated by the conviction that this would promote the production of strong, healthy off-spring.

Spartan women themselves may have been among the most vocal mouthpieces of this ideology. A section of Plutarch's work devoted to the sayings of Spartan females is dominated by fervent pronouncements about their sons. One of the speakers, when asked by a woman from Attica why Spartan women were the only ones who dominated men replied, 'Because we are the only women that give birth to men' (*Moralia* 240e, 6). Their pride in their sons seems to have been closely bound up with their enthusiastic espousal of Sparta's military ethos. Probably the most famous of these pronouncements is the one attributed to a woman who hands her son his shield as he goes off to war and tells him to come back 'either with it or upon it' (241f, 16). A glorious death in battle, if the sayings can be believed, was what every devoted Spartan mother dreamed of for her son: 'I bore him so that he might die for Sparta, and now my wishes are fulfilled' (241c, 8). Cowardice could provoke a mother into a dreadful humiliation of her son. One unfortunate man, on returning from the war, was asked by his mother 'How does our country fare?'. When he replied that all had perished, she hurled a tile at him and said, 'So they sent you to bring us the bad news!' (241b, 5). Some women, we are told, went so far as to kill their sons when they had been disgraced, and were highly honoured for the deed.

These sayings make chilling reading. If they are at all representative of Spartan womanhood,[13] they suggest that females in Sparta were so thoroughly indoctrinated that they formed an effective branch of a state propaganda machine. They also reveal the existence of an emotional bond between mothers and sons involving a high degree of tension. As Kunstler (1987, pp. 35–6) has argued, the dominance of the mother in a boy's early years, followed by the abrupt and total severance of their relations when he was sent off to barracks, was bound to have had what appears to us to be a very damaging effect on the emotional development of both parties.

The picture of Spartan females which emerges from our sources is a paradoxical one. These women were independent, powerful and outspoken, and could earn for them-selves among outsiders a reputation for promiscuity and lack of restraint. At the same time they occupied an integral place in Spartan society as a whole, and were absorbed into a state-controlled apparatus for breeding the next generation of warriors. There is no need for modern critics to decide which of these pictures is 'true'. The interaction between private and public life would have created for women an institutionalised position that in some senses liberated and in others constrained them. As Hodkinson has pointed out (1989, p. 112), in the last Archaic and early Classical periods there was probably an identity of purpose between the state and the female-influenced household. But in the later fifth century this identity of purpose may have been weakened by the growing importance of wealth and the increasing proportion of it which was controlled by women. The result would have been that, as far as wealthy women were concerned, the balance was tipped away from constraint and towards liberation.

Nor is there any need for modern women to pass a final judgement on whether the

Spartan system was 'good' or 'bad' for females. As Cartledge has remarked (1981, p. 105), they are not likely to be impressed by the emphasis on the child-bearing function, but they will nevertheless appreciate the fact that the peculiarities of Spartan society had ensured that this role was one that carried a high status and a large degree of acknowledged domestic power. It should not be forgotten that this unusual system was dependent on the subordination of a majority of the population, the Helots, roughly half of whom were women. It was also a system whose internal contradictions meant that it was inevitably short-lived.

THE WOMEN OF GORTYN

Like the Spartans, members of the Cretan ruling class were of Dorian stock, and ruled over a much larger native population of serfs who were responsible for cultivating the land. In Crete, as in Sparta, the education system was designed to produce military efficiency, and as far as men were concerned family life was downgraded. At about the age of sixteen boys were enrolled in 'troops', presumably for purposes of military training, and prior to that they seem to have lived communally. All adult citizens belonged to men's clubs to which they were admitted when they left their 'troops'.

The Cretans were renowned among other Greeks for their system of law, and in Gortyn, a town in the southern part of the island, inscriptions have been found recording the most complete law-code to have survived from ancient Greece. The code probably belongs to the fifth century BC, but it represents a revision of previous enactments and customary law dating from the Archaic period or earlier. While not, of course, providing a fully-rounded account of the role of women in Gortyn, it does furnish us with details of a legal framework which, while it incorporated features comparable with ones that existed in both the Spartan and Athenian systems, was nevertheless distinct from both.

Much valuable information about the serf class is derived from the code. A serf could both marry and divorce, and the wife of a serf could possess her own property, in the form of moveables and livestock, which reverted to her in the event of a divorce. When a woman married she came under her husband's master; if there was a divorce she returned either to her former master or to his relatives. A master had a right to any child whose parents were both serfs.

It would be going too far to say that the regulations relating to citizen women were more enlightened than those in Athens, since they were certainly not framed with a view to the well-being of the female population. They may reflect a situation in which power was being transferred to the *oikos* from the wider kinship group, but the process was not yet complete, and consequently a woman was not subordinated to the interests of the *oikos* to the same extent as her counterpart in Athens. Her inheritance rights can perhaps be seen as a survival from a time when the tribal structure had predominated.[14]

In Gortyn the daughter of a man who had died without sons (the equivalent of the Athenian *epikleros*) was known as a *patroiokos*. She could be married at the age of twelve, suggesting that here too her primary task was that of producing an heir. She could be claimed in the first instance by her paternal uncles, and then by her paternal cousins, in order of age. However, if none of the eligible candidates wished to marry her, or if none existed, or if she herself were unwilling to marry the claimant, then she was free to marry 'any she likes of the tribe from among those who apply', although she had to surrender a half of her inheritance to the first claimant whom she herself had turned down. The remnants of a customary rule of tribal endogamy (marriage within the tribe) seem to have been preserved within this system, but it had given way in part to measures which ensured the preservation of the individual *oikos*. It may still have been the custom in the fifth century for women who were not heiresses to marry within the tribe.

A daughter also inherited property, in the form of land, livestock or money, even when she had a brother, but her share was smaller; she received half as much as a son's portion, with houses and large animals being excluded from the reckoning. Like her brother, she inherited from both her father and her mother. But it should be noted that there seem to have been no dowries in Gortyn. A father could make a gift to his daughter on marriage, but only within the prescribed limits of her share of the inheritance; this seems to mean that the gifts were a form of anticipated inheritance, and were not additional to anything to which she might be entitled when her parents died. In Athens the dowry was the medium through which a share in the paternal property was transmitted to a daughter, and since its size was within a father's discretion it could in theory have amounted to a larger proportion of the estate than was stipulated under the Gortynian code. In most cases, however, it seems to have been less (see p. 115), and in the majority of cases it consisted of money rather than land.[15]

In Gortyn a husband and wife shared the income from their joint estates, but the woman retained control of her own property and her husband could not sell or mortgage it. Stiff penalties were imposed on a husband or son who disposed of a wife's or mother's property. When a man died and there were children, his widow could remarry if she wished to, taking her own property with her and anything she had received by way of gift from her husband. A childless widow kept her own property, a half of what she had 'woven' and also a portion of any produce in the house, the rest going to her husband's heir (it is assumed that in the case of a widow with children all the woven material and the produce went to the children). A divorced wife was in a slightly less favourable position; she took her own property, half of what she had woven, and a half of the produce from her own property only. Either party had the right to initiate a divorce: if the husband was responsible he paid a modest amount of financial compensation to his wife.

Adultery and rape were not treated as public offences but as matters calling for private monetary compensation. The scale of compensation was generally the same for both, but in the case of adultery the amount was doubled if the deed had taken place in the home of the woman's father, brother or husband. There was no penalty for adultery between a free man and a non-free woman.

The age at which girls who were not heiresses were normally married is not known. According to the fourth-century historian Ephorus (in Strabo 10.4.20), men in Crete were obliged to marry at the time when they left the 'troops', but they did not live with their wives straight away. The reference in the Gortyn code to adultery taking place in a father's house suggests that it may have been usual for girls to remain with their families when they were first married. Ephorus says that Cretan brides moved into their husband's houses when they were capable of managing an *oikos*, which may indicate that they were fairly young when they married.

14

Women and religion

Religion in ancient Greece was practised in a number of different contexts, ranging from the private rituals which were an everyday feature of the life of the *oikos*, to the great public occasions of the state-organised festivals. *Oikos* and *polis* were linked together by a common thread of religious observance, and women participated fully in the rites that were performed on both these levels. The role which they played in maintaining the cohesion and stability of the family made them indispensable co-operators in its ritual activities, and this role was carried through into the sacred practices that helped to bind the community together. Religion was the one area of public life in which women played an acknowledged part.

Among religious officials, a broad distinction can be made between the people who performed subordinate ritual tasks, and the priest or priestess who supervised a particular cult and offered sacrifices and prayers to the deity whom it honoured. Among the former, the sex of the official was normally determined by the nature of the task performed. The assistants who slaughtered a sacrificial animal, for example, would normally have been male; whereas the weaving of a garment to be offered to a deity was always undertaken by females. As for priests and priestesses, the general rule was that men officiated in the cults of male deities, and women in those of females.

There were, however, a number of exceptions to this rule.[1] Two prominent instances of priestesses assigned to male deities occurred at Dodona and Delphi, oracular shrines where answers to queries addressed to a god were transmitted via a female agent. In both of these sanctuaries the priestesses were non-fertile and celibate. Although life-long celibacy was not a condition commonly imposed by Greek religion, as a temporary state it seems to have been considered important when a human female was called upon to act as the mouthpiece for a god. As a woman, the priestess was available for entry by a male deity; as a woman who had no sexual relations with a mortal man, she was reserving herself for the god alone. Dodona, in north-west Greece, was an oracle of Zeus, and in the Classical period enquiries were presented to the god in writing, scratched on to a lead

27 Bronze statuette of a girl runner, from Albania, *c.*560 BC.

28 A woman taking offerings to a tomb. Athenian white-ground lekythos by the Bosanquet painter, *c.*440 BC.

29 Maenad and satyr. Athenian red-figure amphora by the Kleophrades painter, *c.*490 BC.

32 Central figures from the east pediment of the temple of Zeus at Olympia.
Left to right: Sterope, Oenomaus, Zeus, Pelops, Hippodamia. *c.*460 BC.

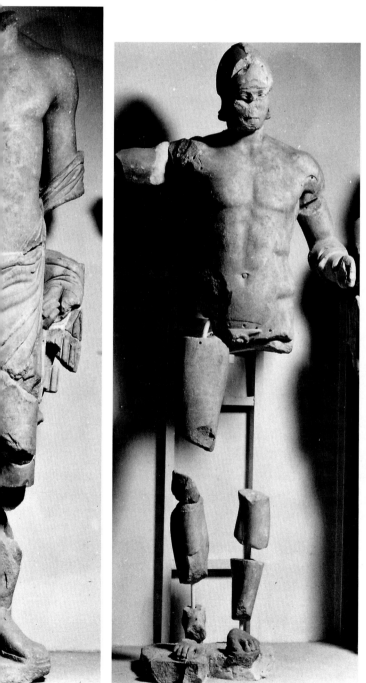

33 Lapiths versus Centaurs: frieze from the temple of Apollo at Bassae, *c.*425 BC.

34 LEFT Bronze statuette of Athena, from the Acropolis, Athens. Early fifth century BC.

35 RIGHT Bronze statuette of Zeus with his thunderbolt, from Dodona, *c*.470 BC.

36 Sculptures from the east pediment of the Parthenon, 430s BC. The central scene of the birth of Athena (sculptures missing) is witnessed by a group of deities. On the far left, horses from the chariot of the sun-god; on the far right, one from the chariot of the moon-goddess.

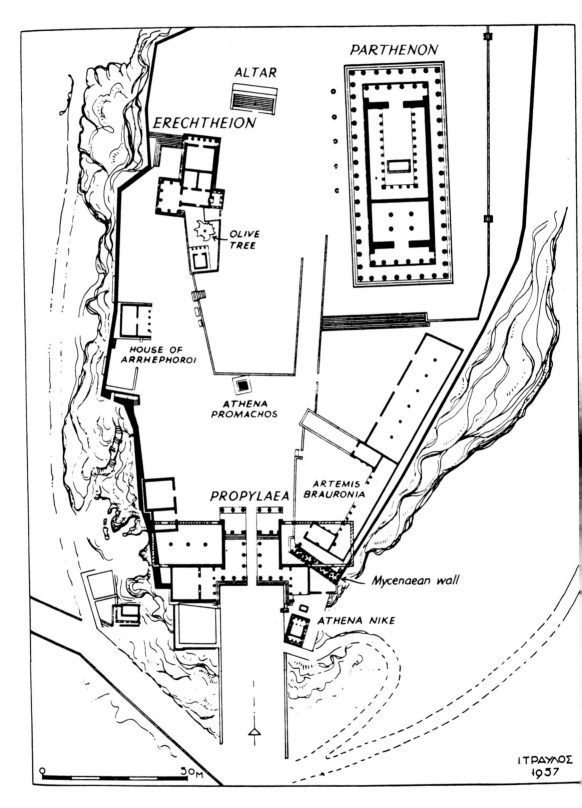

PARTHENON

ALTAR

ERECHTHEION

OLIVE
TREE

HOUSE OF
ARRHEPHOROI

ATHENA
PROMACHOS

PROPYLAEA

ARTEMIS
BRAURONIA

Mycenaean wall

ATHENA NIKE

Ι.ΤΡΑΥΛΟΣ
1957

0   30M

37a Plan of the Athenian Acropolis, showing the position of the Parthenon and Erechtheion (Erechtheum).

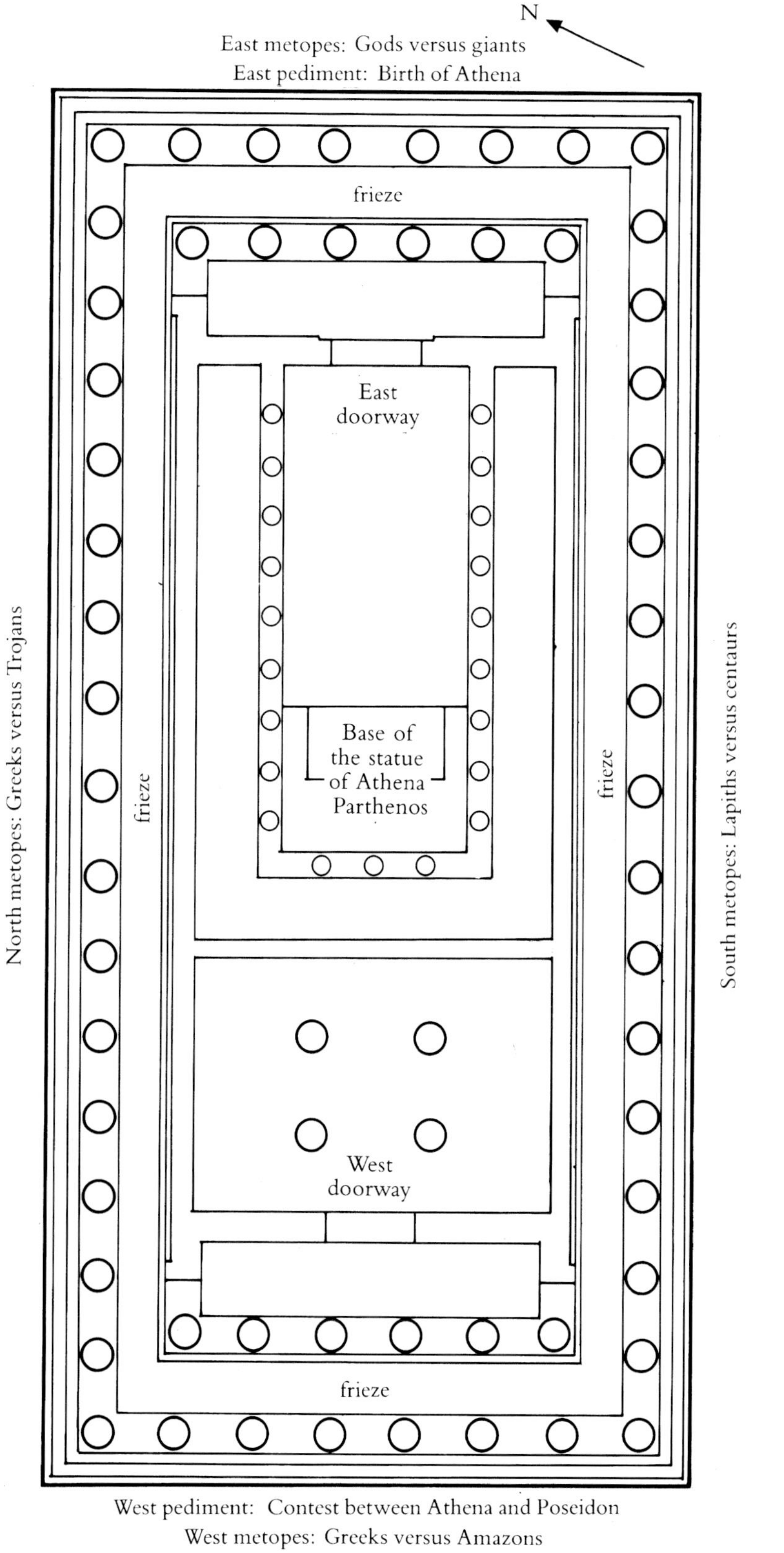

N

East metopes: Gods versus giants
East pediment: Birth of Athena

frieze

East
doorway

Base of
the statue
of Athena
Parthenos

North metopes: Greeks versus Trojans

frieze

South metopes: Lapiths versus centaurs

frieze

West
doorway

frieze

West pediment: Contest between Athena and Poseidon
West metopes: Greeks versus Amazons

37b Plan of the Parthenon showing the position of the pediment sculptures, the metopes and the frieze.

38 'Varvakeion' Athena: a Roman copy of the Athena Parthenos statue.

39 Women in the Panathenaic procession, from the east section of the Parthenon frieze: slab VIII, *c.*440 BC.

40 The 'Ludovisi throne', *c.*460 BC.

41 A nymph from the
Nereid monument, at
Xanthus in Lycia, *c.*400 BC.

42 'Aphrodite' from the east
pediment sculptures of the
Parthenon, 430s BC.

43 Nike untying her sandal, from the parapet of the temple of Athena Nike, Acropolis, Athens, c.410 BC.

44 Venus Genetrix. A Roman copy of a Greek original, perhaps of the fifth century BC.

45 Aphrodite of Cnidus. A Roman copy of Praxitiles' original, c.340 BC.

strip which was then placed in a jar. The priestess, who was an elderly woman, probably extracted the question from the jar along with a symbol which indicated whether the answer was 'yes' or 'no'.

At Delphi, a sanctuary of Apollo which in the Classical Age was the most important of the Greek oracular shrines, the god's possession of the priestess was more dramatic and obvious. Here the method of divination was inspirational: the priestess, who was called the Pythia, went into a trance, and the words which she uttered while in this state were thought to be those of Apollo himself, speaking through her person. According to one writer (Diodorus Siculus 16.26.6), the Pythia had at one time been a young virgin; but by the fifth century she was a woman of at least fifty years of age, who in memory of the earlier custom wore a girl's dress, a garb which would have emphasised her asexuality. Women who had been wives and mothers were not disqualified, but after their appointment they had to cease living with their husbands, if they were still alive, and take up residence in the sanctuary. The method of selecting priestesses is unknown, but writers of the Roman era stress that they were simple peasant women; they were not chosen from a special family or given any particular course of training.[2] In the Classical Age, when the shrine was very busy, there were as many as three Pythias at a time, working on a shift system. These women seem on the face of it to have been invested with considerable political authority, for Delphi was often consulted by representatives of Greek states on matters of the highest public importance. Nowadays it is hard to believe that the Pythia was not being manipulated in some way by the administrators of the shrine, but nothing is known of the process by which Delphic policy was shaped or communicated to the elderly woman who was its mouthpiece.

In Classical Athens, where the position of priestess was the only public office that could be held by a woman, more than forty major cults had priestesses attached to them.[3] Prominent among these was the priestess of Athena Polias, the city's patron deity. This post was always occupied by a female member of the aristocratic clan of the Eteobutadae, who claimed to be descendants of the original royal family of Athens. The priestess officiated at many religious rites and celebrations, including the Great Panathenaea, the most important of the state festivals (see p. 26 and Fig. 1). The fact that she was the only respectable Athenian woman who could be referred to by her personal name in public is indicative of her quasi-masculine status. On occasions she seems to have exerted political influence; in 480 BC, for example, when the Persian army was advancing on Athens, the priestess's announcement that the cake offered to the sacred snake on the Acropolis had been left untouched helped to determine the decision to evacuate the city (Herodotus 8.41).

All Greek women, whether free or slaves, were eligible for initiation into the Eleusinian Mysteries (see p. 43). The administration and conduct of the Mysteries were dominated by male officials, but the chief priest (or *hierophantes*) was assisted in the initiation ritual by two priestesses, the *hierophantides*. The chief priestess of Demeter at Eleusis, who came from one of the local aristocratic families, was also present at the initiation, and seems to have had a starring role in the ritual enactment of the myth. Like the *hierophantides*, she held her office for life, and the significance of her position was acknowledged in the public records of Eleusis, where events were dated by the name of the priestess and the year of her tenure in which they occurred.[4]

In Athens there was one important ritual role for which a woman qualified by virtue of her husband's office. The Basilinna (or Queen), wife of the Archon Basileus (or King Archon), an annually selected magistrate, presided with her husband at the spring festival of Dionysus known as the Anthesteria. On the second day of the festival she performed a ritual which involved making secret offerings to the god on behalf of the city (Demosthenes 59.73–9). Later on the same day she was 'married' to Dionysus, and was joined with him in a sacred union. No details of this rite are recorded, but it may have included an enactment of sexual intercourse in which the Archon Basileus was dressed up as the god Dionysus.

The performance of services on behalf of the dead continued to be an important aspect of women's religious activities in the Classical as in the Archaic Age (see p. 72–3). In the funerary scenes depicted in Classical vase paintings, women predominate and are shown engaged in the rituals carried out both before and after the interment of the body. They are seen washing, anointing and dressing the corpse. At the *prothesis*, the formal laying out, the chief female mourner is generally represented clasping the head of the dead person in both hands, while others stand beside the bier with arms raised, tearing their hair or striking their heads and breasts. Women also appear far more frequently than men as the bearers of offerings of food, wine, oil and garlands to tombs (Fig. 28), which suggests that the duties owed to the dead during the period of mourning and at certain annual festivals fell largely to the females of the family.

In the Classical Age, however, there were a number of states where the role played by women at funerals had become somewhat circumscribed as a result of restrictive legislation. The earliest laws on which we have detailed information are those introduced in Athens in the late Archaic period by the lawgiver Solon. In accordance with these, the laying out of the body had to take place inside the house, and the procession to the cemetery had to be conducted before dawn. Only women who were close relatives or who were aged at least sixty could attend the laying out, take part in the funeral procession, and enter the house of the dead person after the funeral. Lacerations and the singing of specially-composed laments were forbidden. Women were not allowed to visit the tombs of people to whom they were not related, except at the time of interment; and limits were placed on the quantity of offerings which could be presented at the tomb.[5] Similar legislation was enacted at Delphi, at Iulis, on the island of Ceos and elsewhere in the course of the sixth and fifth centuries BC.[6]

The legislators who introduced measures such as these may have been motivated chiefly by the desire to curb ostentatious display at funerals and hence limit the opportunities for self-aggrandisement available to aristocratic families. But, whether intentionally or otherwise, the laws also had the effect of curtailing one of the few areas of activity which brought social prominence to women. Funerals, as well as providing women with an emotional outlet, also presented them with an arena in which they could demonstrate the public significance of their domestic concerns. In partially privatising these ceremonies, the legislators may have been seeking to control an element within society which was seen as representing a focus of resistance to the new political order. As Alexiou (1974, pp. 21–2) has pointed out, their role in funerary ritual gave women in the Archaic period an important position in the religious and social life of the aristocracy, and blood feuds between rival clans may sometimes have been fuelled by calls for revenge included in their lamentations. A literary example of this theme is to be found in Aeschylus's *Libation Bearers* (306–478), where, in a long lament sung at the tomb of Agamemnon, Electra and the female chorus with steadily mounting intensity spur Orestes on to avenge the murder of his father.

The increasing emphasis in the late Archaic Age on the institutions of the *polis*, and on the role of the nuclear family as its fundamental social unit, may well have produced a desire to limit the power of women in an area of religious activity which gave prominence to aristocratic kinship interests. But legislation had the effect of toning down rather than abolishing altogether women's participation in funerary rites. In a city such as Athens, where in the course of the fifth century the impulse towards revenge was to a large extent successfully subsumed within the judicial system of the democratic *polis*, there was probably a significant though gradual change in the function of funerary practices. But, as Alexiou (1974, p. 23) has suggested, there would have been some more remote areas where restrictive legislation failed to penetrate, and where women at funerals continued to give voice to traditional concerns.

In Athens and in other Greek states, women were active as worshippers in a large proportion of public cults, and their performance of subordinate ritual tasks commenced when they were still quite young (see pp. 134–5). Religion was the one area of activity where a section of the population that had been ideologically confined to the private sphere was allowed to emerge into public prominence. Superficially, this anomaly can be explained by the fact that the Greek pantheon included female deities who had to be served by women. More fundamentally, the role accorded both to the goddesses and to their women worshippers can be seen to entail an acknowledgement of the social significance of the female principle. Religion was a dangerous area for men, for it involved demonstrations of female power on both the divine and human levels. Through their mythological construction of the goddesses they sought to contain and control that power in its divine dimensions (see Chapter 3). The complexity of the religious response to the power possessed by real women can be illustrated by focusing on two very different examples of women's rites – the festival of the Thesmophoria and the ecstatic cult of Dionysus.

THE THESMOPHORIA

The festival of the Thesmophoria was celebrated in many parts of the Greek world in honour of Demeter, goddess of corn and cultivation (see pp. 40–3). It took place in October/November, shortly before the planting of the seed-corn. Unlike the Adonia (see pp. 37–8) and the women's rites of Dionysus, it occupied a central place in the state religion; and whereas men were occasionally admitted to the ranks of the women worshipping Adonis and Dionysus, in the case of the Thesmophoria they were rigorously excluded. This sexual taboo, which was not a particularly common one in Greek religion,[7] provides Aristophanes with the plot for his comedy *The Thesmophoriazusae* ('Women celebrating the Thesmophoria'). The tragedian Euripides has heard that in the course of the Thesmophoria the women of Athens are going to condemn him to death for the way in which he slanders them in his work. He persuades an elderly relative, Mnesilochus, to infiltrate the festival disguised as a woman and speak in his defence. Even on the level of fantasy, such an infringement of the taboo cannot be allowed to go unpunished, and Mnesilochus is eventually uncovered (quite literally), and made to suffer the humiliation of being tied to a plank and exposed to public gaze still wearing his yellow dress.

In Athens, the Thesmophoria lasted for three days, and seems to have been limited to the wives of Athenian citizens. The site for the festival was somewhere on the Pnyx Hill, where the Assembly of citizens, the central institution of Athenian democracy, also met. The women slept there in makeshift huts during the period of the celebration. As Burkert (1985, p. 242) points out, for many this would probably have been their only opportunity to spend some time away from their homes and families. On the first day of the festival, which was called the *Anodos* (or 'Way up'), a procession of women carrying sacred objects wound its way up the hill to the festival site. On the second day, called the *Nesteia* or 'Fast', no solid food was consumed, and the women sat on the ground on withies and other plants. In these rituals they were probably re-enacting the grief of Demeter at the loss of her daughter Persephone. But a later writer, Diodorus, tells us that the women were seeking in this way to 'imitate the ancient way of life' (5.4.7), so that there may also have been an allusion to the primitive condition of society prior to the discovery of agriculture. The final day of the festival, called the *Kalligeneia* or 'Bearer of beautiful offspring', was a time of joy, when the women celebrated with sacrifices and feasts the fertility ensured to them by Demeter.

This, in broad outline, was the Thesmophoria's programme of events. But the rites performed there, referred to as 'women's mysteries', were evidently meant to be kept secret; and for this reason it is unclear on what day the most important ritual took place. At some time prior to the celebration – exactly when is not certain[8] – piglets and phallic cakes had been deposited in underground caverns or chambers on the site. In the course of the festival, women called *Antletriae*, or 'Bailers', who had remained chaste for three days, descended into the chambers and brought up the rotting remains. These were then placed on altars, and were later mixed with the seed-corn before it was planted. It was believed that in this way the fertility of the crops would be promoted.[9]

This ritual may on one level have preserved a memory of the prehistoric use of compost. But it undoubtedly carried a symbolic significance as well. Persephone's descent into the Underworld and her subsequent resurrection were mirrored, in the ritual, by the transfer into and out of the ground of material which, though decaying itself, would nevertheless foster new growth. Piglets were included among this material because they symbolised fertility, an association presumably inspired by pigs' prolific breeding habits. But the fact that the word for piglet, *choiros*, could also be used as a slang word for a vagina adds another layer of meaning;[10] the combination of piglets and phallic cakes may signify a coming together of the human sex organs. This suggests that human reproduction was seen both as a parallel with the germination of corn and, to judge by the name given to the last day of the festival, as an objective of the ritual.[11]

As a major state festival, the Thesmophoria was accorded a high degree of official encouragement. In Athens, husbands were required to pay the expenses incurred by their wives in the course of the celebration (Isaeus 3.80), while the location of the festival site close to the men's place of assembly indicates that the Thesmophoria was seen as a comparable institution, central to the well-being of the state. While it was being conducted, any Assembly meeting that needed to be held took place in the theatre rather than on the Pnyx. For this short period, the men were displaced, and the women took over their position at the core of the city's civic life. One can easily imagine that men might for this reason see the Thesmophoria as something of a threat. This is borne out by some of the mythology surrounding the festival. Battus, the legendary king of Cyrene in Libya, was said to have been castrated by women celebrating the Thesmophoria when he tried to spy on their activities (Aelian, fragment 44); and Aristomenes of Messenia, who on one occasion came too close to the celebrations, was taken prisoner by women brandishing sacrificial implements and torches (Pausanias, 4.17.1). The threat posed to the life of Euripides by the female worshippers in Aristophanes' *Thesmophoriazusae* reveals, on the level of conscious fantasy, a similar paranoia concerning the implications of this women-only event.

Modern interpretations of the festival's significance display a marked degree of ambivalence. Some critics have seen it as a manifestation of a male attempt to control women's fertility. Golden (1988) suggests that the symbolism of the pig, an animal which in ancient Greece was to be found in both a wild and a domesticated condition, may denote a ritual taming of women's sexual organs, which must be brought into an institutionalised setting before they can yield beneficial increase. For Detienne (1989, p. 129), the Thesmophoria expresses 'the contradictions within a society and system of thought that deliberately relegates the female sex to the periphery of the politico-religious space but finds itself led, by certain limitations inherent in its own values, to give women a determining role in the reproduction of the entire system'.

These contradictions are apparent also to Zeitlin (1982, p. 149) when she comments on the conjunction of chastity and obscenity inherent in the rituals. The theme of chastity emerges in the stipulation of three days' purity for the 'Bailers', and in the fact that the plants on which the women sat on the second day of the festival were believed to repress sexual appetite (Aelian 9.26). But the piglets and phallic cakes represent an element of obscenity, and this emerges even more strikingly in the ritual utterance of obscene words by the women, an event that occurred at some stage in the celebrations (Diodorus 5.4.7). For Zeitlin, this paradox expresses the 'double bind' which 'demands chastity from the wife and yet insists on her sexual nature'. The Thesmophoria recognised the importance of women's sexuality, but at the same time placed limits on its exercise.[12]

Interpretations such as these accurately reflect the official nature of the festival. The Thesmophoria did not, like the Adonia or the rites of Dionysus, offer women a rare opportunity to break out of the social constraints imposed upon them and give vent to strong emotions of grief and rapture. The emphasis was instead on their role within the community. But the sense of identity and power which they may have derived from this should not be overlooked. Zeitlin recognises that, in spite of its intimations of male control, the ritual and its associated narrative were 'equivalent to the initiation of the female into her own interior space, into the mysteries of female life in which Demeter and the women of the Thesmophoria take part' (1982, p. 144). For Burkert (1985, p. 245), the festival permitted, 'once in the year at least', the establishment of a society of women through which they were able to demonstrate their independence and responsibility. The notion of the Thesmophoria as a piece of female counter-culture emerges most clearly, in ancient literature, in the male perception of threat. In modern works, it is best expressed by Winkler when he draws our attention to the possibility that 'women saw in their religious actions involving grain and sprouts a celebration of their female power over life and sexuality within the peripheral and annoying constraints of male pretensions' (1990, p. 189).

WOMEN WORSHIPPERS OF DIONYSUS

Dionysus, the god of wine and drama, represented above all the principle of transcendence. Through wine-drinking, through theatre and its masks and through ecstatic religious worship, human beings experienced a power which caused them to surrender their normal identities and understandings. Evidence exists which indicates that the worship of Dionysus had been established in Greece as far back as the Bronze Age; and myths which stress his 'foreignness', picturing him as an exotic and orientalised deity who had newly arrived in Greece, can perhaps best be interpreted as symbolising the god's otherness, his ability to transform human consciousness. They do not necessarily tell us anything about his historical origins.[13]

The motifs of resistance and madness which are a feature of many of the myths probably carry a similar psychological import. The most celebrated of these stories is preserved in Euripides' play the *Bacchae*, which opens with a speech in which Dionysus explains that he is a child of Zeus and a princess of Thebes named Semele, who died on the day he was born. After travelling through Asia and winning many followers, he has returned to his birthplace. He has chosen this as the first Greek city to receive his cult because he wishes to vindicate his mother and punish her sisters for their refusal to accept his divine paternity. The sisters have been driven mad, and with the entire female population of the city have rushed out on to the mountainside to celebrate the mysteries of the god whom hitherto they have rejected. The play culminates in the horrific dismemberment of the king Pentheus, an enemy of the new cult, by a band of women led by Semele's sister Agave, who is Pentheus's own mother.

Several of these narrative features are repeated in the story of the daughters of Minyas, legendary king of Orchomenus, who had refused to take part in Dionysus' rites. When the god made his presence felt by causing ivy and vine tendrils to sprout from their looms and serpents to appear in their wool-baskets, one of the sisters, Leucippe, surrendered her son for sacrifice, and the women ran off to join the other worshippers on the mountain (Aelian, *Var.Hist.* 3.42). Myths such as these seems to describe the dangerous level of possession which can afflict those people who attempt to deny the power of the god. More specifically, it is through his effect on women that Dionysus' terrifying ability to overturn the normal order of things is demonstrated. The beings whose incorporation into the civilised state is signified by their dual role as workers at the loom and loving mothers can, under the influence of an angry god, be transformed into vicious murderers of their own offspring and haunters of the wild countryside beyond the city's boundaries.

On some levels, Dionysus held a separate appeal for males and females. It was through his patronage of wine-drinking that he was most clearly distinguished as a god of masculine concerns. Wine was certainly not forbidden to Greek women, but its consumption was not encouraged (Aelian *Var.Hist.* 2.38, Athenaeus 429a–b, 440f–442a). It was seen primarily as a man's drink, and was an important accompaniment of social interaction: among upper-class males the symposium or drinking party was a vital arena for the formation and conduct of political friendships. In Athens the second day of the Anthesteria, a spring festival of Dionysus, was devoted to a drinking contest in which the new wine was tested; male citizens, slaves, and boys who had reached the age of three were eligible to attend, but there is no indication in any of the sources that citizen women were present on this occasion, although they took part in other festival events.

It was in the ecstatic rites of Dionysus that women emerged into prominence. These cult practices can be distinguished both from the masculine rituals of the god and from the women-only festivals of Demeter, in that they took place beyond the confines of the organised state religion, and were apparently regarded with considerable suspicion by some members of the male population. The participants were known as Maenads (*mainades* or 'mad women'), a word which signifies possession by a god but which at the same time carries derogatory connotations, implying masculine disapproval of un-controlled female behaviour. During the Classical Age there appear to have been very few male adherents of these rites.

However, the number of women involved can never have been very large, since the rites were not celebrated in every part of Greece. Maenadism is known to have been practised in Boeotia, at Delphi (where the worshippers were known as Thyiades), in certain cities of Asia Minor,[14] and in some areas of the Peloponnese. There is little evidence to indicate the existence of the cult in Classical Athens, although the large number of Maenads depicted on drinking vessels and the focus placed upon their activities by Euripides would certainly seem to suggest that the phenomenon excited a high degree of interest. The cult of the Thraco-Phrygian god Sabazius, which was in many respects very similar to that of Dionysus, had been established in the city by the mid-fourth century BC (Demosthenes, *On the Crown* 259–60), and it is by no means impossible that Dionysus too was being worshipped ecstatically by small groups of women.[15] Pausanias, writing in the second century AD, refers to parties of Athenian women whom he calls Thyiades 'who go every other year with the Delphian women to Mount Parnassus and there celebrate the rites of Dionysus' (10.4.2); and in speaking of the dances which these worshippers perform at fixed stages on the route from Athens to Delphi he implies that the custom was a long-established one. It may have already been a feature of religious worship in the fifth century BC.

There is very little reliable evidence for the activities of Maenads during the Classical Age. Euripides' *Bacchae*, produced in about 405 BC, is by far the most detailed source, but the play has a substantial mythological content which makes the task of extracting hard data on contemporary cult practice a very difficult one. The rites, moreover, were secret, and it is more than likely that a good deal of male fantasy had collected around them. Apart from the *Bacchae*, vase paintings of the sixth and fifth centuries constitute our most significant source. But here the Maenads are often shown mingling with Satyrs, the part-human, part-animal creatures who in myth are the companions of Dionysus' revels, which suggests that like the *Bacchae* these visual accounts are in some respects highly imaginative. The notion of the exuberant and unrestrained female, so graphically expressed in some of these paintings, is one that has always had an erotic appeal for the male imagination, and may have prompted some of the more highly-coloured renderings.

The *Bacchae*'s most circumstantial account of Maenadic practices is to be found in a report delivered to King Pentheus by a herdsman who has witnessed the activities of the Theban women in the mountains (664–774). He insists that the Maenads had not been drinking or engaging in illicit sexual activity; but their appearance was unusual, for their hair was loose, they wore fawnskins and garlands of leaves, and were wreathed in snakes that licked their cheeks. Some of the women who had left newborn children at home carried young gazelles or wolf cubs which they fed at their own breasts. By wielding their *thyrsoi* (their sacred wands) they could produce from the ground streams of water, wine, milk or honey. As soon as the Maenads realised that they were being spied on by the herdsman and his companions, they raced away, and began tearing apart grazing cattle with their bare hands, and stripping the flesh from their bones. Then like a force of enemy soldiers they fell on two local villages and looted them. They bore away the booty on their shoulders, and could even carry fire on their heads without burning their hair. When attacked by the outraged inhabitants they easily put them to flight, for the spears thrown by the villagers drew no blood, while their own *thyrsoi* inflicted savage wounds.

Some of the items in this account are attested by other sources and can probably be accepted as genuine features of Maenadic worship. Animal skins and *thyrsoi*, ritual chants and frenzied dancing to the music of drums and flutes (thrillingly evoked in one of the choral odes of the *Bacchae*, lines 152–69) were doubtless all common elements. Snake-handling is more dubious, since it is ignored by most of the literary sources, although it features in a number of the vase paintings, and according to Demosthenes (*On the Crown* 260) formed a part of the rituals of the god Sabazius. Possibly only the more fanatical worshippers were to be found indulging in this practice. The ability to carry fire is mentioned only in the *Bacchae*, and can probably be discounted. Many modern critics have accepted the authenticity of a two-stage sacrificial practice involving *sparagmos* (the tearing apart of wild animals, witnessed by the herdsman) and *omophagia* (the consumption of the raw flesh, which is described by the chorus, lines 137–8). However, as Henrichs (1978, p. 144) has pointed out, an inscription from Miletus dating to the third century BC suggests that pieces of raw meat (*omophagion*), presumably cut from an animal sacrificed in the normal way, were handled rather than eaten by worshippers of Dionysus. Seen in this light, the rite seems much less spontaneous and savage than the one outlined by the mythological narratives.

Given the sensational nature of the herdsman's account, it is interesting that he should go out of his way to contradict the accusations of excessive drinking and sexual licence which have been made against the Maenads. As we have seen, the consumption of large quantities of wine was an element in some of the masculine rites of Dionysus. His worship was also in some contexts accompanied by symbolic sexual references: the Athenian Anthesteria featured a form of sacred marriage (see pp. 161–2), while in some of the rural wine festivals, attended as far as we know by both men and women, phallus-shaped images were carried in procession through the streets. It seems more than likely that male anxiety about the antics of the Maenads would have conjured up visions of outrageous drunkenness and debauchery; but in fact there is very little evidence in any of the sources to indicate that their ecstasies were alcohol-induced, or that their rites involved the use of sexual symbols, let alone the real thing. Keuls (1984) and McNally (1978) have both made the point that in the vase paintings which depict the erotic pursuit of Maenads by Satyrs the women are rarely seen to be reciprocating the passion of the rampant males: in many of the scenes they are actively resisting, and are using their *thyrsoi* as phallic weapons (Fig. 29). Unlike the women-only festivals of Demeter (see pp. 164–5), the female rites of Dionysus seem to have had very little in the way of sexual content; on the evidence of the vase paintings, there may even have been a conscious opposition to male erotic activity.

There seems to be little basis for the suggestion made by Dodds (1951, pp. 270–82) that the initial impetus for these rites had been provided by spontaneous manifestations of collective hysteria. References to Maenadic activity in later Hellenistic literature tend to convey an impression of a reasonably restrained and well-regulated cult. For example, Diodorus Siculus in the first century BC speaks of regular biennial festivals, where girls uttered the ritual chant of 'Euai!', while married women performed sacrifices and sang hymns to Dionysus (4.3.2–3). While we cannot be sure that the evidence provided by later authors can be applied to the fifth and fourth centuries BC, it may well be the case that the altogether more awe-inspiring nature of the practices described by Euripides is to be accounted for by the dramatic character of his work and not by the greater intensity and abandon of worshippers during his time.

This is not to say that ecstasy was not a genuine feature of the cult. Plutarch recounts a heart-warming tale about the Delphian Thyiades which dates back to the time of the Sacred War in the fourth century BC. A party of devotees who were still in a state of trance wandered one night into the village of Amphissa, and in their exhaustion flung themselves down to sleep in the market place. The local women, fearing that the sleeping worshippers might be maltreated by the soldiers stationed in the village, formed a circle around them and stood there in silence until they awoke. Then they offered them food and hospitality, and escorted them safely to the frontier (*On the bravery of women* 249e–f).

Numerous modern scholars have discussed the attractions which the cult must have held for women. Not only did it provide them with a temporary respite from the routine and isolation of their domestic existence, but it also allowed them, through their experience of ecstasy, to escape into a mode of self-expression which gave free rein to pent-up emotions and hostilities. In the Thesmophoria the women's awareness of their own value would have been rooted in their knowledge of the significance accorded to their role by the male-dominated community; in the Dionysiac celebrations, by contrast, it would have been inspired by their participation in rituals of rebellion against male authority. Inscriptions from Miletus and Magnesia which probably date to the third century BC reveal that the cult was tolerated and even to some extent encouraged by local communities, and that celebrants were sometimes honoured by their cities after their deaths.[16] But even if men were not actively hostile to the cult, its peripheral character would have served to create a conscious sense of opposition to male values.

A number of commentators have drawn attention to the light which is thrown on Dionysiac worship by I. M. Lewis's study of ecstatic religious phemonena. Lewis believes that a system of possession serves to alleviate some of the grievances experienced by oppressed women in male-dominated societies; but at the same time the system is only able to function because the men recognise that it furnishes a controllable safety valve for potentially destructive emotions. 'From this perspective, the tolerance by men of periodic, but always temporary, assaults on their authority by women appears as the price they have to pay to maintain their enviable position' (Lewis, 1971, p. 86). This account helps to illuminate the apparently anomalous male responses – anxiety and suspicion coupled with tolerance – which Maenadic activity seems to have evoked. It also suggests that Dionysiac worship may, through its provision of a licensed outlet for rebellion, have formed an element in the preservation of male supremacy.

However, if the cult did fulfil this function, then it has to be admitted that its effectiveness must have been very limited, since all the evidence indicates that participation was never very large-scale or widespread. In a penetrating study Zeitlin (1982) has analysed an aspect of the cult's impact which would have furthered male interests in a more pervasive way. She points out that Dionysiac worship incorporated rituals of inversion (such as abandonment of home and children, demonstrations of aggression, and eating of raw flesh) which would have conformed to the male view of women's nature as a subversive and less fully integrated element in society. In this way, the ideological antithesis of masculine restraint and feminine lack of control would have been reinforced: 'disorder is a vital and necessary pole of order' (1982, p. 132). Although the participants themselves may well have derived prestige and emotional release from the rituals, within the society as a whole they could have contributed to male cultural domination: 'the claims made for the cult as an expression of freedom for women and an opportunity to reverse their low social status can be balanced out by less favourable effects, ones which would support a negative ideology of the female as unruly and disorderly' (1982, p. 134). It may have been this reinforcement of an existing ideology, rather than any safety-valve effect, which represented the main value of the cult in men's eyes. The release from tension would only have involved a very small number of women, whereas potentially the whole of the female population could be contained within the ideology.

PART IV

IDEAS ABOUT WOMEN
IN THE
CLASSICAL AGE

The subordinate status of Greek women involved both a material and an ideological dimension. Sometimes these two factors reinforced each other, as for example when the idea that women were naturally wild and unrestrained was used to justify male control of their property and persons, or, alternatively, when women's tenderness was presented as a reason for their exclusion from the world of public affairs. But sometimes the ideas which men constructed might have the effect of masking material reality: this, it has been suggested, may have been the case with the ideal of female seclusion, which was probably more talked about than practised.

Many elements in the ideological view of women have already been discussed. The medical writers, for instance, expressed the concept of a distinctively female physiology, and their diagnoses were sometimes governed by their belief in the primacy of the child-bearing function. The notion that women were less capable than men of controlling their sexual appetites appears to have been widespread, and was most vividly voiced in comic plays. Xenophon, among others, expounded a view of the sexual division of space and labour, focusing on a dichotomy in which the outdoor, public world belonged to men, and the domestic and private interior was the sphere of women. This dichotomy, he emphasised, was not merely a human convention, but was part of the natural order of things: 'activities designed by God in such a way that one sex naturally excels the other are set down as honourable by the law' (*Oeconomicus* 7.30).

In this Part, rather than attempting a summary of these ideological positions, I shall be discussing in detail the ideas about women which are encountered in two of the most conspicuous intellectual media of the Classical Age, drama and philosophy. As both registers and critiques of current values and attitudes, these media were particularly powerful. Both were liberated to a large extent from the obligation to describe women, to say what their lives and behaviour were like in reality. In drama men portrayed women as they might be, and in philosophy they constructed theories about how they ought to be: in both cases beliefs about the essential nature of women were brought into play.

15

Women in drama

All the complete plays which have survived from ancient Greece were written by Athenians. The tragedies of Aeschylus, Sophocles and Euripides were produced between about 490 and 406 BC, while the comedies of Aristophanes were performed in the later years of the fifth and early years of the fourth century. From fragments and references it is known that many other dramatists were at work in Athens during this period; but it would be fair to say that these four were among the most valued. There were also playwrights in other cities, but it appears that the dramas of the Athenians were prized throughout the Greek world, and were staged in states other than Athens.

In Athens, plays were presented in the context of two religious festivals, both of them honouring the god Dionysus. The City Dionysia, held in March, was a great civic occasion, at which a number of official ceremonies were performed in addition to the plays. It lasted five days, and included competitions for tragedy and comedy. The Lenaea, which took place in January, was a more low-key affair, and may have been devoted primarily to comedy. Although the issue does not fundamentally affect our interpretation of the plays, it would be of considerable interest to know whether women were able to attend these festivals. When, for example, Euripides was composing a speech in which Medea passionately proclaimed the wrongs of women, or when Aristophanes was inventing a plot in which Athens' female citizens went on a sex strike, did these playwrights expect women to be part of the audience which would watch these scenes? Unfortunately, although on balance the evidence seems to favour female attendance, the question cannot be answered categorically.[1] It is difficult to believe that women were positively excluded from dramatic festivals when they played such an important part in other religious events; but it may have been the case that the audiences were predominantly male, and that women were not actively encouraged to attend.

The possibility that plays may have been written for primarily male audiences seems particularly intriguing in view of the prominent position occupied by women in their content. Only one extant play, Sophocles' tragedy *Philoctetes*, has no female characters, and in many of them women have a central and determining role. Indicative of this importance is the fact that the titles of over half the surviving tragedies consist either of a woman's name or of a designation for a group of women. Sometimes information is available which tells us that the role of a particular female in a pre-Classical myth has been either expanded or radically altered in the dramatic version produced in the Classical Age: for example, Medea's wilful slaughter of her own children was probably an episode invented by Euripides (see also p. 16, for the changing role of Clytemnestra in the story of Agamemnon's murder). Comic writers had an even freer hand with their characters, since they invented their own plots, which were often gloriously surreal. Although in many of Aristophanes' plays female characters are peripheral, the plots of three of them, *Lysistrata*, *Thesmophoriazusea*, and *Women in the Assembly*, revolve entirely around the activities of women.

In both tragedy and comedy, conflicts between male and female characters often form the focus of the action. The ideological separation of masculine and feminine spheres in fifth-century Athenian society made gender relations a fruitful base for the exploration of other differences: men and women, to borrow a famous expression used by Lévi-Strauss, were 'good for thinking with'. Ideas about sexual difference formulated in the course of these explorations should not necessarily be seen as straightforward reflections of current ideology. The plays performed within the elaborate civic framework of dramatic festivals could be transgressive in their impact (see Goldhill, 1987), and tended to question rather than endorse traditional values. In fifth-century Athens rapid political and social change had generated an intellectual atmosphere in which thinkers were challenging assumptions about the natural basis for conventional divisions within society (see p. 181), and these tensions were both reflected and engendered in the plays of the period. In particular, the questioning of notions about the 'naturalness' of sexual divisions (see p. 171 for Xenophon's version) found an outlet in drama. The probing nature of this process means that no one play can be expected to present a unified and static view of female/male interactions; and this is even less feasible in relation to the dramatic corpus as a whole, which contains plays written by different authors at different historical moments.

Nevertheless, the plays which deal with gender conflict share certain broad narrative devices. Often a situation is envisaged in which actions performed by male characters provoke an intrusion by women into the public arena, a turn of events which involves the assumption by the women of masculine modes of behaviour. This transgression of normal sexual boundaries on the part of the females is sometimes seen to result in a partial feminisation of the males. Sexual role-reversals of this kind are represented most explicitly in comedy, where they are accompanied by cross-dressing. But they are also present in tragedy, although here the emphasis is usually on the female side of the process – on the women's usurpation of masculine roles.

In the first play of Aeschylus's *Oresteia* trilogy, for example, the queen Clytemnestra is repeatedly represented as having behaved in a masculine fashion during her husband Agamemnon's lengthy absence at the Trojan War. At the beginning of the play, the watchman says of her, 'That woman – she manoeuvres like a man' (*Agamemnon* 11),[2] and there are many items in her conduct which an audience of Athenians would have identified as masculine: choosing her own sexual partner (she is living with her husband's cousin, Aegisthus), ruling over Argos while Agamemnon is away, and finally securing political power for herself by murdering her husband when he returns from Troy.

Agamemnon, on the other hand, performs an action which he himself has already identified as feminine: when he comes back in triumph from Troy, and Clytemnestra urges him to walk on a crimson carpet, he replies angrily '. . . you treat me like a woman' (918–19). But he is ultimately persuaded, and 'treading on tapestries' he enters the palace, where he is immediately butchered. This temporary reversal of roles heralds a more protracted disruption of the 'natural' order. The victorious Clytemnestra rebukes the chorus of citizens for responding to her like a desperate woman, and declares that she has a heart of steel (1401–3); while her consort Aegisthus, who planned but did not carry out the killing, is taunted by the chorus as 'You woman . . .' (1625). In the second play of the trilogy, *The Libation Bearers*, this partnership of masculinised female and feminised male is brought to an end. Clytemnestra and Aegisthus are murdered by the queen's son Orestes, who has been spurred to action by the loss of his patrimony, by his disgust at the rule of a 'brace of women', and by Apollo's insistence that he avenge his father's death (299–304). The final play, *The Eumenides*, gives a dramatic account of Orestes' trial for murder in Athens. When he is eventually acquitted (see pp 27–8), he is able to return home to take up his birthright as king of Argos; and the Furies, the female demons who have mercilessly hunted him down for his crime against his mother, are at last persuaded to take up a more nurturing role as powerful protectors of Athenian fertility. With this resolution, the conventional sexual division of labour is restored. Clytemnestra is dead, patriarchal government has been reinstated, and the Furies, an active female force, have been excluded from the administration of justice – where their commitment to the rights of kin manifested itself as an ethic of vengeance – and relocated in a more domestic setting.

In Sophocles' tragedy *Antigone*, the heroine rebels against the law of the state by attempting to perform funeral rites for her dead brother, who in a decree introduced by her uncle King Creon has been refused burial on the grounds that he was a traitor. Antigone's sister Ismene pleads with her not to overstep the normal bounds of female behaviour: 'Remember we are women,/ we're not born to contend with men' (61–2); and Creon, justifying his refusal to pardon Antigone, urges that 'we must defend the men who live by law,'/ never let some woman triumph over us' (677–8). Although Antigone is engaged in traditional areas of female activity – mourning the dead, defending the interests of the family – she is asserting herself in a masculine fashion in order to do so. At the same time Creon feels that his own manhood is being threatened: 'I am not the man, not now: she is the man/ if this victory goes to her and she goes free' (484–5).[3] Both parties come to grief. Antigone is condemned to a living death – she is walled up in an underground vault – and hangs herself. Creon's son Haemon, Antigone's betrothed, and his wife Eurydice both commit suicide.

Euripides in his tragedy *Medea* envisages a conflict between female and male which is provoked by divergent attitudes to the marital bond. When her husband Jason abandons her so that he may make an advantageous marriage to a princess, Medea takes control of her own affairs with ruthless efficiency, and in plotting her revenge adopts a behavioural ethos conventionally associated with the archetypal male hero: 'Let no-one think of me/ as humble or weak or passive; let them understand/ I am of a different kind: dangerous to my enemies,/ Loyal to my friends. To such a life glory belongs' (807–10).[4] If Medea had been a warrior going off to war, these words would have seemed admirable to most Athenians. The terrible irony of her declaration is that she is not about to fight a battle, but to murder the princess, the princess's father and her own dearly loved children, because this is the most effective way she knows of punishing Jason. Medea's transgression of the sexual boundary involves adherence to a code of public morality which has horrific results when transported into the private sphere of existence. Jason, on the other hand, who stars elsewhere in myth as the classic he-man, is represented here as insensitive, calculating and rather stupid; he, of course, has been far from 'loyal to his friends'. In abandoning Medea, he has broken his oath, an essential item in the traditional hero's moral equipment. Medea however has remained true to hers – she has fulfilled her vow to win revenge.

Women are particularly prominent in the plays of Euripides, and a number of them in addition to *Medea* contain allusions to sexual boundary crossing. In *Hippolytus* (see pp. 31, 38–9), Phaedra's dreadful passion for her young stepson reduces her to a fevered state in which she longs to escape to the masculine environments of the hunt or the racetrack (*Hippolytus* 215–31). In *Electra*, Orestes seems hesitant and cautious when he returns from exile to win vengeance for his father's death, and it is his sister Electra who displays the resolution and conviction which one would expect of a hero. The *Bacchae* offers the most explicit allusions to role reversal. When the ecstatic women worshippers of Dionysus take to the hills, they abandon the conventional role allotted to females within the ordered culture of the city. At first their relationship with the natural world still embraces a nurturing function, and those who have left newborn babies behind at home now suckle young gazelles and wolf-cubs (699–72). But when they are pursued by a group of herdsmen, in their frenzy they begin to imitate masculine behaviour: they hunt down animals, sack and plunder villages and defeat men in a pitched battle (728–64). Conversely, their persecutor King Pentheus seems to be fascinated by the activities which he is so anxious to suppress, and his identification with the Bacchae comes to the surface when he agrees to dress up as a woman so that he can spy upon their rituals (821–38). He is mistaken for a wild animal, and his own mother Agave leads the band of manic women who like hunters tear him limb from limb.

Although Euripides was apparently notorious in the Classical Age for his depiction of passionate and violent women, not all his heroines fit into this mould. But even his restrained and gentle female characters display a courage which throws into relief the failings of the men with whom they come into contact. Alcestis, in the play of that name, is an ideal wife – noble, dignified, devoted to her family, a superb manager of the household. When the Fates, prompted by the god Apollo, offer her husband Admetus an escape from imminent death if he can find someone to die on his behalf, Alcestis volunteers for the role. Although the grief that Admetus then experiences seems genuine, he is nevertheless shown to be a cowardly and selfish man who is obsessed with his own suffering. *Iphigenia in Aulis* features another act of self-sacrifice, this time performed by a young woman on behalf of her country. When a prophet announces that the Greek army can only sail to Troy and conquer it if the daughter of King Agamemnon is sacrificed to Artemis (see p. 29), Agamemnon himself responds in a weak and vacillating fashion. But Iphigenia conquers her initial horror and in the end goes willingly to her death, displaying a brave unthinking patriotism that is in stark contrast to the base self-seeking motives of the men for whom she is prepared to giver her life.

The three comedies in which Aristophanes places women at the centre of the action all juxtapose a female takeover of masculine prerogative and masculine space with a temporary feminisation of a male character. In the *Lysistrata*, the women of Athens interfere in one of the most crucial aspects of male policy-making, the handling of decisions about war and peace. By refusing to perform their sexual duties as wives, and by invading the Acropolis and taking control of the Athenian treasury, they eventually succeed in bringing the Peloponnesian War to an end. In one of the confrontations which precede this happy outcome, an Athenian magistrate is dressed up in a woman's veil, given a basket of wool to card (531–5) and made to listen to a lecture on the political applications of women's domestic skills (see p. 144). The *Thesmophoriazusae* features a more protracted piece of cross-dressing (see p. 163). In this play, the fantasy involves the trespass by a male disguised as a woman into space temporarily monopolised by females celebrating a women-only festival. But this is in the nature of an imaginative counter-invasion, for in real life the Thesmophoria involved a female incursion into the Pnyx, an area normally devoted to the political decision-making of men (see p. 164). The playwright reminds his audience of this fact when he pictures the women staging a mock Assembly meeting, in which they make speeches about the crimes of Euripides. In *Women in the Assembly*, it is one of the regular meetings of the Assembly which is infiltrated by women dressed up in their husbands' clothes. There they succeed in getting a motion passed that management of the city's political and economic affairs should be handed over to its female residents. In the meantime, the husband of the women's ringleader Praxagora has been forced to put on his wife's dress and slippers in order to leave the house.

This recurrent theme of sexual boundary-crossing may well represent an element deriving from the traditional religious framework for the performance of Athenian drama. Rituals in which men and women imitated each other in their dress and behaviour are known to have been a feature of a number of religious festivals, and they were also present in some of the initiation rites associated either with the onset of puberty or with marriage. The explanation which is usually offered for these practices is that they represented a temporary assumption of an 'otherness' which social convention required one to banish from one's ordinary life, and that the ritualised putting aside of this inverse role helped to reinforce the unambiguous nature of one's subsequent sexual identity.[5] This function of reinforcement could also be attributed to a number of Athenian tragedies. On a superficial level plays such as *Medea* or the *Bacchae* might easily be seen as cautionary tales, designed to bring home the message that women who invade masculine areas of activity wreak terrible havoc in their families and communities. Some members of an Athenian audience may well have been satisfied with this simple reading of the tragedies. But the complex handling of the theme of role reversal precludes single, exclusive interpretations. The multiplicity of meanings which it creates takes the theme far beyond its original purpose of ritual reinforcement.

Straightforward cautionary interpretations are ruled out, on a basic level, by treatments of female characters which seem in some respects to be sympathetic. Antigone provides the most obvious example of a woman who can be viewed as a victim of oppressive male behaviour. But Phaedra too is a victim, a passive instrument in Aphrodite's scheme for punishment, who has battled bravely against the transgressive sexual desires inflicted upon her. Only when she overhears a passionate outburst against the female sex uttered by Hippolytus, who would like to abolish the necessity for women, does Phaedra decide to commit suicide and at the same time punish her cruel stepson by leaving behind a note accusing him of seduction (*Hippolytus* 373–731). Even Clytemnestra is motivated at least in part by her desperate anger at the sacrifice of her daughter Iphigenia; while Agave's murder of her son is committed unwittingly, at the behest of a god, as a result of that same son's persecution of her religious observances.

The most explicit statement of the social repression experienced by women is put into the mouth of Medea, who is impelled by her husband's desertion into an embittered outpouring on the wrongs suffered by members of her sex (230–58). 'Surely, of all creatures that have life and will, we women/ Are the most wretched.' Women, she says, are forced to accept as masters of their bodies men whose characters are totally unknown to them. If the man turns out to be bad, his wife cannot reject him, and divorce only brings disgrace. A husband who is tired of his home can find diversions elsewhere, but a wife is compelled to look to one man alone. Nor is her life free from danger, for marriage brings with it all the perils of childbirth. The sympathy which Medea's plight evokes in the chorus and in many members of the audience at this point in the play is not entirely dissipated even at the moment when the heroine is on the verge of murdering her children. The playwright graphically represents the agonising mental processes which Medea must go through before she can steel herself to perform the deed (*Medea* 1021–80). The fact that Euripides has been judged by modern critics to be both a misogynist and a feminist is indicative of his multi-layered approach to his female characters. Medea is not the only Euripidean woman who, while conforming to the ideological stereotype of the dangerous and excessive female, is capable at the same time of appearing justified in her actions.

To modern spectators of Greek drama the framing of ideas about women may well appear to be the most significant issue raised by these plays. Some people will applaud their acknowledgement of women's power, others will be horrified by the violence with which this power is so often associated. It is unlikely, however, that the dramatists themselves were consciously addressing 'the problem of women'. Their treatment of female characters must be viewed within the broader context of their construction of gender relations, a perspective which Shaw has adopted in his discussion of the 'female intruder' (1975). According to this analysis, the clash between the sexes in Greek drama can be equated with a wider conflict between the public and private spheres – in Greek terms, between *polis* and *oikos*. When women cross the boundary between the male and female realms, they are often doing so in defence of the interests of the household, which are being threatened by actions performed by men in the public arena. According to Shaw, one of the playwrights' objectives in dramatising female intrusions is to demonstrate the limitations of the 'civic virtues' which men have cultivated in their political operations.

This is a useful analysis, but as Foley (1982a) has pointed out, it fails to take account of the complexities of the dialectical opposition between household and state. The *polis* is never entirely public and the *oikos* never entirely private – what touches one sphere inevitably touches the other, and in this way their interdependence is demonstrated. In the words of Goldhill, who is here endorsing Foley's view, 'Attic drama plays out the recognition of the tension between, on the one hand, the assumed continuity of *oikos* and *polis* as institutions of power and, on the other hand, the conflicts of interest between *oikos* and *polis*, which seems to set them in opposition to each other' (1986, p.114).

The assumption of continuity to which Goldhill refers is rooted in part in the male's position as ruler of both *polis* and *oikos*. Actions which spring from his conviction that the public sphere can command priority over the private precipitate opposition which exposes clashes of interest. Clytemnestra, for example, reacts in response to the sacrifice of her daughter Iphigenia, organised by Agamemnon so that the Greeks might conquer Troy – and so that he might protect his own political position (*Agamemnon* 211–13, *Iphigenia in Aulis* 446–50). When Antigone buries her brother she is breaking a law which, according to Creon's own account, has been enacted in the interests of stability and strong government (*Antigone* 162–210). As far as Antigone is concerned, this law is incompatible with higher obligations towards a family's dead, but Creon fails to recognise this conflict, believing that the family is subordinate to its ruler and his wider political affiliations (*Antigone* 640–67). In Euripides' *Medea*, the heroine is incensed by her husband's lack of personal loyalty, while Jason maintains that he has ended their marriage in order to secure, through his new alliance with the royal family, prosperity and public esteem for his sons (551–68). In plays such as these the public and private spheres are shown to be bound together by relations which are both reciprocal and oppositional. In focusing on the point of interaction between them, Athenian tragedy explores a set of contradictions for which Athenian law, by establishing public masculine control over private female behaviour, had attempted to find a simple solution.

Similar tensions are highlighted in the comedies which feature female incursions. In the *Lysistrata*, the men conducting the Peloponnesian War are represented as denying women's right to an opinion on this issue, believing that females have no contribution to make to the war effort. They take the subordinate status of the family so much for granted that they fail to see any link between private and public spheres; and it is the heroine Lysistrata who points out to them that the women opposing the war have contributed their sons to its operations (*Lysistrata* 507–20, 587–90). In *Women in the Assembly*, the women are motivated in part by their recognition of a rather different connection between public and private: the items of male mismanagement which have driven them to take over the Assembly include the use of public money to line individual pockets (206–7). Even the women in the *Thesmophoriazusae* who want to lynch Euripides are reacting to a public event. They are enraged by the fact that as a result of public theatrical performances their peaceful management of their households has been disrupted; because of the suspicions which the playwright has aroused, male authority has been asserted in an area where women previously exercised an unofficial and craftily concealed sway (see p. 144).

Continuity of *polis* and *oikos* is also implied by the outcome of many of these plays. The actions which women take in defence of their private values frequently have disastrous repercussions in both public and domestic spheres. This dual effect is often reinforced by the siting of the family/state conflict within a single household. When Clytemnestra murders her husband she is also killing a king; Agave's unwitting onslaught on an oppressive ruler is also an attack on her son; and Antigone's close relationship with Creon means that her defiance of his political authority culminates in the destruction of Creon's own family. Sometimes these reverberations involve the denial of a woman's maternity, and hence the betrayal of the very values which she was seeking to defend. Both Medea and Agave murder their sons, while Clytemnestra's response to her daughter's death brings her ultimately into conflict with her son. Antigone, through her excessive devotion to her dead brother, stifles her own potential for marriage and childbirth; her loyalty to the household into which she was born prevents her from making the transition to another man's household on which the reproduction of society depends. She is referred to on a number of occasions as a woman who will be married to Death (e.g. 891, 1205), and her over-valuation of her own kin is emphasised when, as she goes to her death for the sake of her brother, she declares that she would not have performed this act for a husband or a child (905–12). Even the noble Lysistrata adopts a strategy – the ban on sex – of which the ultimate conclusion would be the extinction of the households which she is determined to defend; while the legislation in favour of free love which is introduced by the female infiltrators in *Women in the Assembly* will have the effect of demolishing the nuclear family (635–7).

This complex dialectical relationship between public and private spheres was symbolised by the conventional organisation of theatrical space. The backdrop in a theatre usually represented the front of a house, which stood as a barrier between the open space of the exterior public world and the hidden regions of the private interior. In this respect the two were visibly opposed to each other. But the backdrop had a door in it, through which female characters in particular made their exits and entrances. Clytemnestra, for example, appears at the door with her crimson carpet in order to greet Agamemnon, who has arrived on the scene from the wider world of public affairs (Aeschylus' *Agamemnon* 855). The backdrop which divides men and women becomes the focal point of their confrontations – the point at which public and private concerns intersect.

Although gender conflict is a theme common to all the plays which have been discussed, its specific ramifications are worked out in different ways. Comic drama, as one might expect, offers its audience some reassurance. Greek comedy is a genre rooted in the carnival atmosphere generated by religious rites of renewal, when restraints are removed, roles reversed, and figures of authority mocked, but on an essentially temporary basis. Similarly, many of Aristophanes' plays envisage a situation in which the world is miraculously turned upside down, subjected to rigorous scrutiny, and then restored to normality. For this reason it has often been suggested that his comedies are fundamentally conservative in their impact, in spite of their forceful satire. It is certainly true that Aristophanes is in no sense advocating any radical re-ordering of society. In the *Lysistrata*, for example, the women's seizure of power is the miraculous event through which a temporary inversion is effected, and is not to be seen as a serious project. But when at the end of the play the world is turned the right way up again, it is not exactly the same as it was before. A specific political problem – the conduct of a highly damaging war – has been solved, and this renewal of civilised order has been achieved through the application of feminine values derived from the domestic domain.

Aeschylus' *Oresteia* trilogy also seems to envisage a resolution of the conflict between public and private spheres, although in this instance the specific issue which is being explored – the transition from a family-based to a state-based system of justice – has implications which extend well beyond the immediate political context. But other tragedies carry the crisis through to its bitter end. At the close of the *Antigone* a king has been ruined, his wife and son are dead, and a woman who should have been a source of new life has hung herself in an underground chamber: in this play, it seems, the conflict is irresolvable. Euripides' treatment of the theme is similarly open-ended, but he views the problem from a different perspective. His searing critique of the masculine ethics around which political order is structured – ethics exhibited by characters such as Jason, Agamemnon and Pentheus – raises pressing issues of personal morality. In his works the emphasis shifts, and he focuses to a far greater degree than either of his fellow tragedians on those areas of individual experience with which codes of behaviour shaped in the public sphere are so ill-equipped to deal.

Zeitlin (1990) has argued that Athenian drama was an institution designed primarily for the education of male citizens in a democratic state, and that the prominence of the feminine principle in the theatre has to be analysed in this context. Women, she believes, are being represented not for their own sake, but because of what they reveal about the male identity. Zeitlin rightly points out that women characters regularly serve as the catalysts through which the consequences of male actions are made to rebound on to their original perpetrators: women's sufferings generally lead to disasters which occur before those of the males and help to precipitate them. It is because 'the woman is assigned the role of the radical other' (1990, p. 68) that she can be used in this way to examine and reconstruct male behaviour and values. This function is underlined by the ritual aspects of Greek theatre. Women literally did not represent themselves in Greek drama, but were impersonated by male actors; and theatrical space was dominated by the public arena of the orchestra and the stage, while the house, the feminine sphere, remained hidden and mysterious.

As Zeitlin suggests, the otherness of women is a prominent aspect of tragic drama, one that complicates the challenge to public values which females represent. When women break out of the domestic interior, they tend to pass not merely into the public arena but also beyond it, entering the realms which exist beyond the civilisation and order of the *polis*. Antigone and the Bacchae both go outside the walls of the city in a literal sense, while Phaedra longs to do so; but these are by no means the only female characters who are associated with the wildness of the natural world. Medea's otherness is also demonstrated by her foreignness, which she herself stresses at the end of her 'wrongs of women' speech (252–8), and by her skills as a sorceress. In addition, many of these women have strong links with the divine realm of being. Clytemnestra can be seen on one level as an instrument of divine retribution (e.g. *Agamemnon* 1497–504); Antigone believes herself to be acting in defence of unwritten laws ordained by the gods (*Antigone* 450–7); and the actions of the Bacchae are the medium through which the power of the god Dionysus is demonstrated. Medea, as so often, provides the most striking example: at the conclusion of the play she is swept away to safety in the chariot of her grandfather, the Sun-god.

The relationships which all these women bear to spheres – natural, foreign or divine – which exist beyond the boundaries of male political order provide another reason why gender conflict cannot be reduced to a simple clash between private and public. Private experience is only one of the hidden dimensions which men are forced to confront when they are opposed by women. This analysis tends to confirm Zeitlin's notion of drama as an essentially male project. The focus is on the masculine sense of identity and the crises which it undergoes when the boundaries it has created are undermined. The masculine *polis* invents itself by establishing what it is not – by constructing areas of difference and separating them off from itself. The women who represent these differences erupt into the *polis* from the inside – from the domestic interior – but also from the realms which exist on the outside. When boundaries are crossed in this way they may be re-established or they may be moved. In either case they are re-assessed.

Nevertheless, the fact that Athenian dramatists felt able to project these notions of difference on to their female characters indicates the existence of a general sense of anxiety about women, stemming from an awareness of the anomalous position which they occupied in Athenian society. Moreover, we cannot be sure that all the male members of an audience would have been willing to accept the challenge to their own sense of identity which the plays were offering. Aristophanes' account of the Athenian response to Euripides' dramas would certainly seem to suggest that some men preferred to see these as 'plays about women'. If women themselves attended theatrical performances, they may well have reacted in the same way. Our ignorance on this last point must remain a source of regret. The presence of women in the audience would not in any way contradict Zeitlin's view of drama as a male project, for women living in patriarchal societies are often compelled to be consumers of a male-centred culture. But it would be of great interest to know whether they were in a position to derive their own meanings from a project in which they played so vital a role.

16

Women and the philosophers

Prior to the fourth century BC, gender issues had apparently excited little interest among Greek philosophers. Some of the scientific thinkers of the sixth and early fifth centuries BC had made use of the idea of a basic antithesis between male and female, the most prominent example being found in the Table of Opposites produced by a group of Pythagoreans. They included in their list of ten pairs of opposite principles at work in the universe the categories male and female, limited and unlimited, right and left, light and darkness, and good and evil (recorded by Aristotle in *Metaphysics* 986a). The association between men and women and right and left was also to be found in the work of some early fifth-century thinkers – Parmenides, for instance, seems to have believed that the sex of a child was determined by the place which it occupied on the right or left side of the mother's womb (frag. 17). Pronouncements such as these suggest that a number of philosophers subscribed to the notion of gender difference as a fundamental element in a world order founded on the interaction of opposed substances or forces. By the second half of the fifth century thinkers known as the Sophists were arguing that values and institutions which were assumed to be grounded in 'nature' were in reality social constructs, an approach which may well have influenced the dramatists' questioning of conventional gender distinctions. But the fragments of the Sophists' work that survive give no indication of a specific interest in the male/female antithesis. It is only in the writings of the fourth-century philosophers Plato and Aristotle that we find detailed discussions of gender relations, a subject on which they came to widely differing conclusions.

PLATO

In his dialogue *The Republic*, which was probably completed by about 380 BC, Plato outlines his prototype for an ideal state. The society described by Socrates, a character in the dialogue, is a thoroughly hierarchical one, in which duties and privileges are distributed in accordance with a rigid class system. The population is to be divided into three groups, a ruling class, a soldier class and a class which provides for the economic needs of the community. Rulers and soldiers, who are to be known collectively as the Guardians, will constitute a small and politically dominant élite; and it is to the organisation of this joint group that Plato devotes the bulk of his discussion.

As one of the characters in the dialogue comments, the Guardians are not destined to lead particularly pleasurable lives: their political privileges are not to be matched by any economic advantages. The Guardians are to own no private property apart from the most basic essentials (416d–e); all things, including women and children (423e–424a), are to be held in common. The language employed by Plato at this stage in his argument will be offensive to many modern readers, but the explanation which he offers (451c–456a) for the introduction of this revolutionary proposal throws a rather different light on this aspect of his programme.

Plato believes that the only innate differences between males and females are reproductive ones, and that these offer no barrier to women's equal participation in the highest positions within the state. In an earlier section of *The Republic*, the Guardians have been compared with watchdogs: should female watchdogs, Socrates now asks, perform the same duties as the males, or should they be kept at home on the grounds that the bearing and rearing of puppies incapacitates them for other roles? The answer, of course, is that duties should be shared, although it must be borne in mind that the females will not be quite so strong as the males. The same is true of human beings, Socrates states: males and females have no distinct qualifications for particular pursuits, although men will in general display more natural aptitude for all tasks than women. It follows that there is no one function in society which should be reserved for either women or men: both sexes are equally eligible for selection as Guardians.

The expression of natural male superiority which is inserted into this argument certainly detracts from the egalitarian nature of its conclusion; but it should be noted that Plato is not suggesting that all men are able to do everything better than all women. The same range of natural abilities is to be found in both sexes. Some women have an aptitude for medicine, others for athletics, others for soldiering, and others for philosophy, just as among men (455e–456a). But within any one area of natural ability, the females will always on average be outclassed by the males. Hence, within the Guardian class (it is implied, though not openly stated) the men will on average be superior to the women. However, the great majority of men will not be admitted to the class at all, because they lack the necessary strength, courage and philosophical temperament (375a–376c): in terms of their natural abilities, then, these men will be inferior to the women who do gain admission to the class. Nor will the 'inferiority' of the female Guardians mean that they will be relegated to the most lowly offices of state, for in a later section of *The Republic* (540a–c) Plato specifically includes women among those Guardians who have achieved a knowledge of the Good and therefore qualify to serve as rulers.

Equality of opportunity to enter the Guardian class entails equality of education for both sexes within the class. Women will be given both a physical and an intellectual education. They will exercise naked in the gymnasium alongside the men, and will receive a military training. There will be no sexual division of labour among those who participate in the state education programme: women will undertake exactly the same duties as the men, including warfare; but since they are physically weaker they will be given a lighter share of the tasks (456b–457b).

Having established these points, Plato returns to the subject of marriage and family life (457c–462e). Both of these institutions are to be abolished: men and women will not be divided up into separate households, but will live, eat and train communally. Naturally, they will be sexually attracted to one another, but they cannot be allowed to mate indiscriminately. Festivals will be organised at which partners who have been previously selected for their breeding potential will be brought together, the individuals themselves being under the illusion that they have won this privilege in a lottery. Young men who have distinguished themselves in warfare or in their other duties will be rewarded with more frequent opportunities for sexual intercourse with female Guardians. The children who are the product of these state-regulated unions are to be placed in nurseries and brought up by nurses drawn from outside the Guardian class. Mothers will be taken into the nurseries to feed the babies, but none of them will know her own child, and this will be the only contribution which they make to childcare activities.

Eligibility for mating rituals will be restricted to females between twenty and forty and males between twenty-five and fifty-five years. Guardians who have passed these age limits will be allowed more freedom of choice where sexual intercourse is concerned, but only on condition that any children that are conceived are disposed of through abortion or exposure. In order to avoid the danger of incest occurring, a man will call all the offspring born between seven and ten months after he has participated in a mating festival sons or daughters, and all the children will call him father: there will be a ban on intercourse between 'fathers' and 'daughters' and also between 'mothers' and 'sons'.

This radical re-ordering of society offers, according to Plato, two principal advantages. It allows the state to institute a system of eugenic breeding; and it produces social cohesion by eradicating the diverse loyalties and individual acquisitiveness generated by the nuclear family. The new regime will do away with 'the political dissension that occurs when different people call different things "mine", dragging off to their own private houses whatever they can acquire for themselves alone, and when each man has his own wife and children, and his own private pleasures and pains' (464c–d). A third advantage is implied by Plato's introductory section on sexual equality: the abolition of the family will have the effect of liberating women from domestic concerns, so that their talents can be employed solely in the interests of the state.

Although the programme is revolutionary, in a Greek context it may not have been entirely novel. In about 392 BC the comic poet Aristophanes had produced the play *Women in the Assembly*, in which the government of Athens is handed over to its female citizens, who promptly introduce a measure establishing community of property and of wives and children. It is possible that the abolition of the family and equality of opportunity for women were ideas which were under general discussion in intellectual circles at this time. But Aristophanes may have been thinking specifically of Plato's ideas; he is known to have been acquainted with the philosopher, and could have had a preview of some of the proposals which he was going to put forward in *The Republic*.

The fact that a version of these proposals was incorporated into the plot of a comic play should not be taken as evidence of their general acceptability. 'The world turned upside down' is a common theme in comedy (see p. 179), and it is precisely because they are so outrageous and improbable that rule by women and its associated communism are featured in the play. There can be little doubt that Plato's ideas would have seemed shocking to most Athenians – a reaction which is anticipated by the character of Socrates when he introduces them in the dialogue (450a–451a, 457c–d). But that they were under discussion at all is indicative of a concern about the role of women in the state which may not have been confined to Plato and his circle.

Equality of education, of employment opportunities and of political and military rights are all principles which will find a ready acceptance in many quarters today, even though we are still a long way from achieving them.[1] It goes without saying that Athenian women enjoyed none of these advantages. In Plato's scheme, men and women are also awarded the same sexual and property rights, although he introduces both items in what will appear to many modern readers to be a very negative way, by denying sexual freedom to members of both sexes who are within the prescribed age limits for child-bearing, and by abolishing the right to own property. It is worth bearing in mind, however, that the disabilities imposed on men by these measures are very similar to the disabilities which Athenian women suffered from in real life. Moreover, one aspect of the programme would have represented an advance for Athenian women, since it is implied that once they have passed the age of forty women will be able to choose their own sexual partners.

Other items in the programme are still capable of arousing tremendous controversy. The abolition of the mothering role, which in Plato's terms is an integral element in the eradication of the sexual division of labour, is probably the most problematical proposal for most readers; and the premise on which it is based – that the physiological differences between men and women are of no relevance in a social and political context – is still very much debated. Plato is the only Greek author known to us who explicitly rejects the concept of a fundamental antithesis between male and female. His general interest in gender issues was not, however, uncharacteristic of the age in which he lived. When Plato was a young man the parameters of the relations between men and women were being explored by Euripides in a number of his plays; and the privatisation of male concern that is discernible in both the literature and the visual arts of the late fifth and early fourth centuries suggests that in some respects the gender gap may have been narrowing. Plato responds to this development not by re-assessing the male relationship to the private sphere of existence, but by abolishing the private sphere altogether, thereby catapulting women into the public domain. One of his motives for introducing this measure stems from a negative view of the role of women: wives and children constitute an area of loyalty which distracts men from the interests of the community. But the motive to which he gives most prominence seems on the face of it to be far more positive: women themselves have a potential for service to the community which under existing social arrangements is being allowed to go to waste. Neither of these motives springs, of course, from a concern for the personal happiness of either women or men. For Plato, the good of the state is the only object worthy of consideration.

There is no denying that in setting out his programme Plato sometimes lapses into language and attitudes which seem to contradict his espousal of the principle of equality. He speaks of the 'community' (450c) and the 'possession and use' (451c) of wives and children. These expressions derive from a male-centred view of the world, but they do not accurately reflect the substance of his system; there is no suggestion that men are to have any more freedom and control in the matter of sexual relationships than women, so that Plato might just as well have spoken of the 'community' or 'possession and use of husbands'. His statement that in any one area of natural ability women will always be outclassed by men also stems from a deep-seated male prejudice; but the inference which he draws from it is far more positive – since women have no abilities which are peculiar to themselves, there is no reason why they should be limited to a domestic role and excluded from activities traditionally associated with the male.

Since Plato's object in introducing female emancipation was to benefit the state and not women themselves, we should not be surprised if his personal attitude to women is not all that modern feminists might desire. It is the system itself, and not the philosopher's attitudes, which should be the focus of our criticism. Here the objections are more fundamental. Plato's idea of women's liberation is to convert women into honorary men. He ascribes such a low value to women's traditional functions and qualities that he sees no reason why their role should not – within the Guardian class – be abolished. Other writers, such as Hesiod (see p. 22), had only fantasised about the existence of a world without women, but Plato sees it as a theoretical possibility, since in his ideal state Guardian women are, in all but their child-bearing function, identical to men.

Recognising that the burden of childcare is one of the chief obstacles lying in the way of female emancipation, Plato takes steps to remove it. This does not, of course, entail an insistence that the burden should be shared with men, for their involvement in the private sphere is to be reduced to a minimum and not augmented. Nor can the need for childcare be ignored altogether, for although he is not prepared to admit this openly, people are not like watchdogs, and human offspring require a prolonged period of care and nurturing. Plato's solution is to hand the job over to women from another class. There can be no doubt that the nurses who look after the Guardian children are to be drawn from the class of economic providers – and in this sector of society, we can safely assume, the age-old sexual division of labour will continue to flourish. The system as a whole is one that can only function within a set of rigidly hierarchical structures in which all forms of non-intellectual labour (apart from military defence) are devolved downwards to a subordinate class comprising the majority of the population. In Plato's state, top girls will indeed get the top jobs, but only at the expense of the women beneath them in the social hierarchy. What he envisages is not, after all, a transformation of gender relations, but only, in the words of one modern feminist, 'a change in the genitalia of the people at the top'.[2]

In his last dialogue, the *Laws*, written shortly before his death in 347 BC, Plato produced a second prototype for a reformed society. The constitution proposed for this imaginary state is a more moderate one, and his programme of female emancipation is also considerably modified. Children of both sexes are still to receive the same education and military training, and women are to dine in public messes – although in both the schools and the messes the sexes are now to be segregated (780b–781d; 794c; 804d–806c). Women will also have access to public office. As in *The Republic*, it is the waste of talent involved in the neglect of women's education which chiefly concerns him: 'for thus for the same expense and trouble there arises and exists in nearly every instance only half a state instead of a whole one' (805a). However, marriage and family life are to be reinstated (773e–776b); indeed, they are to be made semi-compulsory, in that men over the age of thirty-five who fail to marry will be compelled to pay annual fines. Women will apparently have no equality of choice where marriage-partners are concerned, since marriages are to be arranged by their fathers and the prospective grooms; and dowries are to be abolished, so that women will behave less oppressively and men will be less subservient (see also p. 116). In his old age, it seems, Plato was less willing to contemplate radical social change, and as a result his latent misogyny became far more visible.

ARISTOTLE

Although Aristotle had been a pupil and friend of Plato for twenty years, in his later thinking he departed from Platonic doctrine in a number of respects, and his views on the nature and proper role of women are radically different from those of his master. His concept of the inherent physiological inferiority of the female (see p. 106) was matched by his belief that women differed fundamentally from men in their psychological characteristics and social competence.

According to Aristotle, women are capable of achieving the virtues of self-control, courage and justice, but whereas in males these qualities are associated with the ability to command, in females they involve a capacity for subordination. 'A man would be thought a coward if he were only as brave as a brave woman, and a woman a chatterer if she were only as restrained as a good man' (*Politics* 1260a; 1277b). Like Xenophon (see p. 140), he believes that men and women complement each other within the private relationship of marriage: 'human beings cohabit not merely to produce children but to secure the necessities of life. From the outset the functions are divided, the husband's being different from the wife's; so they supply each other's deficiencies by pooling their personal resources. For this reason it is thought that both utility and pleasure have a place in conjugal love' (*Nicomachean Ethics* 1162a).[3] This amicable partnership between male and female contributes to the well-being of the community as a whole: 'The community needs both male and female excellences or it can only be half-blessed' (*Rhetoric* 1361a).

But in a marriage as in a community the male is naturally the dominant partner: 'The association between husband and wife is clearly an aristocracy. The man rules by virtue of merit, and in the sphere that is his by right; but he hands over to his wife such matters as are suitable for her ... In some cases, however, it is the wife that rules, because she is an heiress; such rule, then, is based not on merit but on wealth and power, just as it is in oligarchies' (*Nicomachean Ethics* 1160b).[4] Aristotle's one implied criticism of the existing treatment of women is that their education has been neglected: the goodness of the state depends in part on the goodness of its women, and they should be given a training in community values (*Politics* 1260b). But it is not envisaged that this education will take them out of their traditional domestic role; rather that it will better equip them to perform this role in accordance with the needs of the community.

In the *Politics* (1259a–1260a), Aristotle identifies three basic relationships of domination and subordination existing within the household, and compares them with three different types of political authority. The relation of master to slave is like a tyranny, because it is a rule exercised in the master's own interests. The relation of a father to his children is like a monarchy, because the father rules by virtue of a superiority deriving from their difference in age, and takes the interests of his children into account. The relation of husband to wife is 'political' (that is, democratic): it is true that political rule generally involves an interchange of roles between ruler and ruled, with the aim of creating relationships of equality; but in the case of husband and wife the distinction between superior and inferior is permanent. Wives, in other words, will never be able to take over their husbands' 'office', and assume control of the household.

The justification for this state of affairs appears to be that in women the deliberative faculty 'lacks authority' (1260a), whereas in children it is merely undeveloped. Aristotle seems here to be attributing to women an inherent intellectual passivity, but the precise significance of the expression is not at all clear. Nor is it particularly easy to understand why he likens the relationship between husband and wife to a political democracy in which some of the citizens are destined never to hold office. He may by this analogy have intended to express the complementary but nevertheless permanently asymmetrical character of their roles – women are separate, inferior, but equal. However, this is not stated explicitly, and the whole argument is extremely unsatisfactory. In other areas of research Aristotle shows himself to be a scrupulous empirical scientist, but where relations between the sexes are concerned his assumption that women are naturally subordinate seems to be based on nothing more substantial than his belief that the existing household is a natural entity capable of meeting some essential human needs.

17

Women in Classical sculpture

MORTAL WOMEN

In the sculpture of the fifth and fourth centuries BC there is no equivalent of the Archaic *kore* figure (see pp. 92–4). Women are less frequently depicted than men, and ordinary mortal women – as opposed to goddesses and characters from myth – are particularly thin on the ground. Since sculpture was almost always displayed publicly, either in religious sanctuaries or in civic centres, this reluctance to represent real-life females can be seen as one facet of the constraints being placed on women's public appearances during the Classical Age. Certainly one would not expect women who were recognisable as individuals to make much of an appearance, since portraiture was rare in a society where stress was placed on collective rather than on personal achievement, and very few men were honoured in this way. But the female type, so strongly represented in the previous era by the *kore*, is also by and large absent, while the male type continues to have a vigorous existence, most notably in the ubiquitous athlete or warrior figure. On the Athenian Acropolis, male statues of this kind were set up in place of the *kore* figures damaged in the Persian invasion; the stress being placed on Athena's masculine qualities in visual representations of the period seems to have been matched by a masculinisation of her chief residence in Athens.[1]

This dearth of large-scale statues of mortal women makes a study of the construction of gender differences in sculpture rather difficult. But a comparison between the statue in Fig. 30, and one of the renowned Riace warriors (Fig. 31), or Myron's famous Discus-thrower, serves to illustrate a few basic points. Most obviously, the traditional distinction of nude male and clothed female was still being maintained in the fifth century, as was the legs apart/legs together distinction observed in Archaic statues (see pp. 92–3). The male figures now have their arms raised from their sides, and are actively involved in the world, either as soldiers (the Riace figure originally carried a shield and sword), or as athletes. While the woman is on display and invites the spectator to look at her, the males are absorbed in what is going on around them and are oblivious of observation. This is a mark of gender difference which can be found in the visual art of many cultures, not least our own, and it has been tellingly summed up by John Berger (1972, p. 97) in the phrase 'men act and women appear'.

These male figures offer two examples of the 'heroic' male nude commonly represented in the fifth century BC. In the case of the discus-thrower, the nudity is socially realistic, since athletes performed naked; but this is certainly not true of the Riace warrior, since men did not go naked into battle. It seems more than likely that the essential nature of the male figure was being highlighted in these nude representations (see p. 93); but we must also take into account the possibility that for Greek men they may have contained an element of eroticism. We have been educated to see the antique male nude as a symbol of the nobility of the Greek cultural achievement, and for this reason we are often scarcely aware of the fact that we are looking at statues of men whose clothes have been removed. A Greek man would certainly have responded to these works in quite a different way from ourselves; and sexual arousal may well have been part of that response. Nevertheless it is apparent that the typical male pose is active rather than passive. The male nude may have been a sexual image for the Greeks, but he cannot be described as a sexual object.

Mythological as opposed to real-life women give us rather more to go on in the way of large-scale sculptural representation. These narrative scenes are particularly useful, since they show women and men together so that the gender differences emerge all the more clearly. One example is provided by the sculptures from the east pediment of the temple of Zeus at Olympia, created in the 460s (Fig. 32). These represent the preliminaries of a chariot race between king Oenomaus and the hero Pelops, who had to win the contest in order to gain the hand of the king's daughter Hippodamia. In the end he succeeded only by cheating, for he had bribed Oenomaus's charioteer to replace the chariot's axle-pin with a piece of wax, causing the king to crash and be killed. In the sculptural group the central figure of Zeus is flanked by Pelops on one side and Oenomaus on the other; beyond them are Oenomaus's wife, Sterope, and the bride-to-be, Hippodamia, next to the horses and chariots. The familiar polarities of nude/clothed, legs apart/legs together, and active/passive distinguish the males from the females. It has been pointed out that part of the interest of this scene lies in the varying degrees of knowledge possessed by the participants, and in the sense of psychological conflict which this creates.[2] In this context, it is worth noting that it is through the two women, and in particular through the positioning of their arms, that tension and anxiety are expressed. While the men reach out with their arms into the outside world, the women are turned in on themselves: Hippodamia fiddles nervously with her robe, while Sterope clutches herself convulsively. Men act, while women reflect the emotional consequences of their actions, could be said to be one of the implications of this scene. In Hippodamia's case, our perception of the passivity of her role is reinforced by our knowledge that she is not just a spectator of the contest but also the prize to be awarded to its winner.

This atmosphere of highly-charged immobility gives way, in the sculptures of the temple's west pediment, to one of frenzied activity. The two scenes are linked, however, by their shared theme of marriage. Around the central figure of the god Apollo rages the battle between the Lapiths and the Centaurs, the part-horse, part-human monsters who had disrupted the wedding feast of the Lapith king by attempting to rape all the females present. The Lapiths' strenuous and successful defence of their womenfolk provided

Classical sculptors with one of their most popular subjects. For them, it doubtless symbolised the struggle between civilisation and barbarism; but it is significant that in this particular narrative civilised society is represented by the institution of marriage, which is under threat from the bestial and promiscuous sexuality of the Centaurs. Women feature here as the objects of male conflict and beneficiaries of male protection. Their utter passivity is emphasised not, as in the case of Hippodamia, by a self-absorbed quiescence, but by their gestures of frantic helplessness.

The Amazons are a group of mythological mortal women who clearly depart from the norm of female passivity (see pp. 58–62). The story of their battle against the Greeks was another very popular subject in Classical art, and it often appeared side by side with that of the Lapiths and Centaurs, as for example in the metopes of the Parthenon (see pp. 191–3), in the wall-paintings of the sanctuary of Theseus in Athens,[3] in the frieze of the temple of Apollo Epicurius at Bassae (Figs 10 and 33) and in the reliefs of the Mausoleum of Halicarnassus. There is a striking contrast in the two episodes between women who are active and women who are passive, between women who fight and women who are fought over. These polarities were matched in the narratives by opposing outcomes, for the Amazons were beaten by the Greeks, while the Lapith women were rescued and restored to an ordered existence. Again, marriage can be seen as one of the themes that links the two scenes: women who are active and refuse to marry (as the Amazons did) are ultimately overpowered by men, while women who are passive are rewarded with male protection within marriage and the blessings of civilised life.

The *stele*, or carved gravestone, was the only sculptural medium in which real-life women were depicted with any frequency in the Classical Age. From about 430 BC onwards it became common for gravestones in Athens to be decorated with domestic scenes in which the deceased were shown as in life, either bidding goodbye to members of their family, or engaged in characteristic activities. The appearance of this type of representation is indicative of a growing acknowledgement of the private dimensions of human experience. Both men and women were commemorated in this way, and although deceased males might also appear in their public role as soldiers – particularly if they had died in battle – there were few references in the reliefs to the political side of men's activities. The domestic scenes involved either all-male, all-female or mixed family groups.

Although cemeteries are generally associated with the more personal aspects of people's lives, they are also public places, and this was particularly true in ancient Greece, where tombs were placed on either side of the roads leading out of a city. The images on gravestones were therefore intended in part for public consumption, and it is not surprising that they should sometimes have been used to advertise the deceased person's conformity to a collective ideal. In the case of females, this might entail a statement about their reproductive and nurturing capacities, and it was relatively common for women to be shown with babies or young children (Fig. 26). There might also be oblique allusions to their sexual identity – in one famous Athenian gravestone dating to about 400 BC (Fig. 25), a woman named Hegeso is seen seated on an elegant chair, selecting jewellery from a casket held by a slave-girl, an image which also refers indirectly to her husband's ability to maintain her in a leisured and affluent lifestyle. Intimate though many of these scenes are, they do not contain any realistic portraits, and the facial features are idealised and empty of emotion. On the other hand, the tenderness of gesture or attitude which is displayed in many of the mixed groups (Fig. 24) suggests quite strongly that male values at this time were beginning to embrace the notion of devotion to family.

THE GODDESS IN SCULPTURE: ATHENA AND THE ATHENIAN ACROPOLIS

In the Athenians' visual representations of their patron goddess they were confronting the paradox implicit in a patriarchal society's worship of a powerful female deity. Often the difference between Athena and ordinary mortal women was emphasised by high-lighting the goddess's more masculine qualities, so that she was identified as a special case rather than a role model. In this context it is interesting to compare a bronze statuette of Athena, originally equipped with spear and shield, and a statuette of Zeus in which the god is seen in an almost identical warlike pose, on the verge of hurling a thunderbolt (Figs 34 and 35). The conventional distinction of nude male, clothed female has been maintained in these pieces; but in all other respects Athena can be seen to be imitating the outgoing and aggressive stance of the male deity.

The complexity of the artistic responses to Athena can best be observed in her most prominent sanctuary, the Athenian Acropolis. This had been devastated by the Persians in 480 and 479 BC, and was redeveloped by the Athenians between about 460 and 405 BC (Fig. 37a). It forms one of the most compelling visual statements about a Greek goddess ever made, and since so much of it has either survived or has been described for us by ancient authors, it is worth spending some time exploring its themes.

On entering the sanctuary, a visitor was immediately confronted by a thirty-foot (9 metre) bronze statue of Athena Promachos (Champion) complete with shield, helmet and spear. This image of the warrior-maiden, surrounded by war trophies, would have dominated the nearby processional way. Looking to the right, the spectator saw in the west pediment of the Parthenon a set of sculptures illustrating the contest between Athena and Poseidon (see p. 26 and Fig. 37b) for the post of patron deity of Athens. This story would have provided an appropriate reminder of how Athena had acquired her pre-eminent position in the city. But it also represented a victory of a female over a male deity, and would have been read in relation to the narrative of the western metopes, the rectangular slabs below the pediment, which depicted the battle between Greeks and Amazons. There can be little doubt that by this time the Amazon story, together with the episodes represented in the other metopes of the building, was being seen as a mythical analogue of the victory of Greek order and self-control over the arrogance and excess displayed in the Persian invasion which had destroyed the Parthenon's predecessor.[4] But the episodes had further statements to make about the character of a civilised society and of the forces which were opposed to it. In the case of the Amazons, women who had assumed a masculine lifestyle and evaded the constraints of marriage were being identified as the barbarians.

An ancient tour of the Parthenon began, then, with a representation of likeness and difference. As a female warrior who repudiated marriage, Athena was like the Amazons. But she was different because she could get away with it: Athena won and the Amazons lost; female dominance in the divine sphere is counterbalanced by the suppression of female aggrandisement in the human sphere. From the west end, the spectator moved along either the north or the south side of the building, where the narratives in both sets of metopes served to reinforce this notion of difference. Both described the successful defence of marriage, the institution rejected by Athena. In the Trojan War, the subject of the north metopes, marriage was being defended against an outsider, Paris, who had subverted civilised marriage-exchange systems by stealing a wife: in one scene, which showed Aphrodite interceding with Menelaus on Helen's behalf, the prelude to the reinstatement of the marriage was represented. The objective in the battle between Lapiths and Centaurs, depicted in the south metopes, was the defence of marriage against promiscuous and random sexual activity (see p. 190): here, as in other fifth-century representations of this episode, the wedding theme was stressed by the transfer of the battle to a domestic setting (indicated by the presence of wine jars) and by the inclusion of women in the scene.[5] In both these narratives, then, marriage was being viewed as a model of the civilisation whose values were being championed.

The Parthenon metopes served as a frame for the frieze, which was viewed through the building's outer columns. A number of scholars have suggested that in the Panathenaic procession depicted here the spectator was being presented with a heroised image of the Athenian *polis*: hence the city's infantry soldiers, for example, have been equipped with horses.[6] This transfer of heroic values to the *polis* was made visible in that the eye passed from the individualised scenes of legendary conflict shown in the outer metopes to the representation of the citizen collective in the frieze – the *polis* was wrapped around with the heroic tradition. Moreover, the heroic values underpinning the *polis* were seen to include a belief in marriage as a civilising and cohesive force.

At the eastern end of the building the contradiction created by these references to marriage on a virgin goddess's temple was resolved. The east pediment told the story of Athena's birth from her father's head, an event which helped to confirm Zeus in his rule (see p. 28), and which was seen here as central to an orderly universe: the birth scene was framed by a representation of the planetary system, symbolised by the chariots of the Sun-god and Moon-goddess (Fig. 36). The metopes below, which depicted the battle of the Gods and Giants, illustrated the goddess's subsequent defence of her father's regime. In interpreting these episodes one can make use of the analysis which Vernant applies to the goddess Hestia (see pp. 45–6). On the human level, daughters have to be given away in marriage, and other men's daughters have to be imported into the *oikos* in order to reproduce it; but on the divine level the relationship between father and daughter need not be fractured, because at the end of the day the divine household is self-sufficient (see pp. 21–2). Athena's virginity makes her different, but ultimately it serves the same end as marriage among the humans – the maintenance of the male-dominated household.

The eastern section of the frieze contained a representation of the only female participants to appear in the procession (Fig. 39). Their calm dignity presents a strong contrast to the frenetic activity of the horsemen and charioteers of the earlier sections; but there are reasons to believe that, just as the young males in the frieze are presented in their definitive role as warriors, so there are allusions to the definitive role of these young women, that of the wife-to-be. Like brides, they move in procession towards a door – in this case, that of the temple itself. The seating arrangements of the Olympians towards whom they are walking produce quasi-marital pairings: in one case the marriage is a reality, and Hera is seen making the gesture which is symbolic of the bride (Fig. 7). Athena's position next to the robe reminds the spectator of her supervision, as goddess of weaving, of the most characteristic activity of the married woman; while the presence of Hephaestus on her other side calls to mind the pseudo-sexual relationship of this couple (Fig. 1; see p. 28). But there is one small reminder of the goddess's virginity: she holds the Gorgon's head, the centrepiece of her aegis, defensively over her genitals. Although in this scene Athena's affinity with the young mortal women who lead the procession seems to be acknowledged, her difference is not to be forgotten.

Inside the temple this sense of difference was vastly augmented. Here the spectator came face to face with Phidias's Parthenos, a gold-and-ivory statue which was over forty feet (12.3 metres) in height (Fig. 38). The discourses of the metopes were repeated in the decoration of this colossal image: Greeks versus Amazons were depicted on the outside of her shield, Gods versus Giants on the inside; while Lapiths and Centaurs waged war around the rim of her mighty sandals. This is the Virgin Warrior, the daughter who in the idealised world of the gods does not have to be given away in marriage. The need for marriage has been displaced downwards, on to an imperfect human world: the relief on the statue's base represented the creation of Pandora, the first woman and, of course, the first wife. In Athena, the dangerous femininity of Pandora's daughters has been transformed, to produce a goddess who is loyal to the male in all things – apart from marriage (see p. 28).

In moving from the Parthenon to the smaller temple of the Erechtheum, dedicated to Athena Polias, the spectator encountered an expression of a femininity more akin to that of ordinary mortal women (Figs 2, 37). An olive tree in a court at its western end marked the spot where the contest between Athena and Poseidon, represented in the Parthenon's west pediment, had actually been staged. This allusion to Athena's association with the fertility of the earth was reinforced by a number of myths identifying the precinct of the temple as the location for the upbringing of Erichthonius (see p. 28), the child born from the ground and reared by Athena. The building was also the site of many of the religious activities performed by young Athenian women (see pp. 134–5); and its feminine character was established visually by the porch of the Caryatids (see p. 93), who bear a striking resemblance to the women on the Parthenon frieze. In passing from the Parthenon to the Erechtheum, one moves from a goddess represented primarily as different, to one associated with the major stages in a woman's life, maidenhood and motherhood. However, when the Erechtheum is viewed in the context of the sanctuary as a whole, it has to be admitted that it is the Warrior Maiden who is dominant on the Athenian Acropolis. The Erechtheum is an exquisite building, but it is the mighty Parthenon, with all its masculine associations, which leaves the most lasting impression.

THE ARRIVAL OF THE FEMALE NUDE

In the latter half of the fifth century a partial erosion of the nude male/clothed female distinction occurred when fine clinging drapery was introduced in some of the sculptural representations of women. This permitted a greater concentration on the details of the female anatomy, and a number of narrative devices were employed in order to justify the flattening of a woman's dress against her body. In the work known today as the Ludovisi throne (Fig. 40), a female who may be the goddess Aphrodite is being lifted out of a pool of water, providing an early example of the wet T-shirt effect; while in the case of the surging figure from the Nereid Monument (Fig. 41), it is a combination of wind and water which has exposed the woman's form. The arrangement of the drapery clothing the Victory from the temple of Athena Nike (Fig. 43) has been produced by a pose which, as Pollitt (1972, p. 115) has commented, is only 'vaguely functional'. This woman's gratuitous action of untying her sandal has served to create a suggestive shadowy hollow between her thighs, a motif which was to become common in the Hellenistic era.

It is tempting, when contemplating the gradual emergence of the female nude in Greek art, to see it as a sign of an improved social status for women. Nudity was a long-established convention in the representation of the Greek male, and men unquestionably had a higher status than women in Greek society. Certainly, the proliferation of the male nude must indicate that the meaning of nudity for the Greeks was in some ways very different from the one which it has for us; and this impression is strengthened by the fact that most of the female near-nudes produced in the fifth century were goddesses. In these circumstances it is difficult to believe that nudity in itself was seen as something which degraded women.

However, a study of the reclining goddess from the east pediment of the Parthenon (Fig. 42) reveals that, whatever female nudity may have meant for the Greeks, its arrival did not necessarily mark an erosion of gender difference in the visual arts. The voluptuous figure of the goddess, who is probably Aphrodite, is revealed through the softness and strategic bunching of her garment, and through the device of the 'slipped strap'. This piece provides an illustration of the air of passivity and availability which often accompanies these more sensual treatments of the female form. If one compares it with the Riace warrior (Fig. 31), it is apparent that the distinction of passive/active, self-conscious/unaware has by no means been abandoned.

The sexual invitation seems to be made explicit in the case of the figure known to us as Venus Genetrix (Fig. 44).[7] The offer of fruit to the spectator is reminiscent of the pose of the archaic *kore* figures (see p. 93); but here the symbolism of the offer is spelt out for us, and it seems to speak more of sensuality than of fertility. The goddess's robe is drawn tightly across her thighs, there is a pronounced gather between her legs, and the bodice has slipped to reveal a breast. The gesture of removing her mantle leaves us in little doubt that what she is offering is herself, and that she is to be consumed along with the fruit. This statue furnishes an example of what in modern parlance is called the 'come-on', where the gaze of the spectator is openly acknowledged and accepted.

It was not until the end of the Classical Age that the statue which may well have been the first large-scale female nude was produced. Known as the Aphrodite of Cnidus, it was the work of the renowned Athenian sculptor Praxiteles, and is dated to about 340 BC (Fig. 45). In its day, this statue caused a great sensation. According to the Roman writer Pliny the Elder (*Natural history* 36.20–1), Praxiteles offered it for sale, along with a more conventional clothed piece, to the people of Cos, who chose the more 'decent' of the two alternatives. The nude version was eventually sold to the city of Cnidus, on the west coast of Asia Minor, where it became a great tourist attraction. We are told that the king of Bithynia on one occasion offered to discharge the whole of Cnidus's national debt in return for the Aphrodite, but the Cnidians sensibly rejected the deal.

In Cnidus the statue was displayed in a specially-constructed shrine, designed so that it could be viewed from both the front and the rear. Both Pliny (*Natural history* 36.21) and Lucian (*Essays on portraiture* 4) mention an apparently well-known story about a man who fell in love with the Aphrodite, and having contrived to get locked into her shrine overnight made a sexual assault on the statue, leaving a stain on it. There can be little doubt that this erotic response was one which the sculptor had consciously provoked. The excuse which he is offering for Aphrodite's nudity is that she is taking a bath (indicated by the water urn and towel by her side), while her pose suggests that she has been caught unaware by an intruder. This device, which was to be repeated many times in later Greek art, places the statue firmly in the genre of voyeurism, or 'lawless seeing'. It is clear that Aphrodite does not want to be looked at, that the spectator's view is illicit; but at the same time the fact that her attention has been engaged by the intruder assures the spectator that he himself is unseen and safe. The head is turned away, but the body is wide open to the spectator's gaze, and the hand which ineffectually tries to hide the genitals only serves to draw attention to them.

The advent of the female nude, and the increasing sensuality which can be discerned in the treatment of many male nudes, are two of the most striking developments in mid fourth-century sculpture. They indicate that some of the most significant gender distinctions of early Classical sculpture were beginning in some contexts to be broken down. This tentative coming together of male and female images, which was to become much more marked in the Hellenistic period, suggests that a subtle shift in gender relations was already occurring towards the end of the Classical Age.

A number of factors probably contributed to this process. The ideal of female seclusion was coming under growing pressure in the fourth century as political upheavals and accompanying economic problems forced women out of the home (see pp. 137–8), and greater contact between the sexes would have produced a change in male attitudes to women. At the same time ordinary male citizens were being increasingly excluded from the sphere of public achievement as a result of gradual professionalisation in the political and military fields and the encroachments of external powers – of Persia in the eastern Aegean and Philip of Macedon on the mainland. Both of these developments would have meant that the realm of the private was no longer identified as exclusively female, and that men were more able to acknowledge the emotional and sensual aspects of their experience and to express their erotic appreciation of the female form. New religious attitudes were also emerging, for similar reasons, and the possibility of establishing a personal rather than a collective relationship with a great goddess like Aphrodite was beginning to be envisaged.

POSTSCRIPT

18

The Hellenistic Age

One of the most famous Greek pronouncements about women, that their 'greatest glory is to be least talked about among men, whether in praise or blame' (Thucydides 2.46), occurs at the end of a speech which is often viewed as a stirring statement of the ideals of Athenian democracy. The speech's relationship with reality is questionable on a number of levels, and it would be misleading to view either its overall picture of Athenian life or its specific allusion to Athenian women as a straightforward expression of Greek values.[1] Nevertheless, it establishes a link between democratic ideals and the subordination of women which is suggestive of a broad historical relationship. The intensification of the patriarchal system which had begun in the Archaic period, when social and political functions were being transferred to the male-dominated institutions of the *polis*, reached its peak in mid fifth-century Athens. Here, the existence of democratic privileges and duties heightened the awareness of a gulf between masculine and feminine spheres of operation, and at the same time generated tensions in which gender difference was identified as a source and symbol of a range of conflicts.

But the era which saw the tightening of the ideological constraints on women was also the era when these constraints were subject to the greatest challenge. The speech containing the reference to women's glory was supposedly made by the Athenian statesman Pericles at the funeral of the men who had died in the first year of a war that was to give rise to large-scale disruptions. During the Peloponnesian War the changing perceptions of both female and male roles produced a shift in gender relations which was maintained during the difficult years that followed Athens' defeat and the destruction of her empire (see p. 195). Social dislocation was by no means confined to Athens: in the fourth century the political and economic instability experienced in many parts of Greece was associated with the gradual disintegration of the *polis* system, which had played so crucial a part in shaping the lives and representations of Greek women.

On the mainland, political disturbance culminated in the conquests of Philip II of

Macedon, who was assassinated two years later, in 336 BC. He was succeeded by his twenty-year-old son Alexander, who in 334 brought one of his father's long-term projects to fruition by launching an invasion of the Persian Empire. By the time of his death in 323 Alexander the Great's military genius had won for him a vast realm, extending from Egypt to north-west India. But he had appointed no successor to his position; and the half-century which followed was occupied with a series of complex and bloody struggles between his generals. Three major kingdoms emerged from the carve-up of Alexander's empire, each headed by a dynasty founded by one of these generals: Egypt was ruled by the Ptolemies, Asia (centred on Syria and Mesopotamia) by the Seleucids, and Macedonia and Greece by the Antigonids. During the next century the balance of power between these kingdoms was precariously maintained; but they were considerably weakened by border wars, by internal dynastic struggles and by independence movements. In the second century BC the long-drawn-out process of absorption into the Roman Empire began. It was completed in 30 BC, when Cleopatra VII, the last Ptolemaic ruler of Egypt, committed suicide.

Clearly, the Hellenistic Age inaugurated by Alexander's conquests was a period of large-scale political and social upheaval. Considerable numbers of Greeks from the mainland migrated to Egypt and Asia where, together with the descendants of the men who had been fighting there since Alexander's time, they formed a new governing class which dominated the local, working populations. They were backed by a large middle class of Greek soldier-farmers, who gave military service to the king in return for land. Greek was the official language of the new kingdoms, and many of their cultural institutions were adaptations of ones that had existed in Classical Greece. But the system of government was far from Greek. The Hellenistic kings were absolute monarchs, who ruled personally (with the help of large Greek bureaucracies), and were the source of all law. In the cities which they founded many of the features of the Greek *polis* – agora, councils, magistrates – were reproduced; but the cities were centres for a purely local administration, and had no political independence. Only on the Greek mainland, where the control of the Antigonids was in some areas very weak, did the *polis* retain anything like its former vigorous existence.

The degree of change experienced by women in the course of these transformations would have varied considerably in accordance with the region or class in which they were living. But in general it can be said that there was an erosion of the asymmetry between the sexes during the Hellenistic Age, and a consequent improvement in the status of women. In the political arena, the most spectacular advance was made by the women of the Hellenistic royal families. The last Cleopatra was exceptional, in that she ruled Egypt directly; but a number of her predecessors wielded considerable influence as the wives or mothers of kings. Outside the royal circle genuine political competence was an impossibility for members of both sexes; but this in itself would have fostered a willingness to extend 'paper' privileges to females, and we know of a few instances from cities in Asia and Greece where women were awarded honorary citizenship or even magistracies. Of more significance were the rights which women acquired to own and control property. Papyrus documents from Egypt reveal that during this period women were able to act as sellers and purchasers, as lessors and lessees of land, and as bestowers and receivers of legacies.[2] In some parts of Greece women are recorded in inscriptions as landowners, as borrowers of money and as slave-owners; and some of the females of Sparta are known to have been conspicuously wealthy (see p. 156).

Legal and economic rights were matched, in some areas, by greater personal freedom.

Poems such as Theocritus' *Idyll* 15, which recounts the conversation of two respectable Greek housewives making their way through a festival throng in the streets of Alexandria, suggest that there had been a relaxation of the physical and ideological constraints on women. Male poets were exhibiting a growing interest in women's private lives; and at the same time a new generation of female poets, such as Erinna, Nossis and Anyte, was beginning to give voice to women's feelings. Some of the new philosophical movements – Epicureanism, Cynicism, and Neopythagoreanism – included a few women among their adherents; and, on a more basic level, there is evidence to show that in some places girls were being educated outside the home, in elementary schools. The gender gap had by no means been eradicated, but female and male roles were now seen as less clearly distinct. This development is reflected in Hellenistic art, where the representation of both the male and the female nude is often handled with overt displays of eroticism. In Ptolemaic Egypt the goddess Isis was being reshaped as a deity with wide-ranging functions, and her cult was attracting numerous worshippers of both sexes.

A network of factors lay behind these changes. Though in lesser numbers than men, women too were migrating from the Greek mainland to Egypt and Asia, either with their husbands or as independent workers. This increased mobility would in many cases have involved social displacement and financial hardship, as women moved outside the scope of the protection traditionally provided by their families. But the loosening of generational ties, and the rupture of the close relationship between family and *polis*, would also have led to a weakening of some of the social controls over women. Perhaps the most potent factor of all was the disbarment of the male citizen from active political involvement. Communal values were disappearing, and were being replaced by an ideology of individualism, which produced a focusing of cultural attention on private experiences and emotions, and made the attainment of personal happiness a legitimate aspiration. The domestic sphere was increasingly recognised as an object of male concern, and as a result the parameters of the private and public domains became blurred.

The extent to which these changes affected the everyday lives of women and men should not be exaggerated. Nor should the resulting shift in gender relations be seen as an entirely new phenomenon. The gradual privatisation of male interests had been discernible even in the culture of late fifth-century Athens, and in the fourth century it had become more pronounced (see above, pp. 143, 179, 184, 190, 195). Outside Athens, masculine and feminine spheres may always have been less sharply differentiated, and it is possible that if we possessed adequate sources for other Classical *poleis* the developments of the Hellenistic Age would appear rather less dramatic. Nevertheless, the scale of the political transformations occurring in the new era was undeniably large, and it is difficult to believe that this would not have accelerated the process of change in the construction of gender roles. At the very least, this process enables us to know a little more about 'what women were doing' during the Hellenistic Age. But, sadly, the voices that speak of these doings are still predominantly male.

Notes

Introduction

1. This expression is used by the anthropologist Edwin Ardener (1975b, p. 22) in referring to an analysis presented in an earlier article (1975a). In the latter he argues that the analytic tools which a male-centred intellectual tradition has supplied to social anthropologists equip them only to respond to the world-views of male informants, and neither to hear nor to understand the views held by women.

I WOMEN IN MYTH

1 Myth: an introduction

1. See S. Freud (1922). The fact that in visual images the Gorgon has a gaping mouth, and that the Greek word *stoma* denotes both a mouth and either the cervix of the uterus or the lips of the vulva, lends some plausibility to Freud's theory. For Freud, the snaky hair of the Gorgon symbolises both pubic hair and, in a typically Freudian piece of acrobatic thinking, a multiplication of penises.

2. For one version of this theory, see Guthrie (1950), pp. 27–35.

3. For discussions of the evidence, and a résumé of recent references, see Ehrenberg (1989), pp. 66–76, and Goodison (1989), pp. 4–11.

4. For example, see Ehrenberg (1989), pp. 63–6.

5. Bamberger (1974), p. 267.

6. For a much fuller discussion of this symbolisation, see Ortner (1974).

7. I would not want to suggest that in this play Euripides is 'for' civilisation and 'against' nature: the work is far more complex than this. See pp. 175–80.

8. For a useful discussion of liminality, see Friedrich (1978), pp. 132–3.

2 Creation myth

1. For more on Metis and the birth of Athena, see p. 28. For a useful analysis of Hesiod's creation myth, see Arthur (1982).

2. It is worth noting, however, that Zeus has only one legitimate son, Ares the god of war, who is represented as a brainless hooligan who is quite unloved by his father. There is no danger that anyone will ever conspire to make him the king of heaven.

3. There is, for example, a supreme irony in the fact that the lady with the scales of justice who stands on top of the Old Bailey in London is lending her good name to a judicial system still notorious for its exclusion of women. For a very detailed treatment of the use and abuse of women in monuments, see Warner (1985).

4. All translations from Hesiod are by Dorothea Wender, in *Hesiod and Theognis*, Penguin Books, 1973.

5. In many of the Greek myths relating to sacrifice, there is the implication that the life of an animal has to be paid for with the life of a human being: see, for example, the myth of Iphigenia (p. 29), or the one which explains why Athenian girls have to go to Brauron (p. 30). Hunting, which was still an important source of meat in the Archaic and Classical Ages, did of course sometimes claim human lives, so that there is a certain factual truth in the idea. But there is also a metaphorical truth: it is death that sustains our lives, and we pay for this ultimately with our own deaths – meat-eating means that we are not immortal, and so it distinguishes us from the gods.

6. Compare this sentiment with the one expressed in Euripides' *Hippolytus*, where the hero asks why the gods did not arrange things so that men could go to temples and buy their sons: 'Then they could live at home like free men – without women' (*Hippolytus* 616–24).

3 The Olympian goddesses: virgins and mothers

1. Herington (1955), pp. 6–15 and 43–7, suggests that by the fifth century BC there was no separate cult of Athena Parthenos. He believes that both of the two main temples on the Acropolis, the Parthenon and the so-called Erechtheum, were linked to the cult of Athena Polias; but that in the Parthenon the emphasis was on the goddess's manifestation as a virgin warrior.

2. Translation by Dorothea Wender, *Hesiod and Theognis*, Penguin Books, 1973.

3. All translations from Homer are by Richmond Lattimore: *The Iliad of Homer*, University of Chicago Press, 1951; *The Odyssey of Homer*, Harper and Row, 1965.

4. Translations from *The Eumenides* are by Robert Fagles, *The Oresteia*, Penguin Books, 1977.

5. See *Homeric Hymns* 28 and Pindar's *Olympian Odes* 7.34–8.

6. The tendency of men to upstage or appropriate women's creative powers is something that anthropologists have detected in ritual practices like that of the *couvade*, the stylised enactment by males of pregnancy, labour and giving birth, at a time when a female member of the family is actually going through these experiences. Some feminists would claim that the male domination of gynaecology springs from a similar desire to usurp female reproductive functions. On this subject in general, see Halperin (1990, p. 143), and the references cited there.

7. All translations of Homeric hymns are by Apostolos N. Athanassakis *The Homeric Hymns*, Johns Hopkins University Press, 1976.

8. See Sophocles' *Electra* 563–76.

9. See Euripides' *Iphigenia in Tauris* 26–41.

10. According to the gynaecological treatise *On the diseases of virgins*, from the corpus of Hippocratic writings, objects were offered to Artemis at the onset of menstruation. What precisely this was intended to achieve is not completely clear from the passage: see the discussion by King (1993), pp. 113–15.

11. Brauron's association with a goddess who imposes penalties on young women is also suggested by the belief that Iphigenia, one of Artemis's best-known victims, had died and been buried there after escaping from Tauris: see Euripides' *Iphigenia in Tauris* 1464.

12. The ages of the 'bears' – five to ten – may seem to make them a bit too young for an initiation into adult life, since girls were normally married at about the age of fourteen (see p. 119). Sourvinou-Inwood (1988, pp. 25–30) suggests very plausibly that the time spent at Brauron should be regarded as a ritual preparation for the premenstrual stage, when the girls would go through a process of maturation culminating in the menarche. This would inevitably lead in most cases to marriage and childbirth. That women's reproductive role was an important element in the site's associations is confirmed by the records of dedications made there, many of which came from women who had undergone childbirth. The number of young girls who actually went through the initiation is uncertain. At one time a spell at Brauron seems to have been regarded as an essential step for all young girls before they were married, but by the fifth century BC this was certainly no longer the case, and the rites seem to have involved only a representative group.

13. There were a number of important cults of Artemis in the Greek cities on the western coast of Asia Minor, and this tends to bear out the view that she may originally have been a non-Greek deity whose worship spread across the Aegean to mainland Greece. It is possible that she was related to Cybele, the Anatolian mother goddess.

14. See Seltman (1952) and Burkert (1979), p. 130.

15. See Euripides' *Iphigenia in Tauris*, 1464–7. For further discussion, see p. 111.

16. Early temples of Hera existed also at Perachora, Tiryns, Olympia, and Paestum (in southern Italy).

17. Translation by David Barrett (1964), in Aristophanes, *The Wasps. The Poet and the Women. The Frogs*, Penguin Books. The *Thesmophoriazusae* has in this version been given the title *The Poet and the Women*.

18. In Hesiod's version, Zeus and Hera have only three children: according to him, Hephaestus (and not Typhoeus) is the child to whom Hera gives birth when she seeks to rival her husband in single-handed reproduction (*Theogony* 928).

19. Pausanias 1.20.3.

20. Translation by C.M. Bowra (1964), *Pindar*, Oxford at the Clarendon Press, p. 389.

21. The text of Empedocles is in G.S. Kirk, J.E. Raven and M. Schofield (1983), *The Presocratic philosophers*, Cambridge University Press, frag. 349, lines 20–4.

22. In spite of her femininity, the birth of Aphrodite from a purely male substance points to a masculine element in her make-up. This surfaces again in the strange cult of the bearded Aphrodite, which according to a number of sources was practised in Cyprus. A statuette found at Perachora, near Corinth, and dating to the early seventh century BC, seems to relate to a similar cult. It shows a bearded female figure rising from what looks like a scrotal sac, and has been identified by some as the bearded Aphrodite emerging from Uranus' genitals: see Payne (1940), plate 102, no. 183a.

23. See Burkert (1979), pp. 107–8.

24. See Detienne (1977), pp. 116–31.

25. Translation by J.F. Nims, in D. Grene and R. Lattimore, eds., *The complete Greek tragedies. Euripides III*, University of Chicago Press, 1958.

26. Translation by Gilbert and Sarah Lawall (1986), in Euripides, *Hippolytus*, Bristol Classical Press.

27. Translation of Sappho, fragment 2, by Josephine Balmer (1992), in *Sappho. Poems and fragments*, Bloodaxe Books, no. 79. For a more detailed treatment of Sappho's invocations of Aphrodite, see p. 87–8.

28. It has often been pointed out that the pattern of growth in the Mediterranean is not entirely in accordance with this interpretation. When the seed-corn is planted in the autumn, it begins to sprout after a few weeks, and growth is well under way by the following spring. For this reason, Nilsson (1940, pp. 51–2) suggested that Persephone's descent into the Underworld represented the storage of grain in underground containers during the summer months, while her resurrection was the bringing up of grain for sowing in the autumn. This is an attractive solution, but there is no getting round the fact that Persephone is said to return in the spring-time. The myth can probably not be made to square exactly with real life, but perhaps the hazards of the winter months – the fear of blight or frosts – would have meant that it was not until the

spring that people would have been reasonably sure that Persephone had returned as corn.

29. For a detailed discussion of the whole question of initiation, see Mylonas (1961), pp. 261–85.

30. Burkert (1983, pp. 60–7) takes this argument further and maintains that the advance of civilisation as a whole was thought of as requiring the confinement of sexual activity to certain well-defined and limited areas.

31. For a much fuller discussion of this aspect of Artemis, see King (1993). As King points out elsewhere (1987, p. 120), women were generally excluded from all culturally significant acts involving bloodshed, including sacrifice. Women were not prohibited from attending sacrifices, but usually they could not perform them.

32. In myth there are a number of daughters who are notable for their loyalty to their fathers: witness, for example, Athena's closeness to Zeus, Antigone's devotion to the blinded Oedipus (Sophocles' *Oedipus at Colonus*), and Electra's passion for vengeance against the murderers of Agamemnon (Aeschylus' *Libation Bearers*, and Sophocles' and Euripides' *Electra*).

33. For much fuller discussions, see Leach (1969) and Warner (1976). According to Leach, this model for bridging the gap between gods and men is most likely to be employed in aristocratic societies, where it is possible for illegitimate sons born to women of the lower classes to be elevated to the ranks of the élite to which their fathers belong.

4 *Women in the poems of Homer*

1. The most common view is that the Trojan War took place in about 1250 BC, and that politically speaking it was a fairly minor event.

2. All translations of the *Iliad* quoted here are from the version by Richmond Lattimore, *The Iliad of Homer*, University of Chicago Press, 1951.

3. See, for example, Kakridis (1971), pp. 68–75.

4. All translations of the *Odyssey* are from the version by Richmond Lattimore, *The Odyssey of Homer*, Harper and Row, 1965.

5. Chronologically, Odysseus visits Circe before he reaches Calypso's island; but in the narrative the Circe episode comes later, since it is recorded in an extended flashback.

6. Penelope's apparent ignorance of her husband's identity has been the subject of much discussion. Some critics believe that in a scene where she interviews the disguised Odysseus (Book 19) the poet wishes to convey the impression that she has in fact recognised her husband. For a recent argument in favour of this view, see 'Penelope's cunning and Homer's', in Winkler (1990), pp. 129–61; and for one against it, see Murnaghan (1987), who believes that Odysseus' willingness to withhold vital knowledge from his wife is indicative of her lack of control over events. What seems certain is that the poet is not prepared to be explicit on the subject. See Katz (1991) for a discussion of 'the disjunction between the two conflicting directions of narrative action' (p. 10); and Felson-Rubin (1994), pp. 4–5.

7. See Foley (1978).

8. See Felson-Rubin (1994), pp. 38–9.

5 *Amazons*

1. Diodorus Siculus 17.77.1; Strabo 11.5.4; Curtius 6.5.24–32; Plutarch, *Life of Alexander* 46.

2. See Strabo 11.5.1, and Diodorus 2.45.3 and 3.53.3.

3. *Airs, waters, places* chap. 17.

4. See Pindar, *Nemean Odes* 3.38, and Euripides, *Heracles* 409.

5. See, for example, Plutarch, *Life of Theseus* 26, Pausanias 1.2.1, Isocrates *Panath.* 193.

6. See Aeschylus, *Eumenides* 685–90, Plutarch, *Life of Theseus* 27, Lysias 2.4–6.

7. See Pausanias 5.11.6 and Quintus Smyrnaeus 1.18–810.

8. See Tyrrell (1984, p. xiii and p. 129, n.1) for a résumé of modern theories about the origins of the Amazons myth.

9. The author of *Airs, waters, places* gives a similar account to Herodotus, and tells us that Sauromatian women in his own day were not allowed to lay aside their virginity until they had killed three men in battle. For Sauromatian female burials see Sulimirski (1970), pp. 34 and 105–6.

10. During the Gulf War of 1991 British newspapers were full of photographs of women soldiers among the US forces. Some future reader might well, in the absence of other information, imagine that women formed the major element in those forces.

11. Boardman (1982) points out that the earliest certain references to the Amazon attack on Athens date from the 460s BC, and speculates that the whole episode may have been invented after the Persian invasion of Greece, in order to provide a mythological precedent. The idea that the Amazons, like the Persians, launched their attack on the Acropolis from the Areopagus hill may have been invented by the tragedian Aeschylus when he wrote the play *The Eumenides* (lines 685–90).

12. For more detailed discussions of the negative implications of the myth, see du Bois (1979), Merck (1978), and Tyrrell (1984).

II THE ARCHAIC AGE 750–500 BC

6 *Women in an age of transition*

1. See, for example, Murray (1980), p. 39, and Morris (1986).

2. See Engels (1980) for a detailed calculation of the effects of regular female infanticide.

3. For further discussion of these developments, see p. 75. Exceptions to the general rule that daughters did not inherit are to be found in Sparta and Gortyn; see p. 155–6, and p. 159.

4. For examples of both endogamy and exogamy among the aristocratic families of later Archaic Greece, see Lacy (1968), pp. 67–8. Tyrants too frequently made alliances through marriage exchanges with rulers of other states.

5. This outline is based on the accounts of the system given by Lacey (1966) and Morris (1986), pp. 105–15. I am in agreement with these two authors when they maintain that there is no good evidence for the existence of the dowry in Homeric Greece. For a summary of opposing arguments in favour of the dowry, see Morris.

6. For a more detailed discussion of the way in which this system operated in Classical Athens, see pp. 115–6.

7. Both exceptions relate to societies which were probably atypical. The law-code of Gortyn, in Crete, prescribed the payment of financial compensation by a wife's seducer to the aggrieved husband, but does not set down any punishment for the wife; while in Sparta, where the attitude to marital fidelity was a highly unusual one, adultery was not recognised at all. See pp. 154, 159.

8. For further discussion of funeral scenes on Archaic pots, see Coldstream (1968) and Ahlberg (1971). See pp. 162–3, for the restrictive legislation on funerary practice introduced in some areas in the late Archaic period.

9. See Plutarch, *Life of Solon* 12.1.

10. These laws were still in force in the fourth century, and are discussed in more detail in Part III: see pp. 162–3 (funeral rituals), pp. 125–6 (women's adultery), and pp. 117–8 (the *epikleros*).

11. For a further discussion of these developments, see Sussman (1978).

7 *Women and the poets*

1. Two of the poets referred to in this section – Semonides and Archilochus – may not have been 'lyric' poets in the strict sense, in that their poems may not have been performed to the accompaniment of a lyre. They could have been accompanied by some other instrument, or sung or recited without musical backing. But this is an area of great uncertainty, and 'lyric poetry' is a convenient shorthand expression to describe the shorter and more personal poems being written at this time.

2. See Lloyd-Jones (1975), p. 23.

3. Translation by Lloyd-Jones (1975).

4. Translation by C.M. Bowra, in *Greek lyric poetry*, Oxford University Press, 1961, p. 32. The numbering of the Alcman poems quoted is the one given by D.A. Campbell (1987), in *Greek lyric*, vol. 2, Loeb edition.

5. The numbering of the Anacreon poems is the one given by Campbell (1987): see previous note.

6. Translation by Burnett (1983), p. 80. The numbering of the Archilochus poems is the one given in M.L. West ed. (1989), *Iambi et Elegi Graeci*, vol. 1, Oxford, Clarendon Press.

7. This translation of Alcman and the ones that follow are by Campbell (1987): see note 4 above.

8. Translation by Campbell (1987): see note 4.

9. Translation by Burnett (1983), p. 87.

10. But see p. 105 for other evidence relating to the encouragement of female homosexuality in Sparta.

8 *Women as poets: Sappho*

1. *Palatine Anthology* 9.571.

2. Aelian, fragment 187.

3. As Dover (1978, p. 182) points out, the late date for these adverse comments can probably be explained by the influence exerted by the social, moral, and cultural attitudes of Classical Athens on the conventional morality of the Hellenistic Age. Archaic Lesbos may have possessed quite different standards.

4. Translation by Josephine Balmer (1992), in *Sappho. Poems and fragments*, Bloodaxe Books. The numbering of the Sappho fragments is the one given by Campbell (1982) in *Greek lyric*, vol. 1, Loeb edition.

5. *Supp.Lyr.Graec.* S261A.

6. Philostratus, *Life of Apollonius* 1, mentions a woman named Damophyla, from Pamphylia in Asia Minor, who was a disciple of Sappho's; but this is a late source and very unreliable.

7. In D.A. Campbell (1987), *Greek lyric*, vol. 2, Loeb edition.

8. For a discussion of the distinction between the *threnos*, the set dirge, and the *goos*, the improvised lament, see Alexiou (1974), pp. 11–14.

9. See pp. 162–3, for the restrictions imposed from the late Archaic age onwards on the singing of laments by women.

10. See p. 38, for the *Iliad* episode. For a detailed discussion of the complexities of Sappho's response to Homer in this poem, see Winkler (1990, pp. 167–76).

11. This contrast is more apparent in the Greek, where the gender of the 'some' mentioned three times in the first verse is masculine.

12. I am very grateful to Margaret Williamson for giving me a preview of her detailed analysis of this poem, which will appear in her forthcoming book *Sappho's immortal daughters*.

13. See, for example, Denys Page (1955), who believes that the speaker is expressing the jealousy she feels when she sees her lover talking to a man. George Devereux (1970) goes further, and sees the poem as describing a pathological case of penis-envy.

9 *Women in stone*

1. See Richter (1968), p. 4, for a discussion of the significance of the *korai* statues displayed on the Athenian Acropolis.

2. It is possible that these inhibitions did not exist in Sparta, where women may have performed athletics and appeared at public festivals in the nude – see page 152. But this was very unusual, and was seen as shocking by other Greeks.

Even today, female nudity is something that is publicly displayed only in certain fairly well-defined areas, such as art galleries, advertisements, and newsagents' shelves. In ancient Greece there were far fewer public outlets for visual representation; and these occurred in contexts where we would still today not expect to encounter female nudity, namely, religious worship and the honouring of the dead.

3. See, for example, Pollitt (1972), pp. 6–7.

III THE CLASSICAL AGE 500–336 BC

10 *Women's bodies*

1. See the reference cited by Lloyd (1983), pp. 72–3.

2. For women as fillies, see, for example, Euripides, *Hecabe* 142, and *Andromache* 621; see also p. 79, for Anacreon's extended use of the metaphor. For marriage as something that tames, see, for example, Homer, *Iliad* 18.432, and Euripides, *Medea* 804. Calame (1977, vol. 1, pp. 411–20) provides a full discussion of this metaphorical usage.

3. See Parker 1983 (p. 102, n. 113) for the tentative suggestion that the three 'polluted' days which occurred in Athens at the end of each month may have had a connection with menstruation.

4. Translation by I.M. Lonie in *Hippocratic writings*, edited by G.E.R. Lloyd, Penguin, 1978.

5. See Lefkowitz (1981, p. 12–25), where a full discussion of this diagnosis and its ideological implications is provided. Celibacy does not appear to be regarded as the only cause of 'the wandering womb'; but it is the one most frequently cited.

6. Lefkowitz (1981, pp. 16–17) cites the examples of the crazed wanderings of Io, in Aeschylus' *Prometheus Bound*,

and of the ecstasies of the women worshippers of Dionysus, in Euripides' *The Bacchae*, to illustrate the point that
'hysteria' among women is also a preoccupation of fifth-
century tragedians. In both these cases, the women are
brought to their senses by men – Io, significantly, when she
is made pregnant by the god Zeus.

7. Translated by Lonie. See note 4 above.

8. See Golden (1984), p. 313.

9. For other references to women's addiction to sex, see
Aristophanes, *Thesmophoriazusae* 477–96, and *Women in the
Assembly* 877–1111; and Euripides, *Trojan Women* 665–6,
and *Medea* 569–73. For Tiresias' pronouncement, see
Hesiod, fragment 275.

10. For evidence that the *erastes* might sometimes be a
married man, see Xenophon, *Symposium* 2.3 and 4.12–16,
and *Hellenica* 6.4.37. This is implied also by Plato, in *Laws*
841d. A marriage contract from Hellenistic Egypt, dating
to 92 BC, contains a clause which makes it unlawful for the
husband to have either a concubine or a boy lover: see
Pomeroy (1984), pp. 87–9.

11. For recent discussions of this subject, see Dover, 1978,
pp. 60–109; Foucault, 1979, pp. 77–131, on the construction of sexuality in general, and 1987, pp. 187–203, on
ancient Greece in particular; and Halperin, 1990,
pp. 15–40.

12. In this analysis I am closely following that of Halperin
(1990), pp. 31–2.

13. See Plato's *Symposium* 184d–185b.

14. For an elaboration of this argument, see Halperin
(1990), pp. 18–21.

15. The idea did not apparently gain general acceptance
until some time later. See Galen, *On the seed* 2.1.

16. Translation by Robert Fagles, in Aeschylus, *The Oresteia*, Penguin Books, 1977.

17. See Censorinus, *De die nat.* 5.4 and 6.4; Aristotle, *On
the generation of animals* 722 b10.

18. See Eyben (1980/81), pp. 5–7.

19. See Lysias, ed. Th. Thalheim, editio maior, Teubner,
1901, pp. 347–8. For fuller discussions of these questions,
see Nardi (1971), pp. 82–115, and Eyben (1980/1), p. 21.

20. See Garland (1990), p. 65. In this work (pp. 59–99),
Garland provides a detailed account of childbirth in
ancient Greece.

21. See Kurtz and Boardman (1971), p. 139.

22. Epigram by Perses of Thebes, probably written in the
second half of the fourth century BC. Preserved in the
Palatine Anthology 7.730. Translation by Peter Wigham, in
The Greek Anthology, edited by Peter Jay, Penguin, 1981,
no. 55.

23. Golden (1981, p. 318, n. 7) has produced a statistically-
based estimate of six confinements per woman; while
Angel (1972, p. 94, table 28), has proposed, on the evidence of pelvic scars found on female skeletons, an average
of 4.6.

24. For an illustration of a birthing stool, see Garland
(1990), p. 70.

25. For the *ololuge*, see the *Homeric hymn to Apollo* 119. The
ritual bath is described in Callimachus, *Hymn to Zeus*
15–17. For swaddling, see Plutarch *Moralia* 3e, and Soranus, *Gyn.* 2.14.2. The symbols pinned to doors are mentioned by Hesychius, *Lexicon*.

26. For the text of the law, see Parker (1983), p. 336.

11 *Women in Athenian law and society*

1. See Just (1989), pp. 34–6.

2. See Kuenen-Janssens (1941), p. 194.

3. We know of some cases where women were engaged
in transactions which clearly involved more than the value
of a *medimnos*: see Schaps (1979), pp. 52–6. Schaps has
suggested that such a transaction was only made void if it
was challenged in the courts by the *kyrios*, and that the
transaction was not in itself illegal.

4. See Harrison (1968), p. 52. Foxhall (1989, p. 37) believes that he probably did need the woman's consent.

5. See Schaps (1979), p. 78, and Golden (1990), pp. 132–5.

6. See Schaps (1979), pp. 79–80.

7. See Harrison (1968), pp. 55–6.

8. The position when a widower was left with daughters is
uncertain.

9. See Harrison (1968), pp. 144–9, and Just (1989), p. 87.

10. The infrequency with which property was transmitted through the *anchisteia* probably explains why there are
very few references in literature or inscriptions to women
as landowners. Schaps (1979, pp. 5–6) believes that most of
the references which do occur in inscriptions can be explained by the fact that a husband's land had been mort-
gaged for his wife's dowry; that is, the land was being used
as a guarantee of the repayment of the dowry in the event
of a divorce.

11. The rules relating to the *epiklerate* are complex and in
some ways quite difficult to understand. For fuller discussions, see Harrison (1968), pp. 9–12 and 132–8; and
Schaps (1979), pp. 25–47.

12. What happened when the deceased had more than
one daughter is not absolutely clear, but there is evidence
to suggest that they shared the property, and were claimed
in marriage by relatives in order of succession. See Harrison (1968), p. 134.

13. See Harrison (1968), pp. 309–11.

14. See Isaeus 10.12. Harrison (1968, p. 135) suggests that
only one son of the *epikleros* could succeed to his maternal
grandfather's estate, and that this was by way of posthum-
ous adoption into his grandfather's *oikos*; the situation is,
however, unclear.

15. For further discussion of the question of a surplus of
marriageable females, and the possibility that this may have
been avoided by exposure of girl babies, see pp. 130–1.

16. Plutarch (*Life of Cimon* 4.7) considers it highly unusual
that Elpinice, the sister of the Athenian general Cimon,
married in accordance with her own free will.

17. See Thompson (1967).

18. For a summary of these arguments, see Patterson
(1981), pp. 3 and 97–105. The law was introduced at a time
when the existence of a large population of resident aliens,
and the involvement of many Athenians in overseas activities, would have meant that even citizens from the lower
classes were in a position to marry non-Athenians. The law
may have been intended to deal with quite a pressing
problem of marriage outside the citizen community: an
anticipated surplus of Athenian women who could not be
settled in families may have been perceived as part of this
problem.

19. See, for example, Aeschylus, *Seven against Thebes*
752–6; Euripides, *Medea* 1281; Pindar, *Pythian Odes*
4.254–5; and Sophocles, *Antigone* 569, *Oedipus Rex* 1211,
1257, 1485, and 1497–8, and *Women of Trachis* 31–3.

20. For the theme of abduction, see also Sourvinou-Inwood (1973, p. 17).

21. For funerals, see Alexiou (1974), who shows that the same parallels can be found in Greek rituals today; Jenkins (1983), pp. 141–2; Redfield (1982), pp. 188–9; Seaford (1987), pp. 106–7; Holst-Warhaft (1992), p. 41, who discusses the similarity between wedding songs and funeral laments in the modern Greek folk tradition; and Rehm (1994). For sacrifices, see Foley (1982b); Jenkins (1983), p. 141; Burkert (1983), p. 63; and Golden (1988), pp. 11–12.

22. Translation by E.F. Watling, in Sophocles, *Electra and other plays*, Penguin Books, 1953. Other tragedies in which a wife is expected to share her home with a concubine are Aeschylus' *Agamemnon* (Clytemnestra and Cassandra), and Euripides' *Andromache* (Hermione and Andromache). In the former, the wife murders the concubine, in the latter she fails in the attempt.

23. On the bigamy question, see Harrison (1968), pp. 16–17. For concubines in general, and the rights of their children, see Just (1989), pp. 52–62. Whether illegitimacy was, in normal circumstances, a disqualification for citizenship is a hotly disputed question. Just is inclined to believe that it was, and that the law introduced in the Peloponnesian War conferred citizen rights on the children of Athenian concubines only. Those who, like Pomeroy (1975, p. 67), maintain that illegitimacy was not a disqualification think that the effect of the law was to give citizenship to the children of foreign concubines; that is, the Periclean law on citizenship was for the time being relaxed. Even if this were the case, it does not follow that the relationships were recognised as marriages.

24. Aristophanes, *Clouds* 1083–4. Most commentators accept that this was in reality a punishment for adultery, but Cohen (1985) believes that it may have been a product of Aristophanes' over-fertile imagination.

25. For other references to women's adultery in Aristophanes, see *Lysistrata* 107, *Thesmophoriazusae* 340–4 and 477–501, and *Women in the Assembly* 523–5.

26. See Harrison (1968), pp. 43–4.

27. Translation by H. Lloyd-Jones in Lefkowitz and Fant (1982), pp. 19–20.

28. For a full discussion of this practice, see Schaps (1977).

29. Translation by A.H. Sommerstein, in Aristophanes, *Lysistrata* etc., Penguin Books, 1973.

12 The lives of women in Classical Athens

1. See Lacey (1968, pp. 105–6), who believes that the exposure of healthy legitimate children of either sex was probably limited. Some support for this view can be derived from Aristotle, who refers to a 'regular custom' forbidding the exposure of children who are not deformed (*Politics* 1335b); and from Isocrates, who includes the disposal of infants in a recital of the horrendous iniquities perpetrated in the past by non-Athenian states (*Panathenaecus* 121–2).

2. For a full discussion of women's names, see Golden (1986).

3. As Cole (1981, p. 226) has pointed out, the only substantial piece of evidence, a fifth-century vase painting which seems to show a girl being led to school, could be interpreted as a representation of an educated courtesan.

4. For a more detailed discussion of these vase paintings, see Cole (1981), pp. 223–4. Caution is necessary when using vase paintings as evidence of real-life activity: there are no clear indicators in the paintings that these are to be interpreted as citizen women, and the viewer may have been intended to see them as educated courtesans or as Muses.

5. See Bérard (1989), p. 91, for a discussion of a vase painting which may show a musical entertainment in the home. But see note 4.

6. For a discussion of these vase paintings, see Arrigoni (1985), pp. 166–9 (athletics) and pp. 173–4 (swimming). Arrigoni is inclined to believe that the swimming girls are Athenian, but is more sceptical about the 'athletes'. See Kahil (1983), pp. 235–8, and Sourvinou-Inwood (1988), pp. 130–4, for discussions of the fragments from Brauron; Sourvinou-Inwood is responsible for the suggestion that the nudity of some of the girls had a ritual significance.

7. This translation is based on the version of the text suggested by Sourvinou-Inwood (1988, pp. 136–52).

8. For a discussion of these mysterious rituals, see Robertson (1983).

9. For this reason, it seems very unlikely that any one Athenian woman would have performed all the roles mentioned by the chorus, and there is probably a degree of comic exaggeration in their recital. The spell at Brauron would have involved the largest number, but even here only a small fraction of Athenian girls could have undertaken this service. The sanctuary is very modest in size, and has not provided a large number of finds. The girls who did go to Brauron may, however, have been regarded as representatives of their age group: Sourvinou-Inwood (1988, pp. 113–14) has suggested that a certain number of girls from each of the ten tribes of Athens may have been selected.

10. See Euripides, *Children of Heracles* 777–83; 'On the windy mountain ridge the shrill voices of maidens echo to the rhythmic beat all night of dancing feet.'

11. See Pomeroy (1975), pp. 58–9, for an excellent summary of the principal positions in this debate.

12. For men as shoppers, see Aristophanes *Wasps* 493–9 and *Women in the Assembly* 817–22; and Theocritus 15.15–20. In rural Greece today it is still common for men to do the shopping.

13. See Gould (1980, p. 47) for an interesting discussion of Demosthenes 47. Similar accusations of intrusion are made in Demosthenes 21.79 and 37.45–6.

14. See in particular Gomme (1925), pp. 7–8.

15. Dubisch (1986, p. 200) points out that in a modern Greek village in the Cycladic islands, the state of a woman's home is thought to reflect her moral character; if she has looked after it properly, then she has not had time to get into mischief. Hirschon (1978, p. 83) informs us that at one time among Greeks living in Turkey quickly-prepared dishes were referred to as 'prostitutes' food'.

16. For ribbons, see Demosthenes, 57.31 and 34; garlands, Aristophanes, *Thesmophoriazuae* 448; vegetables, *Thesmophoriazusae* 387 and *Wasps* 497; and bread, *Wasps* 1390–1. See Cohen (1989), pp. 7–9, for a comprehensive survey of women's activities outside the home.

17. The countrywoman's freedom to move outside the home may have been similar to that which Dubisch (1986, p. 200) describes as belonging to a woman in rural Greece today: 'She works in the fields when necessary, she feeds the chicken and the pig, she attends religious festivals. But these are all activities connected with her role as maintainer of the house in both its physical and spiritual aspects.'

18. Translation by J.F. Nims, in *Euripides III. The Complete Greek tragedies*, University of Chicago Press, 1958.

19. Translation by Philip Vellacott, in Euripides, *The Bacchae and other plays*, Penguin Books, 1973.

20. For a discussion and plans of excavated houses, see Walker (1993).

21. This suggestion is made tentatively by Finley (1981, p. 159), and far more positively by Stone (1977) in relation to the high mortality rate in England in the period 1500 to 1800.

22. Golden makes reference here to studies carried out in modern societies where abortion is permitted.

23. Translation by Philip Vellacott, in Euripides, *The Bacchae and other plays*, Penguin Books, 1973.

24. Some prominent examples are Agamemnon and Iphigenia, Agave and Pentheus, Medea and her sons (parent/child murder); and Oedipus and Laius, and Orestes and Clytemnestra (child/parent).

25. For family burial, see Garland (1985, pp. 125–76). For grave-reliefs and privatisation, see Humphreys (1983, p. 111). See p. 190 for more information on gravestones.

26. For male prostitution, see Aeschines 1.74. For the tax on prostitutes, see Aeschines 1.119–20. For the 'red-light' districts, see the sources cited by Halperin (1990), p. 183, n. 29.

27. Translation by Halperin (1990), pp. 92–3.

28. Translation by Halperin (1990), p. 100. Halperin argues that this 'democratising initiative' (whether introduced by Solon or not) was intended 'to shore up the masculine dignity of the poorer citizens . . . and to promote a new collective image of the citizen body as masculine and assertive' (pp. 102–3).

29. See Halperin (1990), pp. 109–12 for a more detailed discussion of the different types of prostitutes.

30. See, for example, Lysias 4.7, Isocrates 7.48, and Aeschines 1.42.

31. See Lysias 7.41, and 24.6; and Demosthenes 53.29.

13 *Sparta and Gortyn*

1. See Redfield (1977–8), who, like Aristotle (see pp. 155–6), is inclined to see women's power as ultimately damaging to the Spartan state.

2. Pausanias, for example, records (3.13.7) that at a sanctuary of Dionysus in Sparta women who were called 'Daughters of Dionysus' used to run races.

3. See Edmonson (1959). We can compare this practice with the one at Elis (see p. 33), where sixteen matrons of excellent repute oversaw the girls' foot-races held at Olympia in honour of Hera.

4. For a detailed discussion of the bronzes, see Arrigoni (1985), pp. 156–8. For the girl runners at Olympia, see p. 33.

5. See Dover (1978), pp. 185–96.

6. See Cartledge (1981), pp. 94–5.

7. Hodkinson (1989), p. 120, no. 70, has suggested that marriages may have been subject to increasing parental control in the fifth century, when considerations of wealth and status were beginning to influence marriage practice. See p. 156.

8. Brides at Argos wore false beards: see Plutarch, *Moralia* 245f.

9. See Vidal-Naquet (1981, p. 155).

10. See Hodkinson (1989), p. 109; and Cartledge (1981), pp. 101–2.

11. For discussions of the land ownership question, see MacDowell (1986), pp. 89–110, and Hodkinson (1989), pp. 80–1.

12. Herodotus (6.57.4), in the fifth century, says that if the brotherless heiress had not been betrothed by her father the kings were responsible for deciding who had the right to marry her; whereas according to Aristotle, if her father had not left instructions in his will the heir (*kleronomos*) of his estate gave her in marriage to whomever he liked. MacDowell (1986, pp. 107–8) believes that the new arrangement described by Aristotle may have been introduced in the late fifth century BC. He points out that in Aristotle's account there is an apparent contradiction in that he mentions both an 'heir' (presumably the male next-of-kin) and an 'heiress', and suggests that the property may have been divided in some way between the two.

13. Many of the sayings cannot be definitely dated to the Classical period, and their authenticity is in any case debatable. But it is likely that they 'were shaped by realities of Spartan life' (Kunstler, 1987, p. 35).

14. See Willetts (1967), pp. 11 and 21–2. Leduc (1992, pp. 254–72) suggests an alternative explanation. With the emergence of the *polis*, a matrimonial system had been adopted in Gortyn which ensured that land was transmitted without regard to sex; whereas the Athenians in the same situation had chosen a system whereby wealth other than land was transmitted – through the institution of the dowry – without regard to sex. In the latter case, since wealth was eventually passed on to a woman's sons, citizenship was opened up to men who did not own land. In the case of Gortyn, citizenship continued to be tied to the ownership of land.

15. Willetts (1967, p. 22) believes that the provision which stipulated that the daughter's share of the inheritance should be half a son's portion was a new one, and that previously she may have received more.

14 *Women and religion*

1. See Holderman (1985) for a detailed discussion of sex differentiation among religious officials. A few goddess cults were served by priests: for example, at Old Paphos in Cyprus there was a priest of Aphrodite. Sex differentiation occasionally extended to admission to sanctuaries (see Holderman, 1985, pp. 318–19). For example, there was a sanctuary of Persephone at Megalopolis which women could enter at any time, but which men could only enter once a year (Pausanias 8.31.8).

2. See Parke (1967), p. 73.

3. See Gould (1980), p. 50, n. 92, and the reference cited there.

4. See Mylonas (1961), p. 231.

5. Demosthenes 43.62 and Plutarch, *Life of Solon* 21.4.

6. See Garland (1989), pp. 3–15. Caraveli (1986) has pointed out that the laments for which women in rural Greece are still renowned are often frowned upon by their menfolk, ostensibly because they believe that lamentations imposes too great an emotional strain on the women.

7. It is uncertain whether there was any corresponding taboo affecting women in Athenian religion, but they may have been excluded from the drinking rituals held on the second day of the Anthesteria, and possibly from the dramatic festivals (see pp. 166, 172). For exclusions in other parts of Greece, see Parker (1983, pp. 83–5).

8. Modern suggestions range from two days to four months – the latter being the period which would have elapsed if the objects had been placed in the ground at the festival of the Scira (see n. 12).

9. The nature of the underground depositories used in Athens is not known, since the exact site for the Thesmophoria has not been located. But evidence from elsewhere suggests that they might consist either of natural clefts in the rocks, or of underground chambers. See Burkert (1985), p. 243. The most detailed source for the rite of the piglets and cakes is the scholiast on Lucian *dial.mer.* 2.1 (Rabe 275.23–276.28).

10. See Henderson (1975, pp. 131–2) and Golden (1988). This *double entendre* becomes the basis of an extended 'joke' in a scene from Aristophanes' *Acharnians* (729–835), where a Megarian tries to sell his young daughters in the market disguised as pigs.

11. Winkler (1990, p. 198) notes that the combination of piglets and phallic cakes involves a structured contrast, not just between female and male, but also between raw and cooked, and nature and culture. The mixture is therefore a powerful amalgamation of opposites.

12. Obscenity and chastity were accorded ritual significance in other women-only festivals celebrated in Athens. Women attending the Scira, a festival of Demeter held at harvest-time, were required to remain chaste, and they are said to have eaten garlic in order to discourage the attentions of their husbands. At the Haloa, a secret rite performed by women at Eleusis in honour of Demeter and Dionysus, the women carried models of the male and female sexual organs, drank large quantities of wine and used foul language.

13. See Henrichs (1993) for a summary of recent interpretations of Dionysus.

14. See Kraemer (1979), p. 66, for inscriptional evidence for the cult in Magnesia and Miletus.

15. See Kraemer (1979), pp. 60–5, for a discussion of the evidence relating to Athens.

16. See Henrichs (1978), pp. 124, 130 and 148.

IV IDEAS ABOUT WOMEN IN THE CLASSICAL AGE

15 *Women in drama*

1. Much of the evidence is discussed by Henderson (1991), who believes that women did attend dramatic festivals. For evidence in favour of female attendance, see Plato, *Gorgias* 502b–d and *Laws* 658a–d; and Aristophanes, *Peace* 962–7. Contrary evidence can perhaps be derived from Aristophanes, *Thesmophoriazusae* 383–97, *Peace* 50–53, and *Birds* 793–6; and from Menander *The Grouch* 965–7.

2. Translations of the *Oresteia* are by Robert Fagles, in Aeschylus, *The Oresteia*, Penguin Books, 1977.

3. Translations of the *Antigone* are by Robert Fagles, in Sophocles, *The Three Theban Plays*, Penguin Books, 1984.

4. Translations of *Medea* are by Philip Vellacott, in Euripides, *Medea and other plays*, Penguin Books, 1963.

5. See pp. 153 and 207, Sparta and Gortyn, n. 9. For religious festivals, see Zeitlin (1990), p. 66, n. 8.

16 *Women and the philosophers*

1. Since many of the issues raised by Plato are still of considerable relevance, it seems valid to discuss his ideas in the context of a question which would have been meaningless to Greeks in the fourth century BC, but which has been much debated in recent years – can Plato be regarded as a feminist? For discussions which focus on this question, see in particular Wender (1973), Annas (1981, pp. 181–5), Vlastos (1989), and Lefkowitz (1989).

2. P. Bunkle, 'A history of the women's movement', *Broadsheet*, part 1, Sept. 1979, p. 27.

3. Translation by J.A.K. Thomson, in *The ethics of Aristotle*, Penguin, 1976.

4. Translation by Thompson: see note 3.

17 *Women in Classical Sculpture*

1. For the *kore* figures on the Acropolis, see p. 92. For the statues which were there in the Classical Age, see the account by Pausanias, *Description of Greece* 1.22.4–28.3. See p. 191 for the stress on Athena's masculine qualities.

2. See, for example, Pollitt (1972), pp. 33–5.

3. These paintings do not survive, but they are referred to by Pausanias, 1.17.

4. See Castriota (1992), pp. 134–74.

5. See B. Cohen (1983).

6. See, for example, Osborne (1987).

7. The 'Venus Genetrix' is a Roman copy of a Greek work, and the date of the original is not certain; but many of the stylistic traits belong to the fifth century. See Ridgway (1981), pp. 198–201.

POSTSCRIPT

18 *The Hellenistic Age*

1. See Goldhill (1986), pp. 109–11.

2. See Pomeroy (1984), pp. 115–21, 156–60 and 172.

Bibliography

G. AHLBERG (1971) *Prothesis and ekphora in Greek geometric art* Paul Astroms Forlag. (funerary ritual)

M. ALEXIOU (1974) *The ritual lament in Greek tradition* Cambridge University Press.

J.L. ANGEL (1972) 'Ecology and population in the eastern Mediterranean' *World Archaeology* 4, pp 88–105.

J. ANNAS (1976) 'Plato's *Republic* and feminism', *Philosophy* 51, pp 307–21.

J. ANNAS (1981) *An introduction to Plato's Republic*, Clarendon Press, pp 181–5.

L. ARCHER, S. FISCHER, and M. WYKE (1994) *Women in ancient societies: an illusion of the night* Macmillan.

E. ARDENER (1975a) 'Belief and the problem of women', in S. Ardener (1975), pp 1–17.

E. ARDENER, (1975b) 'The "problem" revisited', in S. Ardener (1975), pp 19–27.

S. ARDENER, ed. (1975) *Perceiving women* Malaby Press.

S. ARDENER (1978) *Defining females. The nature of women in society* Croom Helm.

G. ARRIGONI, ed. (1985) *Le donne in Grecia* Editori Laterza.

M. ARTHUR (1973) 'Early Greece: the origins of the western attitude toward women' *Arethusa* 6, pp 7–58.

M. ARTHUR (1977) 'Politics and pomegranates: an interpretation of the Homeric hymn to Demeter' *Arethusa* 10, pp 7–47.

M. ARTHUR (1982) 'Cultural strategies in Hesiod's *Theogony*: law, family and society' *Arethusa* 15, pp 63–82.

J. BAMBERGER (1974) 'The myth of matriarchy: why men rule in primitive society', in Rosaldo and Lamphere (1974), pp 263–80.

S. BARNARD (1978) 'Hellenistic women poets' *Classical Journal* 73, pp 204–13.

A.S. BECKER (1993) 'Sculpture and language in early Greek ekphrasis: Lessing's *Laokoon*, Burke's *Enquiry*, and the Hesiodic descriptions of Pandora' *Arethusa* 26, pp 277–93.

C. BERARD (1989) 'The order of women', in C. Bérard and others, *A city of images. Iconography and society in ancient Greece*, Princeton University Press, 1989, pp 89–107. (the representation of women in Attic vase-painting)

J. BERGER (1972) *Ways of seeing* BBC/Penguin.

A.L.T. BERGREN (1983) 'Language and the female in early Greek thought' *Arethusa* 16, pp 69–95.

J. BLOK and P. MASON (1987) *Sexual asymmetry. Studies in ancient society*, Gieben.

S. BLUNDELL (1986) *The origins of civilisation in Greek and Roman thought* Croom Helm.

J. BOARDMAN (1982) 'Herakles, Theseus and Amazons', in D.C. Kurtz and B. Sparkes, *The eye of Greece. Studies in the art of Athens*, Cambridge University Press, pp 1–28.

A. BRELICH (1969) *Paides and parthenoi* Edizioni dell'Ateneo (initiation rituals)

P. BURIAN, ed. (1985) *Directions in Euripidean criticism* Duke University Press.

W. BURKERT (1979) *Structure and history in Greek mythology and ritual* University of California Press.

W. BURKERT (1983), trans. P. Bing *Homo necans. The anthropology of ancient Greek sacrificial ritual and myth* University of California Press.

W. BURKERT (1985), trans. J. Raffan, *Greek religion* Harvard University Press.

A.P. BURNETT (1983) *Three Archaic poets: Archilochus, Alcaeus, Sappho* Duckworth.

C. CALAME (1977) *Les choeurs de jeunes filles en Grèce archaique* Edizioni dell'Ateneo e Bizzarri.

A. CAMERON and A. KUHRT, eds. (1993) *Images of women in antiquity* Routledge.

E. CANTARELLA (1987) *Pandora's daughters. The role and status of women in Greek and Roman antiquity* Johns Hopkins University Press.

A. CARAVELI (1986) 'The bitter wounding: the lament as social protest in rural Greece', in Dubisch (1986), pp 169–94.

T.H. CARPENTER and C.A. FARAONE, eds. (1993) *Masks of Dionysus* Cornell University Press.

A. CARSON (1990) 'Putting her in her place: women, dirt and desire', in Halperin, Winkler and Zeitlin (1990), pp 134–69.

P. CARTLEDGE (1981) 'Spartan wives: liberation or licence?' *Classical Quarterly* 31, pp 84–105.

D. CASTRIOTA (1992) *Myth, ethos and actuality. Official art in fifth century Athens* University of Wisconsin Press.

L.L. CLADER (1976) 'Helen: the evolution from divine to heroic in Greek epic tradition' *Mnemosyne* supplement 42.

G. CLARK (1989) *Women in the ancient world. Greece and Rome. New surveys in the Classics* no. 21. Oxford University Press.

K. CLARK (1956) *The nude. A study of ideal art* John Murray.

B. COHEN (1983) 'Paragone: sculpture versus painting. Kaineus and the Kleophrades Painter', in Moon (1983), pp 171–92.

D. COHEN (1985) 'A note on Aristophanes and the punishment of adultery in Athenian law' *Zeitschrift der Savigny-Stiftung fur Rechtsgeschichte* 102, pp 385–87.

D. COHEN (1989) 'Seclusion, separation, and the status of women in Classical Athens' *Greece and Rome* (2nd series) 36, pp 3–15.

D. COHEN (1991) *Law, sexuality and society. The enforcement of morals in classical Athens* Cambridge University Press.

J.N. COLDSTREAM (1968) *Greek geometric pottery* Methuen.

S.G. COLE (1981) 'Could Greek women read and write?', in Foley (1981a), pp 219–45.

S.G. COLE (1984) 'The social function of rituals of maturation: the Koureion and the Arkteia' *Zeitschrift fur Papyrologie und Epigraphik* 55, pp 233–44.

P. CULHAM (1987) 'Ten years after Pomeroy: studies of the image and reality of women in antiquity', in Skinner (1987), pp 9–30.

J. DEJEAN (1990) *Fictions of Sappho: 1546–1937. Women in culture and society.* University of Chicago Press.

M. DETIENNE (1977), trans. J. Lloyd *The gardens of Adonis: spices in Greek mythology* Harvester Press.

M. DETIENNE (1979), trans. M. Muellner *Dionysus slain* Johns Hopkins University Press.

M. DETIENNE (1989) 'The violence of well-born ladies: women in the Thesmophoria', in M. Detienne and J.-P. Vernant, eds., *The cuisine of sacrifice among the Greeks*, trans. P. Wissing, University of Chicago Press, 1989, pp 129–47.

G. DEVEREUX (1970) 'The nature of Sappho's seizure in fr. 31 LP as evidence of her inversion' *Classical Quarterly* (new series) 20, pp 17–31.

S.K. DICKISON (1973) 'Abortion in antiquity' *Arethusa* 6, pp 159–66.

E.R. DODDS (1951) *The Greeks and the irrational* University of California Press.

W. DONLAN (1985) 'The social groups of Dark Age Greece' *Classical Philology* 80, pp 293–308.

K.J. DOVER (1973) 'Classical Greek attitudes to sexual behaviour' *Arethusa* 6, pp 59–73.

K.J. DOVER (1974) *Greek popular morality in the time of Plato and Aristotle* Blackwell.

K.J. DOVER (1978) *Greek homosexuality* Duckworth.

K. DOWDEN (1989) *Death and the maiden. Girls' initiation rites in Greek mythology* Routledge.

J. DUBISCH, ed. (1986) *Gender and power in rural Greece* Princeton University Press.

P. duBOIS (1978) 'Sappho and Helen' *Arethusa* 11, pp 89–99.

P. duBOIS (1979) 'On horse/men, Amazons and endogamy' *Arethusa* 12, pp 35–49.

P. duBOIS (1982) 'On the invention of hierarchy' *Arethusa* 15, pp 203–20.

P. deBOIS (1991) *Centaurs and Amazons. Women and the prehistory of the great chain of being* University of Michigan Press.

P.E. EASTERLING (1987) 'Women in tragic space' *Bulletin of the Institute of Classical Studies* 34, pp 15–26.

C. EDMONSON (1959) 'A graffito from Amyklai' *Hesperia* 28, pp 162–4.

M. EHRENBERG (1989) *Women in prehistory* British Museum Press.

D. ENGELS (1980) 'The problem of infanticide in the Graceco-Roman world' *Classical Philology* 75, pp 112–20.

E. EYBEN (1980–81) 'Family planning in Graeco-Roman antiquity' *Ancient Society* 11–12, pp 5–82.

E. FANTHAM (1975) 'Sex, status and survival in Hellenistic Athens. A study of women in New Comedy' *Phoenix* 29, pp 14–74.

N. FELSON-RUBIN (1994) *Regarding Penelope. From character to poetics* Princeton University Press.

M.I. FINLEY (1955) 'Marriage, sale and gift in the Homeric world' *Revue Internationale des Driots de l'Antiquité* 3.2, pp 167–94; reproduced in M.I. Finley (1981) *Economy and society in ancient Greece*, edited by B.D. Shaw and R.P. Saller, Chatto and Windus, pp 233–45.

M.I. FINLEY (1975) *The use and abuse of history* Chatto and Windus.

M.I. FINLEY (1978) *The world of Odysseus* Penguin.

M.I. FINLEY (1981) 'The elderly in Classical antiquity' *Greece and Rome* 28, pp 156–71.

H.P. FOLEY (1978) '"Reverse similes" and sex roles in the *Odyssey*' *Arethusa* 11, pp 7–26.

H.P. FOLEY (1981a) *Reflections of women in antiquity* Gordon and Breach.

H.P. FOLEY (1981b) 'The conception of women in Athenian drama', in Foley (1981a), pp 127–68.

H.P. FOLEY (1982a) 'The "female intruder" reconsidered: women in Aristophanes' *Lysistrata* and *Ecclesiazusae' Classical Philology* 77, pp 1–21.

H.P. FOLEY (1982b) 'Marriage and sacrifice in Euripides' *Iphigenia in Aulis' Arethusa* 15, pp 159–80.

H.P. FOLEY (1985) *Ritual irony. Poetry and sacrifice in Euripides* Cornell University Press.

H.P. FOLEY, ed. (1994) *The Homeric hymn to Demeter. Translation, commentary, interpretive essays.* Princeton University Press.

E. FOX-GENOVESE (1982) 'Placing women's history in history' *New Left Review* 133, pp 5–29.

L. FOXHALL (1989) 'Household, gender and property in Classical Athens' *Classical Quarterly* (new series) 39, pp 22–44.

M. FOUCAULT (1979), trans. R. Hurley *The history of sexuality. Vol. 1: An introduction* Allen Lane.

M. FOUCAULT (1987), trans. R. Hurley *The history of sexuality. Vol. 2: The use of pleasure* Penguin.

M. FOUCAULT (1988), trans. R. Hurley *The history of sexuality. Vol. 3: The care of self* Penguin.

J.G. FRAZER (1957) *The Golden Bough. A study in magic and religion* Abridged edition. Macmillan.

S. FREUD (1922) *Medusa's head*, reproduced in the *Standard edition of the complete psychological works*, Hogarth Press, 1955, vol. 18, pp 273–4.

E. FRIEDL (1962) *Vasilika. A village in modern Greece* Holt, Rinehart and Winston.

P. FRIEDRICH (1978) *The meaning of Aphrodite* University of Chicago Press.

J. GARDNER (1989) 'Aristophanes and male anxiety – the defence of the *oikos' Greece and Rome* (2nd series) 36, pp 51–62.

R. GARLAND (1985) *The Greek way of death* Duckworth.

R. GARLAND (1989) 'The well-ordered corpse: an investigation into the motives behind Greek funerary legislation.' *Bulletin of the Institute of Classical Studies*, 36, pp 1–15.

R. GARLAND (1990) *The Greek way of life: from conception to old age* Duckworth.

L. GERNET (1981) 'Law and pre-law in ancient Greece', in L. Gernet, *The anthropology of ancient Greece*, trans. J. Hamilton and B. Nagy, Johns Hopkins University Press, 1981, pp. 143–215.

M. GODELIER (1981) 'The origins of male domination' *New Left Review* 127, pp 3–17.

M. GOLDEN (1981) 'Demography and the exposure of girls at Athens' *Phoenix* 38, pp 308–24.

M. GOLDEN (1984) 'Slavery and homosexuality' *Phoenix* 38, pp. 308–24.

M. GOLDEN (1986) 'Names and naming at Athens: three studies' *Echos du Monde Classique* 30, pp 245–69.

M. GOLDEN (1988) 'Male chauvinists and pigs' *Echos du Monde Classique/Classical Views* 32, new series, 7, pp 1–12.

M. GOLDEN (1990) *Childhood in Classical Athens* Johns Hopkins University Press.

S. GOLDHILL (1984) *Language, sexuality, narrative: the 'Oresteia'* Cambridge University Press.

S. GOLDHILL (1986) *Reading Greek tragedy* Cambridge University Press.

S. GOLDHILL (1987) 'The Great Dionysia and civic ideology' *Journal of Hellenic Studies* 107, pp 58–76.

S. GOLDHILL (1991) *The poet's voice. Essays on poetics and Greek literature* Cambridge University Press.

A.W. GOMME (1925) 'The position of women in Athens in the fifth and fourth centuries BC' *Classical Philology* 20, pp 1–25.

L. GOODISON (1989) 'Death, women and the sun: symbolism of regeneration in early Aegean religion' *Bulletin of the Institute of Classical Studies* supplement 53.

J. GOODY (1983) 'From brideprice to dowry?', in J. Goody, *The development of the family and marriage in Europe*, Cambridge University Press, 1983, Appendix 2, pp 240–61.

R.L. GORDON, ed. (1981) *Myth, religion and society* Cambridge University Press.

J. GOULD (1980) 'Law, custom and myth: aspects of the social position of women in Classical Athens' *Journal of Hellenic Studies* 100, pp 38–59.

F.T. GRIFFITHS (1981) 'Home before lunch: the emancipated women in Theocritus', in Foley (1981a), pp 247–73.

W.K.C. GUTHRIE (1950) *The Greeks and their gods* Methuen.

J.P. HALLETT (1979) 'Sappho and her social context' *Signs* 4, pp 447–64.

D.M. HALPERIN (1990) *One hundred years of homosexuality (and other essays on Greek love)* Routledge.

D.M. HALPERIN, J.J. WINKLER, F.I. ZEITLIN, eds. (1990) *Before sexuality: the construction of erotic experience in the ancient Greek world* Princeton University Press.

A.E. HANSON (1990) 'The medical writers' woman', in Halperin, Winkler and Zeitlin (1990), pp 309–38.

A.E. HANSON (1991) 'Continuity and change: three case studies in Hippocratic gynaecological therapy and theory' in Pomeroy (1991), pp 73–110.

R. HARRIOTT (1985) 'Lysistrata: action and theme', in Redmond (1985), pp 11–22.

W.V. HARRIS (1982) 'The theoretical possibility of extensive infanticide in the Graeco-Roman world' *Classical Quarterly* 32, pp 114–16.

A.R.W. HARRISON (1968) *The law of Athens: the family and property* Clarendon Press.

K. HASTRUP (1978) 'The semantics of biology: virginity', in Ardener (1978), pp 49–65.

C.M. HAVELOCK (1982) 'Mourners on Greek vases: remarks on the social history of women', in N. Broude and M.D. Garrard, eds., (1982) *Feminism and art history: questioning the litany*, Harper and Row, pp 45–61.

J. HENDERSON (1975) *The maculate muse. Obscene language in Attic comedy.* Yale University Press (2nd edition, 1991, Oxford University Press).

J. HENDERSON (1980) 'Lysistrata: the play and its themes', in J. Henderson, ed., *Aristophanes: essays in interpretation*, Yale Classical Studies, vol. 26, pp 153–218.

J. HENDERSON (1991) 'Women and the Athenian dramatic festivals', *Transactions of the American Philological Association* 121, pp 133–47.

A. HENRICHS (1978) 'Greek maenadism from Olympias to Messalina' *Harvard Studies in Classical Philology* 82, pp 121–60.

A. HENRICHS (1982) 'Changing Dionysiac identities', in B.F. Meyer and E.P. Sanders, eds., *Jewish and Christian self-definition. Vol. 3: Self-definition in the Graeco-Roman world*, SCM Press, 1982, pp 137–60.

A. HENRICHS (1993) 'He has a god in him: human and divine in the modern perception of Dionysus', in Carpenter and Faraone (1993), pp 13–43.

C.J. HERINGTON (1955) *Athena Parthenos and Athena Polias* Manchester University Press.

R. HIRSCHON (1978) 'Open body/closed space: the transformation of female sexuality', in Ardener (1978), pp 66–88.

S. HODKINSON (1989) 'Inheritance, marriage and demography: perspectives upon the success and decline of Classical Sparta', in A. Powell (1989) *Classical Sparta: techniques behind her success*, Routledge, pp 79–121.

E.S. HOLDERMAN (1985) 'Le sacerdotesse: requisiti, funzioni, poteri', in Arrigoni (1985), pp 299–344. (priestesses)

G. HOLST-WARHAFT (1992) *Dangerous voices: women's laments in Greek literature* Routledge.

D.O. HUGHES (1978) 'From brideprice to dowry in Mediterranean Europe' *Journal of Family History* 3, pp 262–96.

S.C. HUMPHREYS (1983) *The family, women and death. Comparative studies* Routledge and Kegan Paul.

S.C. HUMPHREYS (1993) *The family, women and death. Comparative studies.* 2nd edition. University of Michigan Press.

L. IRIGARAY (1985), trans. G.C. Gill *Speculum of the other woman* Cornell University Press.

I. JENKINS (1983) 'Is there life after marriage? A study of the abduction motif in vase-paintings of the Athenian wedding ceremony' *Bulletin of the Institute of Classical Studies* 30, pp 137–45.

R. JENKYNS (1982) *Three Classical poets: Sappho, Catullus and Juvenal* Duckworth.

J.P. JOHANSEN (1975) 'The Thesmophoria as a woman's festival' *Temenos* 11, pp 78–87.

C. JUNG and C. KERENYI (1963) *Science of mythology. Essays on the myth of the divine child and the Mysteries of Eleusis* Ark.

R. JUST (1989) *Women in Athenian law and life* Routledge.

L. KAHIL (1983) 'Mythological repertoire of Brauron' in Moon (1983), pp 231–44.

J.T. KAKRIDIS (1971) *Homer revisited* Gleerup.

M. KATZ (1991) *Penelope's renown: meaning and indeterminacy in the Odyssey* Princeton University Press.

E. KEULS (1984) 'Male-female interaction in fifth century Dionysiac ritual as shown in Attic vase-painting' *Zeitschrift für Papyrologie und Epigraphik* 55, pp 287–96.

H. KING (1993) 'Bound to bleed: Artemis and Greek women', in Cameron and Kuhrt (1993), pp 109–27.

H. KING (1987) 'Sacrificial blood: the role of the *amnion* in ancient gynaecology', in Skinner (1987), pp 117–26.

M. DEFOREST (1993), ed. *Woman's power, man's game. Essays on Classical antiquity in honour of Joy K. King* Bolkazy-Carducci.

R.S. KRAEMER (1979) 'Ecstasy and possession: the attraction of women to the cult of Dionysus' *Harvard Theological Review* 72, pp 55–80.

R.S. KRAEMER (1992) *Her share of the blessings. Women's religions among pagans, Jews, and Christians in the Graeco-Roman world* Oxford University Press.

L.J. KUENEN-JANSSENS (1941) 'Some notes on the competence of the Athenian woman to conduct a transaction' *Mnemosyne* (3rd series) 9, pp 199–214.

B. KUNSTLER (1987) 'Family dynamics and female power in ancient Sparta', in Skinner (1987), pp 31–48.

D.C. KURTZ and J. BOARDMAN (1971) *Greek burial customs.* Thames and Hudson.

W.K. LACEY (1966) 'Homeric *hedna* and Penelope's *kyrios*' *Journal of Hellenic Studies* 86, pp 55–68.

W.K. LACEY (1968) *The family in Classical Greece* Thames and Hudson.

E. LEACH (1969) *Genesis as myth and other essays* Jonathan Cape.

M. LEFKOWITZ (1973) 'Critical stereotypes and the poetry of Sappho' *Greek, Roman and Byzantine Studies* 14, pp 113–23.

M. LEFKOWITZ (1981) *Heroines and hysterics* Duckworth.

M. LEFKOWITZ (1986) *Women in Greek myth* Duckworth.

M. LEFKOWITZ (1989) 'Only the best girls get to' *Times Literary Supplement* May 5–11.

M.R. LEFKOWITZ and M.B. FANT, eds. (1982) *Women's life in Greece and Rome* Duckworth.

M.R. LEFKOWITZ and M.B. FANT, eds. (1992) *Women's life in Greece and Rome* 2nd edition. Johns Hopkins University Press.

I.M. LEWIS (1971) *Ecstatic religion: an anthropological study of spirit possession and shamanism* Penguin.

S. LIPSHITZ, ed. (1978) *Tearing the veil. Essays on femininity* Routledge and Kegan Paul.

G.E.R. LLOYD (1983) *Science, folklore and ideology. Studies in the life sciences in ancient Greece* Cambridge University Press.

H. LLOYD-JONES (1975) *Females of the species: Semonides on women* Duckworth.

N. LORAUX (1985) 'La cité, l'histoire, les femmes' *Pallas* 32, pp 7–39.

N. LORAUX (1987), trans. A. Forster *Tragic ways of killing a woman* Harvard University Press.

N. LORAUX (1993), trans. C. Levine *The children of Athena. Athenian ideas about citizenship and the division between the sexes* Princeton University Press.

S. LOVIBOND (1994) 'An ancient theory of gender: Plato and the Pythagorean table' in Archer, Fischer and Wyke (1994), pp 88–101.

D.M. MACDOWELL (1986) *Spartan law* Scottish Academic.

S. MCNALLY (1978) 'The maenad in early Greek art' *Arethusa* 11, pp 101–36.

G.H. MACURDY (1932) *Hellenistic Queens* Johns Hopkins Press.

J.R. MARCH (1989) 'Euripides' "Bacchae": a reconsideration in light of vase-paintings' *Bulletin of the Institute of Classical Studies* 36, pp 33–66.

J.D. MARRY (1979) 'Sappho and the heroic ideal: *erotos arete*' *Arethusa* 12, pp 71–92.

J.R. MARTIN (1985) *Reclaiming a conversation. The ideal of the educated woman* Yale University Press.

P. MASON (1987) 'Third person/second sex. Patterns of sexual asymmetry in the *Theogony* of Hesiodos', in Blok and Mason (1987), pp 147–89.

M. MAUSS (1925) *The gift*, in translation by I. Cunnison, Free Press, 1954.

M. MERCK (1978) 'The city's achievements. The patriotic Amazonomachy and ancient Athens', in S. Lipshitz (1978), pp 93–115.

P. MILLETT (1984) 'Hesiod and his world' *Proceedings of Cambridge Philological Society* (new series) 30, pp 84–115.

W.G. MOON (1983) ed. *Ancient art and iconography* University of Wisconsin Press.

I. MORRIS (1986) 'The use and abuse of Homer' *Classical Antiquity* 5, pp 81–138.

I. MORRIS (1992) *Death-ritual and social structure in Classical Antiquity* Cambridge University Press.

S. MURNAGHAN (1987) 'Penelope's *agnoia*: knowledge, power and gender in the *Odyssey*', in Skinner (1987), pp 103–15.

O. MURRAY (1980) *Early Greece* Fontana.

G.E. MYLONAS (1961) *Eleusis and the Eleusinian Mysteries* Princeton University Press.

J.F. NAGY (1981) 'The deceptive gift in Greek mythology' *Arethusa* 14, pp 191–204.

E. NARDI (1971) *Procurato aborto nel mondo Greco-Romano* Dott. A. Giuffre.

J. NEILS (1992) *Goddess and polis. The Panathenaic festival in ancient Athens* Princeton University Press.

M.P. NILSSON (1940) *Greek popular religion* Columbia University Press.

M.P. NILSSON (1950) *The Minoan-Mycenean religion and its survival in Greek religion* Gleerup.

S.M. OKIN (1979) *Woman in western political thought* Princeton University Press.

S.D. OLSON (1989) '*Odyssey* 8: guile, force and the subversive poetics of desire' *Arethusa* 22, pp 135–45.

S.B. ORTNER (1974) 'Is female to male as nature is to culture?', in Rosaldo and Lamphere (1974), pp 67–87.

R. OSBORNE (1985) *Demos: the discovery of classical Attica* Cambridge University Press.

R. OSBORNE (1987) 'The viewing and obscuring of the Parthenon frieze' *Journal of Hellenic Studies* 107, pp 98–106.

R. PADEL (1993) 'Women, model for possession by Greek daemons', in Cameron and Kuhrt (1993), pp 3–19.

D. PAGE (1955) *Sappho and Alcaeus* Oxford University Press.

H.W. PARKE (1967) *Greek oracles* Hutchinson University Library.

R. PARKER (1983) *Miasma. Pollution and purification in early Greek religion* Clarendon Press.

C. PATTERSON (1981) *Pericles' citizenship law of 451–50* The Ayer Company.

C. PATTERSON (1985) '"Not worth rearing": the causes of infant exposure in ancient Greece' *Transactions of the American Philological Association* 115, pp 103–23.

C. PATTERSON (1987) '*Hai Attikai*: the other Athenians', in Skinner (1987), pp 49–67.

C. PATTERSON (1991) 'Marriage and the married woman in Athenian law', in Pomeroy (1991), pp 48–72.

H. PAYNE (1940) *Perachora: the sanctuaries of Hera Akraia and Limenia* vol. 1. Clarendon Press.

J. PERADOTTO and J.P. SULLIVAN, eds. (1984) *Women in the ancient world: the Arethusa papers* A collection of papers from *Arethusa* vols 6 and 11. State University of New York Press.

P. PERLMAN (1989) 'Acting the She-bear for Artemis' *Arethusa* 22, pp 111–33.

J.J. POLLITT (1972) *Art and experience in Classical Greece* Cambridge University Press.

S.B. POMEROY (1975) *Goddesses, whores, wives and slaves* Robert Hale.

S.B. POMEROY (1984) *Women in Hellenistic Egypt* Schocken.

S.B. POMEROY, ed. (1991) *Women's history and ancient history* University of North Carolina Press.

F.J.P. POOLE (1981) 'Transforming "natural" women: female ritual leaders and gender ideology among Bimin-Kuskusmin', in S.B. Ortner and H. Whitehead, eds. (1981) *Sexual meanings: the cultural construction of gender and sexuality*, Cambridge University Press, pp 116–65.

A. POWELL (1990), ed. *Euripides, women and sexuality* Routledge.

K.J. RECKFORD (1964) 'Helen in the *Iliad*' *Greek, Roman and Byzantine Studies* 15, pp 5–20.

J. REDFIELD (1977/8) 'The women of Sparta' *Classical Journal* 73, pp 146–61.

J. REDFIELD (1982) 'Notes on the Greek wedding' *Arethusa* 15, pp 181–201.

J. REDMOND (1985) *Drama, sex and politics* Themes in drama no. 7. Cambridge University Press.

R. REHM (1994) *Marriage to death. The conflation of wedding and funeral rituals in Greek tragedy* Princeton University Press.

A. RICHLIN, ed. (1992) *Pornography and representation in Greece and Rome* Oxford University Press.

G.M.A. RICHTER (1968) *Korai. Archaic Greek maidens* Phaidon.

B.S. RIDGWAY (1981) *Fifth century styles in Greek sculpture* Princeton University Press.

N.J. RICHARDSON (1974), ed. *The Homeric hymn to Demeter* Clarendon Press.

N. ROBERTSON (1983) 'The riddle of the Arrhephoria at Athens' *Harvard Studies in Classical Philology* 87, pp 241–88.

M.Z. ROSALDO and L. LAMPHERE (1974) *Woman, culture and society* Stanford University Press.

A. ROUSSELLE (1988), trans. F. Pheasant *Porneia. On desire and the body in antiquity* Blackwell.

J. RUSSO (1973/4) 'Reading the Greek lyric poets (monodists)' *Arion* (new series) 1, pp 707–30.

G.E.M. DE STE. CROIX (1970) 'Some observations on the property rights of Athenian women' *Classical Review* (new series) 20, pp 273–8.

W. SALE (1961) 'Aphrodite in the *Theogony*' *Transactions of the American Philological Association* 92, pp 508–21.

L. SAXONHOUSE (1985) *Women in the history of political thought* Praeger.

D. SCHAPS (1977) 'The woman least mentioned: etiquette and women's names' *Classical Quarterly* 27, pp 323–30.

D. SCHAPS (1979) *The economic rights of women in ancient Greece* Edinburgh University Press.

PAULINE SCHMITT PANTEL (1992) *From ancient goddesses to Christian saints* Vol. 1 of *A history of women in the west*, edited by G. Duby and M. Perrot. Harvard University Press.

R.A.S. SEAFORD (1987) 'The tragic wedding' *Journal of Hellenic Studies* 107, pp 106–30.

R.A.S. SEAFORD (1994) *Reciprocity and ritual. Homer and tragedy in the developing city-state* Clarendon Press.

R. SEALEY (1990) *Women and law in Classical Greece* University of North Carolina.

C. SEGAL (1974) 'Eros and incantation: Sappho and oral poetry' *Arethusa* 7, pp 139–60.

C. SEGAL (1978) 'The menace of Dionysus: sex roles and reversals in Euripides' *Bacchae*' *Arethusa* 11, pp 185–201.

C.T. SELTMAN (1952) 'The wardrobe of Artemis' *Numismatic Chronicle* 12, pp 33–51 (on the statue of Artemis at Ephesus).

H.A. SHAPIRO (1992) 'Eros in love: pederasty and pornography in Greece', in Richlin (1992), pp 53–72.

M. SHAW (1975) 'The female intruder: women in fifth-century drama' *Classical Philology* 70, pp 255–66.

G. SISSA (1990a), trans. A. Goldhammer *Greek virginity* Harvard University Press.

G. SISSA (1990b) 'Maidenhood without maidenhead: the female body in ancient Greece', in Halperin, Winkler and Zeitlin (1990), pp 339–64.

M. SKINNER (1987), ed. *Rescuing Creusa: new methodological approaches to women in antiquity*

Special issue of *Helios* (new series 13.2). Texas Tech University Press.

P. SLATER (1971) *The glory of Hera. Greek mythology and the Greek family* Beacon Press.

A. SNODGRASS (1974) 'An historical Homeric society?' *Journal of Hellenic Studies* 94, pp 114–25.

J.M. SNYDER (1989) *The woman and the lyre. Women writers in Classical Greece and Rome* Bristol Classical Press.

C. SOURVINOU-INWOOD (1973) 'The young abductor of the Locrian pinakes' *Bulletin of the Institute of Classical Studies* 20, pp 12–21.

C. SOURVINOU-INWOOD (1988) *Studies in girls' transitions: aspects of the arkteia and age representation in Attic iconography* Kardamitsa.

C. SOURVINOU-INWOOD (1990) 'Ancient rites and modern constructs: on the Brauronian bears again' *Bulletin of the Institute of Classical Studies* 37, pp 1–14.

E.S. STIGERS (1981) 'Sappho's private world', in Foley (1981a), pp 45–61.

L. STONE (1977) *The family, sex and marriage in England, 1500–1800* Weidenfeld and Nicolson.

T. SULIMIRSKI (1970) *The Sarmatians* Thames and Hudson.

L.S. SUSSMAN (1978) 'Workers and drones: labour, idleness, and gender definition in Hesiod's beehive' *Arethusa* 11, pp 27–41.

L.K. TAAFFE (1993) *Aristophanes and women* Routledge.

W.E. THOMPSON (1967) 'The marriage of first cousins in Athenian society' *Phoenix* 21, pp 273–82.

W.B. TYRRELL (1984) *Amazons: a study in Athenian myth-making* Johns Hopkins University Press.

A.-M. VERILHAC and C. VIAL (1990) *La femme dans la monde Méditerranéen. Vol. VIII: la femme Grecque et Romaine. Bibliographie* Travaux de la maison de l'Orient, no. 19.

J.-P. VERNANT (1980) 'Marriage', in J.-P. Vernant, *Myth and society in ancient Greece*, trans. J. Lloyd, Harvester Press, 1980, pp 45–70.

J.-P. VERNANT (1983) *Myth and thought among the Greeks* Routledge and Kegan Paul.

J.-P. VERNANT (1991) *Mortals and immortals. Collected Essays* Princeton University Press.

H.S. VERSNEL (1992) 'The festival for Bona Dea and the Thesmophoria' *Greece and Rome* 39, pp 30–55.

P. VIDAL-NAQUET (1981) 'The Black Hunter and the origin of the Athenian *ephebeia*', in Gordon (1981), pp 147–62.

G. VLASTOS (1989) 'Was Plato a feminist?' *Times Literary Supplement* March 17–23.

M.E. WAITHE (1987) *A history of women philosophers. Vol. 1: 600 BC–500 AD* Martinus Nijhoff Publishers.

S. WALKER (1993) 'Women and housing in Classical Greece: the archaeological evidence', in Cameron and Kuhrt (1993), pp 81–91.

M. WARNER (1976) *Alone of all her sex: the myth and cult of the Virgin Mary* Weidenfeld and Nicolson.

M. WARNER (1985) *Monuments and maidens* Weidenfeld and Nicolson.

D. WENDER (1973) 'Plato: misogynist, paedophile, and feminist' *Arethusa* 6, pp 75–90.

R.F. WILLETTS, ed. (1967) *The law-code of Gortyn. With introduction, translation and commentary* Walter de Gruyter.

D. WILLIAMS (1993) 'Women on Athenian vases: problems of interpretation', in Cameron and Kuhrt (1993), pp 92–106.

M. WILLIAMSON (forthcoming, 1995) *Sappho's immortal daughters.*

S.F. WILTSHIRE (1976) 'Antigone's disobedience' *Arethusa* 9, pp 29–36.

J.J. WINKLER (1981) 'Gardens of nymphs: public and private in Sappho's lyrics', in Foley (1981a), pp 63–89.

J.J. WINKLER (1990) *The constraints of desire. The anthropology of sex and gender in ancient Greece* Routledge.

J.J. WINKLER and F.I. ZEITLIN (1990) *Nothing to do with Dionysus. Athenian drama in its social context* Princeton University Press.

F.I. ZEITLIN (1978) 'The dynamics of misogyny: myth and mythmaking in the *Oresteia*' *Arethusa* 11, pp 149–84.

F.I. ZEITLIN (1981) 'Travesties of gender and genre in Aristophanes' *Thesmophoriazusae*', in Foley (1981a), pp 169–217.

F.I. ZEITLIN (1982) 'Cultic models of the feminine: rites of Dionysus and Demeter' *Arethusa* 15, pp 129–57.

F.I. ZEITLIN (1985) 'The power of Aphrodite: eros and the boundaries of self in the *Hippolytus*', in Burian (1985), pp. 52–111.

F.I. ZEITLIN (1990) 'Playing the other: theater, theatricality and the feminine in Greek drama', in Winkler and Zeitlin (1990), pp 63–96.

M. ZOGRAFOU (1972) *Amazons in Homer and Hesiod* Athens.

Quotation acknowledgements

The author and publishers would like to thank the following for permission to use quotations from printed books. (See text and notes for page/line references.)

Bloodaxe Books Ltd:
Extracts reprinted by permission of Bloodaxe Books Ltd from *Sappho: Poems and Fragments* translated by JO BALMER (Bloodaxe Books, 1992).

Gerald Duckworth and Company Ltd:
A.P. BURNETT, 1983, *Three Archaic Poets.*
M.R. LEFKOWITZ AND M.B. FANT, 1982, *Women's Life in Greece and Rome.*
H. LLOYD-JONES, 1975, *Females of the Species.*

Robert Fagles:
ROBERT FAGLES (transl.), 1977, *Aeschylus: The Oresteia,* (Penguin Books) © Robert Fagles 1966, 1967, 1975, 1977.
ROBERT FAGLES (transl.), 1984, *Sophocles, The Three Theban Plays* (Penguin Books), © Robert Fagles, 1982, 1984.

HarperCollins Publishers
The Odyssey of Homer, translated with an introduction by RICHMOND LATTIMORE, 1965, (Harper Perennial, a division of HarperCollins Publishers), copyright © 1965, 1967 by Richmond Lattimore.

Harvard University Press:
Reprinted by permission of the publishers and the Loeb Classical Library from D.A. CAMPBELL, *Greek Lyric,* vol. 2, Cambridge, Mass.: Harvard University Press, 1987.

Johns Hopkins University Press:
APOSTOLOS N. ATHANASSAKIS, *The Homeric Hymns.*

Illustration acknowledgements

The author and publishers would like to thank the following for permission to publish photographs.

Abbreviations:

BM   By courtesy of the Trustees of the British Museum.

SB   Photograph by the author.

1   BM.
2   SB.
3   Olympia Museum, Greece.
4   H.L. Pierce Fund. Courtesy, Museum of Fine Arts, Boston. Acc. 00.330.
5   James Fund and by Special Contribution. Courtesy, Museum of Fine Arts, Boston. Acc. 10.185.
6   Ephesus Museum, Turkey. Inv. 718.
7   BM.
8   BM. B210.
9   BM. E140, side A.
10   BM. Sculpture 534.
11   Staatliche Antikensammlungen, Munich, inv. 2342.
12   Antikensammlung, Staatliche Museen zu Berlin – Preussicher Kulturbesitz. F 1887, side A.
13   Antikensammlung, Staatliche Museen zu Berlin – Preussicher Kulturbesitz. Sk 1800.
14   National Archaeological Museum, Athens. No. 3851.
15   Acropolis Museum, Athens. No. 670.
16a Acropolis Museum, Athens. No. 680.
16b Photo DAI Athens, Schrader 47. No. 672 in Acropolis Museum, Athens.
17   Tarquinia Museum, Italy, RC 2984.
18   BM, E 815.
19   Tarquinia Museum, Italy.
20   BM, 1920.12–21.1.

21   Bari Museum, Italy, 4979.
22   BM, B 332.
23   All rights reserved, Metropolitan Museum of Art, New York, 31.11.10.
24   National Archaeological Museum, Athens, P 695 (I 221).
25   National Archaeological Museum, Athens, NM 3624.
26   Photo DAI Athens, Ker. 2620.
27   BM, sculpture 208.
28   National Archaeological Museum, Athens, 1935.
29   Staatliche Antikensammlungen, Munich, inv. 2344.
30   BM, 192.
31   Museo Nazionale, Reggio Calabria.
32   Olympia Museum, Greece.
33   BM, sculpture 522.
34   National Archaeological Museum, Athens, 6447.
35   National Archaeological Museum, Athens, 16546.
36   BM.
37a After J. Travlos.
37b Drawn by Sue Bird.
38   National Archaeological Museum, Athens, NM 129.
39   BM.
40   SB.
41   BM, no. 909.
42   BM.
43   Acropolis Museum, Athens, 973.
44   Musée du Louvre, inv. MA 525. Cliché des Musées Nationaux, Paris.
45   Monumenti Musei e Gallerie Pontificie, Vatican City, inv. 812.

Index